# Multicultural Autobiography

# Multicultural Autobiography: American Lives

*Edited by James Robert Payne*

THE UNIVERSITY OF TENNESSEE PRESS / KNOXVILLE

A preliminary version of Raymund A. Paredes's essay, "Autobiography and Ethnic Politics," appeared in *A/B: Auto/Biography Studies* 3 (1987): 18–25. José David Saldívar's essay, "The School of Caliban," was published in different form in his *The Dialectics of Our America* (Durham, NC: Duke University Press, 1991). Quotations from the "Diary [of] George W. Cable 1888–1889[,] 1890–1891" in James Robert Payne's essay, "George Washington Cable's 'My Politics,'" are used with the permission of the Manuscripts Section, Howard-Tilton Memorial Library, Tulane University.

The paper in this book meets the minimum requirements of the American National Standard for Permanence of Paper for Printed Library Materials. ∞ The binding materials have been chosen for strength and durability.

Library of Congress Cataloging in Publication Data

Multicultural autobiography: American lives / edited by James Robert Payne.
     p.      cm.
  Includes bibliographical references and index.
  ISBN 0–87049–739–1 (cloth: alk. paper)
  ISBN 0–87049–740–5 (pbk.: alk. paper)
  1. Autobiography. 2. American prose literature—Minority authors— History and criticism. 3. Minorities—United States—Biography—History and criticism. 4. Authors, American—Biography—History and criticism. I. Payne, James Robert.
PS366.A88M85     1992                                          91-27130
818' .08—dc20                                                        CIP

# Contents

# Acknowledgments

I wish to acknowledge the help and friendship of colleagues who discussed aspects of this project with me, who offered valuable specific suggestions, and who gave me warm encouragement: William L. Andrews, University of Kansas; Richard Barksdale, University of Illinois, Champaign-Urbana; Carlos R. Hortas, Hunter College, City University of New York; Amy Ling, Trinity College; James Olney, Louisiana State University; Marco Portales, Texas A&M University; John M. Reilly, State University of New York, Albany; Joseph T. Skerrett, University of Massachusetts, Amherst; and the late Darwin T. Turner, University of Iowa. My wife and colleague at New Mexico State University, Avis Kuwahara Payne, helped me very substantially and greatly encouraged me at every stage. I wish to acknowledge, too, the kindness and guidance of James L. Woodress, University of California, Davis, who directed my dissertation on American autobiography.

With regard to my contribution to this collection, I wish to offer special thanks to Anne G. Jones, University of Florida, for prompting my interest in Cable, and to John Lowe, Louisiana State University, for discussing southern literature with me on a number of enjoyable occasions. I am also grateful to SallyAnn Harris Ferguson, University of North Carolina, Greensboro, for many stimulating discussions of southern authors. A grant from the College of Arts and Sciences Research Center, New Mexico State University, allowed me to study Cable's papers at Tulane University, and a National Endowment for the Humanities Travel to Collections Grant permitted a visit to Harvard University to study Cable's manuscripts there. I sincerely appreciate this research support and the confidence it represents.

Thanks are due to Stan Ivester of the University of Tennessee Press for the expert copyediting which made this a better book. Finally, it is a special pleasure to convey sincere appreciation to Carol Orr for her extremely helpful suggestions throughout the course of this project, for her unfailing support, and for her faith in this book.

—*James Robert Payne*

# Multicultural Autobiography

# Introduction

*James Robert Payne*

My introduction is not meant to be a guide to the general field of autobiography, for which I refer readers to James Olney's unsurpassed *Autobiography: Essays Theoretical and Critical* (1980), nor to the field of American autobiography per se.[1] Instead, my discussion is limited to, first, an overview of key earlier studies in the field of American autobiography, with particular reference to the multicultural concerns and values represented by *Multicultural Autobiography*. Second, I consider the circumstances of the conception of this book and its purposes. Finally, I briefly introduce each of the essays and suggest some of the ways in which they interrelate, though I am sure readers will find many other important relationships and telling points of difference among them.

American autobiography has been the subject of major scholarship and criticism since the 1960s. At the opening of that decade, Louis Kaplan published his landmark *Bibliography of American Autobiographies* (1961), a work which, it seems to me, always beckons us toward the fuller and more inclusive studies toward which we are still working.[2] There followed in the 1960s two important book-length studies, Robert F. Sayre's *The Examined Self: Benjamin Franklin, Henry Adams, Henry James* (1964) and Daniel B. Shea's *Spiritual Autobiography in Early America* (1968).

Sayre noted a special relationship between the emergence of recognizing autobiography as a distinct genre and the establishment of the United States as a political entity, observing that "The 'founding' of autobiography as a designated and conscious genre fell within the early years of the Republic, and its growth, coinciding with the spread of the romantic movement, has also coincided with the growth of the United States" (33). In an important later article, "Autobiography and America," James M. Cox expands on the idea that there is an affinity between self-writing and America and reminds us "that an astonishingly large proportion of the slender shelf of so-called American classics is occupied by autobiographies" (12). Sayre traces a central aspect of the tie between autobiography and America to nonconformist religious traditions that predate the American Revolution, noting that "in accordance with the Puritan precept that literature be useful, . . . authentic personal experience had greater prestige than poetry or any variety of fiction" (35).

Basing his generalizations about American autobiography on personal narratives of mostly elite men of Anglo-Saxon ancestry of the northeastern United States, Sayre found *The Confessions of St. Augustine* and *The Autobiography of Benjamin Franklin* to be "the most important models for autobiography in America" (3). The religious conversion narrative and, even more, the secular success narrative traditions that Sayre found so central for American self-writing are certainly antecedent in some respects to a number of autobiographies discussed in this volume, as we see in Frances Smith Foster's, Richard Tuerk's, and Fred Gardaphe's contributions. They do not, however, prove especially helpful in reading a number of others, including works discussed by A. LaVonne Brown Ruoff, Stephen H. Sumida, and Sau-ling C. Wong. With our present hindsight, we may argue that large generalizations such as that on "the most important models for autobiography in America" may just be too precariously balanced atop too narrow a definition of "America" and "American."[3] The American autobiographical criticism that is needed now, I believe, is suggested more by Shea's approach in *Spiritual Autobiography in Early America*.

In his preface, Shea admirably hesitates to attempt overarching generalizations about early American autobiography, noting that "General descriptions [of personal narratives] may well remain useful; yet they may also seem empty or stale when applied to the persistent singularity of many individual narratives" (vii). Shea cautions us further to remember that literary "conventions are always more apparent from a distance" (ix). In my planning for and work on *Multicultural*

*Autobiography* I have striven to keep Shea's wise counsel here always in mind. I have, to be candid, found it more helpful than the example of those who seek a more or less all-inclusive paradigm for "American literature" or "American autobiography."

In addition to making important distinctions between the personal writing of Quakers and Puritans in British colonial America, Shea suggests the differential effect of the two traditions on subsequent American self-writing. While most studies tend to privilege the Puritan heritage, in its quiet insistence on the *differences* between Quaker and Puritan life-writing at the headwaters of the formal and systematic study of American autobiography, Shea's work foreshadows our present-day awareness of the need for pluralist approaches.

Our understanding of American life-writing as a distinct category of study was enlarged in the 1970s by three important books: Thomas Cooley's *Educated Lives: The Rise of Modern Autobiography in America* (1976); Mutlu Konuk Blasing's significant, though often overlooked, *The Art of Life: Studies in American Autobiographical Literature* (1977); and G. Thomas Couser's *American Autobiography: The Prophetic Mode* (1979).

Like Shea, Cooley usefully focuses on a particular period of autobiography, the post–Civil War era. Where Shea (and, to a great extent, Sayre) reveals the impact of dominant religious trends on autobiography, Cooley demonstrates the impact of the new, post–Civil War psychology on the personal narratives of such classic Gilded Age figures as Henry Adams, Mark Twain, William Dean Howells, and Henry James. Cooley's account of how the new developmental psychology displaced the older psychology, which taught "that character is inviolable" (19), is a significant context for Keith Byerman's essay in this volume, with its interpretation of Du Bois's view of personality as "pre-modern." Byerman argues that Du Bois followed the older psychology in regarding his personality as not formed through outside circumstances but as essentially unchanging through life. Though derived mostly from analysis of self-writings of white men of privileged class, generalizations about American autobiography presented in *Educated Lives* are particularly helpful for many works of the post–Civil War and modern eras.

In his 1979 book, *American Autobiography: The Prophetic Mode*, G. Thomas Couser anticipates Albert E. Stone's *Autobiographical Occasions and Original Acts* (1982) in his laudable attempt to work beyond the usual focus on self-writings of elite white males and deal with a relatively broad and diverse range of American autobiographical writings, including works of Frederick Douglass, Louis Sullivan, Gertrude Stein, Malcolm X, and many others. Couser finds "a coherent tradition—perhaps the mainstream of American autobiography from the Puritans to the present" reflected in personal narratives of the (British) colonial figures Thomas Shepard, Increase Mather, Jonathan Edwards, John Woolman, Benjamin Franklin, proceeding through such nineteenth- and twentieth-century authors as Thoreau, Whitman, and Henry Adams, as well as those mentioned above. In this, his first of two books on American autobiography, Couser finds the particular characteristics of the self-writing tradition in which he is interested to derive from the writers' tendency "to assume the role of prophet in writing autobiography" and notes that the "tradition of prophetic autobiography has its roots in Puritan literature." Further, he observes that "the source for the distinctive concerns and literary strategies of the prophetic autobiographers can be located in their Puritan attitudes toward themselves and their history" (3). Although in his 1989 book *Altered Egos* Couser takes a very different approach to American autobiography, as discussed below, I have quoted at some length here from his 1979 study because it exemplifies to a degree a recurring tendency to find basic patterns of American literature, including and perhaps especially autobiography, to be more or less traceable to (British) colonial Puritan antecedents.[4] While the desire to find patterns is understandable, it would seem premature, and in a way, unfair, to attempt far-reaching generalizations about "American literature" before the many neglected traditions beyond that of the

Anglo-American are more thoroughly explored. It would be a little like deciding an important election before all the precincts were heard from. The basic purpose of *Multicultural Autobiography* is to present reports from more precincts, some rarely heard from (or listened to).

In the introduction to her 1977 study *The Art of Life*, Mutlu Konuk Blasing deals with the question of relationships between Puritan and secular colonial self-writing and later American autobiography:

> the range of such possible connections suggests that in tracing a tradition of personal literature in America one is dealing less with direct influences and more with a series of responses to essentially similar social, spiritual, and literary experiences. (xii)

This seems to me to be a very helpful observation, for it suggests that similarities between post-colonial American personal narratives, such as those discussed in Couser's *American Autobiography* and other studies that point to the Puritan heritage, may derive, to some extent, not so much from "descent" or direct influence but from production under similar social circumstances.

Blasing's *The Art of Life* is an eclectic study, designed to demonstrate varied approaches to what she perceives as a very wide-ranging body of American autobiographical literature. Blasing's definition of autobiography as a work "in which the hero, narrator, and author can be identified by the same name" (xi) allows her to address poetry, such as Whitman's "Song of Myself" and Williams's *Paterson*, and other works not generally included in studies of autobiography as well as traditionally recognized texts of the American autobiographical canon.[5] Blasing's view that "the term 'autobiographical' . . . does not imply any particular standard of 'truth' to the 'facts,' since the recording of a life necessarily represents . . . fictionalization— to a greater or lesser degree" (xi) places her, in some respects, with "the trend in recent autobiography studies . . . to erode the distinction between fiction and nonfiction" (Couser, *Altered Egos* 18).[6]

In line with the recent trend of applying poststructuralist approaches to criticism of American autobiography, two studies are particularly notable: Joseph Fichtelberg's *The Complex Image: Faith and Method in American Autobiography* (1989) and Couser's *Altered Egos: Authority in American Autobiography* (1989). Of the two, *Altered Egos* is more helpful from the standpoint of present-day efforts to acknowledge a broader range of American literatures springing from diverse American cultural groups.

*Altered Egos* brings recent critical and theoretical trends in autobiography studies into focus for a relatively wide range of American life-writing. In addition to considering the current tendency "to erode the distinction between fiction and nonfiction," Couser notes how—contrary to the older, conventional wisdom—autobiography may be regarded as not so much "*produced* by a pre-existent self but as *producing* a provisional and contingent one" (18, 19). After exploring the problematics of "authority" in a selection of autobiographies springing from diverse cultural groups, Couser concludes, "The authority of autobiography never resides exclusively in the text or the self, or even in the correspondence between them; rather it is something negotiated and renegotiated, between the autobiographer and others—collaborators, editors, critics, biographers, historians, and lay readers" (253). Couser differentiates his approach in response to varied American traditions in order to deal with such particular issues as collaboration in relation to American Indian and slave narratives as well as problems associated with "biculturalism" in Chicano and Chinese-American autobiography. Because of Couser's sensitivity to the varied ways in which diverse cultural conditions affect the production and reception of autobiography, parts of *Altered Egos* provide worthwhile context for certain essays in this volume, especially those in the American Indian, Chicano, and Chinese-American areas.

Using Nietzsche's *Ecce Homo* as a point of departure, in

*The Complex Image* Joseph Fichtelberg explores how the self-writer, "by retelling his life to himself, . . . comes to know himself in and through the act of revision" (16). Though granting that in the twentieth century it may be impossible to ascribe a "millennial identity" or "national soul" (213) to the United States, Fichtelberg locates a "millennial" pattern in American autobiography in the self-writings of Walt Whitman, Thomas Shepard, John Woolman, Benjamin Franklin, Frederick Douglass, Gertrude Stein, and others. Each of the millennial autobiographers, through their revisions, sought to promulgate a particular ideal for America. In some respects, the "millennial" pattern recalls the "prophetic mode" which G. Thomas Couser explored in his 1979 book *American Autobiography*.

As much as by any other study, the present volume was inspired by Albert E. Stone's *Autobiographical Occasions and Original Acts: Versions of American Identity from Henry Adams to Nate Shaw* (1982). A passage early in Stone's study helped to crystalize my varying dissatisfaction with earlier work in the field, which Stone describes as involved in "building generalizations about American autobiography and culture on the foundation of a relatively few classics, a single theme, rhetorical stance, or historical period. In this process certain texts become elevated to the status of canonical works" (18, 19). In planning and commissioning essays for *Multicultural Autobiography*, I tried to keep in mind Stone's reminder that "the whole oratorio [of American autobiography] is . . . composed of separate Songs of Myself" and that we must "learn to read these scores as individual stories *and* cultural narratives . . ." (26, 27, emphasis added). I think that the essays of *Multicultural Autobiography* fit this dictum. In a more general way, *Autobiographical Occasions* provided an example of an attempt to acknowledge and study autobiographies of many Americans of extremely varied social and cultural backgrounds.

An obvious difference that sets *Multicultural Autobiography* apart from not only Stone's study but most other books on American autobiography is the attempt in this volume to bring together different critical voices, each speaking from an area of expertise on a particular American cultural tradition. I believe that, at the present scholarly-critical moment, it is not really possible for a single critical voice to put forth a credible, full-scale study of American autobiography if American cultural diversity is to be acknowledged and if American autobiographies are to be studied as specific "cultural narratives" as well as "individual stories," as Stone rightly proposes.

At present, the approach in autobiography studies that seems to me most productive is that which is sensitive to particular American cultural traditions, as evidenced by such important recent work as William L. Andrews's *To Tell a Free Story: The First Century of Afro-American Autobiography, 1760-1865* (1986), William Boelhower's *Immigrant Autobiography in the United States: Four Versions of the Italian American Self* (1982), Joanne M. Braxton's *Black Women Writing Autobiography: A Tradition within a Tradition* (1989), H. David Brumble III's *American Indian Autobiography* (1988), and Arnold Krupat's *For Those Who Come After: A Study of American Indian Autobiography* (1985). These works exemplify scholarship and criticism well attuned to autobiography as both "cultural narrative" and "individual story," to borrow Stone's words again. None of them proposes an overarching thesis or inclusive paradigm for "American autobiography" as a "whole." I see *Multicultural Autobiography* as part of the present trend represented by these works. *Multicultural Autobiography* is meant as a contribution to the broadening and deepening of our understanding of autobiographies of disparate American cultures, considered in the spirit of Henry Louis Gates, Jr.'s reminder in *Figures in Black* "that what we have for too long called 'the tradition' is merely one tradition of several and that we have much to learn from the systematic exploration of new canons" (58).

The actual beginnings of *Multicultural Autobiography* go back to Paul Lauter's invitation to me to participate in the Reconstructing American Literature Institute at Yale in 1982. At that institute, scholars such as Elizabeth Ammons; Houston Baker; Juan Bruce-Novoa; Mary Anne Ferguson; Ann Fitzgerald; Henry Louis Gates, Jr.; Carlos Hortas; Annette Kolodny; Paul

Lauter; Amy Ling; Peggy McIntosh; Annette Niemtzow; A. LaVonne Brown Ruoff; Mary Helen Washington; Ana Zentella; and others helped me to discover "whole new continents and worlds" of American literature beyond the restricted canon.

The approach I have adopted for this collection is modeled on the Reconstructing American Literature Institute: no a priori critical or theoretical orientation has been imposed on contributors. And yet the contributors have drawn freely on the rich criticism and commentary on the genre of autobiography that has blossomed in recent years. As at the Yale conference, every attempt has been made to invite contributions from the widest possible range of American traditions, contributions from scholars generally recognized as being highly fluent in the language(s), the idiom, of the autobiographical literatures they write about.

In *For Those Who Come After*, Arnold Krupat has pointed out the bicultural nature of Native-American autobiography (xii); A. LaVonne Brown Ruoff and other scholars remind us that American Indian nationalities are diverse, that it is of course a mistake to regard American Indian culture as monolithic.[7] In her contribution for this volume, Ruoff focuses on an autobiographer of the Osage culture, John Joseph Mathews. Mathews provides a clear example of bicultural autobiography, as Ruoff shows through her discussion of his use of traditional Osage material along with literary techniques of Thoreau and John Muir in the production of *Talking to the Moon* (1945), a text Ruoff describes as "the most sophisticated and polished autobiography by an Indian author to be published up to 1945." Perhaps the most moving plea, though indirect, for acknowledgment and acceptance of the pluralism of American cultures surfaces in one of Ruoff's quotations from an early section of *Talking to the Moon*, in which Mathews laments the loss of the traditional Osage religion: "The passing of a concept of God seems to be almost as poignant as the passing of a species" (84). Mathews's use of the ecological trope in his lamentation on the Osage culture prefigures significant present-day critical trends, as suggested again in Ruoff's concluding point in which she reiterates how Mathews, like Thoreau and Muir, sought "a harmony with nature," as had been achieved by the traditional Osage. In the course of explicating *Talking to the Moon*, Ruoff gives us fresh contexts for *Walden* (1854) and Muir's *My First Summer in the Sierra* (1911) as well.

In "Autobiography after Emancipation: The Example of Elizabeth Keckley," Frances Smith Foster points out that autobiography is now recognized by many critics "as the fountainhead of African-American literature"; yet scholarship has tended to concentrate on pre–Civil War, modern, and contemporary narratives. Foster's purpose "is to suggest something of the in-between," the period after the Civil War but before the end of the century, a period of American autobiography when, as Foster notes, "the form and functions of the antebellum slave narrative [were adapted] to the experiences and intents of the postbellum era." Foster compares Elizabeth Keckley's rise from obscurity to the rise of Benjamin Franklin or Abraham Lincoln. Keckley's rise was even more remarkable than theirs, considering that she was a black woman and a former slave. Finding significant difference between pre– and post–Civil War black autobiography, Foster shows how Keckley's narrative "is more assertive and more critical than those published during slavery" and how Keckley evinced greater "optimism and faith in the American dream" than is typical of twentieth-century black autobiography. Foster hypothesizes that cultural change in America following the Civil War may have allowed "readers to tolerate . . . even admire, a young girl's decision to become a fighter and not a fugitive."

Foster's account of Keckley's difficulties in controlling how her autobiography would be published and marketed is the first of several accounts in this volume of problems experienced by ethnic minority and women autobiographers in controlling the circumstances of the publication, presentation, and reception of their narratives. In some ways comparable to Foster's account of the consequences of Keckley's lack of power in relation to her publisher are Fred Gardaphe's account of Jerre Mangione's difficulties in controlling the generic designation of his *Mount Allegro* (1943) and Sau-ling C. Wong's report of Maxine Hong Kingston's readers' negative response to the publisher's classification of *The Woman Warrior* (1976) as autobiography. Analogous to Keckley's publisher's obtuseness in overriding her rights as author is an older critical tendency, as detailed and criticized by Foster, which displaced Keckley as the central figure in her own autobiography.

As Foster demonstrates with Keckley, and as I attempt to show with Cable, Keith Byerman shows how W. E. B. Du Bois employed autobiographical narrative to establish "control over the image of himself." Increasingly marginalized in his old age because of his radicalism, Du Bois, Byerman argues, used his "final text of lives and texts" to "demonstrate . . . that his radicalism places him at the center rather than on the edge of American principles" and to show that he "has been a central part of American history." Even though Du Bois incorporated sections of a number of his earlier texts in composing his *Autobiography*, Byerman finds it to be essentially a traditional "narrative with a strong inner form," in which the "self" is treated as an "essence," not the result of a "process." Like Keckley, Du Bois, as Byerman argues, incorporated verifiable material of public history, the "dates, people, places, organizations" that fill *The Autobiography* to support the authority of his personal, subjective narrative. In contrast with such "discontinuous" personal narratives as Mary Antin's *The Promised Land* (1912) and M. E. Ravage's *An American in the Making* (1917), as described by Richard Tuerk in this volume, in his "final text," Byerman argues, Du Bois presents a life in which the last stage "completes a circle" that began in his childhood. In Byerman's trenchant summary of his thesis, the young Du Bois, "who learned lessons of democracy, reason, and opportunity in America's heartland has become the old man who must embrace foreigners because they are the ones fulfilling America's promise and ideals."

Although the notion that distinctive cultures of American regions or sections may produce distinctive autobiography is relatively new and questioned by some Americanists, the possibility that there may be a characteristically southern American autobiographical tradition has already generated several important essays, including William L. Andrews's "In Search of a Common Identity: The Self and the South in Four Mississippi Autobiographies," William Howarth's "Writing Upside Down: Voice and Place in Southern Autobiography," Elizabeth Fox-Genovese's "Between Individualism and Community: Autobiographies of Southern Women," and James Olney's "Autobiographical Traditions Black and White." In his introduction to *Located Lives: Place and Idea in Southern Autobiography* (1990), the collection that includes the last three essays mentioned above, J. Bill Berry notes that *Located Lives* contributors "see a strong, coherent tradition of autobiography by southern black writers," while "[t]here is less agreement concerning a tradition of autobiography by southern whites" (xiv). Berry sees "the central problem of southern autobiography" as "a tension between American ideas and an overlapping, sometimes reinforcing, but often conflicting set of southern values and loyalties" (xv).

In "George Washington Cable's 'My Politics,'" I examine how Cable, except for Mark Twain probably the most highly regarded southern author of his day, subtly revised his political memoir to minimize negative reactions he thought it might engender among fellow southerners. During difficult post-Reconstruction days, Cable in "My Politics" criticizes political white supremacy and advocates civil rights for African Americans. Although many readers regard Cable as an author who wrote against the grain of his native South, one of the significant themes that comes through in this memoir is that he was actually a loyal southerner, but a southerner who had a larger view of the South than did many people of his day. Cable's larger view is suggested in a number of ways, including his account of how he grew to regard African Americans as fellow "Southerners," entitled to the same rights as other Americans. Finally, I explore possible reasons why Cable suppressed "My Politics" after he had done so much painstaking revision.

Richard Tuerk's essay "At Home in the Land of Columbus"

seems to me to exemplify well, within the compass of European-American immigrant autobiography, the comparative approach in American cultural studies, as called for by Henry Louis Gates, Jr.; Paul Lauter; A. LaVonne Brown Ruoff; and other scholars at present.[8] Rather than seeking to impose an inclusive thesis for European-American autobiography, Tuerk locates at least two contrasting types of European immigrant autobiography, personal narratives such as those of Jacob Riis and Louis Adamic that present a life perceived as continuous, and narratives of "discontinuous" lives, such as those described in self-writings of Mary Antin and M. E. Ravage. Tuerk notes that, like the Benjamin Franklin of *The Autobiography*, Riis reveals "in his early chapters set in Denmark that he contained the seeds of what he later became." Riis's sense of a "continuous" life is thus comparable to Du Bois's life story, where the "end" was "in the beginning," as described by Byerman. A basis for Louis Adamic's perception of his life as continuous is suggested in Tuerk's telling quotation from *My America* (1938) in which Adamic calls for "recognition of the fact that America is not purely an Anglo-Saxon country" (218). Adamic evidently felt it unnecessary to abruptly change to accommodate his view of Anglo-Saxon ways, since "American" is not synonymous with "Anglo-Saxon."

In contrast to Riis's and Adamic's life stories, Tuerk offers self-writings of Mary Antin and M. E. Ravage, who perceived their life courses as relatively "discontinuous." For Antin, life in America was like a "rebirth," following her childhood in Russia, where her chances were limited by anti-Semitism and Old World patriarchy. For Ravage, Tuerk notes, "rebirth" was painful and "involved a complete remaking, even of his soul." The possible pain of assimilation is touched on again, in a very different context, in Raymund A. Paredes's essay, "Autobiography and Ethnic Politics: Richard Rodriguez's *Hunger of Memory*." Tuerk concludes with some provisional remarks on possible religious, ethnic, and personal factors that might explain why the "two visions" of life he describes "should be so different."

After suggesting in his essay "My House Is Not Your House" some of the oral and folk roots of Italian and Italian-American narrative, Fred L. Gardaphe employs an extended figure of "houses," "four prototypes of Italian-American houses as metaphors for possible readings of Italian-American writings. . . . the house as shrine . . . as villa . . . as *palazzo* . . . as embassy." Gardaphe uses this trope in his extended discussion of the self-writings of Jerre Mangione, doubtless the most prominent Italian-American autobiographer. In charting Mangione's development from feeling under the sway of Old World *destino* to experiencing relative "freedom" in America, Gardaphe builds on brief sketches of personal narratives of earlier Italian immigrants, including those of Constantine Panunzio, Pascal D'Angelo, and Rosa Cavalleri. These autobiographies are little known to most American readers and clearly deserve more attention. Like most of the essays in this volume, Gardaphe's contribution is richly heuristic, suggesting both directly and indirectly numerous avenues for further study.

Gardaphe notes that, despite self-writings of such "*prominenti*" as Cellini, Vico, Croce, and others, whose experience "differs greatly from that of the immigrant," "Italian-American autobiographers . . . can be seen as creating a new tradition . . . [which] in the minds of most Italian immigrants, is considered 'American.'" Thus, for certain traditions alluded to in *Multicultural Autobiography*, the genre identity "autobiography" seems to mark a work as more an "American" rather than "Old World" conception, as we see even more definitely in Wong's essay on Chinese-American autobiography. Gardaphe's many citations to Italian-language sources, like Wong's listing of Chinese-language sources, as well as Paredes's and Saldívar's use of Spanish-language materials, demonstrate beyond any question that English is only one American language and that Americanists will have to move beyond traditional graduate-school French, German, and Latin if we are to make even a gesture toward mastery of our field.

In his essay "The Ghetto and Beyond" Steven J. Rubin touches on one of the major roots of the present-day resurgence of ethnic consciousness: how events of public history may pull one into a sense of ethnic identity, even if one had not previously been nourishing such an identity. In his study of self-writings of contemporary American-Jewish writers, Rubin shows how "the most common elements" of "the autobiographic works of [Alfred] Kazin, [Meyer] Levin, [Irving] Howe, and [Herbert] Gold are those associated with the two most significant occurrences in recent Jewish history: the extermination of six million European Jews and the establishment of the state of Israel." These historical events led to a renewal of a sense "of peoplehood and . . . acceptance of Jewish identity," even among such figures as Howe, for whom religion had not before held high priority. Rubin summarizes the pattern he finds in first-generation American-Jewish autobiographies as consisting of accounts of early "feelings of isolation, an identity crisis marked by the pull of dual loyalties, a journey (either physical or spiritual) of 'return' to a place or culture of personal significance, a renewed connection with one's people, and finally a better understanding of self in relation to the group." The pattern is comparable, I believe, to the life course Gardaphe finds running through Mangione's Italian-American narratives. Borrowing some of Tuerk's terminology, one could say that Rubin gives us self-writers who discover, rediscover, or construct "continuity" where there had been some degree of "discontinuity" in relation to personal cultural antecedents. A discovery of "continuity" is suggested in Rubin's quotation from *A Margin of Hope* (1982), in which Howe tells how he came to find that ". . . the Yiddish poets helped me to feel at ease . . . with my past. . . . [They] . . . helped me strike a truce with, and then extend a hand to, the world of my father" (267, 269).

With "Protest and Accommodation, Self-Satire and Self-Effacement, and Monica Sone's *Nisei Daughter*," Stephen H. Sumida contributes an essay in one of our most neglected American traditions, the Japanese-American area, which has often been consigned to a monolithic "Asian-American" category. Sumida places his thesis on how Sone's "very discourse changes as her remembrance moves from early childhood . . .

through World War II and the Japanese-American internment,"
within a context of analysis and criticism of other Japanese-
American self-writings and fiction as well as contrasting Chinese-American works. His detailed text and extensive notes
and bibliography suggest many opportunities for further work.

In exploring the tragic and shameful episode in American
history when "nisei citizenship, their birthright, had been revoked by their fellow Americans, no matter that such an act
was illegal," Sumida shows how Sone substantiates her autobiography by interweaving events of public history with her
personal account. In this respect, Sumida's study of *Nisei
Daughter* is comparable to Foster's analysis of Keckley's *Behind the Scenes*, Byerman's discussion of Du Bois's *Autobiography*, and Rubin's approach to American-Jewish self-writings,
all of which reveal a strong interest in interrelationships between personal stories and collective and public history. In his
analysis, Sumida shows how Sone's choice and description of
personal life events of Japanese Americans ultimately reveal
the "failure" of the "internment . . . to tear apart the community, family, and Japanese-American individual." Sumida's
concluding reminder of the need to "define 'American' not by
race but by histories of diverse peoples' experiences, deeds,
lineages, intellectual and cultural developments, and by their
histories of integration (not assimilation)" provides in effect,
I think, a focused reiteration of the theme and purpose of
*Multicultural Autobiography*, with its exploration of personal
"histories of diverse peoples."

Sau-ling Cynthia Wong's essay "Autobiography as Guided
Chinatown Tour? Maxine Hong Kingston's *The Woman Warrior* and the Chinese-American Autobiographical Controversy"
raises and critiques a bedrock issue for multicultural studies.
Is it fair for readers to expect or assume that Kingston, as an
autobiographer, will somehow represent in a "typical" or "authentic" or "positive" way her cultural background, perhaps
with the cultural "outsider" reader in mind? Wong shows how
appeals for ethnic loyalty from other members of the Chinese-
American community, from within the "family," as one reader

of this essay put it, may seemingly attempt to subvert or question a woman's intention to express individual experience and imagination in autobiography. Yet as we follow Wong's analysis of criticism of *The Woman Warrior* (1976) by some members of the Chinese-American community as not "representative" and not an authentic portrayal of actualities of the community, we learn that perceived expectations and possible assumptions of non-Chinese readers may be the source of some of the negative response to the book. Wong argues that a number of Kingston's critics felt that a Chinese-American autobiographer has an obligation to present a carefully mediated, "responsible" view of life within the Chinese-American community, almost a carefully "guided Chinatown tour," in Wong's phrase. Kingston's situation, as described by Wong, seems comparable to that of George Washington Cable as he sat down to revise "My Politics," evidently feeling vulnerable to criticism from fellow southerners, that is, from within the cultural "family," as I detail in my contribution to this volume.

Wong develops her argument within a rich context of discussion of other Chinese-American narratives, most of which are virtually unknown to most readers in this country. As signaled by Wong's essay, this body of American literature invites further studies on its own terms rather than attempts to fit it to preconceived patterns developed perhaps more for American literatures springing from Atlantic coast immigrations.

Raymund A. Paredes's "Autobiography and Ethnic Politics" reveals significant political implications and dimensions of ethnic American autobiography. Focusing on Richard Rodriguez's *Hunger of Memory* (1981), probably the most widely known Mexican-American personal narrative, Paredes interrogates the stance of the "quintessentially modern literary figure: the solitary observer, immune to involvement in anything he surveys." Paredes's critique not only illuminates his chosen textual subject but helps us, if we read with imagination and empathy, to estimate and perhaps change or extend what we are doing as readers of and writers about American cultures. Paredes's implication that writers and scholars may have some obligation to foster "political action on behalf of" oppressed groups they study and may seem in a sense to "represent" is important and challenging, especially at present, when "multicultural studies" appear to be in fashion.

Indirectly, in the course of his analysis of *Hunger of Memory*, Paredes projects an ideal of potential Mexican-American self-writing, narratives that may convey "legends," "*corridos*," "stories of the Mexican Revolution," bilingual narratives that might delineate a "consciously ethnic" persona able "to function successfully in several communities simultaneously." As I derived this ideal of pluralism from Paredes's essay, I thought ahead to José David Saldívar's discussion of Ernesto Galarza's *Barrio Boy* (1971), which in some ways approximates the type of narrative Paredes seems to indirectly call for.

Sharing an interest with Raymund Paredes in the varying interpretive potentialities of the figure of Caliban, from Shakespeare's *The Tempest*, José David Saldívar states his purpose in "The School of Caliban: Pan-American Autobiography" as first to "trace the cultural reworkings of *The Tempest* by three prominent Caribbean writers" and then to "try to establish the literal and figurative centrality of Caliban to a line of Chicano/a and African-American writers not usually seen as instances of Calibanic inheritance: Ernesto Galarza, Richard Rodriguez, Cherrié Moraga, and Houston Baker, Jr." If Prospero in *The Tempest* may suggest the European colonialist in the New World, and Caliban the exploited, colonized American, the Caribbean authors Saldívar addresses, George Lamming of Barbados, Aimé Césaire of Martinique, and Roberto Fernández Retamar of Cuba, project in their writings an opportunity, Saldívar argues, "to rethink our American culture and identify from the perspective of the Other, a protagonist excluded, ruled, exploited, Caliban." In assessing autobiographies of Rodriguez, Galarza, Moraga, and Baker "within Fernández Retamar's Calibanic frame of reference," Saldívar projects a detailed, highly illuminating contrast between "the alienated Ariel intellectual-writer who sides with . . . Prospero" and those who reveal "signs of independence," as represented by the last three autobiographers mentioned above.

Saldívar's inclusion of American authors not of the United States restores to us the knowledge, often overlooked, that political boundaries may seriously obscure our perception of cultural relationships. His grouping of autobiographical works by authors of several cultural groups under the sign of Caliban may be compared to earlier efforts, discussed above, to find common patterns in American autobiography. That Saldívar's endeavor does not strain to be so all-encompassing seems to me a virtue, as does his direct consideration of class factors in finding relationships between members of different American groups. It might be noted, too, that Saldívar's inclusion and discussion of Baker's *Modernism and the Harlem Renaissance* (1987) provides refreshingly explicit acknowledgment of the autobiographical potential of literary criticism.

Finally, as I read and reread the essays in this volume, I am struck not only by the cultural diversity present but by the cultural diversity absent. Studies of personal histories of Arab Americans, immigrants from East India and Korea, Irish Americans, Puerto Ricans—another volume and still another could be made from possible studies forgone here because *Multicultural Autobiography* is only one book. I hope that readers who may feel the absence of an essay on autobiography of a particular American cultural group may be inspired to produce new work to deepen still further our understanding and discussion of American life writing. There is much work, much exploration, to be done before we decide what is the "essential" American language and character. My guess is that, as we increase our ability to hear the nuances of a variety of American cultures, we will wish more and more to "encourage and sustain a truly comparative and pluralistic notion of the institution of literature" (Gates xx), and, more specifically, of American literatures.

## Notes

1. An important new collection of essays on *American Autobiography* (1991), edited by Paul John Eakin, appeared when *Multicultural Autobiography* was being copyedited. In my view, *American Autobiography* complements *Multicultural Autobiography* in a number of useful ways.
2. Mary Louise Briscoe extended Kaplan's work with her *American Autobiography, 1945–1980: A Bibliography* (1982).
3. See Robert F. Sayre's "*The Examined Self* Reexamined: A Reintroduction, 1987," in the 1988 edition of *The Examined Self*, for a somewhat comparable discussion of Sayre's ground-breaking study of American autobiography.
4. Sollors discusses this tendency and, in some respects, exemplifies it in *Beyond Ethnicity*, 6, 54–56, et passim.
5. Blasing's definition is essentially similar to Philippe Lejeune's definition of autobiography in "Le Pacte autobiographique" (1973), which appears in English translation in *On Autobiography* (1989), edited by Paul John Eakin. See Lejeune 4–26, 29–30, et passim.
6. On this point, see Mansell 115–32; de Man 919–30; Fleishman 15–19; Egan 14–23 et passim; Eakin, *Fictions in Autobiography*, 184–91 et passim; and Adams 9–16.
7. See Ruoff, *American Indian Literatures* 1–2 et passim for a suggestive, brief summary of American Indian cultural diversity.
8. See Gates 55, 58, et passim; Lauter 48–96; and Ruoff and Ward, "Introduction" to *Redefining American Literary History* 1–5.

# Selected Bibliography

Adams, Timothy Dow. *Telling Lies in Modern American Autobiography.* Chapel Hill: U of North Carolina P, 1990.

Andrews, William L. "In Search of a Common Identity: The Self and the South in Four Mississippi Autobiographies." *Southern Review* 24 (Winter 1988): 28–46.

———. *To Tell a Free Story: The First Century of Afro-American Autobiography, 1760–1865.* Urbana: U of Illinois P, 1986.

Berry, J. Bill, ed. *Located Lives: Place and Idea in Southern Autobiography.* Athens: U of Georgia P, 1990.

Blasing, Mutlu Konuk. *The Art of Life: Studies in American Autobiographical Literature.* Austin: U of Texas P, 1977.

Boelhower, William. *Immigrant Autobiography in the United States: (Four Versions of the Italian American Self).* Verona: Essedue, 1982.

Braxton, Joanne M. *Black Women Writing Autobiography: A Tradition within a Tradition.* Philadelphia: Temple UP, 1989.

Briscoe, Mary Louise, et al., eds. *American Autobiography, 1945–1980: A Bibliography.* Madison: U of Wisconsin P, 1982.

Brumble, H. David, III. *American Indian Autobiography.* Berkeley: U of California P, 1988.

Bruss, Elizabeth W. *Autobiographical Acts: The Changing Situation of a Literary Genre.* Baltimore: Johns Hopkins UP, 1976.

Cooley, Thomas. *Educated Lives: The Rise of Modern Autobiography in America.* Columbus: Ohio State UP, 1976.

Couser, G. Thomas. *Altered Egos: Authority in American Autobiography.* New York: Oxford UP, 1989.

———. *American Autobiography: The Prophetic Mode.* Amherst: U of Massachusetts P, 1979.

Cox, James M. "Autobiography and America." *Virginia Quarterly Review* 47 (1971): 252–77. Rpt. in James M. Cox, *Recovering Literature's Lost Ground: Essays in American Autobiography.* Baton Rouge: Louisiana State UP, 1989. 11–32.

de Man, Paul. "Autobiography as De-Facement." *Modern Language Notes* 94 (1979): 919–30.

Eakin, Paul John, ed. *American Autobiography: Retrospect and Prospect.* Madison: U of Wisconsin P, 1991.

————. *Fictions in Autobiography: Studies in the Art of Self-Invention.* Princeton: Princeton UP, 1985.

Egan, Susanna. *Patterns of Experience in Autobiography.* Chapel Hill: U of North Carolina P, 1984.

Fichtelberg, Joseph. *The Complex Image: Faith and Method in American Autobiography.* Philadelphia: U of Pennsylvania P, 1989.

Fleishman, Avrom. *Figures of Autobiography: The Language of Self-Writing in Victorian and Modern England.* Berkeley: U of California P, 1983.

Fox-Genovese, Elizabeth. "Between Individualism and Community: Autobiographies of Southern Women." Berry 20–38.

Gates, Henry Louis, Jr. *Figures in Black: Words, Signs, and the "Racial" Self.* New York: Oxford UP, 1987.

Gunn, Janet Varner. *Autobiography: Toward a Poetics of Experience.* Philadelphia: U of Pennsylvania P, 1982.

Howarth, William. "Writing Upside Down: Voice and Place in Southern Autobiography." Berry 3–19.

Jelinek, Estelle C. *The Tradition of Women's Autobiography: From Antiquity to the Present.* Boston: Twayne, 1986.

Kaplan, Louis, et al. *A Bibliography of American Autobiographies.* Madison: U of Wisconsin P, 1961.

Krupat, Arnold. *For Those Who Come After: A Study of American Indian Autobiography.* Berkeley: U of California P, 1985.

Lauter, Paul. "The Literatures of America—A Comparative Discipline." In Lauter, *Canons and Contexts.* New York: Oxford UP, 1991. 48–96.

Lejeune, Philippe. *On Autobiography.* Ed. Paul John Eakin. Trans. Katherine Leary. Minneapolis: U of Minnesota P, 1989.

Mansell, Darrel. "Unsettling the Colonel's Hash: 'Fact' in Autobiography." *Modern Language Quarterly* 37 (1976): 115–32. Rpt. in *The American Autobiography: A Collection of Critical Essays,* ed. Stone. 61–79.

Olney, James. "Autobiographical Traditions Black and White." Berry 66–77.

————, ed. *Autobiography: Essays Theoretical and Critical.* Princeton: Princeton UP, 1980.

————. *Metaphors of Self: The Meaning of Autobiography.* Princeton: Princeton UP, 1972.

————, ed. *Studies in Autobiography.* New York: Oxford UP, 1988.

Ruoff, A. LaVonne Brown. *American Indian Literatures: An Introduction, Bibliographic Review, and Selected Bibliography*. New York: MLA, 1990.

Ruoff, A. LaVonne Brown, and Jerry W. Ward, eds. *Redefining American Literary History*. New York: MLA, 1990.

Sayre, Robert F. *The Examined Self: Benjamin Franklin, Henry Adams, Henry James*. 1964. New introd. Sayre. Madison: U of Wisconsin P, 1988.

Shea, Daniel B. *Spiritual Autobiography in Early America*. 1968. New preface and bibliog. supp. by Shea. Madison: U of Wisconsin P, 1988.

Smith, Sidonie. *A Poetics of Women's Autobiography: Marginality and the Fictions of Self-Representation*. Bloomington: Indiana UP, 1987.

Sollors, Werner. *Beyond Ethnicity: Consent and Descent in American Culture*. New York: Oxford UP, 1986.

Spengemann, William C. *The Forms of Autobiography: Episodes in the History of a Literary Genre*. New Haven: Yale UP, 1980.

Spengemann, William C., and L. R. Lundquist. "Autobiography and the American Myth." *American Quarterly* 17 (1965): 501–19.

Stone, Albert E., ed. *The American Autobiography: A Collection of Critical Essays*. Englewood Cliffs: Prentice, 1981.

———. *Autobiographical Occasions and Original Acts: Versions of American Identity from Henry Adams to Nate Shaw*. Philadelphia: U of Pennsylvania P, 1982.

Taylor, Gordon O. *Chapters of Experience: Studies in 20th Century American Autobiography*. New York: St. Martin's, 1983.

Weintraub, Karl Joachim. *The Value of the Individual: Self and Circumstance in Autobiography*. Chicago: U of Chicago P, 1978.

# John Joseph Mathews's
# *Talking to the Moon:*
# Literary and Osage Contexts

*A. LaVonne Brown Ruoff*

## I

American scholars have increasingly emphasized the importance
of American autobiographies to the study of American culture.
In "Autobiography and the Making of America," Robert F. Sayre
attributes this to American autobiographers having "generally
connected their own lives to the national life or to national
ideas" (149). Like their white and African-American counterparts, Native Americans have emphasized the connection between their lives and the larger community. Although their life
histories emphasize the interrelationship between the individual
and the tribe more than that with the United States as a nation,
they also stress the impact of Indian-white relations on Indian
life. Recognizing that life histories constitute one of the major
genres of American-Indian literatures, scholars such as H. David
Brumble III, Arnold Krupat, Gretchen Bataille, Kathleen Mullen
Sands, Lynne O'Brien, and Ruoff have increasingly turned their
attention to the study of life histories and autobiographies.[1] Because American-Indian written autobiographies reflect not only
the personal and tribal history of the author but trends in popular literature and in Indian-white relations, they form a rich re-
source. This essay will focus on John Joseph Mathews's *Talking
to the Moon* (1945), a highly sophisticated literary autobiography, and will discuss its place in the history of American-Indian
autobiography. It will also examine the extent to which the
form and content of Mathews's *Talking to the Moon* were influenced by Henry David Thoreau's *Walden* (1854) and John
Muir's *My First Summer in the Sierra* (1911) as well as by Osage traditions and history.

Full-length confessions or autobiographies in the Western European literary mode are not part of American-Indian oral literary tradition. However, Brumble indicates in *American Indian Autobiography* that Native-American preliterate autobiographical narratives include a variety of forms designed to convey specific information or achieve a particular purpose. Among these are coup tales, which describe feats of bravery; tales of warfare and hunting; self examinations, which might consist of confessions required for participation in rituals or accounts of misfortunes and illnesses; self-vindications; educational narratives; and tales of acquisition of powers (22–33). Even today some Indians may decline to write or narrate full-length autobiographies because their tribes consider it inappropriate for individuals to speak about themselves in an extended fashion until after they have achieved a status acknowledged by the tribe.

American-Indian life histories and autobiographies often blend a mixture of tribal myth, ethnohistory, and personal experience. This mixed form was congenial to Indian narrators and authors accustomed to viewing their lives within the history of their family, clan, band, or tribe. In her introduction to *Life Lived like a Story*, Julie Cruikshank provides a contemporary example of this perspective. To her questions about secular events, three Athabaskan/Tlingit women responded by telling traditional stories because "these narratives were important to record *as part of*" their life stories. Their accounts included not only the personal reminiscences we associate with autobiography but also detailed narratives elaborating mythological themes, genealogies and lists of personal and place names that had both metaphoric and mnemonic value. She notes that these women talked about their lives using an oral tradition grounded in local idiom and a mutually shared body of knowledge (2).

In the early nineteenth century, publication of full-length American-Indian life histories was stimulated by the popularity of captivity and slave narratives. In the East and Midwest, it also resulted from renewed interest in "the noble savages," who no longer threatened whites because the Indians had been pacified or, under the provisions of the 1830 Indian Removal Bill, forcibly relocated to Indian Territory, now Oklahoma, and other areas west of the Mississippi. As Indians were removed, whites increasingly wanted to read about the vanished "noble savages" or about assimilated Indian converts to Christianity. Published in response to this interest, nineteenth-century American-Indian autobiographies became forceful weapons in Native Americans' never-ending battles against white injustice.

In 1833, the narrated American-Indian autobiography, a major literary form in the late-nineteenth and twentieth centuries, was introduced with the publication of *The Life of Ma-ka-tai-me-she-kia-kiak or Black Hawk*. Narrated by Black Hawk (Sauk) to translator Antoine Le Claire and revised for publication by John B. Patterson, this popular book went through five editions by 1847. The earliest published full-life autobiographies written by American Indians were *A Son of the Forest* (1829) by William Apes (Pequot, b. 1798) and *The Life, History and Travels of Kah-ge-ga-gah-bowh* (1847) by George Copway (Ojibwa, 1818–69). Like the slave narrators, Apes and Copway consciously modeled their autobiographies on the spiritual confessions and missionary reminiscences popular with white readers. The spiritual confessions linked Indian autobiographers to Protestant literary traditions and identified these authors as civilized Christians whose experiences were as legitimate subjects of written analysis as the experiences of other Christians. Apes, Copway, and later American-Indian autobiographers, like the slave narrators, used personal and family experiences to illustrate the suffering their people endured at the hands of white Christians.[2]

Because he was apprenticed to whites after age four and was not raised in a traditional Indian culture, Apes, unlike later autobiographers, does not include a tribal ethnohistory in *A Son of the Forest*. This book is primarily devoted to Apes's spiritual journey toward salvation and to strong statements about white injustice to Indians. More representative of the evolving form of American-Indian written autobiographies than Apes's self-published *A Son of the Forest* was Copway's *The Life, History and Travels of Kah-ge-ga-gah-bowh* (1847). This popular autobiography went through six editions in one year. Although Copway used the structure of the spiritual confession and missionary reminiscence, he blended these with Ojibwa myth, ethnohistory, and personal experience. Copway also introduced descriptions of childhood experiences and portraits of family life designed to counteract the stereotype of Indians as "red devils" intent on killing as many innocent whites as possible.

From the early nineteenth century through the 1960s, more American-Indian life histories or autobiographies were published than any other genre of Native-American literature. However, subsequent Indian autobiographers abandoned the religious narrative as a model and in its place used versions of the blend of mythology, ethnohistory, and personal experience that Copway initiated. Instead of personal religious experience, Indian autobiographers emphasized tribal culture and history and Indian-white relations. *Life among the Piutes* (1883) by Sarah Winnemucca (Paiute, ca. 1844–91), exemplifies this shift in perspective. During most of the nineteenth century, Winnemucca was the only Indian woman writer of personal and tribal history. Her *Life among the Piutes* is particularly interesting for her characterization of her childhood terror of whites, her discussion of the status of women in Paiute society, and her descriptions of her role as a liaison between Indians and whites.

To the descriptions of tribal ethnohistory and growing up within a tribal culture included in earlier Indian autobiographies, later writers added accounts of Indian children's adjustment to white-run schools. *The Middle Five* (1900) by Francis La Flesche (Omaha, 1857–1932) exemplifies this trend. The most influential and widely read Indian autobiographer in the early twentieth century was Charles Eastman (Sioux, 1858–1939), who wrote two autobiographies. *Indian Boyhood* (1902), written for his children, describes his life as a traditional Sioux boy from infancy to age fifteen. *From the Deep Woods to Civilization* (1916) is a progress autobiography that traces Eastman's struggles to succeed, from his first days in a white school to becoming a medical doctor and an internationally known spokesperson on Indian issues. It also reflects his growing sense of Indian-ness and disillusionment with white society.

## II

Mathews's *Talking to the Moon* differs from most earlier Indian autobiographies because it is a spiritual autobiography of a specific period in the author's life rather than a life history of growing up Indian or of adjustment to contact with non-Indians and their institutions. Unlike Copway and later Indian autobiographers, Mathews did not grow up within a tribal culture. Consequently, *Talking to the Moon* is not an exploration of Mathews's ethnicity but rather a chronicle of his attempts to find himself at a crucial time in his life through rediscovering the land, animals, and people of his native Oklahoma. In the course of this rediscovery, Mathews pays tribute to the Osage, whose traditional life had undergone tremendous change. One-eighth Osage by blood, Mathews spent his youth and much of his adult life after 1932 living among and working with them. Most of his books were devoted to describing their lives, heritage, and history.

While *Talking to the Moon* does contain the blend of myth, history, and personal experience that characterizes American-Indian autobiographies, it is modeled not on these books but rather on the works of Thoreau and John Muir. Mrs. Elizabeth Mathews makes this clear in her foreword to the 1981 reprint of her husband's book: "this is John Joseph Mathews's *Walden*. It is a book that a Thoreau or a Muir might write, but it is a *Walden* of the plains and prairies, of the 1930s and 1940s, by a Native American" (ix). By incorporating many elements of the form and content of Thoreau's *Walden* and Muir's *My First Summer in the Sierra*, Mathews deliberately places *Talking to the Moon* within a received literary tradition, which he adapts to incorporate as-

pects of Oklahoma and Osage culture and history. The result
is the most sophisticated and polished autobiography by an
Indian author to be published up to 1945.

Mathews (1894–1979) was raised in Pawhuska, the Osage agency
in Indian Territory. He was descended from the union between
A-Ci'n-Ga and William Shirley Williams, an early missionary to
the Osage who later became famous as a mountain man. Their
daughter Sarah married John Mathews, a trader among the Osage, and bore him William Shirley, John Joseph's father. By the
time John Joseph was born, the Mathews family had become one
of the wealthiest families in Pawhuska and lived in a house located approximately a hundred yards from the Osage council
house. Though not as fluent in Osage as his father, Mathews did
speak the language. He did not, however, participate in clan ceremonies because his Osage lineage was matrilineal and Osage
clans are patrilineal (Wilson,"Osage Oxonian" 266–70). Young
Mathews came to know the Osages well through his associations
with them in his father's store and through his visits with them
out on the prairies. In his introduction to *The Osages* (1961),
Mathews describes his boyhood fascination with Osage culture and characterizes his relationship to it as an observer but
not a participant. As a frightened little boy alone in his bed-
room, he listened to the "long, drawn-out" Osage chants, broken by weeping: "It filled my little boy's soul with fear and
bittersweetness, and exotic yearning, and when it had ended
and I lay there in my exultant fear-trance, I hoped fervently
that there would be more of it, and yet was afraid there might
be" (ix).

After attending private and parochial elementary and jun-
ior high schools, Mathews graduated from the public high
school in Pawhuska, where the majority of the students were
non-Indian. In 1914, he entered the University of Oklahoma
at Norman to study geology. During World War I, Mathews
left to enlist in the cavalry, later transferring to the aviation
branch of the Signal Corps. After service in France, he returned to the university and graduated in 1920. He then entered Oxford University to study natural science, receiving his
BA in 1923. That same year he enrolled in the School of In-

ternational Relations in Geneva, from which he received a certificate. While in Geneva, Mathews met his first wife and served as an occasional correspondent for the Philadelphia *Ledger* at the League of Nations. After leaving Geneva, he traveled over Western Europe, Britain, and North Africa. He later settled with his wife in Los Angeles, where he became a realtor. When his marriage ended in 1929, he returned to Pawhuska.

Mathews attributed his decision to return from his overseas travels to an incident that occurred during a hunting trip in North Africa during the late 1920s when Arab tribesmen raced through his camp firing their Winchesters and then dismounted to join the party for dinner. Their actions reminded Mathews of the day in his childhood when breechclouted Osage warriors surrounded him on the Prairies, shooting off their guns in what the author called "joy shooting." The incident made Mathews wonder what he was doing in North Africa: "Why not go back to the Osage? They've got a culture. So I came back; then I started talking with the old men" (Logsdon 71). Mathews's reimmersion in Osage culture came in 1931, when, following the death of Major Laban J. Miles, agent to the Osage during the early reservation period, the author inherited Miles's journals. In order to complete *Wah'Kon-Tah* (1932), a fictionalized account of Osage life since 1878 based on Miles's diaries, Mathews isolated himself in an abandoned house twenty miles from Pawhuska, where curious Osages dropped by to give him additional information (Wilson, "Osage Oxonian" 274). The fondness for solitary living that the author developed during this period made him decide to build a cabin on his Osage allotment. There he wrote *Sundown* (1934), a novel that focuses on a mixed-blood hero who rejects his Osage heritage for the white world and whose dreams of glory end in an alcoholic daze. *Sundown* incorporates many aspects of Mathews's own life and reflects his continuing commitment to telling the story of the Osage.

During the 1930s, Mathews was increasingly drawn into Osage affairs. Elected to the Osage tribal council in 1934, he served two terms and often acted as one of the tribe's chief representatives in difficult business negotiations. He was largely responsible for obtaining government funds to establish the Osage Tribal Museum, which opened in 1938 as the first tribally owned and operated museum in the country (Wilson, "Osage Oxonian" 277–79). After writing a biography of his friend, E. W. Marland, entitled *Life and Death of an Oilman* (1951), Mathews devoted himself to research on his major work, *The Osages: Children of the Middle Waters* (1961). In his *The Underground Reservation*, Terry P. Wilson praises *The Osages* as a tribal history conceived from a Native-American viewpoint, combining documentary and oral research, and written with Indians as the primary actors (x). This lengthy history is one of the primary sources of information about the tribe.

The period of his life covered by *Talking to the Moon* begins after the publication of *Wah'Kon-Tah*. Undoubtedly, Mathews's interest in what motivates humankind, his need to understand our relationship to nature, and his desire to observe nature closely led him to choose Thoreau's and Muir's works as his literary models. Like these authors, he withdrew from cities to overcome the separation he felt between himself and nature. For Mathews, this process involved restoring his relationship to his Oklahoma homeland and with the animals and humans, such as the Osage, cowboys, and ranchers, who inhabited it. Twenty-eight-year-old Thoreau settled near Walden Pond in 1845 and remained for two years. Thirty-eight-year-old Mathews settled and remained ten years in the "blackjacks" near Pawhuska, a region named for the tough oaks that covered the sandstone region. Clearly Mathews identified with Thoreau's statement of why he settled near Walden Pond: "I went to the woods because I wished to live deliberately, to front only the essential facts of life, and see if I could not learn what it had to teach, and not, when I came to die, discover that I had not lived" (89). The influence of Thoreau's *Walden* is clearly reflected in Mathews's statement that he returned to the blackjack region in order to become part of the balance:

> . . . to learn something of the moods of the little corner of the earth which had given me being; to learn something of the biological progression and

mysterious urge which had inspired it, until the biological changes within myself had dimmed the romance of it. I had kept my body fit and ready, but my perceptive powers had been dulled by the artificialities and crowding and elbowing of men of Europe and America, my ears attuned to the clanging steel and strident sounds of civilization, and the range of my sight stopped by tall buildings and walls, by neat gardens and geometrical fields; and I had begun to worship these things and the men who brought them into being—impersonalized groups of magicians who never appeared to my consciousness as frail, uninspiring individuals. (*Talking to the Moon* 2–3)

Mathews had long realized that the wonders of civilization, as well as "war and unnatural crowding of men, slavery, group fanaticism, and social abnormalities, were inspired by the biological urge manifesting itself in progression, as were the dreams of the few who created beauty, comfort, and tragedy" (3). He emphasized that he did not return to the blackjacks because of political convictions but rather to devote a few years to pleasant and undisturbed living. There Mathews felt he might come to understand the relationship between humankind's primal and creative urges: "I realized that man's artistic creations and his dreams, often resulting in beauty, as well as his fumbling toward God, must be primal, possibly the results of the biological urge which inspires the wood thrush to sing and the coyote to talk to the moon" (3). Unlike Thoreau and Muir, Mathews settled in a place where as a child he had felt a oneness with the ridges and prairies. The influence of Thoreau's *Walden* and Muir's *My First Summer in the Sierra* is reflected as well in the organization and content of *Talking to the Moon*. Mathews follows Thoreau's example by organizing his autobiography by seasons, which allows both authors to describe not only their observations of nature but their personal growth in terms of natural cycles. The focus of Muir's book is on the description of the changes in nature during a single summer and of his maturation during that period. Mathews follows Muir's example in using a month-by-month structure, which he bases on the Osage months of the year.

Mathews also includes topics similar to those treated by Thoreau and Muir. All three authors share a strong sense of place, revealed in Thoreau's loving descriptions of the area around Walden Pond, Muir's ecstatic word landscapes of the majestic Sierra Nevada, and Mathews's poetic descriptions of the ridges and prairies in eastern Oklahoma. Both Thoreau and Mathews chronicle the changes these places undergo through the seasons and years, emphasizing that these areas transcend and reflect time while Muir recounts in diary form his daily observations of his summer in the Sierra.

Thoreau examines the Walden Pond area and the soil of his beanfield to trace their history; Muir speculates about the origin of the boulders deposited in the high mountains during the glacial period. Similarly, Mathews analyzes with the eye of the scientist and verbal landscape artist the limestone ridges and his post oak to learn the history of the rain, drought, and fire they endured over the passage of time. For Mathews, the ridges and the blackjacks link primordial nature with contemporary life. At the beginning of his book, Mathews focuses his description of the ridges on the blackjack oaks, whose dead limbs slant downward, "hard and tough as steel lances," protecting them from harm. In earlier days, buffalo rubbed against the trees to scratch their itching hides; now cows hide in their groves to deliver calves. Mathews's description of the blackjacks parallels Muir's numerous tributes to the fir, juniper, and pine trees of the Sierra.

Mathews's careful descriptions of animals, birds, and insects also reflect the influence of Thoreau and Muir. Thoreau's observations on his brute neighbors include his famous description of the mock heroic battle of the red and black ants. In attempting to come close to nature, Thoreau became an amateur scientist, observing under a microscope the movement of ants on a piece of wood, while Muir risked his life to observe a bear up close. Mathews is as curious about the creatures of nature as his predecessors were. Some of his experiments reveal a scientific detachment, as he himself seems to acknowledge. One is his futile attempt to tame a coyote whelp, which spent her days looking out of the pen with her yellow-green eyes filled with "hatred and courage" (121). Mathews coldly comments that "She taught me nothing except the fact that even at her age her mother was still interested in her and made valiant attempts to save her. She also confirmed my experiences that coyotes suffer and die in silence and thus do not endanger the other members of the band by calling for help" (123). Another example is his setting a chicken loose out on the prairie near a coyote den to determine the mother's reaction. Although the mother coyote clearly sees the chicken, she pretends the fowl is not there. The coyote both fascinated and frustrated Mathews, whose attempts to outthink it usually ended in failure. Like the Osage, Mathews regarded the coyote as "a symbol of cupidity and double-dealing" (188). For Mathews these episodes exemplify the eternal battle between the intellect of humankind and the instinct of the animal as humans vainly and destructively attempt to control nature and all its creatures. Mathews is more conscious than Thoreau and Muir that his own efforts to control nature disturb the balance.

During his first year in the blackjacks, Mathews lived as part of this balance and was proud of his harmony with the life around him. However, under the influence of the Planting Moon (April), he broke the truce: "After bringing pheasants, guineas, and chickens to the ridge, I had to fight for the survival of my charges against my predacious neighbors, which was probably a more natural state and in the end more satisfying than the 'friends and neighbor' idea'" (59). The presence of his charges whetted the predators' desires and sharpened their cunning. He and the predators were caught in a struggle, pitting their wits against one another. Mathews wonders whether his position was unnatural since he did not live off the land; thus, he was then not part of the economic struggle of the ridge which results in the balance. Mathews vividly depicts this battle with predators in the chapter entitled "Little-Flower-Killer Moon" (May), in which he tells how he emptied the cylinder of his revolver into a skunk that slaughtered many of his chickens "from sheer lust." Mathews emphasizes that the skunk behaved abnormally, killing for enjoyment rather than survival and leaving behind his headless victims. Nevertheless, Mathews confesses that, when he held the muzzle of his gun to the skunk's head and emptied the cylinder, he gloried "in the nauseating musk odor that hung on the heavy air of night, transforming its glory with the sharp explosions that broke the silence of the ridge into a symbol of the mighty power of *Homo sapiens* when aroused and announcing his entrance into the struggle" (65). For Mathews, the episode reveals the desire for revenge that lurks just beneath humankind's civilized veneer. He also acknowledges that this tragedy resulted from his bringing the chickens to his land, an act that interfered with the balance.

Like Thoreau and Muir, Mathews emphasizes sensory experience in nature, particularly hearing and sight. Just as Thoreau devotes a whole chapter of *Walden* to "Sounds" and gives detailed descriptions of animal sounds in "Winter Animals," and as Muir catalogs the animal and human sounds of the Sierra sheep camp, so Mathews includes descriptions of sounds: the April sounds of bird songs filled with "injured innocence and pessimism" (50) and of long cattle trains that "come screaming into the little loading pens and stand panting from their exertion as the cattle bawl and the boys shout as they unload them" (51). Mathews follows the examples of Thoreau and Muir in his emphasis on sight as well. Thoreau, in his chapter on "The Ponds" in *Walden* vividly describes the colors of shore and water while Muir, in *My First Summer in the Sierra*, paints verbal landscapes of the magnificent grandeur of this mountain range. Although Mathews includes far less geographic and landscape description than Thoreau and Muir, he includes some lovely descriptive passages in his chapter "Little-Flower-Killer Moon" of the thousands of little flowers that die away in May and of the flowering weeds that replace them, reinforcing the theme of the fragility of life in the cycles of nature elaborated in that chapter. Equally beautiful are the pictures of the prairies awash in the old-gold color of sunflowers, butterflies, and goldfinches that Mathews creates in the chapter called "Yellow-Flower Moon" (August). However, in both of these chapters Mathews uses these descriptions as introductions to his observations on insects, birds, animals, and men, which are the focus of his interest.

Another parallel to Thoreau and Muir is Mathews's description of his living accommodations. For Mathews, as for Thoreau, his cabin and cultivated land represent personal space between the town and the wild. Whereas Thoreau recounts his labors in planting his garden and tilling his beanfield, Mathews describes his in planting kafir, a grain sorghum, for the prairie chickens and trees and shrubbery for his yard. Thoreau plants to eat while Mathews plants to encourage the presence of fowls and to shade himself from the parching Oklahoma sun and winds. Just as Thoreau pauses in tilling his beanfield to observe the hawks flying above him, Mathews pauses in his planting to observe the mockingbirds' return, the prairie chickens' dances, and the cocks' fights. Unlike Thoreau, Mathews does not use the description of building his cabin as a jumping-off point for discussing the history of man's attitude toward shelter. Instead, he uses it to introduce the human inhabitants of the ridges and prairies—Virgil, the most efficient hand on the ranch and Mathews's house builder, and other ranch hands who question why Mathews builds on a high ridge far from arable land and why he plans to live alone. Their attitudes set Mathews's own in relief.

There are parallels as well in the three authors' treatment of such subjects as solitude, neighbors, and visitors. For example, all three enjoy occasional visits with friends. Thoreau keeps three chairs for company; Mathews keeps a bountiful supply of food for his city guests. Mathews's descriptions of his pleasures in cooking echo those of Thoreau and Muir on bread making. The three authors also create memorable portraits of their visitors and neighbors. However, Muir and Mathews do not denigrate their neighbors or companions as does Thoreau in his description of the hapless Irish bogsman, John Field, whom he calls "honest, hardworking, but shiftless" (173). Muir has little in common with his campmates, who are oblivious to the beauties of nature. He refers to Delaney as Don Quixote, because his sharp profile resembles that of the Spanish knight, and to Billy, the tobacco-chewing shepherd and camp butcher, as Sancho Panza. However, Muir is sympathetic to the hard life that Billy led.

Mathews creates several vivid portraits of locals. Especially memorable is that of Les Claypool, a former cowboy whose face was "like weathered granite"; "his steel-gray eyes and his silence, as he looked at his great gold watch with the hunting case," caused Mathews to feel like a guilty schoolboy when he was late for a meeting. Claypool staunchly clung to the past and resisted change. Thirty-eight years after he quit working on cattle drives and after he became a car owner, Claypool still kept his horse saddled, ready for emergencies.

*Talking to the Moon* shows the influence of Thoreau's *Walden* in its purpose, general structure, and content, and of Muir's *My First Summer in the Sierra* in its detailed, scientific descriptions of nature and sympathetic portraits of local characters. While it is clear that Mathews wished to write *Talking to the Moon* within the tradition of the pastoral, spiritual autobiography popularized by Thoreau and Muir, it is equally clear that he wishes to distinguish his work from theirs by adding an emphasis on Indian history and culture largely absent from their books. The difference in the focus of the autobiographies is evident in the authors' choice of titles. Whereas Thoreau and Muir select titles that refer to the places where they renewed themselves in nature, Mathews chooses one that alludes to the Osage's interrelationship with their natural gods. In *Walden*, Thoreau makes only a few fleeting references to the Indians near Concord, their simple shelters, and the ancient civilization that inhabited the soil Thoreau tills in his beanfield. Although Muir includes more descriptions of Indians he encounters in the Sierra, he is equally detached from them as people. This is especially clear in his comments about the Indian member of his sheep camp. Describing how the men chatted during breakfast, Muir remarks that the "Indian kept in the background, saying never a word, as if he belonged to another species" (10). Unlike Billy, the shepherd, the "Indian" is neither given a name nor described in a character sketch. Later in *My First Summer in the Sierra*, Muir expands his reaction to Indian silence in the description of another Indian who arrived unobserved, "as motionless and weather-stained as an old tree-stump that had stood there for centuries. All Indians seem to have learned this wonderful way of walking unseen,—making themselves invisible like certain spiders I have been observing here" (53). Muir also mentions the Digger Indians who inhabit the area and gives a short biography of Old Tenaya, the Yosemite chief and namesake of the basin.[3]

By stressing the Indian heritage of the blackjack region, Mathews makes *Talking to the Moon* an account of the changes in the Osage culture that had survived for centuries as part of the balance of the blackjacks and prairie as well as an account of the changes in nature and himself. Mathews's sensitivity to the Osage is evident in his decision to pay tribute to his tribal ancestry not by exploring his own ethnicity as a mixed-blood but rather by focusing on the tribe's myths, history, customs, and elders. In fact, he does not mention his own Osage heritage, although his wife does in her foreword to the 1981 edition. As Terry P. Wilson points out in "The Osage Oxonian," Mathews was well aware of the antagonism of a faction of Osage full-bloods toward mixed-bloods. The full-bloods had not forgotten the fraud perpetuated in 1906, when many whites had their names included on the Osage rolls in order to get allotments of Osage land. Mathews realized that, although his own identity as an Osage was not tainted in this way, he was always "suspect in the minds of some." According to Wilson, the author's "elections to the tribal council said less about his identification as an Indian in the eyes of the Osages and more about their respect for his education, familiarity with the complexities of white society, and devotion to the tribe's interests." Wilson correctly concludes that this "reluctant dependence on Mathews and other mixed-bloods is typical of the ambivalence in most tribes and many Indian organizations" ("Osage Oxonian" 269).

Undoubtedly, Mathews realized that exploring his own ethnicity in this autobiography would have resulted in severe criticism from the Osages and would have undercut his efforts on their behalf. Instead, he chose to focus on recording what he learned from the Osages and on creating memorable portraits of tribal members. Mathews was all too aware that, since the beginning of the reservation period in 1878, the Osages had endured traumatic changes in their culture. In 1907, Oklahoma became a state and the Osage Nation reservation became Osage County. Unlike other Indian tribes in Oklahoma, the Osage had retained the mineral rights to their lands after allotment. The discovery of oil on Osage lands in 1897 led to boom times in the 1920s that threatened to extinguish traditional Osage culture and values. Oil companies, entrepreneurs, and scalawags poured into Osage County to take advantage of the Osages' oil and their new-found wealth. During what Mathews calls in *The Osages* the "Great Frenzy," some Osages spent their money freely. Other Osages were defrauded or murdered for their lands and oil money.[4] Still others succumbed to alcoholism. By 1932, when Mathews settled in his cabin in the blackjacks, the boom of the 1920s was over. As Mathews notes in *The Osages*, the oil royalties peaked in 1925 at $13,000 per capita but slipped in 1932 to $712 (775).

The traditional Osage were, in Mathews's view, the human inhabitants of the blackjack region most in tune with the land. The key to this oneness with nature was their religion:

> He [the traditional Osage man] built up in his imagination the Great Mysteries and he walked, fought, hunted and mated with the approval of them. When the Force urged him to expression, he turned his eyes to Grandfather the Sun; the colors he saw under his closed eyelids, he put into beadwork, quillwork, and painting, as inspirations from one of the greatest manifestations of the Great Mysteries, the sun, Father of Father Fire, impregnator of Mother Earth." (*Talking to the Moon* 221)

The Osage tribe symbolized the universe, and the Osages divided themselves and their universe into two parts: man and animal, spiritual and material, sky (Chesho; Sky People; Peace Division) and earth (Hunkah; Earth People; War Division). The Osage conceived of the moon as a woman because she periodically appeared twelve times a year; because of the moon's power over the earth; and because when she dominated the ridges, there was no disturbance by the male element: "Grandfather the Sun has gone to rest and even Father the fire is dim in her presence, as though out of a traditional understanding and deference, like a great warrior in camp where woman is supreme." As a good woman should, she leaves at dawn, taking her children, the stars, so as not to disturb Grandfather the Sun when he takes over the male world of daytime (33). Mathews incorporates the Osage concept of the moon as a woman into many chapters of *Talking to the Moon*. The opening passage of the chapter called "Single Moon by Himself" (January) illustrates how Mathews uses Osage concepts of the Moon Woman to set the mood: "The Moon Woman floats by herself now. There are no babies or fruits or flowers, say the Osage, and the Moon Woman is lonesome. She is not so gay and temperamental but dull and moody. Snow may stay on the ground for a long time, and there will be no sun, and the days as much alike, cold and gloomy. The moon is sometimes called Frost-on-Inside-of-Lodge Moon and long ago was known as the Hunger Moon" (210).

For Mathews, traditional Osage life achieved a balance in nature which the white man never gained and which the Osage themselves lost when they were forced to abandon the old, free life and substitute the peyote cult or Christianity for the gods of their ancestors. Mathews describes the balance the Osage achieved in the chapter on the Planting Moon (April), the time for female ceremonies of planting and growth. Using Osage-style English, Mathews retells old Ee-Nah-Apee's story about Osage planting customs, which exemplify the tribe's belief in balance:

> Purty soon womens go to them little—hills, I guess, and they make hole with that pole on south side of that there hill. They used to say Grandfather sure would see them holes in them hills on south side, that-a-way. We put corn in them hills, in them little holes; and when we have all of 'em with corn in it, we put our feets on it. We stand on them little hills and make drum against the earth with the poles and sing purty song. (48)

The women stamp the hills with the left foot for Chesho and the right for Hunkah. That the Osage have moved from these customs into the world of the white man is demonstrated by

Ee-Nah-Apee laughing when she told the story, as "though she were embarrassed by recalling such primitive things that the tribe was now attempting to put away forever" (48). The Osage recognized that the nature of the world and humankind included both of these polarities, which must be kept in balance. They also recognized that at various times one would dominate the other. Certainly this division of the Osage into Chesho (associated with peace and thought or imagination) and Hunkah (associated with war and physical action) influences Mathews's attitudes toward his own state of mind, which moves between these polarities. When the author first moved to the blackjacks, he exulted in the physical: "I wanted to express my harmony with the natural flow of life on my bit of earth through physical action" (16). The planting song of the Osages runs through his head, stimulating him to the physical action of planting trees and shrubs. Another example of action during a Hunkah state of mind is his narrative, in the chapter called "Deer Breeding Moon" (October), of joining in a hunt to track down a bear which had killed some of a neighbor's sheep: "Bear hunting, with its frenzied action and the deep voices of the bloodhounds echoing from the savage walls of the mountain canyons, awakens every nerve to incautious action" (168). He notes that, ten years later, his desire for action had been tempered. In the chapter "Single Moon by Himself" (January), Mathews describes his thoughts as "Chesho, as they should be, and there are no longer Hunkah thoughts of youth and action, when Single Moon by Himself comes to the blackjacks, and I am inside the dark little sandstone house by the fire" (224).

Among the several Osage myths that Mathews blends into *Talking to the Moon* is that of the spider, the Osage symbol that Mathews uses on the spines of the books he has authored. Mathews indicates that the spider was formerly a clan symbol but is now used by a woman's secret society. According to the story, members of a clan could not make up their minds about which animal to choose as a symbol suitable to great warriors. During their search, they rejected many animals until one of their leaders walked into a spiderweb. The spider persuaded them to accept it as their symbol: "I am a little black thing; I have not the strength, the courage, the beauty of those you talk about, but remember this: wherever I go I build my house, and where I build my house all things come to it" (142). Mathews also comments on the Osage use of the coyote in their stories that "depend on dignity made ridiculous as a basis for humor." The coyote also appears as a warning for children that they should never think of themselves as being shrewder than others, since "one may be outwitted through one's own vanity" (188). For the Osage, the coyote was an indicator of something astir on the prairie, either enemy, friend, or quarry. They mimicked his yelping to deceive enemies: "He was an important person in the scheme of things, but he hadn't the proper virtues for symbolism" (189).

Mathews's most extended treatment of Osage history and culture is contained in the chapter "Buffalo-Pawing-Earth Moon" (June), focusing on the month when the Ee-lon-shescha, male ceremonial dances, are held at the villages of the three active branches of the original five physical divisions of the Osage.[5] He vividly evokes the color and customs of these dances, describing the different costumes and steps used by dancers from various clans, the honoring songs, giveaways, and the storytelling. Mathews's activities and observations during the ceremonies reveal his relationship to the tribe. While he does not participate in the ceremonies, he observes proper etiquette by giving money to the drum keeper to help support the ceremonies and then joins the old men, who evidently welcome him: "Here I pick up many stories of the jealousy between the Peyote factions, and laugh with them over the stories of dignified men being humiliated. I like the sound of their voices and the graceful movements of their hands as they talk, in this setting of colorful activity" (79). To illustrate Osage storytelling, Mathews recreates a scene in which an elder describes, in Osage dialect and within the hearing of the subject's grandson, how an arrogant Osage male was humiliated in the midst of his bragging. While the proud Osage was in the middle of a speech designed to impress some Sioux visitors, a louse crawled up his eagle feather headdress: "At the same time he finish his talkin' that feather make bow, ain't it? That little eagle feather make bow with louse ridin' on it—sure was funny" (81). The story exemplifies Indians' use of humorous stories to enforce approved behavior.

Mathews confesses that he has never grown tired of watching the dancers, whom he has watched since he was a small boy—"a time when they wore nothing except breechcloths, moccasins, silver arm bands, and scalplocks and carried hand mirrors and war axes." Then the dancers were tall and lean. But now, despite the fat bellies and flabby arms and gorgeous costumes, "the dance is grave and the figures graceful, and in its dignity and fervency the dance is still a prayer" to Wah'Kon-Tah of the old religion, "not withstanding the symbols of peyote with which they adorn themselves" (83). He comments that the June dances, which originally had ritual but at the time he describes had only social significance, and the gossip at the dances about conflict between peyote factions reinforce his sense of the drama in the world represented by the relentless movement of Christianity: "I feel the earth's drama all about me, but the conflict between Christianity and the old religion of the Osages forces itself upon my attention . . ." (84). Mathews feels extremely fortunate to witness the last struggle of a native religion and believes that his daily life in the blackjacks was as influenced by this as by any other struggle for survival: "The passing of a concept of God seems to be almost as poignant as the passing of a species" (84).

Mathews illustrates this passing of the old religion, along with his own determination to preserve its artifacts, by recreating a scene between himself and the second son of Spotted Horse. The young man brings his father's message that, although it is all right to have a sacred medicine bundle in the Osage museum Mathews that is to establish, he should not open it: "He says you alltime ask too many questions about them bundles, he says. You oughtn't do that; it's bad. He says you' sure die if you fool with them things. Osage have put them bad things away, he says" (85).

The confusion into which Christianity and industrialization have thrown the Osage is only part of that tribe's tragedy. Although old men lamented the destruction of the social structure, they lamented even more the consequent end of the tribe as a unit and the loss of their individual immortality. Their consciousness points out to them "the end of their race, the end of their god, the complete assimilation of their children, and the end of their immortality. It is the sheet-water of oblivion that washes their moccasin prints from the ridges and agitates their last thoughts" (86).

Because the old Osage chief, Eagle-That-Gets-What-He-Wants, feared that tribal traditions would disappear from memory, unremembered by young Osage eager to adopt white ways, he arranged for his wife to interpret his accounts of Osage oral traditions, which Mathews wrote down. The chief's story about Tze Topah, his uncle and the chief of the Little Osages, illustrates how the Osage used oral tradition to keep their history and culture alive in the memories of their people. When old Tze Topah realized he would die soon, he spent many hours telling people what he knew and did when young. Unable to tell his stories to a band out hunting, Tze Topah dressed in his war finery and rode through the band's camp, singing so that all people would stop their work to hear his song and so that they would know him and remember him as long as they had tongues to talk and their children ears to hear.

For Mathews, the peyotism of the Native American Church represents a blend of Osage religion and Christianity. Many of the Osage elders felt that the religion of their god, Wah'Kon-Tah, was not strong enough to stand up against Christianity and therefore should be put aside. Mathews emphasizes that the Osage "adopted the Man on the Cross because they understand him. He is both Chesho and Hunkah. His footprints are on the peyote altars, and they are deep like the footprints of one who has jumped" (239). Mathews enlivens his discussion of Osage culture with a series of verbal portraits of Osage elders. Many of these are contained in the chapter "Yellow-Flower Moon" (August), in which he describes how he helped an artist commissioned to paint the pictures of the old men for the Osage Museum. The proud Osage elder, Claremore, insists on posing for days in full regalia despite the withering July heat. The teasing Abbott, a member of the Osage tribal council, comments that the portrait of Claremore looks like a "white man that lost his money. Maybe someday when I look at it, I shoot myself" (131). When Abbott poses for his own portrait, Mathews brings the desired twinkle to the council member's eye by recalling the story of how Abbott, who was always in debt, told a butterfly that landed on his shoulder, "'Pay you next week'" (131). The incident also illustrates Mathews's rapport with the Osage elders. Other examples of Indian humor are provided by Nonceh Tonkah, the only elder to wear a scalplock. The old man instructs his daughter in Osage to tell the artist to bring his daughter to Nonceh Tonkah in exchange for his posing. The elder also asked the artist if he wants Nonceh Tonkah's head when he dies. His patronizing daughter refuses to translate these unseemly remarks. Mathews creates another memorable portrait in his characterization of Louie, a Cherokee who talks to owls, explaining that he does not have to hide from the owls because "'them owls don't care 'bout nothin' when they do this here big talkin'.'" Louie hoots at the owls in a coaxing, seductive tone which they answer in kind (41). For Mathews, Louie embodies the unity between the Indian and nature.

### III

Like Thoreau and Muir, Mathews sees himself as a mediator between man and nature. However, whereas Thoreau eschews identification with the purely natural man represented by Indians and non-Indian woodcutters, and Muir feels a bond with his shepherd but not with the Sierra Indians, Mathews praises both Indians and other men of nature for achieving a natural balance through instinct that he can achieve only through intellect. Each of the three writers attempts to achieve a balance between the polarities of the intellectual or imaginative and the physical or instinctual. Thoreau's concept of nature and of the balance between the polarities is rooted in the Romantic attitudes toward nature expressed by writers like Goethe and Wordsworth. As James MacIntosh points out, Thoreau shares with these writers a "powerful wish to love nature and even to merge with it, with a consciousness, sometimes explicit, sometimes concealed, of separation" (20).[6] MacIntosh notes that Thoreau shares the Romantics' secret fear of the destructiveness of nature—the natural cycle of growth, decay, death, and rebirth—and that he is wary both of the existence of nature within himself and of his realization that nature can sometimes exist as power or chaos rather than as life or growth. For Goethe, Wordsworth, and Thoreau, repeated experience is a "necessary way to enlightenment and truth" (57). They are attracted by the "world of generation that brings pleasure and peace to the men of restless mind because it is both ordered and alive" (58).

Muir shares with the Romantics an ability to express ecstasy in the presence of the natural sublime. Like Thoreau, he was influenced by both Wordsworth and Emerson. Harold P. Simonson suggests in "The Tempered Romanticism of John Muir" that the author tried in his work to reconcile the conflicting ideas that pertained, on the one hand, "to nature that conforms to the mind's eye and projects the drama of one's developing self; and, on the other hand, to nature as divine emanation, as revelation, as topological figure presupposing a distinctly separate and sovereign God" (228). Simonson comments that Muir attempted to verify nature's higher laws, as did Thoreau, and found his epiphany in nature. Although Muir has less fear of the destructiveness of nature than Thoreau, he is nevertheless aware of its darker side. Simonson concludes that, despite Muir's affirmations about the flow and unity of nature's laws, Muir retained a dualized Christian cosmology, in which the soul is a divine spark known in a rapt state of wildness, and body was the bondage of society and morality, symbolized by life in the lowlands (239).[7]

Mathews's sense of balance is rooted not only in the literary traditions represented by Thoreau and Muir but in the oral traditions of the Osage. Like Thoreau and Muir, he too deals with issues of duality—between the primal and the ornamental (a term he takes from Thoreau) or intellectually creative. Strongly influencing his thought, however, are the Osage principles of Chesho (sky, passivity, peace) and Hunka (earth, action, war), which one must learn to balance. However, Mathews seems far less fearful of the dark side of nature than do Thoreau and Muir. In the chapter "The Single Moon By Himself" (January), Mathews comments on the constant battle to keep the balance:

> The peace of my ridge is not a peace but a series of range-line skirmishes and constant struggle for survival. The balance is kept by bluff and a respect for that power which backs it up, and it utilizes and protects an area large enough and fruitful enough to sustain that power. The laws of the earth for survival are laid down, and man is not far enough away from the earth to supersede them with those of his own creation; he can only go back to the earth to ascertain where he has diverged from the natural processes. (226)

Thoreau and Muir lament that America destroys its soul and the land in its quest for material and industrial wealth. While recognizing these dangers, Mathews is also deeply concerned about the possible extinction both of Osage culture as a result of white pressure and of the free world as a result of World War II. Writing in 1942, when the survival of freedom in the United States and Europe was very much in doubt, Mathews concludes that the human race cannot have lasting peace, even though organized warfare seems to be human-created and therefore may be human-controlled: "Forced peace, which is the only kind of peace man can conceive of now in his present stage of development, cannot last any longer than the powers that impose it" (226).

All three authors want to merge with and yet remain separate from nature. The differences between the philosophical positions of Thoreau and Mathews are exemplified in their attitudes toward hunting. In the chapter on "Higher Laws" in *Walden*, Thoreau stresses that hunting and fishing are usually a young man's introduction to nature. If he has the seeds of a better life in him, a man "distinguishes his proper objects, as a poet or naturalist it may be, and leaves the gun and fishpole behind" as did Thoreau himself (179). Meat eating, Thoreau feels, is a throwback to savage cannibalism—a reminder of a primitiveness that man must overcome. Muir treats the subject indirectly, through his description of the hunting techniques of David Brown, a gold miner and renowned bear hunter. Mathews, on the other hand, regards hunting as a form of ornamental play, a reminder of man's struggle for survival. The instinct to hunt remains strong in Mathews despite his progression to a sense of community with humanity and its renewal in nature. In the chapter "Deer-Breeding Moon" (October), Mathews describes the revitalizing power of a bear hunt:

> Somewhere ahead of that excited chorusing was a great black beast whose ancestors far back in time once hunted man, and man has a racial memory of having been the delicate, thin-skinned hunted instead of the hunter, which adds zest to bear hunting; the racial memory of the scratching and sniffing at his cave barrier is still deep in man's soul. (168)

Thoreau, Muir, and Mathews use the cycles of nature as a framework for describing their own cycles of maturation and renewal, recalled for the benefit of the reader. All three authors emphasize, as did Wordsworth before them, that humanity must progress from physical to spiritual perceptions of nature but that close observation of the physical is a necessary stage to reaching the spiritual. Early in *Talking to the Moon*, Mathews stresses that, although humankind has the same natural urges as other species, he goes farther by acknowledging the progression of life through his dream of God. Mathews's attempts to protect his fowls from predators made him part of the life struggle and of the balance of the ridge: "Thus, I achieved a greater harmony with my environment and found that there is no place for dreams in natural progression, and it seems to me that I realized for the first time that with responsibility come enemies" (60).

As the time and the seasons come and go, Mathews, like the other inhabitants of the ridges and prairies, is changed. Although he no longer wants to battle the natural elements, he becomes restless because just living and filling up his days are not enough: "First, I had to have responsibility and disturb the balance of the blackjacks: then, after a few years, I extended my activities beyond the ridges" (125). Unlike Thoreau, he did not move away from his retreat, but instead he entered the world of social service by becoming a member of the Osage tribal business committee and a member of the Oklahoma Board of Education.

In explaining why he left Walden Pond, Thoreau says that "perhaps it seemed to me that I had several more lives to live, and could not spare any more time for that one. It is remarkable how easily and insensibly we fall into a particular route and make a beaten track for ourselves" (259). Urging his readers to be a "Columbus to whole new continents and worlds within you," Thoreau wants them to open new channels, "not of trade, but of thought" (258). Thoreau yearns for truth rather than for love, money, or fame. For Muir, the exploration of the Sierra Nevada is the first excursion into a sublime land, which ends only because the coming fall and winter necessitate his bringing the sheep back down from the mountains, not because he was psychologically ready to leave unspoiled nature. He remained in the Sierra for ten years.

Like Thoreau, Mathews matures sufficiently to end his isolation. He had begun to reenter the world of social responsibility by becoming a member of the Osage tribal council and running, unsuccessfully, for the school board. His decision to conclude his retreat is dramatized in his vain attempt to enlist in active service during World War II, described in the last chapter, "The Light-of-the-Day-Returns or Coyote-Breeding Moon" (February). Turned down, Mathews was forced to recognize that he had indeed moved from the active Hunkah world to the inactive Chesho world. His "Chesho thoughts have the same roots as his Hunkah thoughts and the same roots as the Hunkah actions in all species, even though inspired by the Force as an urge to immortality" (242). Not satisfied to feel and enjoy the flood of emotion that living inspires and expresses in action, he now wants to express the subtleties of world symbols.

In his conclusion, Mathews seems to take up the challenge offered by Thoreau to seek out new worlds of thought, which he will express in words, so that people will not only know that a great ego passed that way but that Mathews "heard the wood thrush at twilight—the voice disembodied in the dripping woods—that I have heard the coyote talk to the moon and watched the geese against a cold autumn sunset" (243). By writing *Talking to the Moon*, Mathews recaptures the experience of renewal in nature earlier described by Thoreau in *Walden* and Muir in *My First Summer in the Sierra*. He also immortalizes in poetic prose the traditions of his beloved Osage, who achieved a harmony with nature that the three authors sought and that humankind must seek if we are to survive.

## Notes

1.  H. David Brumble III has published two indispensable guides to the field: *An Annotated Bibliography of American Indian and Eskimo Autobiographies* and "A Supplement to *An Annotated Bibliography of American Indian and Eskimo Autobiographies*" in his *American Indian Autobiography*. In the latter book, Brumble gives a comprehensive analysis of the attributes and influence of preliterate traditions of Native-American life history and of the role of editors, ghost writers, and amanuenses. In *For Those Who Come After*, Arnold Krupat discusses the literary influences, structure, and role of the editors in several narrated autobiographies. Gretchen Bataille and Kathleen Mullen Sands examine in *American Indian Women: Telling Their Lives* the development of women's life histories and autobiographies. They also discuss the role of the editors and transcribers in shaping these works. Lynne O'Brien briefly surveys the life histories of Plains Indians in her *Plains Indian Autobiographies*. In "Three Nineteenth-Century American Indian Autobiographers," Ruoff traces the influences of the spiritual confession, missionary reminiscence,

slave narrative, and American-Indian oral traditions on the written autobiographies of William Apes, George Copway, and Sarah Winnemucca.

2. For discussions of the influence of the spiritual confession on autobiography, see G. A. Starr, *Defoe and Spiritual Autobiography*. Informative discussions of the forms of slave narratives include William L. Andrews, *To Tell a Free Story*; Stephen Butterfield, *Black Autobiography in America*; Frances Smith Foster, *Witnessing Slavery*; Robert B. Stepto, *From Behind the Veil*.

3. For discussions of Thoreau's and Muir's evolving attitudes toward Indians, see Richard F. Fleck, *Henry Thoreau and John Muir among the Indians* and Robert F. Sayre, *Thoreau and the American Indians*.

4. Linda Hogan (Chickasaw) vividly recreates the dangers to their lives and culture faced by the Osage in her *Mean Spirit* (1990), a fictional account of the oil murders. The fullest historical account of the impact of oil on the Osage is Terry P. Wilson's *The Underground Reservation: Osage Oil* (1985), which focuses on the period from 1875 to the present.

5. For a detailed description of these dances, see Callahan, *The Osage Ceremonial Dance I'n-Lon-Schka* (1990). The name of the dance is variously spelled.

6. For additional discussion of Thoreau's attitudes toward nature and the spiritual versus the physical worlds, see especially Frederick Garber, *Thoreau's Redemptive Imagination*; Stanley Cavell, *The Senses of Walden*; and Sherman Paul, *The Shores of America: Thoreau's Inward Exploration*.

7. Other works dealing with Muir's concepts of nature and his philosophies include Michael P. Cohen, *The Pathless Way*, and John C. Elder, "John Muir and the Literature of Wilderness."

# Bibliography

Andrews, William L. *To Tell a Free Story: The First Century of Afro-American Autobiography, 1760–1865*. Urbana: U of Illinois P, 1986.

Apes, William (Pequot). *A Son of the Forest: The Experience of William Apes, a Native of the Forest*. New York: Author, 1829. Rev. ed. 1831.

Bailey, Garrick. "John Joseph Mathews." In *American Indian Intellectuals*, ed. Margot Liberty. 1976 Proceedings of the American Ethnological Society. St. Paul: West, 1978. 205–14.

Bataille, Gretchen M., and Kathleen Mullen Sands. *American Indian Women: Telling Their Lives*. Lincoln: U of Nebraska P, 1984.

Black Hawk (Sauk). *Black Hawk: An Autobiography*, ed. Antoine Le Claire and John B. Patterson. Originally published as *Life of Ma-ka-tai-me-she-kia-kiak, or Black Hawk*. 1833. New introd. by Donald Jackson. Urbana: U of Illinois P, 1955.

Brumble, H. David, III, comp. *American Indian Autobiography*. Berkeley: U of California P, 1988.

————. *An Annotated Bibliography of American Indian and Eskimo Autobiographies*. Lincoln: U of Nebraska P, 1981.

Butterfield, Stephen. *Black Autobiography in America*. Amherst: U of Massachusetts P, 1974.

Callahan, Alice Anne (Osage). *The Osage Ceremonial Dance I'n-Lon-Schka*. Civilization of the American Indian Series, no. 201. Norman: U of Oklahoma P, 1990.

Cavell, Stanley. *The Senses of Walden*. 1972. Expanded ed. San Francisco: North Point, 1981.

Cohen, Michael P. *The Pathless Way: John Muir and American Wilderness*. Madison: U of Wisconsin P, 1984.

Copway, George (Ojibwa). *The Life, History and Travels of Kah-ge-ga-gah-bowh (George Copway)*. . . . Albany, NY: Weed and Parsons, 1847. Republished as *The Life, Letters and Speeches of Kah-ge-ga-gah-bowh, or G. Copway*. . . . New York: Benedict, 1850; and as *Recollections of a Forest Life; or, The Life and Travels of Kah-ge-ga-gah-bowh, or George Copway*. London: Gilpin, 1851.

Cruikshank, Julie, Angela Sidney, Kitty Smith, and Annie Ned. *Life Lived like a Story: Life Stories of Three Yukon Elders*. American Indian Lives Series. Lincoln: U of Nebraska P, 1991.

Eastman, Charles (Sioux). *From the Deep Woods to Civilization: Chapters in the Autobiography of an Indian.* 1916. Introd. by Raymond Wilson. Lincoln: U of Nebraska P, 1977.

———. *Indian Boyhood.* 1902. New York: Dover, 1971. Introd. by Frederick W. Turner III. Greenwich, CT: Fawcett, 1972.

Elder, John C. "John Muir and the Literature of Wilderness." *Massachusetts Review* 22 (1981): 375–86.

Fleck, Richard F. *Henry Thoreau and John Muir among the Indians.* Hamden, CT: Archon, 1985.

Foster, Frances Smith. *Witnessing Slavery: The Development of the Antebellum Slave Narrative.* Westport, CT: Greenwood, 1979.

Garber, Frederick. *Thoreau's Redemptive Imagination.* New York: New York UP, 1977.

Hogan, Linda (Chickasaw). *Mean Spirit.* New York: Atheneum, 1990.

Krupat, Arnold. *For Those Who Come After: A Study of Native American Autobiography.* Berkeley: U of California P, 1985.

La Flesche, Francis (Omaha). *The Middle Five: Indian School Boys of the Omaha Tribe.* 1900. Foreword by David A. Baerreis. Lincoln: U of Nebraska P, 1978.

Logsdon, Guy. "John Joseph Mathews—A Conversation." *Nimrod* 16, no. 2 (1972): 70–89.

MacIntosh, James. *Thoreau as Romantic Naturalist: His Shifting Stance Toward Nature.* Ithaca: Cornell UP, 1974.

Mathews, John Joseph. *Life and Death of an Oilman: The Career of E. W. Marland.* Norman: U of Oklahoma P, 1951, 1976.

———. *The Osages: Children of the Middle Waters.* Norman: U of Oklahoma P, 1961.

———. *Sundown.* 1934. Introd. by Virginia H. Mathews. Norman: U of Oklahoma P, 1987.

———. *Talking to the Moon.* 1945. Foreword by Elizabeth Mathews. Norman: U of Oklahoma P, 1981.

———. *Wah'Kon-Tah: The Osage and the White Man's Road.* Norman: U of Oklahoma P, 1932, 1968.

Muir, John. *My First Summer in the Sierra.* 1911. Boston: Houghton, 1916, 1979. All citations are to the 1979 edition.

O'Brien, Lynne Woods. *Plains Indian Autobiographies.* Western Writers Series, no. 10. Boise: Boise State College P, 1973.

Paul, Sherman. *The Shores of America: Thoreau's Inward Exploration.* Urbana: U of Illinois P, 1958.

Ruoff, A. LaVonne Brown. "Three Nineteenth-Century American Indian Autobiographers." In *Redefining American Literary History*, ed. Ruoff and Jerry W. Ward, Jr. New York: MLA, 1990. 251–69. The autobiographers are William Apes (Pequot), George Copway (Ojibwa), and Sarah Winnemucca (Paiute).

Sayre, Robert F. "Autobiography and the Making of America." In *Autobiography: Essays Theoretical and Critical*, ed. James Olney. Princeton: Princeton UP, 1980, 146–68.

———. *Thoreau and the American Indians.* Princeton: Princeton UP, 1977.

Simonson, Harold P. "The Tempered Romanticism of John Muir." *Western American Literature* 13, no. 3 (1978): 227–41.

Standing Bear, Luther (Sioux). *Land of the Spotted People.* 1933. Foreword by Richard N. Ellis. Lincoln: U of Nebraska P, 1978.

———. *My People the Sioux.* E. A. Brininstool. 1928. Introd. by Richard N. Ellis. Lincoln: U of Nebraska P, 1975.

Starr, G. A. *Defoe and Spiritual Autobiography.* Princeton: Princeton UP, 1965.

Stepto, Robert. *From Behind the Veil: A Study of Afro-American Narrative.* Urbana: U of Illinois P, 1979.

Thoreau, Henry David. *The Variorum Walden.* Annotated and introduced by Walter Harding. New York: Twayne, 1962. All citations are to this edition.

Wilson, Terry P. (Potawatomi). "Osage Oxonian: The Heritage of John Joseph Mathews." *Chronicles of Oklahoma* 59, no. 3 (Fall 1981): 264–92.

———. *The Underground Reservation: Osage Oil.* Lincoln: U of Nebraska P, 1985.

Winnemucca, Sarah (Hopkins; Paiute). *Life among the Piutes [sic]: Their Wrongs and Claims.* Ed. Mrs. Horace Mann. 1883. Bishop, CA: Chalfant, 1969.

# Autobiography after Emancipation: The Example of Elizabeth Keckley

*Frances Smith Foster*

The increased scholarly attention both to autobiography and to African-American studies which came about in the 1970s proved to be a bonanza for African-American autobiographical studies. Though the Vietnam era fostered this latest revision of the canon, the post–World War II period laid its foundation. Both Marion Starling and Charles Nichols completed dissertations in the 1940s which signaled the first serious literary study of slave narratives. Since then, studies such as my *Witnessing Slavery* (1979); *The Art of the Slave Narrative*, edited by Sekora and Turner (1982); and *The Slave's Narrative*, edited by Davis and Gates (1985) have firmly established the autobiographical works of slaves and ex-slaves as part of the American literary tradition. William Andrews's *To Tell a Free Story: The First Century of Afro-American Autobiography, 1760–1865* (1986) has broken new ground by redefining the terms of bondage and freedom with his concentration upon what he terms the "literary emancipation" of the African-American narrative. Also in the late 1940s, Rebecca Chalmers Barton's *Witnesses for Freedom: Negro Americans in Autobiography* suggested ways of categorizing the many contributions since Booker T. Washington's *Up from Slavery*. Later studies of African-American autobiography such as Butterfield's *Black Autobiography in America* (1974), Smith's *Where I'm Bound: Patterns of Slavery and Freedom in Black American Autobiography* (1974), and Stepto's *From Behind the Veil: A Study of Afro-American Narrative* (1979) have in their own ways responded to Barton's call. Currently, there is unprecedented attention to African-American autobiographies, the genre that many modern critics recognize as the fountainhead of African-American literature.

Scholarly attention, however, has concentrated upon the

antebellum and the twentieth-century African-American autobiographies. My intention with this essay is to suggest
something of the in-between, the period immediately after the
Civil War and before the turn of the century, a period wherein
the genre began to expand in accordance with the changes in
literary form, social environment, and African-American experience. My example is Elizabeth Keckley's *Behind the
Scenes; Or, Thirty Years a Slave, and Four Years in the White
House,* an autobiography published in 1868. It is, in many
ways, representative of the postbellum slave narratives.
Analysis of its form and content reveals much about the assumptions and traditions within which African Americans of
the Reconstruction period wrote and the ways in which their
writings were received. Though representative, it is also a special case. The extreme controversy that its publication engen-
dered gave this work at first unusual notoriety and then
unmerited neglect.

Before focusing upon the example of Keckley's autobiography, however, it will be helpful to briefly review the origins
of African-American autobiography and the place of this form
in literary history. Extant examples are rare, but they are frequent enough for scholars now to understand that as early as
2450 B.C. Assyrians, Egyptians, and Babylonians customarily
inscribed prayers and personal desires upon tombs and pillars.
Though male writers dominate this genre, women did participate. Princess Nj-sedjer-Kai's prayers are inscribed upon a
tomb dated from the Fifth Dynasty, and the "Tale of Ahuri"
(ca. 1570 – 1085 B.C.) is a first-person account of the life of a
pharaoh's daughter (Jelinek 11–12). Autobiographical writing
entered the Greco-Roman tradition several centuries before
Margery Burnham Kempe wrote the earliest extant autobiography in English.[1]

Of course, the originators do not have any privileged influence upon the development or the use of that creation, and
the characteristics by which autobiographies have come to be
evaluated have not been determined by Africans or by British

women. Colonists brought the tradition with them in such forms as criminal, travel, and religious conversion narratives to North America. Here women and men adapted those forms to the experiences that shaped their own realities. In the two most original and important forms, Indian captivity and slave narratives, women and blacks had significant impact. However, literary historians and critics, most of whom have been Anglo males, defined and deified autobiography in their own image. So pervasive has been their influence that until this day most people believe that American autobiography is a legacy from St. Augustine almost directly to Benjamin Franklin. Ignoring the African heritage of Augustine, they have established a canon which privileges the life histories of white men even as they concede that the persistent and provocative contributions of women and persons of color have made autobiography what William Dean Howells in 1909 proclaimed as the "most democratic province of the republic of letters" (798).

In the United States especially, the personal histories of lives lived or, perhaps more accurately, of lives as the authors wished to have readers believe they were lived, have captured the imaginations and offered a forum for an incredible variety of people who would otherwise not have entered the literary realms. Women and men; rich and poor; judges, criminals, and victims; inventors and embezzlers; athletes; entertainers; entrepreneurs; social reformers; and con artists have all contributed to the genre. And since, as William Andrews has reminded us, "Whatever else it is, autobiography stems more often than not from a need to explain and justify the self" (1), it is small wonder that this form would hold a particular attraction for African Americans. Today, scholars and general readers alike know about certain modern African-American autobiographies such as Wright's *Black Boy*, Angelou's *I Know Why the Caged Bird Sings*, and *The Autobiography of Malcolm X*. It is important to recall, however, that African-American autobiography began well before the twentieth century. From the Indian captivity narratives of Briton Hammon (1760) and John Marrant (1785) to the religious experiences of Jarena Lee (1836) and Rebecca Jackson (1830–64), from the travel narratives of Nancy

Prince (1850) and William Wells Brown (1852) to the rags-to-riches sagas of Frederick Douglass (1881) and George Henry (1894), the first-person accounts of African-American lives and times have entertained and informed American readers. Some, particularly the antebellum slave narratives, achieved best-seller status.

Nonetheless, William Dean Howells overstated the case when he announced that autobiography was a genre unrestricted "to any age, or sex, creed, class or color" and asserted that, despite the obscurity or humbleness of an individual, "it needs but the sincere relation of what he has been and done and felt and thought to give him a place with any other in this most democratic province of the republic of letters" (798). The American public certainly knew better. Over fifty years earlier, Ralph Waldo Emerson had complained that "men imagine that books are dice, and have no merit in their fortune; that the trade and the favor of a few critics can get one book into circulation, and defeat another" (138). As the author of many books, the editor of influential journals, and a mentor to at least two African-American writers, Howells was not ignorant of the impact of extraliterary influences upon the publication, distribution, and critical reception of literary texts.

Though contemporary analyses of autobiography still tout autobiography as the "most democratic province," some critics do note the scarcity of women and people of color within this literary republic. Feminist scholars such as Paula Gunn Allen, Estelle Jelinek, Amy Ling, Sidonie Smith, and Domna Stanton have been especially diligent in examining the "female autograph." They and others acknowledge that, in the nineteenth century, racism and sexism made literacy difficult and often illegal for the white women and the people of color who together constituted then, as now, the majority of Americans. Those who were able to write or to dictate their stories generally found few publishing opportunities. And those who both wrote and published their versions of self found that the readers' expectations and prejudices required particular modifications of style and content and even then often distorted what was written.

The commentary that surrounds Elizabeth Keckley's *Be-*

*hind the Scenes* presents particularly striking examples of misreadings that not only distorted her intent but, in order to justify the commentators' conclusions, consistently ignored critical elements of her text. Because of the political prominence of those with whom she interacted and the unfortunate timing of her publication, her work has suffered more radical misinterpretation and neglect than most. Not only was the book misread, condemned, and withdrawn from public circulation but its authorship was attributed to others and Elizabeth Keckley's very existence was denied.[2] Thus, another reason for using this particular work is to argue for its rightful status as an autobiography.

Things should have been different. Elizabeth Keckley's life had all the elements to delight postbellum readers. Having begun life as a poor, friendless, and abused child, she could now survey her history from a position of success achieved by her own hard work, indefatigable determination, and good character. The pattern of her life fit so exactly the prevalent formula for women's fiction that Keckley felt compelled to warn her readers that "My life, so full of romance, may sound like a dream to the matter-of-fact reader, nevertheless everything I have written is strictly true" (xi). In describing her journey from obscurity to prominence, Keckley's autobiography continued the tradition established by Benjamin Franklin and concentrated upon the incidents that molded her character—particularly those that involved political and social leaders. She was an intimate of both the Jefferson Davis household before the secession and the Abraham Lincoln household afterwards. Her narrative would undoubtedly reveal inside— maybe even titillating—information about the defeated president of the Confederacy, the martyred president of the Union and, of course, the notorious Mary Todd Lincoln.

Nineteenth-century readers could consider Keckley's life as a fitting imitation of Lincoln's journey from rail-splitter to president or of Franklin's progress from apprentice to ambassador. Though Keckley had not obtained the status of a Franklin or a Lincoln, that was to her advantage. Her sphere was considered to be entirely different. Elizabeth Keckley was a woman, she was black, she was a former slave. According to the attitudes of that time, her progress was remarkable for one of her ilk.

Elizabeth Keckley had been a valued and loyal slave for thirty years. With her master's permission, she had purchased herself and her son, moved to Washington, D.C., and established a business that employed over twenty people and catered to an elite, white clientele. Not only was Keckley a talented, responsible seamstress but she had served as a family retainer to several prominent figures. In her current position with the Lincolns, Keckley had gone from being nursemaid in a Big House to domestic servant in the Biggest House or, as she describes it and as several newspaper articles had made public, from slave to "friend and confidant" of Mary Todd Lincoln.

Elizabeth Keckley's life contained materials that could be used to delight and instruct nineteenth-century readers. And, in fact, it promised even more. In the postbellum period, when the nation wanted to turn its back on pain and divisiveness and to believe that the American Dream would survive, what better assurance could readers have desired than to be told that former slaves did not blame them for slavery and that, given the chance, they would become industrious, self-sustaining, and loyal servants? Elizabeth Keckley expressed no bitterness over slavery and exhibited no wish to change the basic order of things. She assured her readers that slaveholders were less responsible for slavery than "the God of nature and the fathers who framed the Constitution for the United States" (xii).

It was also more pleasing to her readers that Keckley was not an agitator. She was not publicly identified with the temperance, suffrage, or other reformist movements of that period. Her primary interests outside her job had been her son, who left Wilberforce College to join the Union forces; her church, Washington, D.C.'s socially active but staid Fifteenth Street Presbyterian Church; and her friends who were among the black social elite. She worked quietly but effectively with philanthropists and abolitionists to support the Contraband

Relief Association and the Freedmen's Village, two of the organizations that tried to care for the thousands of slaves and ex-slaves who migrated to Washington during and immediately after the Civil War. Though self-assured and to some a bit arrogant, Mrs. Keckley carefully observed social protocol. Small wonder that she reports many requests to write her life story. A life such as hers could be used to inspire black people, to reassure doubtful whites about the potential of the newly freed slaves, and to prove once again the vitality of the American Dream.

Elizabeth Keckley knew her life achievements were extraordinary. She cherished her reputation in the black community as a brilliant conversationalist and a generous but exacting teacher. She proudly reported that President Lincoln always addressed her as "Madam Elizabeth" (156), and she undoubtedly knew that she had become a legend who caused people to arrive early at church in order to see her "queenly" entrance each Sunday (John Washington 218). Over the years she had carefully preserved memorabilia that included family letters and legal papers, scraps of fabric from garments made for her more famous clients, the glove that Lincoln wore at his second inaugural reception, and various documents from the Confederate Congress. All this, along with her strong sense of historicity, made it inevitable that she would someday write her memoirs.

Often, as Albert E. Stone reminds us, autobiography is "an act deferred, a duty often imposed by fate at the end of a long career and enjoined by family, friends, publishers, and the curious public" (28). When Mary Todd Lincoln's attempt to sell some of her clothing and jewelry became a media circus that many believed not only proved once again her social ineptitude but besmirched her martyred husband's name and embarrassed the country, Elizabeth Keckley believed that it was her duty to try to assuage the damage caused by this "Old Clothes Scandal." She felt that her testimony regarding the motivations for Mary Lincoln's actions, the actual circumstances that transpired, and, especially, Keckley's own role in these events would help squelch the pernicious rumors that threatened both Mary Lincoln's and her own reputation. This then became the occasion that caused her to accede to the "importunities of her friends" and to write her life story. But in Keckley's case, fate, friends, publishers, and the curious public turned against her.

The book she had intended as her autobiography became increasingly sensationalized. James Redpath, her editor, violated her trust by appending, with no attempt to remove the personal elements, Mary Lincoln's letters to Keckley. G. W. Carleton and Company, her publisher, first advertised the book in April 1868 as "A Remarkable Book entitled *Behind the Scenes*" that could not fail "to create a wide world of interest not alone in the book, but in its gifted and conscientious author." By May 13, the work was being promoted by the dual title: *White House Revelations or Behind the Scenes*, and by May 30, the big bold print promised *Behind the Scenes, the Great Sensational Disclosures*, by Mrs. Keckley (John Washington 231–34).

The reading public took its lead from the advertisements. Rather than developing an interest in this "gifted and conscientious author," readers focused upon the book's descriptions of the private affairs of the prominent people with whom she had associated. Whereas Keckley meant to draw aside "the veil of mystery" and bring "the origin of a fact . . . to light with the naked fact itself" (xiv), her readers perceived it as uncovering scandal and publicly, as airing the Lincolns' dirty linen. Though Keckley wrote to help "stifle the voice of calumny," her work raised the volume of the voice. Mary Lincoln was mortified. Robert Lincoln was infuriated. He pressured the publishers to halt distribution, and his friends bought up the remaining copies. Though Elizabeth Keckley had intended the profits to aid Mrs. Lincoln, Mary Lincoln was so outraged that she refused to reimburse Keckley for the expenses she had incurred at Lincoln's request and thereafter pretended not to have known the woman she had formerly called her "dearest friend." Instead of easing Lincoln's financial distress, Keckley found herself facing poverty. Her business lost most of its clients. Her status in the black community declined. Some who had applauded Keckley as an example of black achievement now considered her a disgrace to the race. Because she had been accused of betraying her employers' confidence, they argued that she had imperiled the jobs of similarly employed black people.

Today *Behind the Scenes* occupies a permanent, albeit obscure, niche in Lincoln memorabilia. The letters it contains do provide invaluable information about what has come to be called "The Old Clothes Scandal," and every serious biography of Mary Todd Lincoln quotes material from Keckley's book. According to Dorothy Porter, "Mrs. Keckley's book reveals more clearly the intimate family life of the martyred president and offers a more credible portrait of Mary Todd, than perhaps any other book about the Lincolns" (ii). *Behind the Scenes* also shows up regularly in bibliographies of slave narratives and surveys of early African-American literature. Scholars acknowledge Keckley's work as a contribution to black social history; however, they tend to conclude, as did Vernon Loggins, that Mrs. Lincoln is "really the central figure" of Mrs. Keckley's book (260).

While the book is, as she intended, something more than the personal history of Elizabeth Keckley, to make Mary Lincoln the central figure of the book requires that one ignore not only a substantial portion of the work itself but the author's stated intentions and her own life history. As Loggins himself states, "Considerable comment in *Behind the Scenes* is devoted to Elizabeth Keckley's feelings toward race prejudice. She was a Negro woman proud of her color, and she lost no opportunity to push her race forward" (261). Her narrative is shaped, as was her life, by an unshakable self-confidence and a consistent self-respect. The multiple purposes of *Behind the Scenes* are unified through a structural organization based on the constant repetition of two basic themes: the preeminence of private substance over public appearance and the predestined progress for those who perceived the hidden lessons of experience and acted upon them. At times the Lincolns dominate her narrative as they were dominating her life while she was writing it, but Keckley's narrative presence and her persistent characterization of herself as an exemplar preserve her centrality. When one considers the book as a whole, noting carefully the narrator's stated goals and characterization and her narrative's structure and content, it becomes evident that *Behind the Scenes* is Elizabeth Keckley's *apologia pro sua vita*, an autobiography in the tradition of Benjamin Franklin's, and a testimony to the tenacity of the American Dream during one of the nightmares of this nation's history. As a Reconstruction autobiography, it is a pivotal work in the development of African-American autobiography, adapting the form and functions of the antebellum slave narrative to the experiences and intents of the postbellum era. *Behind the Scenes* is a pivotal work, qualifying in Robert Stepto's terms as a "response" to the slave narratives' "call"; that is, an "artistic act of closure performed upon a formal unit that already possesses substantial coherence" (6).

*Behind the Scenes* is similar to the antebellum slave narrative in its basic intention to provide an insider's account of slavery which would correct the myths and convince the readers of the horrible wrongness of that institution. This resemblance is most obvious in the first third of the book, which recounts Keckley's thirty years as a slave. In describing her experiences and her transformation from chattel to citizen, the author uses the pattern established for the antebellum slave narrative. She creates a protagonist who represents countless other slaves.

The title page of *Behind the Scenes* announces its author as "Elizabeth Keckley, formerly a slave. . . . " In its immediate and prominent acknowledgment of her slave heritage, Keckley's narrative follows the tradition begun with the eighteenth-century publications of Phillis Wheatley and Briton Hammon, who were identified as "a Negro servant to Mr. John Wheatley" and "A Negro Man,—Servant to General Winslow." The authors of antebellum slave narratives rigidly adhered to these two models. Whether fugitives or legally free, authors of antebellum narratives generally emphasized their slave status, identifying themselves, for example, as "Frederick Douglass, an American Slave," "William Wells Brown, a Fugitive Slave," or "Linda Brent . . . a Slave Girl."[3] Keckley begins, as so many others had before her, by expressing the conundrum of being born into a life-denying environment. She says, "I was born a slave . . . therefore I came upon the earth free in God-like thought, but fettered in action" (17). Her early chapters chronicle a series of confrontations between her "God-like thought" and the forces that would deny her such expression. She shows the institutionalized dehumanization by concentrating upon its capricious and brutal punishments, its heartless divisions of families, and its deliberate denial of gentility and virtue to black women. As a slave she lived in Virginia, North Carolina, Mississippi, and Missouri. When she was free, she moved to Washington, D.C. The pattern of her narrative follows the antebellum slave narrative's movement from South to North. Through her personal experiences and those of others she knew, Keckley presents a panoramic view of slavery. Though she assured her reader that her work would paint both the "dark" and the "bright" sides of slavery, it is apparent that the dark side is bondage and the light side is freedom.

The differences between antebellum and postbellum narratives are sometimes subtle, but they are significant. Chief among these are the changes in tone and characterization. Like antebellum narrators, the ex-slaves chronicle the atrocities and deprivations under slavery. However, they are far more likely to reinterpret their earlier hardships in light of the lessons they taught. Keckley cites her slave sufferings as the "fire of the crucible" and declares, "I was a feeble instrument in His hands, and through me and the enslaved millions of my race, one of the problems was solved that belongs to the great problems of human destiny" (xii).

As agents of cosmic truth, the slaves were more than victims. The protagonists could be portrayed in more heroic terms, as persons whose special sufferings endowed them with special attributes. For example, the four-year-old Lizzie Keckley was assigned to watch over her master's infant. Obviously this was a Herculean task for one who was still a toddler herself, and Keckley admits that she was not equal to it. When she rocked the cradle so "industriously" that the baby was tossed out, though the infant was not harmed, the young nursemaid was severely beaten. According to Keckley, this was the first of many punishments she endured. However, in recounting her first beating, she does not linger on the cruelty but emphasizes the overall benefits of her job. In retrospect, her assignment as a nursemaid was generally "pleasant" because she was transferred from the "rude cabin" to her master's household, she received a dress and an apron, and she was promised that if she performed her duties well, she could become the little girl's personal maid (20). She concludes that "notwithstanding all the wrongs that slavery heaped upon me, I can bless it for one thing—youth's important lesson of self-reliance" (19–20).

Although her perspective here might seem to be that of an extremely patient individual, Keckley's is actually more that of an ambitious and calculating hero recounting the cost of her success. Her characterization is not so much nonviolent as nonaggressive, and here again is a subtle but important difference from earlier narrators. Before the war, narrators preferred to present themselves as long-suffering and nonviolent victims of oppression. When all else failed, they resorted to guilt-provoking duplicity and elected to run rather than to fight. Frederick Douglass was one of the few antebellum narrators who confessed to having been physically defiant. In confessing this incident, Douglass emphasizes that he had suffered many inhumane beatings as part of Covey's attempt to break him "in body, soul, and spirit" (66). Finally, when Covey beat Douglass because Douglass was too ill to work and when Douglass's master refused his appeal for protection and forced him to return to Covey, Douglass resolved to defend himself from any further physical assaults. The confrontation with Covey is central to Douglass's narrative; it symbolizes his psychological transformation from chattel to human being. And yet, this passage is very ambiguous. Douglass makes it clear that Covey attacked him and that he fought only in self-defense. Douglass does not assert that he defeated Covey, only that he resisted until Covey was worn out. Moreover, Douglass suggests that, until he wrote his narrative many years later, this confrontation remained secret.

Elizabeth Keckley, on the other hand, recites several instances wherein she fought both her master and a local minister who sought to subdue her "stubborn pride" (36). Though she was not a physical match for these men, she could and did fight back so valiantly that they were exhausted with the struggle. Apparently Keckley also fought with her tongue, for she says that "These revolting scenes created a great sensation at the time, were the talk of the town and neighborhood, and I flatter myself that the actions of those who had conspired against me were not viewed in a light to reflect much credit upon them" (38). Finally, unlike Douglass, Keckley clearly triumphed because she says that each man apologized, promised never to hit her again, and kept that promise.

Given what we know about Douglass's character and his outspokenness in subsequent autobiographies, these differences in self-depictions by two people who in 1868 were friends and colleagues are not easily explained as differences in personality. Rather it is more likely that postbellum narrators were freer to admit their rebelliousness. Abolition had removed the necessity to condemn any form of physical resistance in order to discourage slave insurrections. The cultural context had changed sufficiently to allow readers to tolerate, perhaps even admire, a young girl's decision to become a fighter and not a fugitive. While postbellum readers might consider it unseemly for a black or a woman to raise a hand against a white man, such readers were also likely to appreciate the atrocity of grown men who claimed social leadership assaulting innocent girls.

The postbellum era may have been slightly more tolerant towards slave rebels, but the enormous number of newly freed slaves created considerable concern. This situation required other differences in characterization. Unlike the antebellum slave narrators, who downplayed their individual initiative and self-discipline to enhance their argument against the insidiousness of slavery as an institution, postbellum narrators needed to convince their readers that the former slaves, especially those who had passively endured their bondage, were capable of assuming the responsibilities of freedom. Keckley emphasizes her early determination to gain recognition not solely as a human being but as an individual who deserved respect and compensation for her talents and sacrifices. This emphasis upon talent and potential was partly accomplished by increasing the length of time the narratives covered. Although many narratives, such as those by Douglass, Harriet Jacobs, and J. W. C. Pennington, were written many years after the authors had escaped from slavery, most antebellum works ended soon after their writer's arrival in the North. Postbellum narratives, by contrast, normally went beyond that arrival to describe the actual or anticipated achievements of the former slave.

Keckley's narrative exemplifies this trend from its beginnings. Just as its title echoed those of antebellum narratives by its immediate and prominent identification of its author with slavery, *Behind the Scenes* also modified that form by stressing a movement up from slavery. Keckley's identification as "formerly a slave, but more recently modiste, and friend" and her juxtaposition of "Thirty Years a Slave, and Four Years in the White House" reject a static definition as "slave" or even "former slave." They suggest progressive movement, emphasizing the social distance traveled. Keckley's early ambition to leave the rude cabin foreshadowed the motivation that would propel her into the White House. It symbolized the possible strength of character of her fellow slaves who had endured the crucible and typified that of other black achievers whose autobiographical offerings would follow her model. In this way, *Behind the Scenes* is a prototype for later black success stories such as John Mercer Langston's *From the Virginia Plantation to the National Capitol*, Peter Randolph's *From Slave Cabin to the Pulpit*, and Robert Anderson's *From Slavery to Affluence*.

Finally, African-American autobiographers of the Reconstruction period were free to develop other themes. Publishing as they did after the end of legal slavery, there was no need to plead the antislavery cause. As a postbellum writer Keckley could concentrate upon larger implications of the struggle between good and evil. Keckley's book downplays categories such as North and South, bondage and freedom, and slave and master. It postulates instead the interrelation of the most despised and victimized slave with the most respected and powerful slaveholder. Keckley's emphasis was in keeping with the liberal reconstructionists' goal of mending the tears in the society's fabric while reweaving the pattern in black and white. And, she was freer to enjoy the prerogatives of the autobiographical form.

Several scholars have argued persuasively that the assembly of an African-American author's work—that is, its prefaces, appendices, inscriptions, and such, and the control the author asserts over that assemblage—provide critical information for anyone "who seeks an integrated vision of literary tradition and transition" (Stepto 52). Unlike most antebellum narratives, *Behind the Scenes* does not offer testimonies of authenticity, letters of recommendation, or prefaces from white people. The title page, preface, and even the copyright identify the work as that of Elizabeth Keckley only. Despite the manipulation of the volume's distribution and publicity, Keckley retained control of its narrative voice. It is, therefore, significant that the autobiographical intent evidenced in the text of the work is signaled first by these prefatory documents.

The title page identifies the work as *"Behind the Scenes* by Elizabeth Keckley, formerly a slave, but more recently a modiste, and friend to Mrs. Abraham Lincoln." The title reminds the readers that behind the public performance is unseen but influential activity. It promises a guided tour or an insider's description. The value of such information depends upon the authority of the informant and the extent to which the individual's knowledge exceeds or confirms the audience's. Consequently the role of narrator is critical, and the credentials Keckley presents imply the aspects that she thought most important to authenticate. Keckley had been "a slave," a designation that indicates a social status somewhere between three-fifths human and an article of personal, movable property. Currently she is a "modiste." Keckley is not called a dressmaker, a nurse, or a domestic servant, though in her narrative she frankly reveals that she rendered such services. As a "modiste," she is a designer, artisan, and entrepreneur of women's fashions, an authority on manners and appearances, all of which are connotations more fitting to her concept of her role in the Lincoln household and in Washington society as well. Finally, she is a friend to the former First Lady.

The subtitle, *Thirty Years a Slave, and Four Years in the White House,* defines more specifically the book's intent. The narrator offers thirty years' experience as a slave, four years as a White House retainer, and a privileged association with the widow of the former president. While the life after bondage may have been more unusual, not only are thirty years a lot longer than four but the second mention of slavery reinforces its significance to this work. The subtitle indicates the authenticity of sustained personal experience in two apparently irreconcilably separate areas. It makes clear the social distance the narrator has traveled, from chattel to confidant of the most prestigious and symbolically powerful people in our nation. The subtitle manifests what the nation had come to realize through the War Between the States, the symbiosis of these two entities. Her parenthetical identification presents the author as an exemplary answer to current questions concerning the possible roles of the newly freed slaves and gives a larger interpretation to the meaning of "Behind the Scenes." Ultimately, it reveals the coherent pattern of the book.

The opening lines of her preface reaffirm Keckley's autobiographical intentions: "I have often been asked to write my life, as those who know me know that it has been an eventful one. At last I have acceded to the importunities of my friends, and have hastily sketched some of the striking incidents that go to make up my history" (xi). Keckley refers to her life as a "romance." This does not suggest that she considers her experiences benign or ideal but rather that they exemplify her concepts of human progress. Slavery had robbed her of her dearest right, liberty. Says Keckley, "I would not have been human had I not rebelled . . . " (xii). Nonetheless, she maintained that slavery had been a necessary phase in the moral development of the United States, a phase in which she and other slaves had "aided in bringing a solemn truth to the surface as a truth" (xiii). "Bringing truth to the surface" is the plainly stated but unacknowledged key to *Behind the Scenes*. Keckley's autobiographical intentions were based upon a profound belief in the efficacy of truth.

Elizabeth Keckley's autobiography is structured in the mode of countless other American autobiographies. It establishes its narrator as an individual of insight and integrity, demonstrates the development of a superior character by the endurance of oppression and vilification, and ultimately vindicates her sufferings by the recognition of the rightness of her actions and its accompanying riches and respect. It presents a dualistic philosophy affirming the difference between public appearance and private realities as well as the ultimate revelation of the symbolic importance of real events, an approach that Roy Pascal has demonstrated is basic to autobiography as a genre.

Keckley's autobiography is divided into three parts of five chapters each. Part 1 describes her thirty years as a slave. Part 2 relates important events during her four years as a White House intimate. Part 3 focuses upon her experiences after the assassination of President Lincoln. Her seven months' involvement in the "Old Clothes Scandal" receives only one chapter. Her association with the latter incident had motivated her to publish her narrative when and as she did, but her structure plainly shows that the episode was but a part of the total story she had to tell. It was the overall story, in fact, that she believed would allow the proper perspective from which to view that particular episode. Her interest is not in summarizing each year of her life nor even in reporting her most dramatic experiences. She has omitted many "strange passages" in her history, she says, in order to confine her story to her major interest, "the most important incidents which I believe influenced the moulding of my character" (18). What is important to her is not the surface events but the attitudes and contexts that lay behind those actions.

In chapters 1 through 5, she writes of her family, her childhood, her slave experiences, and her efforts to obtain her freedom. Each episode of her slave experience is used not only to portray the truth about that institution but to show how the institution affected her personality and values. Keckley authenticates her narrative with letters and other documents which offer further context for her actions. They show that the narrator considered herself an integral and dynamic part of the families with whom she interacted. For example, in a letter to her mother Keckley reminds her to "Give my love to all the family, both white and black" (41). In the first section, the narrator emerges as an ambitious, independent, but loyal individual whose industry and integrity were rewarded with freedom.

None of the many incidents reveals the depth of her character as much as her attempts to gain her freedom. Her master refused her first request to buy herself and commanded her to never again bring up that subject. But Keckley persisted. When in exasperation he offered her the fare for the ferry and told her to leave, Keckley refused, telling him that she was perfectly aware of the ease with which she could escape, but since by law she was a slave, she chose freedom only by such means as that same law provided. He named a price. Keckley transformed herself from capital to capitalist by obtaining loans from investors and purchasing herself and her son. The extended description of this episode emphasizes her strength of character and demonstrates one of the sources of Keckley's intense belief in the ultimate triumph of integrity and perseverance.

In the last chapter in Part 1 the narrator tells how she repaid her loans and established her business. Although she describes the discriminatory laws and practices that hindered her progress, Keckley does not campaign against them. Perhaps it was the optimism of the Reconstruction era during which she was writing, but she emphasized the role of her good reputation and her discipline in acquiring the friends she needed to establish herself as dressmaker for Washington's elite. One of the more significant relationships was with Varina Davis. Her situation in the Jefferson Davis household foreshadowed the one Keckley enjoyed with the Abraham Lincolns. Elizabeth Keckley had begun her relationship with Jefferson and Varina Davis in Washington when Varina Davis needed a dressmaker. During the period in which she was employed, Varina Davis came to have, in Keckley's words, "the greatest confidence" in her. When Varina Davis was preparing to assume the role of First Lady of the Confederacy, she urged Keckley to come south with them so they could protect her from the inevitable backlash against free blacks which the war would bring. In the chapter she titles "In the Family of Senator Jefferson Davis," Keckley tries to make it clear that it was her character and not any particular leanings of the Lincolns that gave her access to the White House.

The first part of her book is a success story designed to establish the narrator as an individual whose personal integrity and indomitable spirit resulted in remarkable achievements. The narrator is not an ex-chattel, working the emotions of a readership predominated by those who might sympathize but could never empathize. Rather she is portraying herself as a fellow participant in the American Myth—characterizing herself as what Spengemann and Lundquist call the "Hero" or one who fully enacts prophesies, takes the mythic journey and progresses from low to high, as one who in so doing has won "the right to teach and so to perpetuate a viable tradition" (509).

Keckley's four years in the White House, detailed in chapters 6 through 11, begin shortly after the Lincolns' arrival in Washington, D.C., and end with the assassination of President Lincoln. This section of the narrative, replete with observations, experiences, and personal anecdotes concerning the Lincoln family, echoes her earlier, briefer revelations about the Davis family. In neither case does she divulge private episodes as much as she supplements what is already public knowledge with the behind-the-scenes view. Keckley describes preparations for public appearances, gives glimpses of domestic activities, and sometimes reports conversations that reveal the private intent behind the public words or actions. In essence her narrative offers to the American public verification of the humanity of those known primarily as national symbols. In doing this, however, Keckley inserts a new figure into these family portraits. She herself is an active participant. Frequently she relates conversations she had with the Lincolns or the Davises concerning well-known events. Though the personages often dominate the stage, it is always Elizabeth Keckley, the narrator, who relates and interprets their behavior.

The unifying concept in this section is the relationship between Elizabeth Keckley and Mary Todd Lincoln. Keckley reveals the First Lady as an impulsive, stubborn, and extravagant woman but one who is essentially kindhearted, often misunderstood, and occasionally maligned. Keckley is her stabilizer, her advisor, and her friend. Their relationship is similar to that between Keckley and the Garlands, described in the first section of her book. Keckley had served as nursemaid and companion to Anne Garland from infancy until she had managed to purchase her freedom. Keckley refers to Anne as "my pet" and notes that Anne, too, had been "the cause of great trouble to me" (21). When the Garland family suffered financial setbacks, Keckley had managed to rescue them also. As she reports it, when she and the family joined Mr. Garland in their new home in Mississippi, "we found him so poor that he was unable to pay the dues on a letter advertised as in the post-office for him" (44). Keckley sought work as a seamstress and dressmaker and soon established such a clientele that she was able to keep "bread in the mouths of seventeen persons for two years and five months" (45). The same elements of personal integrity and self-sacrifice that she demonstrated in her relationship with the family of her slave master are prominent in her relationship with the Lincoln family. The same means by which she had enabled the family of her slave master to "move in those circles of society to which their birth gave entrance" Keckley employed on behalf of Mrs. Lincoln's attempts to do likewise (45).

In the second part of *Behind the Scenes*, the First Family is in the foreground, but Keckley presents herself as an essential participant. To Mary Lincoln, "Lizzie" Keckley may have been simply a substitute for the mammy she had left in Kentucky, but Elizabeth Keckley is the narrator and she identifies her position as that of friend and confidant. Clearly she was more than a dressmaker, for she was summoned to perform duties that ranged from combing Mary Lincoln's hair before parties to washing and laying out the body of the Lincolns' beloved son, Willie. Long before the fateful journey to New York, Elizabeth Keckley had become a regular traveling companion, accompanying Mary Lincoln on the triumphant presidential survey of war-torn Virginia and on her sorrowful relocation to widow's quarters in Chicago.

A particular incident in this section exemplifies Keckley's narrative technique. Having already established her roles as costumer and general stagehand, she says, "I had never heard Mr. Lincoln make a public speech, and, knowing the man so well, was very anxious to hear him" (174). Before describing the public appearance that she witnessed, Keckley reminds the reader of her privileged position. She recalls for us that before the speech she had observed Lincoln "looking over his notes and muttering to himself." She knew "that he was rehearsing the part that he was to play in the great drama soon to commence" (175). Later, as she relates the "great drama" of his speech, she says, "I stood a short distance from Mr. Lincoln" (177), and though she does not report the content or the occasion of that particular speech, Keckley does say that, while observing the performance, she suddenly realized the president's vulnerability and had a premonition of his assassination (178). By describing a public appearance that her readers could readily verify and claiming a "sudden thought" which she partially attributes to "remembrance of the many warnings that Mr. Lincoln had received" (178), Keckley establishes sufficient credibility to insure acceptance of her description of the private preparations for Lincoln's public appearance. In so doing, Keckley is also laying the foundation to support her other revelations of behind-the-scenes occurrences. The theme of public performance and private reality is carried out in this reminiscence. Moreover, she as witness, prophet, and narrator is the central figure in this drama.

The assassination climaxes Part 2. Again Keckley juxtaposes public knowledge and personal experience. She begins her description of this event by contrasting the jubilation of the nation which believed the war was over with its reaction to the news that its president had been shot. "A nation suddenly paused in the midst of festivity, and stood paralyzed with horror—transfixed with awe" (184). Having set the stage, Keckley places herself upon it by saying, "At 11 o'clock at night I was awakened . . . with the startling intelligence that the entire Cabinet had been assassinated, and Mr. Lincoln shot. . . . When I heard the words I felt as if the blood had been frozen in my veins" (184). The reader recalls the nation "paralyzed with horror" and can see Keckley, at this point, as part of "the nation." Her blood, like that of her fellow citizens, froze. The tableau thaws and, seeking the truth of the rumor, she goes to the White House where she joins "the outskirts of a large crowd." Like everyone else, Keckley did not know the details immediately, and her reaction is that of the general public. However, a White House emissary soon came for her and, for several days, she is behind the scenes as Mary Lincoln's "only companion, except her children, in the days of her great sorrow" (193). Their shared grief and Mary Lincoln's dependence upon her during that crisis prove their intimate friendship and establish Keckley as Mary Lincoln's mainstay, foreshadowing Keckley's later involvement in the "Old Clothes Scandal." Moreover, in demonstrating that she had been privy to specific details about earlier public occasions, Keckley reinforces her claim to special information which would cast a new light upon the situation that prompted her writing.

The third section begins with preparations for leaving the White House. The narrator carefully details these events partly to establish the position of Mary Lincoln as dependent upon an unsympathetic Congress for her sustenance and upon her "Dear Lizzie" for support. This section continues the pattern of her relationship as guardian and friend to those she served. However, Keckley emphasizes the difference between her morality and strengths and those of Mary Lincoln. For example, when they left Washington, Mary Lincoln felt herself impoverished and was often in tears. Elizabeth Keckley, on the other hand, stood at the window of the Lincolns' new home and thought ethereally about the sunbeams that reflected upon the lake. Confided Keckley, "I wondered how any one could call Hyde Park a dreary place. I had seen so much trouble in my life, that I was willing to . . . slumber anywhere" (214). Unlike Mrs. Lincoln, Mrs. Keckley had developed a greater resistance to adversity.

In an even more revealing incident, Keckley challenges those who might wish to condemn her and her race while excusing Mary Todd. According to Keckley, the Lincolns had not required their son Tad to attend school, and he was almost illiterate. After describing one of Mary Lincoln's frustrated attempts to teach Tad to read, Keckley concluded that, "had Tad been a negro boy, not the son of a President, and so difficult to instruct, he would have been called thick-skulled, and would have been held up as an example of the inferiority of race" (219). Keckley assures her audience that she was not reflecting upon the intelligence of Tad but simply upon the dual standards by which black and white people are judged. In light of the circumstances during which she was writing her book, it takes little effort to discern special significance in her statement that "I only mean to say that some incidents are about as damaging to one side of the question as to the other . . . and if a whole race is judged by a single example of apparent dulness, another race should be judged by a similar example" (220).

In the chapter preceding the "Secret History of Mrs. Lincoln's Wardrobe," Keckley takes what she identifies as "a slight retrospective glance" and describes in great detail her triumphant return as an invited guest in the home of her former owners. Here Keckley reminds us again that through her efforts the family had been able to keep up appearances even while they had no money. Juxtaposed as it is against the events of the following chapter, this is obviously a final attempt to justify her own actions in the "Old Clothes Scandal." As important as it is for characterization, however, it is also thematically significant. It serves as Keckley's vindication and testifies to the general acceptance of her life as a success story. And since she has depicted herself as an exemplar, it is also a testimony to the possibilities of Reconstruction.

In this chapter, Madame Elizabeth is the central figure. The guest of honor, she sits in state while her former owners scurry about to prepare her food and to make her comfortable and "the servants looked on in amazement" (250). She attends social functions with Confederate leaders. Keckley reports that her host, General Meems, joked about the changes in her status, saying, "Why, Lizzie, you are riding with Colonel Gilmore. Just think of the change from Lincoln to Gilmore! It sounds like a dream. But then the change is evidence of the peaceful feeling of this country; a change, I trust, that augurs brighter days for us all" (254). In one of their conversations, Keckley assures her former mistress that she harbors "but one unkind thought" about their former relationship, that she "was not given the advantages of a good education." Her mistress, now the wife of a Confederate general, apologized but asserted that Keckley had not suffered irreparable harm since she got "along better in the world than we who enjoyed every educational advantage in childhood" (257). Miss Anne had acknowledged also that her mother had been "severe with her slaves in some respects," and certainly she had been mistaken in predicting that Keckley would not be "worth her salt." Keckley's forgiveness suggests not only her own magnanimity but the possibilities that the racial animosities of the past can be overcome, that good can ultimately triumph over evil.

In the final chapter of her history, Keckley addresses the controversy that precipitated this book. Though her self-confidence and self-respect remain unshaken, the act she now relates, "The Secret History of Mrs. Lincoln's Wardrobe in New York," is still being played out. Her book is in fact an attempt to direct the final scene. Now, Keckley depicts herself as a supporting character in an unsavory drama which features Mary Lincoln before an audience whose sympathies are not yet determined. In this section, autobiography is subordinated to exposition, and characterization gives way to plot. When the appended letters are considered, the work resembles a cloak-and-dagger drama. Yet, the theme of private substance behind public appearance continues, and Keckley's faith in the efficacy of truth connects this chapter to the rest of the narrative.

The events of this chapter began in March 1867 when Mary Lincoln wrote Elizabeth Keckley that "she had struggled long enough to keep up appearances, and that the mask must be thrown aside" (267). Lincoln was so desperate for money that she had decided to sell her clothing. Keckley reluctantly agreed to help her. She spotlights the ironic reversal that made the widow of a former president petition a former slave for help by saying, "She was the wife of Abraham Lincoln, the man who had done so much for my race, and I could refuse to do nothing for her" (269).

By birth and by marriage, Mary Lincoln was expected to manifest ladylike decorum at all times. Elizabeth Keckley, on the other hand, was not. Still, Keckley reveals herself as the more refined individual. She takes pains to show that the details of Mary Lincoln's plan troubled her from the beginning. For example, Keckley says she "could not understand why Mrs. Lincoln should travel, without protection, under an assumed name" (271). Her consternation over "the strange programme" increased when she arrived in New York to discover that Mary Lincoln was, in fact, incapable of distinguishing appearance from reality. Lincoln's actions become increasingly theatrical, and Keckley acts Sancho Panza to her Quixote. Keckley establishes her superiority when she vetoes Lincoln's decision to dine in public unescorted, saying, "I realize your situation, if you do not" (283). But Keckley's superior understanding did not empower her to control this woman who "was willing to adopt any scheme which promised a good bank account to her credit" (290–91). Despite Keckley's reservations, Mary Lincoln agreed to the suggestions by the broker with whom she contracted the sale, W. H. Brady, that she obtain money from "certain politicians" by writing letters delineating her pecuniary distress and by threatening to go public with those letters if these politicians should refuse to aid their former leader's impoverished widow. So, while Mary Lincoln wrote the letters that helped scandalize her name, Keckley could only stand "at Mrs. Lincoln's elbow" and suggest "that they be couched in the mildest language possible" (294). The plan did not work. The letters became further evidence to political insiders that Mary Lincoln was emotionally unstable. Lincoln then agreed to have the letters published in the newspapers and to put her clothing on public exhibition. On the day the letters were published, Mary Lincoln returned to Chicago, leaving Keckley to deal with Brady, the wardrobe, and the political hornet's nest that Mary Lincoln's actions had stirred. Not only did Mary Lincoln compromise her reputation by this indecorous behavior but Keckley tells us that "Mrs. Lincoln's venture proved so disastrous that she was unable to reward me for my services, and I was compelled to take in sewing to pay for my daily bread" (326).

In reporting the secret history, Keckley shifts from purely first-person narration toward the objective point of view, increasingly relying upon documents to tell the story but never entirely relinquishing her voice. To prove her efforts to counter the scandalous rumors, Keckley summarizes news articles based upon her press releases. She includes letters from prominent African Americans such as Frederick Douglass and Henry Highland Garnet attesting to their willingness to help Lincoln's widow. These letters show that Keckley's loyalty was shared by other African Americans, and, by juxtaposing the eagerness of her race to support the former First Lady during her troubles with the readiness of the white population to castigate her for her failings, Keckley suggests a more ironic interpretation of the "Old Clothes Scandal."

The shift in point of view in this section does several other things. Reliance upon memoranda, letters, and news accounts distances the narrator from events and allows us to see Keckley's helplessness in this situation without diminishing her overall achievements. It allows her to authenticate her account without resorting to a posture of self-defense. Keckley does not have to criticize Mary Lincoln directly, but as she promised in her preface, she could let "the origin of a fact be brought to light with the naked fact itself" (xiv). Just as she tried to salvage a bad situation by persuading Mary Lincoln to couch her letters in the "mildest language possible," Keckley uses the language of others to exonerate herself as gracefully as possible.

Finally, Keckley reports, "As I am writing the concluding pages of this book, I have succeeded in closing up Mrs. Lincoln's imprudent business arrangement" (327). The irony becomes almost too heavy. The former slave has proven more capable of handling business and political affairs than the wife of a United States president. As she ends her narrative, Keckley is confident that she has saved Mary Lincoln from the immediate consequences of her folly and that, by writing the book, she will be able to help her even more.

In spite of the sensationalism of the last chapter and the less charitable comments that Keckley allows herself to make, the third section continues the design of the first two. After chronicling her movement from slavery to freedom and from poverty to affluence, Keckley reveals her current actions as merely another of a series of challenging situations in which she is required to play the facilitating role. In making a public proclamation of her personal experiences, she declares the illusion of appearances and the efficacy of truth. By noting such ironies as the blacks' readiness to assume what was both a civic and moral obligation while the whites bickered among themselves, Keckley echoes the Puritan idea of moral superiority achieved through adversity, a morality, in fact, that some whites had yet to achieve.

As a postbellum narrative, *Behind the Scenes* is more assertive and more critical than those published during slavery. And yet, coming as it does at a time when "The Battle Hymn of the Republic" rang in many ears and many Americans truly believed they were on the verge of a new day, it carries an optimism and faith in the American dream that later works do not. In many ways Keckley's autobiography demonstrates a characteristic that Mary Burger has identified as central to black autobiography, "an effect of celebration in protest and affirmation in negation" (10). It anticipates those later African-American autobiographers who take their tone from the blues and thereby, as Albert Murray phrases it, "affirm not only U.S. Negro life in all of its arbitrary complexities and not only life in America in all of its infinite confusions, [but] affirm life and humanity itself in the very process of confronting failures and existentialistic absurdities" (212). Keckley's autobiography is a literary riff of the kind endemic to those who play major roles behind the scenes and on center stage.

Careful attention to the total structure of *Behind the Scenes*, and especially to the characterization of its narrator, reveals a coherence and purpose heretofore eclipsed by the presence of the book's more spectacular but less important characters. The broader implications of *Behind the Scenes*, as manifested by the author's stated intentions and the repeated motifs, which work "to bring truth to the surface as a truth," reveal this work to be a contribution of singular importance to African-American autobiography and thereby to American literary history.

## Notes

1. *The Revelations of Divine Love* written by Dame Julian (or Juliana) of Norwich sometime around 1373 predates Margery Kempe's work; however, most scholars believe as Estelle Jelinek does that *Revelations* "is more an intellectual treatise than a personal narrative." *The Book of Margery Kempe*, written between 1436 and 1438, is therefore generally acknowledged as the earliest extant autobiographical narrative in English (Jelinek 14, 15).

2.  For an excellent summary of the arguments and a definitive answer to them see John E. Washington, *They Knew Lincoln*. New York: Dutton, 1942.
3.  "Linda Brent" is the pseudonym used by Harriet Jacobs when *Incidents in the Life of a Slave Girl* was published.

# Works Cited

Anderson, Robert. *From Slavery to Affluence: Memoirs of Robert Anderson, Ex-Slave.* Hemingford, NE: Hemingford Ledger, 1927.

Andrews, William. *To Tell a Free Story: The First Century of Afro-American Autobiography, 1760–1865.* Urbana: U of Illinois P, 1986.

Angelou, Maya. *I Know Why the Caged Bird Sings.* New York: Random, 1970.

Barton, Rebecca Chalmers. *Witnesses for Freedom: Negro Americans in Autobiography.* New York: Harper, 1948.

Black Fashion Museum. *Modiste Elizabeth Keckley: From Slavery to the White House.* New York, n.d.

Brown, William Wells. *Narrative of William Wells Brown, a Fugitive Slave.* Boston, 1847.

———. *Three Years in Europe; or, Places I Have Seen and People I Have Met.* London, 1852.

Burger, Mary. "Black Autobiography: A Literature of Celebration." Diss. Washington U, 1973.

Butterfield, Stephen. *Black Autobiography in America.* Amherst: U of Massachusetts P, 1974.

Davis, Charles T., and Henry Louis Gates, Jr., eds. *The Slave's Narrative.* New York: Oxford, 1985.

Douglass, Frederick. *Life and Times of Frederick Douglass,* Hartford, 1881.

———. *Narrative of the Life of Frederick Douglass, an American Slave.* Boston, 1845.

Emerson, Ralph Waldo. "Thoughts on Modern Literature." *The Dial* 1 (1840): 137–58.

Foster, Frances Smith. *Witnessing Slavery: The Development of the Ante-Bellum Slave Narrative.* Westport, CT: Greenwood, 1979.

Franklin, Benjamin. *Autobiography.* Ed. Max Farrand. Berkeley: U of California P, 1949.

Hammon, Briton. *A Narrative of the Uncommon Sufferings, and Surprising Deliverance of Briton Hammon, a Negro Man.* Boston, 1760.

Henry, George. *Life of George Henry together with a Brief History of the Colored People in America.* Providence, 1894.

Howells, William Dean. "Editor's Easy Chair." *Harper's Monthly Magazine* 119 (1909): 795–98.

Jackson, Rebecca. *Gifts of Power: The Writings of Rebecca Jackson, Black Visionary, Shaker Eldress.* Ed. Jean McMahon Humez. Amherst: U of Massachusetts P, 1981.

Jacobs, Harriet. *Incidents in the Life of a Slave Girl.* Boston, 1861.

Jelinek, Estelle. *The Tradition of Women's Autobiography: From Antiquity to the Present.* Boston: Twayne, 1986.

Keckley, Elizabeth. *Behind the Scenes; Or, Thirty Years a Slave, and Four Years in the White House.* New York, 1868.

Langston, James Mercer. *From the Virginia Plantation to the National Capitol; or, The First and Only Negro Representative in Congress from the Old Dominion.* Hartford, CT, 1894.

Lee, Jarena. *The Life and Religious Experiences of Jarena Lee, a Coloured Lady.* Philadelphia, 1836.

Loggins, Vernon. *The Negro Author: His Development in America to 1900.* New York: Columbia UP, 1931.

Malcolm X. *The Autobiography of Malcolm X.* New York: Grove, 1965.

Marrant, John. *A Narrative of the Lord's Wonderful Dealings with John Marrant, a Black.* London, 1785.

Murray, Albert. *The Omni-Americans.* New York: Avon, 1971.

Nichols, Charles. *Many Thousands Gone: The Ex-Slaves' Account of Their Bondage and Freedom.* Bloomington: Indiana UP, 1969.

Pascal, Roy. *Design and Truth in Autobiography.* Cambridge: Harvard UP, 1960.

Pennington, James W.C. *The Fugitive Blacksmith; or, Events in the History of James W.C. Pennington.* London, 1849.

Porter, Dorothy. Introduction. *Behind the Scenes.* By Elizabeth Keckley. New York: Arno, 1968.

Prince, Nancy Gardener. *A Narrative of the Life and Travels of Mrs. Nancy Prince.* Boston, 1850.

Randolph, Peter. *From Slave Cabin to the Pulpit: The Autobiography of Rev. Peter Randolph; the Southern Question Illustrated and Sketches of Slave Life.* Boston, 1893.

Sekora, John, and Darwin T. Turner, eds. *The Art of the Slave Narrative: Original Essays in Criticism and Theory.* Macomb: Western Illinois UP, 1982.

Smith, Sidonie. *Where I'm Bound: Patterns of Slavery and Freedom in Black American Autobiography.* Westport, CT: Greenwood, 1974.

Spengemann, William C., and L. R. Lundquist. "Autobiography and the American Myth." *American Quarterly* 17 (1965): 501–19.

Starling, Marion Wilson. "The Slave Narrative: Its Place in American Literary History." Diss. New York U, 1946.

Stepto, Robert B. *From Behind the Veil: A Study of Afro-American Narrative.* Urbana: U of Illinois P, 1979.

Stone, Albert E. *Autobiographical Occasions and Original Acts.* Philadelphia: U of Pennsylvania P, 1982.

Washington, Booker T. *Up from Slavery: An Autobiography.* New York: A. L. Burt, 1901.

Washington, John E. *They Knew Lincoln.* New York: Dutton, 1942.

Wheatley, Phillis. *Poems on Various Subjects, Religious and Moral.* London, 1773.

Wright, Richard. *Black Boy: A Record of Childhood and Youth.* New York: Harper, 1945.

# The Children Ceased to Hear My Name: Recovering the Self in *The Autobiography of W. E. B. Du Bois*

*Keith E. Byerman*

If the production of autobiographical texts is any sign of self-absorption, then William Edward Burghardt Du Bois was one of the most self-absorbed men in American history. Several of the essays in *The Souls of Black Folk* (1903), *Darkwater* (1920), *Dusk of Dawn* (1940), *In Battle for Peace* (1952), and *The Autobiography of W. E. B. Du Bois* (1968), in addition to the largely autobiographical fictional trilogy *The Black Flame* (1957–61) and the privately printed *Pageant in Seven Decades* (1938) focus on the experiences, career, and ideas of this most distinguished member of the black intelligentsia. Yet, despite his historical significance and his articulation over many decades of his identity and ideas, by the time of his death in 1963 at the age of ninety-five, he had largely become a nonperson to Americans black and white. His increasing association with the Stalinist ideology of the American Communist party (CPUSA) during the late forties and the fifties left him isolated from the mainstream of black political thinking, which was then focused exclusively on the civil rights movement. Even among American leftists, Stalinism had largely been discredited by the purges, the pact with Hitler, and the bloody repressions in East Germany and Hungary. In the face of all of this, Du Bois, at the time he was writing *The Autobiography*, decided to join the CPUSA, emigrated to Ghana, and gave up his American citizenship, all of which suggest his lack of faith in the prospects for racial and economic justice in the United States. He was increasingly harassed by the State Department, watched by the FBI, and even, in 1951, put on trial (and acquitted) for being the unregistered agent of a foreign power. These actions were based on his association with the international peace movement, his advocacy of socialism, and his sharp attacks on American foreign policy, corruption, and racism. In this context, the initial chapters of *The Autobiography* on the Soviet Union and the People's Republic of China, as well as the credo on communism, form an additional gesture signifying his ideological identity.

But to read *The Autobiography* as an apologia for his political position, comparable to Booker T. Washington's *Up from Slavery* as a validation of his accommodationist position or the initial design of *The Autobiography of Malcolm X* as a defense of the Black Muslims, would be an oversimplification. Despite the proclaimed confidence in the ultimate triumph of communism and the strong denunciation of American political activities, a deep anxiety pervades *The Autobiography*. Du Bois clearly sees his increasing marginality in America and seems to write the book in order to understand and overcome it. He seeks to demonstrate, in effect, that his radicalism places him at the center rather than on the edge of American principles, and, perhaps more important, that he himself already has been a central part of American history. He seeks respect and recognition for his life and career at a moment when the nation is making him invisible. In a complex sense, he is writing in what G. Thomas Couser calls "the prophetic mode": "Confronted with a sense of declension or of uncontrollable change, they [prophetic autobiographers] have insisted on their power not only to order their own lives but to influence the course of history" (5). On the surface, certainly, *The Autobiography* does precisely this in criticizing American militarism and virulent anticommunism and in advocating socialism as a solution.

The problem is that Du Bois finds himself, at the end of a long life devoted to fighting racism and oppression, in the ironic position of constructing something like a slave narrative. During the antebellum period, when the nation refused to acknowledge the human reality of the slaves, hundreds of them escaped and created texts which gave them histories and identities. The narratives not only told stories of abuse and immorality that reinforced abolitionist arguments; they revealed the narrators' belief in fundamental American prin-

ciples of freedom, individuality, and literacy. They attributed
to themselves the same moral and political values as their
readers; they were, in other words, good Americans. The flaws
were in their countrymen (and women) who failed to live up
to the democratic and Christian values they proclaimed.

While Du Bois, writing a century later, obviously lives in
very different historical circumstances, the problem of status
within the society is similar. Because the nation has lost its
political and moral direction, it is on the verge of rendering
invisible one of its most valuable native sons. Du Bois seeks,
through his narrative, to regain control over the image of himself. He will recreate his own history as well as that part of
the nation's history through which he has lived. He will impose his own meaning on that history, a meaning that justifies his self-proclaimed importance. As Albert Stone has suggested about *The Autobiography,* "Here, clearly, is a deeply
felt and long-lasting impulse to order time and history around
the self, a desire which unites the diverse aspects of Du Bois's
multifaceted career as historian, sociologist, NAACP official,
and imaginative writer" (32). Du Bois interprets for readers
those events and people that helped make him significant and
those that threatened his status. And, through an intriguing
act of intertextual narcissism, he claims control over his own
previous versions of himself through wholesale incorporation
into *The Autobiography* of sections of the previous self-portraits.[1] The book thus becomes not merely a rereading of personal and national history but a means of recovering and preserving previous meanings of the self.

The nature of the meaning to be imposed is of course crucial.
Du Bois, throughout his career as an autobiographer, seems to
have been aware of the inherent artfulness of the genre. This is
in sharp contrast to his empiricism in historical and sociological
writing. Titles and subtitles of the autobiographical publications
reveal the creative character of the works: *The Souls of Black
Folk: Essays and Sketches; Darkwater: Voices from Within the
Veil; A Pageant in Seven Decades; Dusk of Dawn: An Essay toward an Autobiography of a Race Concept; In Battle for Peace:*

*The Story of My 83rd Birthday;* and *The Autobiography of W. E. B. Du Bois: A Soliloquy on Viewing My Life from the Last Decade of Its First Century.* Each work informs us of its literary as well as historical character.

In the last book, "soliloquy" implies both the isolation and the control that form the work's tension. A soliloquist, alone on the stage or in the speech act, interprets for the audience the meaning of the action. At the same time, however, this speaker is the creation of an author, a character in someone else's story. The interpretive control over the action is only momentary and only one reading of the events. Thus, in choosing such a designation for his narrating self, Du Bois seems to be reinforcing rather than alleviating the uncertainty of his position. The long history implied in the second part of his subtitle ("the Last Decade of Its First Century") strengthens the validity of his speech act but does not give it reality independent of the "play" of which it is a part. In fact, the status of the work is made even more problematic early in the first chapter: "This book then is the Soliloquy of an old man on what he dreams his life has been as he sees it slowly drifting away; and what he would like others to believe" (13). The statement implies a high level of subjectivity, in both remembering and representing the past. Everything in the comment lacks substance; it suggests a surrender to the personal, without conscious control or design. The narrative itself, though, is filled with concrete history: dates, people, places, organizations, conflicts, relationships. Very little of it is dream or drift. This apparent contradiction may be part of the deep design of the text. If the work is called dream or soliloquy, then it is not subject to the rigorous standards of formal argument; a personal view must be granted truth value precisely to the extent that it *is* personal. Readers must acknowledge, unless there is clear evidence to the contrary, that this is really what Du Bois believes. He is thus free to make as thoroughgoing an ideological statement as he wishes without being held rhetorically accountable for it. The concreteness of the history rendered makes his voice authoritative without sacrificing its subjectivity. He grants himself, in other words, the right that the nation denies him to be heard.

Control is exerted in another sense early in the autobiography. A binary opposition is established between the endgame of Du Bois's life and its beginnings. An opening set of chapters concerning his most recent travels, especially to the Soviet Union and China, is matched in length by chapters on his family and childhood in Great Barrington, Massachusetts. Thus, the text begins with an assertion of its own closure. This is a life that has taken its final form and, from that point, can look back to its start. But the implicit completeness is more than formal; it is also thematic. Both the ending and the beginning, joined appropriately by a credo on communism that serves as hyphenation, are utopian visions that emphasize justice, equality, intellect, and, most important, voice.

For Du Bois, the Soviet Union stands for all the virtues that have been lost in Western societies; it is, in fact, the West purified. Economic justice has been achieved; religious superstition has been eliminated; and the people "feel a vested interest in this nation" (35). But special emphasis is given to two key issues for Du Bois's narrative. The first is race: "The Soviet Union seems to me the only European country whose people are not more or less taught and encouraged to despise and look down on some class, group or race" (39). The struggle Du Bois waged all his life has been won under Stalin and Khrushchev. The second issue is freedom of inquiry and expression versus suppression, the fundamental conflict that shapes the narrative. In contrast to America, where voices such as his are stifled or denigrated, the Soviet Union values debate:

> Russians sit and listen long to talks, lectures, expositions; they read books, magazines and newspapers, not just picture books. Each problem of existence is discussed in village and factory. Comments, spoken and written, are welcomed, until every aspect, every opinion has been expressed and listened to, and the matter rises to higher echelons, and is discussed again. (35)

A true democracy is revealed here, in which every voice has weight in the decision-making process. Views are not ignored or suppressed on grounds of race, gender, or ideology.

An important element in this expressive process is the intellectual:

> Above this [the working class] and rising out of it and expressing its thoughts and ideals, rises the real aristocracy of the Soviet Union, the writers and scientists. They get the highest wages, they enjoy such privileges as the law and public opinion allow. How free are they? Science is free from religious dogma and vested interests. The writer has a wide leeway and rich applause, but he is limited by the aims of socialism to serve all and not a few. . . . (36)

The Du Bois who found his scientific research limited by the financial machinations of Booker T. Washington, and his editorial voice at *The Crisis* silenced by policy disputes within the NAACP, sees in the Soviet Union not merely freedom of speech but profound respect for intellectual activity. He is so impressed that he creates the oxymoron of an aristocracy of communism, an image consistent with certain of his lifelong principles, including the idea of a Talented Tenth, educated, thoughtful, self-sacrificing individuals working for the uplift of the masses.[2]

If the Soviet Union represents the best achievement of Western culture, China is a model of the possibilities of nonwhite peoples. Du Bois carefully and repeatedly makes the connection between the black experience in America and external and internal exploitation of the Chinese. He recalls his first visit, in 1936:

> Shanghai was an epitome of the racial strife, the economic struggle, the human paradox of modern life. Here was the greatest city of the most populous nation on earth, with the large part of it owned, governed and policed by foreign nations. . . . Even at that, matters were not as bad as

they once had been. In 1936, foreigners acknowledged that the Chinese
had some rights in China. Chinese who could afford it might even visit
the city race track from which they and dogs were long excluded. It was
no longer common to kick a coolie or throw a rickshaw's driver on the
ground. Yet, the afternoon before I saw a little English boy of perhaps
four years order three Chinese children out of his imperial way on the
sidewalk of the Bund; and they meekly obeyed and walked in the
gutter. It looked quite like Mississippi. (45)

Racial hatred is a universal reality; the need to expose it in all
its ugliness is a universal necessity for true justice: "I used to
weep for American Negroes, as I saw what indignities and repressions and cruelties they had passed; but as I read Chinese
history in these last months and had it explained to me
stripped of Anglo-Saxon lies, I know that no depths of Negro
slavery in America have plumbed such abysses as the Chinese
have seen for 2,000 years and more" (50). Du Bois's own lifetime efforts in history, sociology, and political and social commentary find their equivalent in the truth of Chinese historical studies under Mao Tse-tung.

But this historically exploited nonwhite country has done
more than expose its enemies; it has built an independent nation in defiance of its antagonists. And the principles on which
that building has been done are the ones Du Bois has argued
for consistently: equality, justice, honesty, hard work, and respect for intellect. "China has no rank or classes; her government awards no medals. She has no blue book of 'society.' But
she has leaders of learning and genius, scientists of renown,
artisans of skill and millions who know and believe this and
follow where these men lead" (51). The Talented Tenth has
been enacted in China: "Does your neighbor have better pay
and higher position than you? He has this because of greater
ability or better education, and more education is open to you
and compulsory for your children" (52). Even if Du Bois is a
pariah or nonperson in his own country, he is a prophet on
the world scene. By putting into practice these principles Du

Bois has stood for all his life, China has created a place of security, health, political integrity, and hope. And Du Bois's role has been recognized by the Chinese: "My birthday was given national notice in China, and celebrated as never before; and we who all our lives have been liable to insult and discrimination on account of our race and color, in China have met universal goodwill and love, such as we never expected" (49).

Thus it is that Du Bois begins his narrative by defining what he sees as the great future and his place in it. The Soviet Union and China represent visible proof of the validity of his values and experiences. He is in fact so committed to the positive image of these countries that he has little trouble, despite his peace activities, justifying their violence against others, as in Hungary and Tibet. They are acting on right principles, so their actions must be legitimate.

But while it is essential to establish his worth in the present, Du Bois is equally concerned with his place in the past. In one sense, to identify himself with the communist powers is to reinforce his alien status in his own country. What is necessary is to establish a continuity and harmony of values and ideas, to connect his American past with the global future. To do this, he recreates the Great Barrington of his childhood as a place spiritually consistent with the Soviet Union and China. While it was in many ways a conventional capitalist community, it did not openly display its class differences and conflicts:

> There were differences of property and income and yet all the men
> worked and seemed at least to be earning their incomes. . . . The owner-
> ship of property, of homes and stores, of a few mills of various sorts, was
> fundamental, and the basis of social prestige. Most families owned their
> homes. There was some inherited wealth but not in very large amounts.
> There were no idle rich and no outstanding "society." (78)

Great Barrington was, in essence, a middle-class community not implicated in the economic evils that led Du Bois to communism. While it believed in and practiced capitalist principles, it assumed no fixed class structure:

> The chief criterion of local standing was property and ancestry; but the
> ancestors were never magnates like the patroons of the manors along
> the Hudson to the west; nor were they persons of great prestige and
> learning with aristocratic connections like the residents of Boston and
> eastern Massachusetts. They were usually ordinary folk of solid
> respectability, farm owners, or artisans merging into industry. Standing
> did not depend on what the ancestor did, or who he was, but rather that
> he existed, lived decently and thus linked the individual to the community. (80)

What Du Bois describes here is the essence of bourgeois culture: respectability and responsibility. Such a culture is, from his perspective, fundamentally democratic in that it excludes no one willing and able to meet its standards. He points out, for example, that the local vice of drinking occurred among all classes, usually in the same place.

The democratic principle also applied to race. The old, established black families, including his own, were an accepted part of the community. They owned property, worked as farmers and artisans, and belonged to the Congregational and Episcopal churches. "The colored folk were not set aside in the sense that the Irish were, but were a part of the community of long-standing; and in my case as a child, I felt no sense of difference or separation from the main mass of townspeople" (83). Du Bois reinforces the point by devoting much of the chapter to details of relationships with both his white classmates and the adults of the community.

Even in the discrimination against the Irish, the sources seem more cultural than economic or ethnic. They were Catholic in a Protestant region, ignorant in a place that valued education, and "dirty" and "vulgar" in a community that demanded respectability above all else. They were the true Other, even among the blacks. But even this status was not permanent; Du Bois points out that, as the Irish established themselves and began educating their children, the "better class" of them became integrated into the larger community. In essence, acceptance of a bourgeois cultural hegemony opened opportunities for participation in society. The virtue of Great Barrington, from Du Bois's perspective, seems to have been its authentic effort to live up to its hegemonic ideals.[3]

This is most apparent in the town's politics: "In government, Great Barrington was in theory and largely in practice a democracy of the New England type" (91). In a book largely devoted to demonstrating the importance of voice, democracy is crucial. As a parable of voice, Du Bois narrates the story of the town meetings of his boyhood. Every year, Baretown Beebe, "a particularly dirty, ragged, fat old man," would come out of the hills for the meeting and denounce at length the expenditures for high-school education. "I remember distinctly how furious I used to get at the stolid town folk, who sat and listened to him. He was nothing and nobody. Yet the town heard him gravely because he was a citizen and property-holder on a small scale and when he was through, they calmly voted the usual funds for the high school." The moral of the story can serve as an epigraph for the autobiography: "Gradually as I grew up, I began to see that this was the essence of democracy: listening to the other man's opinion and then voting your own honestly and intelligently" (92).

The story is a parable of the life experience rendered in the book. Du Bois represents his career as devoted to inclusion of those—black Americans, the colonized, socialists and communists, peace advocates—seen as "dirty" and "ragged" outsiders by the respectable of the world. He advocates bringing them in from the "hills" of otherness and letting their views be heard, even if they offend the conventions of society. He claims for them citizenship and "property rights" in their humanity. Moreover, the principle of difference implied in the moral justifies his own dissensions from the views of others in his career. Because he sees himself as "honest" and "intelligent," his disputes with Booker T. Washington, the NAACP, and the American government, among others, are not idiosyncrasies or subversions but deeply respectful expressions of fundamental American values. He dared to have his own opinion, even when the right to do so was questioned; he, therefore, is the true democrat. Finally, as the self writing his autobiography, he knows that he has become, politically speaking, a kind of "particularly dirty, ragged, fat old man," a voice from the wilderness of radicalism. Having been in the past one of the respectable voices of democracy, he has become an object of scorn. He claims, in effect, the right to the same attention that he has so long sought for others. Even if what he does is revile that which others hold sacred, even if he speaks that which they do not want to hear, they have an obligation, as Americans, to listen to him "honestly" and "intelligently."

Thus, the journey to China and the Soviet Union completes a circle that had its beginnings in Great Barrington. The young boy who learned lessons of democracy, reason, and opportunity in America's heartland has become the old man who must embrace foreigners because they are the ones fulfilling America's promise and ideals. Because this is an autobiography defining the self in ideological terms, the coherence of political values—the completing of the circle—becomes the guarantee of identification between the young man and the old one. Though much happens between youth and age, between late nineteenth-century Great Barrington and mid–twentieth-century Moscow, though much education and experience are necessary to get from one to the other, still the end is in the beginning. In this sense, *The Autobiography* is a good old-fashioned narrative with a strong inner form.

The space between youth and age, which makes up the bulk of the story, follows a pattern determined by the opening chapters. Du Bois must always work against those who presume to define and control him and his endeavors; in his heroic struggles, he stands firm for his principles and in the end emerges stronger. These conflicts are consistently over issues of education and expression, and Du Bois never acknowledges being wrong in any of them. His awareness may, at any point, be limited because he lacks information or perspective, but he is always as right as he can be under the circumstances. Such a self-image is neither self-righteous nor egotistical. Because he gained in his childhood certain eternally valid principles, he can never be wrong on fundamental issues. He may be defeated, as he is several times in his life, but that never leads to a questioning of the premises from which he operates. He fails either because the opposition is politically or materially stronger or because victory would come only through moral compromise. Whatever the outcome, Du Bois sees himself gaining greater wisdom for the next struggle (and there is always a next struggle).

Appropriately, the circumstances of Du Bois's education provide the first instance of struggle. In the tradition of African-American personal narrative, from Olaudah Equiano and Frederick Douglass to Malcolm X and Maya Angelou, the means and meaning of acquiring education have been central to the life story. Robert Stepto has even suggested that literacy (and its relationship to freedom) is the fundamental theme of black writing. The role of whites in black education is a frequent issue: Douglass describes the irony of learning the value of reading from a master defending black illiteracy; Malcolm X talks of a high-school teacher who advised him to be realistic and understand that blacks could never aspire to the professions. In Du Bois's case, he both acknowledges and questions white contributions to his academic preparation. He says of his high-school principal: "He suggested, quite as a matter of course, that I ought to take the college preparatory course which involved algebra, geometry, Latin and Greek. If Hosmer had been another sort of man, with definite ideas as to a Negro's 'place,' and had recommended agriculture or domestic economy, I would doubtless have followed his advice, had such 'courses' been available" (101).

In this passage Du Bois's attitude seems much like that of Booker T. Washington, who went to great lengths to express his gratitude to those white men and women who assisted and guided his training. But Du Bois notes that Hosmer and others decide that he should pursue his education in the South, despite his own preference for Harvard. His family resents the idea that a black man's place is in the former slave territory, but Du Bois himself accedes to the notion. Unlike Washington, however, he does not assume a greater white wisdom: "Whether or not I should always live and work in the South, I did not stop then to decide; that I would give up the idea of graduating from Harvard, did not occur to me" (105). Not in a position to reject white guidance, he incorporates it into his own perspective. Moreover, he turns it to his advantage and to a criticism of whites on another level:

> But here and now was adventure. I was going into the South; the South of slavery, rebellion and black folk; above all, I was going to meet colored people of my own age and education, of my own ambitions. . . . But I wanted to go to Fisk, not simply because it was at least a beginning of my dream of college, but also, I suspect, because I was beginning to feel lonesome in New England. Unconsciously, I realized that as I grew older, and especially now that I had finished the public school, the close cordial intermingling with my white fellows would grow more restricted. There would be meetings, parties, clubs, to which I would not be invited. Especially in the case of strangers, visitors, newcomers to the town would my presence and friendship become a matter of explanation or even embarrassment to my schoolmates. I became aware, once a chance to go to a group of young people of my own race was opened up for me, of the spiritual isolation in which I was living. (105–6)

White paternalism provides Du Bois with the opportunity to achieve a level of racial identification that would otherwise not be possible. He speaks shortly after the passage cited above of realizing that the black South could provide "something inherently and deeply my own" (106). The unintended effect of the white gesture, based on racial stereotypes, is to make available to him a profound cultural identity. Like Frederick Douglass, he turns white denial into black affirmation. What makes the realization a part of Du Bois's "double-consciousness"⁴ is its revelation to him of his true condition in that previously pristine world of Great Barrington. He cannot, as an educated adult, be a true native son. His very ambitions for education and a middle-class life exclude him from the community. The existing order can accept him as dependent, powerless, and voiceless, but not as self-defining, even if that definition is coherent with its own. Projecting the image of otherness in the eyes of his erstwhile friends and supporters, he knows that he must look elsewhere to find a true self.

Consistent with this understanding, he proceeds to show how he must work against others, both black and white, to achieve what is right for himself and for the race with which he now identifies. As part of this drama, he repeatedly creates images of homelessness for himself.[5] He is left an orphan when his mother dies; he never feels a part of the Harvard community; Wilberforce College proves an academic disappointment; life at Atlanta University is disrupted by racial violence and conflict with Washington's Tuskegee Machine; and finally, government persecution robs him of security in his old age. Such portraits reinforce the necessity of self-creation; the young man sent away from Great Barrington must always make a place for himself because none is ever granted to him.

These various elements come together in the story of his short time at Wilberforce, the leading college of the African Methodist Episcopal Church. He went there almost directly from the University of Berlin, "with the cane and gloves of my German student days; with my rather inflated ideas of what a 'university' ought to be and with a terrible bluntness of speech that was continually getting me into difficulty" (186). The latter shortly lands him in trouble when he refuses to offer a prayer at a campus religious meeting. This somewhat humorous episode nicely foreshadows the more significant confrontation with Bishop Arnett. What saves him at the beginning is his energy: "I was willing to do endless work when the work seemed to me worth doing" (186). He intended through this effort to make Wilberforce "a great university." To this end, he taught his courses, tried to introduce new material and create a real library, began writing books, and attempted to enhance the cultural life of the institution. But what he confronted was a hierarchy focused on church politics and not on intellectual excellence. Advancement within the college required attendance to the power structure; this Du Bois rejected:

> The bishops and would-be bishops gathered here in force on each commencement where elders and ministers waylaid them in long conferences. The teachers also found it expedient to make powerful acquaintances at these occasions; I in my independence met no one but walked off into the woods as the hosts talked. (187)

Du Bois's resistance to political interaction of this sort becomes open when he leads a faculty revolt against the appointment of Bishop Arnett's unqualified son to an academic appointment at the college. The bishop was a force to be reckoned with: "With little literary ability, he established a sort of school of literature, bringing together and reprinting hundreds of books, pamphlets, and scraps of the writings of American Negro literature. He was a power in Ohio politics. He distributed offices in the church and settled the appointment of teachers at Wilberforce" (190). He is the typical Du Bois antagonist: uncultured in some way, powerful, self-serving, autocratic, and disdainful of idealism.

Against him the young professor feels compelled to act, regardless of the consequences: "Under my impetuous and uncurbed assault, the Bishop had to bend, but I knew well that my days at Wilberforce were numbered" (190). While it may be questioned whether a greater good might have been served by a compromise that would have allowed Du Bois to continue his efforts at the school, such a pragmatic consideration is precisely what he disdains in the retelling. He imagines himself having the "cunning" to help shape the institution but asserts that the end result would not have matched his ideal. The very labeling of the necessary quality as "cunning" suggests a view that accommodation would have violated both his principles and his self-image, an image he seeks to reinforce sixty-five years after the event. Here and throughout the narrative, purity of intention and action marks his heroic persona. The point is not to win the battles but to fight the good fight and to always be "right," even in defeat.

If this episode shows us the impetuous young hero sacrificing all for the sake of principle, the story of the protagonist's relationship with Booker T. Washington reveals the hero as man of reason and science facing forces of deceit and irrationality. He takes special care in defining himself as man primarily committed to the pursuit of truth in a reasoned, scientific way. He seeks the scholar's life in the world of Atlanta University, which he describes as an intellectual and moral oasis where the ideals of goodness, truth, and beauty are carefully and continuously inculcated. He says of the effects the years there had on him:

> They were years of great spiritual upturning, of the making and unmaking of ideals, of hard work and hard play. Here I found myself. I lost most of my mannerisms. I grew more broadly human, made my closest and most holy friendships, and studied human beings. I became widely acquainted with the real condition of my people. (213)

He goes on to describe in considerable detail what the study of human beings meant for him. It was research into various aspects of the conditions of black life, research that resulted in the Atlanta Studies, a series established by Du Bois and funded by Atlanta University and other sources. What Du Bois wishes readers to understand is the pioneering nature of this sociological work, first in its gathering of hard data and second in its depth and breadth. It was to be a hundred-year project, working in ten-year cycles, with constant improvements in research and interpretive techniques. It was to be, in other words, a model in both method and results. It was to be the great lifework: rational, productive, and socially useful in the sense that the facts uncovered could be used to make intelligent social improvements.

But it never fulfilled its promise, not because of any flaws in its conception or execution but because the attempt was made in a world not committed to his principles. To provide an image of this, he tells of his exhibit, based on the Atlanta Studies research, at the 1900 Paris World's Fair. Though given little financial support, little time to prepare, and a very small space at the exposition, he managed to mount an exhibit that was popular and that won a Grand Prize and a Gold Medal for him. Such recognition should have gained considerable attention and funding, but it did not. The reason it failed is an indictment of American culture:

> I did the deed but I did not advertise it. Either I myself or someone for me should have called public attention to what had been done or otherwise it would quickly be forgotten. Indeed the philosophy then current and afterward triumphant was that Deed without Advertising was worthless and in the long run Advertising without Deed was the only lasting value. (221)[6]

Clearly matters become highly problematic when substance itself has lost its relevance. The very notion of self-promotion is antithetical to the values on which Du Bois's research is based and on which this self has constructed its identity. The point is always to reveal substance, not to displace it.

Underlying this question of presentation is another about the nature of the substance studied. The real issue is whether there was any desire to know the truth about black life:

> [T]here was no such definite demand for scientific work of the sort that I was doing, as I had confidently assumed would be easily forthcoming. I regarded it as axiomatic that the world wanted to learn the truth and if the truth were sought with even approximate accuracy and painstaking devotion, the world would gladly support the effort. This was, of course, but a young man's idealism, not by any means false, but also never universally true. (222)

It is important here to clarify what Du Bois accepts and what he questions. The final statement concerns itself with the practicalities of enacting principles in a fallen world; it does not raise doubts about the principles themselves. The issue is not the scientific work, about which he uses words like "truth" and "devotion," but rather his youthful naïveté about the nature of the world.

More troubling, though not commented on in detail, is the response of the scientific community:

> Our reports were widely read and commented upon. On the other hand, so far as the American world of science and letters was concerned, we never "belonged"; we remained unrecognized in learned societies and academic groups. We rated merely as Negroes studying Negroes, and after all, what had Negroes to do with America or science? (228)

Such an observation implicitly calls into question science itself, since it suggests that prejudice can preclude awareness of fact, even in those trained to recognize it. Du Bois here verges on an ideological reading of scientific practice, one in which extrinsic factors produce silences or blind spots to such a degree that whole areas of knowledge are suppressed. He backs away, presumably because to go forward would mean to call into question his own endeavors and values. After all, much of his reputation was based on objective, documentable research and analysis in history and sociology. He consistently in his career distinguished between his writings that were "propaganda" and those that were scientific.[7]

A prominent thread running through this section of *The Autobiography* is Du Bois's relationship with Booker T. Washington. Washington is in many ways the bête noire of the narrative. He frustrates scientific ambitions; he subverts efforts to create a black intellectual journal; he indirectly but persistently questions Du Bois's motives; he resists improvements in black education; he denigrates efforts to gain civil rights; and he, in effect, forces Du Bois to change careers. Such a list implies that the narrative functions as a frontal attack, but Du Bois is much more subtle than that. He never directly accuses Washington of any hostile or unethical act. He works instead by circumlocution, Washington's own favored method. He says that he felt pressure to change the direction of his research, without specifying the source or nature of that pressure. He notes that Atlanta University might have found continuing funding for the Atlanta Studies "if it had not been for the controversy with Booker T. Washington that arose in 1903 and increased in intensity until 1908" (222), but then he immediately shifts to other topics. The attacks on himself and others and certain financial and political manipulations are said to be the work of the Tuskegee Machine. He is cautious in assigning blame: "How much Mr. Washington knew of this work of the Tuskegee Machine and was directly responsible, one cannot say, but of its general activity and scope he must have been aware" (239).

Despite such circumspection, a judgment on Washington is clearly implied; it comes not through assessment of ideas, as it did in *The Souls of Black Folk*,[8] but through comments on character. Washington exhibits traits that are at odds with and morally inferior to those Du Bois grants himself. The first of these is an unwillingness to stand for anything: "It was characteristic of the Washington statesmanship that whatever he or anybody believed or wanted must be subordinated to dominant public opinion and that opinion deferred to and cajoled until it allowed a deviation toward better ways. It was my theory to guide and force public opinion by leadership" (237). According to Du Bois, Washington has no courage or conviction; in fact, such language is irrelevant when discussing him because his nature and his success are based precisely on concealment of whatever real intentions he might have. True leadership is revealed not by conceding existing conditions but by pushing constantly for change. Despite Washington's fame and influence, he lacks, in contrast to Du Bois, the moral fiber of authentic leadership.

Moreover, "it did not seem fair, for instance, that on the one hand Mr. Washington should decry political activities among Negroes, and on the other hand dictate Negro political objectives from Tuskegee" (238). Here timidity becomes hypocrisy. Washington publicly proclaims the need for accommodation, submission, and acquiescence to white southern discrimination but simultaneously builds a political machine that controls black public life. Du Bois's lifelong disdain for conventional politics comes through here. The Tuskegee Machine is a version of Tammany Hall; whatever its achievements, it is, in the Du Boisian moral universe, fundamentally corrupt because it is based on deceit and manipulation. It is a violation of those very principles of honesty, hard work, and sacrifice that Washington himself kept talking about.

Such a machine, in addition to operating dishonestly, also was capable of positive harm. Du Bois tells a story "which always stands in my memory as typical." A well-to-do young black man attempts to improve black life by establishing a self-sufficient community in the South. On the surface, this would seem to fit exactly into Washington's philosophy by encouraging blacks to build their own economic base through self-reliance. But when the man seeks northern financial assistance to begin the project, he is unsuccessful, not because he is opposed, but because Washington says nothing in support of the proposal. After years of futile effort, the man dies of overwork and stress. Du Bois clearly implies that this death is on Washington's head because he used his power improperly. Even though his sin is one of omission (presumably), the fact that his silence can produce such devastating results indicates the extent of both his authority and his irresponsibility. The claim that the story is "typical" impugns Washington's basic character.

The young man is a surrogate of sorts for Du Bois. He, too, is a victim of Washington; not only are his scholarly studies disrupted; his very being is challenged. His underlying objection to his antagonist is that Washington demands absolute conformity to his own views. Since Du Bois defines his essential self in terms of an independent, honest voice, such conformity amounts to virtual extinction. It is especially appropriate, then, that when he recalls negotiations around 1902 for him to move to Tuskegee, he describes his expected role as "ghost writer." To accept a position as an intellectual source for another's expression would mean invisibility. Ironically, the conflict, which leads to the end of the first stage of Du Bois's academic career, results in his taking on a new role, "master of propaganda," at the NAACP.

The struggle with Washington, in which the element of character was central, leads to a question of Du Bois's presentation of his own character. Clearly the issue was important to him as an autobiographer; the editors of the Library of America volume on him have pointed out that the chapter entitled "My Character" is the only wholly new section in *The Autobiography* (1308). The chapter suggests an essential self that has nonetheless had its experience shaped by environmental forces. The key traits of his personality are honesty, vitality, intellectuality, and a desire for control. He shows these traits being tested in matters of money, sexuality, social interaction, and religion; in every case, his qualities hold up under the stress of practical considerations. He displays relatively little concern for finances; as long as he gets income fairly and provides for his family, money is of little concern. He notes, for example, that a bad investment in New York real estate could have been made profitable if he had been willing to let the building be used for questionable purposes. He, of course, preferred to take the loss. "In all of this I had followed the advice of a friend skilled in the handling of real estate but who assumed that I was trying to make money and not dreaming of model housing conditions. As many of my friends have since informed me, I was a fool; but I was not a thief which I count to my credit" (279).

This willingness to sacrifice personal benefits in order to preserve integrity is the pattern of the chapter. He refuses to participate in the adulterous practices of his colleagues at Wilberforce, and he proclaims lifelong marital fidelity despite his frequent associations with intelligent, attractive women in his work. Even his flaws in this regard are markers of integrity. "As a teacher in the rural districts of East Tennessee, I was literally raped by the unhappy wife who was my landlady. . . . A brief trial with prostitution in Paris affronted my sense of decency. I lived more or less regularly with a shop girl in Berlin, but was ashamed" (280). All of these events occurred in his youth and serve effectively to demonstrate simultaneously his lack of priggishness and his fundamental morality.

The examples of money and sexuality suggest that his self-portrait relies on an underlying belief in a rational morality. In this, he seems to be resisting key elements of his own achieved wisdom. The character he presents is, in essence, pre-Freudian and pre-Marxian, despite Freud and Marx being crucial parts of his education and despite his identification of his present self as a Marxist. He reveals this premodern sensibility in his assumption that reason and moral control are basic to personality and not products of underlying nonrational elements, whether psychological or economic. His defects are matters of ignorance and temporarily misguided impulse; his failures are the products of immoral forces at work in the world. Thus, racism, which he persists in seeing as a correctable moral defect, is the cause for his not developing interracial friendships:

> I was on occasion incomprehensibly shy. . . . This in the case of my fellow Negroes was balanced by our common experiences and shared knowledge of what each other had been through; but in the case of white companions, and especially those newly met, we could not talk together, we lived in different worlds. We belonged to no social clubs, and did not visit the same people or even stand at the same liquor bars. We did not lunch together. I did not play cards, and could never get wildly enthusiastic even over baseball. Naturally we could not share stories of sex. Thus I did not seek white acquaintances, I let them make the advances, and they therefore thought me arrogant. In a sense I was, but after all I was in fact rather desperately hanging on to my self-respect. (282–83)

This passage is crucial to understanding Du Bois's self-representation. The self is surrounded by forces—economic, sexual, racial—which threaten it. Only strenuous protective devices—"arrogance," withdrawal, self-control—can prevent its humiliation. This suggests the self as an essence rather than a process; the Du Bois recreated in this chapter does not fundamentally change from childhood to old age. This is not an identity shaped by economic or sexual or even racial forces; it is, rather, one challenged, threatened, and tested by them. They may limit its possibilities and frustrate its desires, but they do not make it what it is. Its achievement should be measured by its inner wholeness, not by its external success or failure.

Such a standard is important in what is dramatized as the greatest struggle of all in *The Autobiography*. In his conflict with the U.S. government over his international peace activities and the government's foreign policy and racial practices, Du Bois represents the government as his most powerful and insidious antagonist. He defines the conflict precisely as one of honesty and individual expression:

> Even if some thought peace at present dangerous and did not believe in socialism, they knew that if democracy was to survive in modern culture and in this vaunted "Land of the Free" and leader of "free nations," the right to think and to speak; the right to know what others were thinking; . . . that this democratic right of freedom of thought and speech must be preserved from Truman and McGrath; McCarran and Smith; from McCarthy and little Georgia's Joseph Wood leading the reactionary slave South—or America was dead. Despite this, most Americans of education and stature did not say a word or move a hand. This is the most astonishing and frightening result of this trial. We five [Du Bois, Kyrle Elkin, Elizabeth Moos, Abbott Simon, and Sylvia Soloff] are free but America is not. The absence of moral courage and intellectual integrity which our prosecution revealed still stands to frighten our own nation and the better world. It is clear still today, that freedom of speech and of thinking can be attacked in the United States without the intellectual and moral leaders of this land raising a hand or saying a word in protest or defense, except in the case of the Saving Few. (388–89)

According to Du Bois, the government's attack itself was dishonest from the beginning. In 1951, the Justice Department claimed that the Peace Information Center and its officials were operating as agents of a foreign power without registering as such. The impression was created in the media that this

power was the Soviet Union, but in the courtroom the pros-
ecution offered no evidence of a connection and claimed that
it did not need to do so. It argued that consistency of views
was sufficient cause for conviction and put witnesses on the
stand, including some formerly associated with the center, to
testify that both the Soviet Union and international peace organizations held the same views as the center. The judge rejected that contention and dismissed the indictment. Behind
the specious charges, Du Bois sees the real attack:

> It was the State Department which started this prosecution to quell
> Communists, and retard the peace movement which was beginning to
> annoy the Pentagon. The inclusion of myself, a Negro, in the dragnet,
> was probably at first fortuitous, but quickly backed by the military as a
> needed warning to complaining Negroes. (389)

Thus, Du Bois creates a moral drama in which the power of
the government is arrayed against a small group precisely because that group is standing for the fundamental principles of
the nation itself. He claims that the government cannot admit that it fears the very freedom it espouses, so it lies and
intimidates to justify suppression. And, even more important
for Du Bois's story, the nation's moral and intellectual leaders, so dependent themselves on democratic freedoms, lack
the courage and integrity to protest such abuses. Among this
group are educated blacks, a contingent that Du Bois himself
virtually created. All have such deep investments in the status quo that they have lost a sense of what it is they are supposed to be about. Moreover, in an age of widespread
anticommunist hysteria, fear and patriotism combine to create ambiguities about moral and political principles; loyalty
to country becomes defined as rejection of certain rights. Du
Bois sees only himself and his "Saving Few" as retaining their
integrity and their commitment to fundamental American
values.

But the price for such integrity is high; as always Du Bois must make a great sacrifice in order to preserve his self-respect. This time the risk is virtual annihilation: "All this made my enemies and the Federal government take a determined stand to insure my destruction" (394). He becomes that "dirty, ragged" man he had earlier described when discussing Great Barrington's town democracy. Though he has been acquitted of any wrongdoing, he reports that the government harasses him in a variety of ways, publishers will not print his work, universities and organizations will not invite him to lecture, and, one of the greatest ironies, the NAACP actively campaigns to deny him speaking opportunities. The net effect is invisibility: "From being a person whom every Negro in the nation knew by name at least and hastened always to entertain or praise, churches and Negro conferences refused to mention my past or present existence" (394).

It is an experience he tries to comprehend and explain in terms of the very history he helped to create:

> It was a bitter experience and I bowed before the storm. But I did not break. I continued to speak and write when and where I could. I faced my lowered income and lived within it. I found new friends and lived in a wider world than ever before—a world with no color line. I lost my leadership of my race. It was a dilemma for the mass of Negroes; either they joined the current beliefs and actions of most whites or they could not make a living or hope for preferment. Preferment was possible. The color line was beginning to break. Negroes were getting recognition as never before. Was not the sacrifice of one man, small payment for this? Even those who disagreed with its judgment at least kept quiet. The colored children ceased to hear my name. (395)

As before, the sacrifice is double-edged. On the one hand, Du Bois loses his place at the head of the race; on the other, he enters a world where race is transcended and thus achieves one of the great goals of his life. Importantly, he believes that the loss of leadership results not from any distance between himself and other blacks ideologically but because the race itself lacks his sacrificial character.[9] He becomes their scapegoat; the ritual, however, is profane because what they are gaining is secular. "Preferment" implies special status and promotion that would come through acceptance of the existing order rather than courageous effort to change it. This result would be gained through the martyrdom of one of the race's greatest men. Because blacks cannot live up to Du Bois's model, they are willing to surrender their own integrity and his being. The one whose actions in the past have helped make possible their present will disappear from their future.[10]

Because the nation, the intelligentsia, and the black race are willing to erase his place in history, Du Bois can depend only on himself to establish his visibility. And because his role in history is one of ideas as well as actions, it is important to preserve his words as well as his experiences. *The Autobiography* does this by incorporating earlier works. Much of this is verbatim use, with occasional rearrangement or updating, and most of it is unacknowledged. In effect, he creates an anthology of his own work in which he reproduces not so much the story of himself as a compendium of self-portraits. Unlike most autobiographical works, which are voiced by a narrating self recalling the experiencing self from a fixed point in the present,[11] Du Bois gives us several narrative selves taking a variety of perspectives in both the past and the present. While it could be argued that this pattern results from a lack of energy in a ninety-year-old man, the shaping of the inclusions connects this activity to other artfulness in the book. Sometimes parts of passages are used and then expanded upon; at other times, long sections will be incorporated; and finally, Du Bois will occasionally call attention to the passage having been written years before. Though the effect is often stylistically jarring, more significantly it creates ideological inconsistencies that one would expect a Marxist and a historian to be sensitive to. After all, the liberal reformer of 1903 took positions not held by either the nationalist of 1940 or the socialist of the 1950s. But perhaps that is the point: the way to demonstrate one's historical reality and the meaning of history for the self is to reproduce the earlier versions of the self, not from a later perspective but from the times and in the terms of those selves. How better to claim one's place in history than by, in documentary fashion, citing the words, ideas, and experiences from those historical moments?

Moreover, while these narrators work from different ideological positions and while their styles are distinguishable, the differences are dialectically related to the coherence of the self they present. From the young Du Bois teaching in rural Tennessee (from *The Souls of Black Folk*) to the ninety-year-old man contemplating his own death (written in 1959–60), there is a consistency of character that, given ideological shifts and changing historical conditions, should not be present. Each narrator is a careful moral observer, concerned with the spiritual implications of the world he sees. And the self portrayed tries to find a place in that world; it is a self certain of its own virtue but uncertain of virtue's effectiveness in the face of ignorance, greed, and racism.

Such a coherence of selves cannot be taken as demonstration that, in some objective sense, the experiencing Du Bois of the 1880s was identical to the Du Bois of 1960, or even that the autobiographer of 1903 is identical to the one of 1960. Rather, the consistency suggests a deep-seated need to represent, to himself and others, an underlying identity transcending ideology and history. The incorporation of earlier texts operates self-reflexively to create an image of wholeness; in an impossible but necessary gesture, he overrides difference and discontinuity in his desire to see the life as a narrative of heroic struggle both in language and action, a narrative which he has constantly retold and which reaches its completion in this final text of lives and texts. On the verge of the dissolution of death and the invisibility of national and racial suppression, Du Bois generates a final permanent portrait of himself as the ultimate American.

## Notes

1.  The editors of the Library of America anthology of Du Bois's works point out that most of *The Autobiography* was previously published

in *Dusk of Dawn*, *In Battle for Peace*, and a 1958 article in *National Guardian* (1308–9). In addition, several passages are taken verbatim from *The Souls of Black Folk* and *Darkwater*.

2. See, for example, "The Talented Tenth" in *The Negro Problem* of 1903. Though Du Bois later modifies some of the more elitist elements of the concept in such works as *Dusk of Dawn*, some version of it persists throughout his career. In *The Autobiography*, it loses its racial connotations and is based instead on political principles.

3. For another reading of the importance of Great Barrington to Du Bois, see Woodard, who interprets the Great Barrington experience as determining Du Bois's ideology.

4. In *The Souls of Black Folk*, Du Bois describes the "peculiar sensation" of "always looking at one's self through the eyes of others, of measuring one's soul by the tape of a world that looks on in amused contempt and pity. One ever feels his twoness,—an American, a Negro; two souls, two thoughts, two unreconciled strivings; two warring ideals in one dark body" (16–17).

5. Compare Albert Stone, who reads *The Autobiography* as controlled by a metaphor of travel.

6. This statement about "Deed" appears deliberately constructed to contrast with the closing statement of the book: "Teach us, Forever Dead, there is no Dream but Deed, there is no Deed but Memory" (423). That which is truly lasting is intratextually set against an illusion of value. As elsewhere, Du Bois asserts the validity of his eternal principles in contrast to the superficial pragmatism of the nation.

7. As one example from late in his life, he comments in the preface to his *Black Flame* (1957–61) trilogy that he would have written a work of history if he had had the time and the resources. Lacking those, he settled for documentary fiction.

8. That Du Bois feels it necessary to treat Washington in detail so often in his writings indicates his significance for Du Bois. The real hostility emerges in the *Black Flame* trilogy, written in the 1950s, which maliciously describes Washington becoming ill while visiting a brothel in New York.

9. For a different view of Du Bois's relationship with blacks during this period, see Horne. His argument that Du Bois remains central to black political experience seems rather clearly contradicted by Du Bois himself.

10. On the relationships of blacks, the American Communist party, and Marxism generally, see Record and Robinson.

11. See Stone: "A narrating self reinvents the historical actor" (13).

## Works Cited

Couser, G. Thomas. *American Autobiography: The Prophetic Mode.* Amherst: U of Massachusetts P, 1979.

Douglass, Frederick. *Narrative of the Life of Frederick Douglass, An American Slave.* 1845. New York: Modern Library, 1984.

Du Bois, W. E. B. *The Autobiography of W. E. B. Du Bois: A Soliloquy on Viewing My Life from the Last Decade of Its First Century.* New York: International, 1968.

———. *The Black Flame: A Trilogy.* New York: Mainstream, 1957–61.

———. *Darkwater: Voices from Within the Veil.* New York: Harcourt, 1920.

———. *Dusk of Dawn: An Essay toward an Autobiography of a Race Concept.* New York: Harcourt, 1940.

———. *In Battle for Peace: The Story of My 83rd Birthday.* New York: Masses and Mainstream, 1952.

———. *A Pageant in Seven Decades, 1868–1938.* N.p.: n.p., 1938.

———. *The Souls of Black Folk: Essays and Sketches.* 1903. Greenwich, CT: Fawcett, 1961.

———. "The Talented Tenth." In *The Negro Problem: A Series of Articles by Representative American Negroes of To-Day.* New York: James Pott, 1903. 33–75.

———. *Writings.* Ed. Nathan Huggins. New York: Library of America, 1986.

Horne, Gerald. *Black and Red: W. E. B. Du Bois and the Afro-American Response to the Cold War, 1944–1963.* New York: State U of New York P, 1986.

Malcolm X. *The Autobiography of Malcolm X.* New York: Grove, 1965.

Record, Wilson. *Race and Radicalism: The NAACP and the Communist Party in Conflict.* Ithaca: Cornell UP, 1964.

Robinson, Cedric. *Black Marxism: The Making of the Black Radical Tradition.* London: Zed, 1983.

Stepto, Robert B. *From Behind the Veil: A Study of Afro-American Narrative.* Urbana: U of Illinois P, 1979.

Stone, Albert E. *Autobiographical Occasions and Original Acts: Versions of American Identity from Henry Adams to Nate Shaw*. Philadelphia: U of Pennsylvania P, 1982.

Washington, Booker T. *Up from Slavery*. New York: Doubleday, 1901.

Woodard, Fredrick. "W. E. B. Du Bois: The Native Impulse: Notes Toward an Ideological Biography, 1868–1897." Diss. U of Iowa, 1976.

# George Washington Cable's "My Politics": Context and Revision of a Southern Memoir

*James Robert Payne*

In his entry for December 18, 1888, in an unpublished diary now in the archives of the Tulane University Library, George Washington Cable noted:

> I have somehow grown very fond of this diary. I feel, when I take it up as if only my nearest and dearest were by and I could talk with the perfect freedom of the most confidential friendship and love. (Diary I, 52)[1]

Cable's reference to his "nearest and dearest" and to "the most confidential friendship and love" may well have been prompted by feelings about his family, from whom he was frequently absent in order to meet the demanding schedule of public readings he committed himself to in the late 1880s. The diary served in part as an outlet during travel for the sort of personal expression that the usually circumspect Cable would reserve for family and intimate friends. Indeed, many of the approximately one hundred manuscript pages of the journal, labeled "Diary George W. Cable 1888–1889 1890–1891," were composed on trains and in hotels during the course of the author's travels to speaking engagements nationwide.

---

Quotations from the "Diary [of] George W. Cable 1888–1889[,] 1890–1891" are included in this essay with the permission of the Manuscripts Section, Howard-Tilton Memorial Library, Tulane University, New Orleans. Material quoted from this diary may not be requoted without written authorization from the Manuscripts Section of the Howard-Tilton Memorial Library.

Following close on the above-quoted expression of the feeling of freedom that may be entailed in diary writing is Cable's striking statement of a sense of the limitations of such expression:

> . . . I wish it were best—as I know full well it is not— that I should be known through & through by all my kind. Not even this diary can or should ever give that knowledge. There are things a man cannot tell even himself. What a farce the confessional must be. (Diary I, 52)

Within the parameters of ideal freedom and actual constraint that he perceived as inherent in the diary form, between December 1888 and January 1889 Cable compiled a personal record that gives us a unique view of significant aspects of the character of the author of *Old Creole Days* (1879), *The Grandissimes* (1880), *Madame Delphine* (1881), and other classic works of American fiction and nonfiction.

In addition to conventional dated journal entries, Cable wrote the first draft of his memoir "My Politics" in the 1888–89 diary. Characterized by Arlin Turner as "a sort of apologia" (introd. to Cable, *The Negro Question* 2), "My Politics" describes the development of his political values and writings against the background of his experience of the Civil War, of the "fierce" days of Reconstruction, and of the post-Reconstruction time during which his rise to prominence as author and civil rights advocate coincided with the period of most extreme suppression of rights of African Americans. Although originally intended by Cable to serve as the introduction to an expanded edition of his collection of essays *The Silent South* (1889), "My Politics" was suppressed during Cable's lifetime as "too personal," in accordance with the advice of his editors (Turner, introd. to *The Negro Question* 2). Arlin Turner drew on "My Politics" for his landmark *George W. Cable: A Biography* (1956), and other scholars have alluded to data from the memoir, especially since Turner's publication of "My Politics" as the lead article in his 1958 edition of Cable's *The Negro Question*. Before deciding to suppress "My Politics," Cable prepared a revised version, a copy of the typescript of which is in the Tulane University Library archives. This typescript revision of "My Politics" is a more circumspect document than the manuscript version written in Cable's diary. Prepared for the public, and evidently allowing for the sensibilities of Cable's fellow southerners, it reflects the parameter of constraint that Cable knew was inevitable in diary writing (Diary I, 52). By comparison, his first draft manuscript version is a more personal document, reflecting the parameter of freedom that Cable posited as an ideal potential for diary composition, a place where he could express himself with "perfect freedom" (Diary I, 52). Arlin Turner published from the typescript and gave the world the more public Cable memoir in *The Negro Question* (1958). Most scholars and general readers, if they know the essay at all, know it in this revised, "public" version. Yet this unique and important testimony by a major post–Civil War southern author is well worth study in its freer, more spontaneous, more personal original version within the context of the diary in which it first appeared. In this essay I will examine "My Politics" in its original context in the diary, and I will explore the significance of key changes Cable made as he revised the manuscript to produce a text geared more for the perceived attitudes of the American public of his day, especially in the South.

Following a strategy comparable to that of such classic conversion narratives as St. Augustine's *Confessions* and Jonathan Edwards's *Personal Narrative*, Cable in "My Politics" reveals how he changed from a youth who believed in and fought for "Slavery and a White Man's Government" (*The Negro Question* 3)[2] to become the prominent author and civil rights advocate who could conclude his political memoir with the statement that "lasting national peace, fellowship, and wealth . . . can never stand on other foundations than equal justice and equal liberty to all people" (*The Negro Question* 25). Offering his own life experience of change especially to his fellow southerners, Cable

relates how he has been where his post-Reconstruction com-
patriots may still feel they are:

> I felt that I belonged, still, peculiarly to the South. I had shared in every
> political error of the "Southerner," and had enjoyed whatever benefits the
> old slave-holding civilization had to offer. As a result duty bound me to
> my best conception of the true interest of the South as a whole— . . . white
> and black. (*The Negro Question* 22)

Having shared in every "sin," every "error" of the old ways,
Cable, like Augustine and Jonathan Edwards, those exemplary
narrators of conversion before him, expresses a feeling of obligation to offer his life experience to his fellows as an example
of the possibility of change. And, indeed, Cable's righteous
political convictions rivaled in passionate intensity the religious convictions of Augustine, Edwards, and other conversion narrators.

Yet while Cable was sensitive to conscience, sensitive to what
he thought was "right," as a well-known author with a large family dependent upon his success, he was attentive, too, to what he
perceived to be the sensibilities of his late nineteenth-century,
essentially genteel, middle-class audience. As we study "My Politics"
in its original context in Cable's diary along with Cable's revisions
from the original manuscript to the typescript, we see how Cable
worked to construct and bolster his public persona as genteel
southern civil rights liberal, we see how Cable strove at times to diffuse points that might be abrasive, especially to fellow southerners,
and we discover fresh and valuable sidelights on his character. That Cable himself evidently half desired and expected
that portions of his diary would be made public is suggested
in the concluding part of his entry for December 18, 1888: "I
wish I could—I wish it were best—as I know full well it is
not—that I should be known through & through by all my
kind" (Diary I, 52).

Ideals of human equality, "equal justice and equal liberty
to all," as he wrote at the end of "My Politics," were things

that Cable strove for. What came naturally and spontaneously to him, as we see in his journal entries that form the immediate context of the original manuscript of "My Politics," was a very keenly felt sense of class and race differences among his fellow citizens. He frequently focused on such differences in his descriptions of fellow travelers, which he wrote in his diary during the trips to fulfill speaking engagements that occupied so much of his time in the late 1880s. On a train bound for Fall River, Massachusetts, on January 8, 1889, Cable saw

> . . . a pretty, large-eyed, bold factory-girl in well fitted and graceful draperies, her dark brown hair knotted *en grecque*; lacking naught but mental & moral refinement. But what a lack. (Diary II, 1)

Within the confidential space of his diary, where he may write with "perfect freedom," Cable records how he associates lack of "mental & moral" qualities with the young woman's working-class status. The entry continues with Cable's description of another passenger who exhibited, in his view, a marked class difference from the "factory-girl":

> How different [was the "factory-girl"] from yonder maiden in the red jacket, whom I heard speak at my back before I saw her, & knew, beyond peradventure, by the voice, that a lady was nigh. (Diary II, 1)

These two entries, while revealing the spontaneous valuation Cable placed on class differences he perceived, are clearly "notebook" raw material for possible transmutation into fiction. A tendency toward spontaneous response to perceived American racial differences is more pronounced in the diary than are demarcation and evaluation of perceived class differences. Thus, in his entry for December 20, 1888, Cable permits himself stereotyped representation of dialect in his recollection of

A very interesting and scholarly-looking colored man, [who] called & by & by wanted my name added to the mayor's . . . recommending him for appointment under govt. Naw, sah! I don't do that kind of business. . . . (Diary I, 57)

Although these passages might be jarring to readers who think of Cable in relation to the liberal, humanitarian public image he so carefully cultivated, the very sharp demarcations of class and race inscribed in the diary entries are of course not remarkable for their time and place, or for that matter, any American time and place. What *is* remarkable is the diary record of how Cable used his self-knowledge of his own spontaneous attitudes and instincts regarding perceived American class and race differences. His self-knowledge yielded such a rigorously insightful entry as that for December 20, 1888:

A thought for tomorrow's speech: Humanity—even Christianity—has never yet produced a *class* of people so noble so wise & so good, that it will not oppress, if it has the power, any distinct class below it toward which it does not cherish a spirit of fraternity, or of which it becomes in any way afraid. (Diary I, 58, B)

For such a conscientious, adamant Presbyterian as Cable to acknowledge that "even Christianity" is to no avail against class and race oppression, that only through the political action he would outline in "My Politics" could groups perceived as different be safe, is highly significant. Such hard-won insights provide the basis for the "My Politics" memoir, the first draft of which begins four pages following the above-quoted entry. In the diary we see clearly that Cable's critical evaluation and proposed remedies for southern civil rights problems were based squarely on self-knowledge, self-knowledge that his regular diary writing in the late 1880s both facilitated and became a repository for. Virtually nowhere in the journal entries do we find significant negative criticism of fellow southerners. On the contrary, despite his detractors' suspicions, what we do find is Cable's direct, unedited, spontaneous expression of feelings of love and concern for his home region.

Just before the beginning of the diary draft of "My Politics," Cable wrote an entry that gives us a tantalizing glimpse of his first meeting with the eminent black fictionist Charles W. Chesnutt. This passage conveys well the tone of Cable's public life and character in the period of composing "My Politics," particularly of his role as increasingly prominent author traveling to fulfill his many speaking engagements.

> As I turned to go to my room [at a hotel in Cleveland] a man said, "Is this"—& I said it was. He said his name was Chestnut. Wanted to go to my room and ask me a question. I thought him an unskilful interviewing reporter and met his proposition coldly. Asked him to state his question. He began, that he had contributed some stories to the Atlantic Monthly—I said, "Come upstairs". Up there he began thanking me for my political papers and surprised me with the statement that he was a "colored man." We talked an hour. He is very bright. Is a court stenographer here. I think he will be very valuable in our Open Letter Club work. (Diary I, 59–60)

The "political papers" that Chesnutt thanked Cable for are the papers whose genesis Cable describes in the "My Politics" memoir, the first draft of which Cable would initiate on the second diary page following the Chesnutt recollection. The Open Letter Club, organized by Cable, was a group of prominent, mostly southern, Americans who wrote articles on political and social issues of the South and then critiqued each other's articles prior to hoped-for publication or presentation. This club epitomized Cable's deep desire to combine some kind of political activity with his belletristic and nonfiction writing career. That Cable invited Chesnutt to join the Open Letter group clearly indicates that he regarded Chesnutt as a kindred spirit, a fellow southern writer who positively acknowledged and defended the New Orleans author's civil rights advocacy and other political expression. And it was evidently Cable's pleasurable recollection of Chesnutt's acknowledgment of his political papers that provided the immediate catalyst to prompt the next significant diary entry: "I ought to be writing 'My Politics,' for Scribner's new edition of my essays. Let's see:" (Diary I, 62).

There follows on pages sixty-two to sixty-seven of the diary the first segment of Cable's manuscript of the "My Politics" memoir, from the beginning to Cable's recollections of the immediate post–Civil War era. In this first segment of "My Politics" Cable recounts his early interest in books and what he regarded as a related orientation toward questions of abstract principle rather than toward concrete events. He recalls his attempt, under his mother's prodding, to memorize the Declaration of Independence and acknowledges that at sixteen he was "reeking with a patriotism of the strongest pro-slavery type" (*The Negro Question* 2). Yet, paradoxically, he notes, "Even then I remember I was puzzled to know how men could declare such ideal truths and yet hold other men in slavery" (*The Negro Question* 2). Cable completed this first segment of his draft of "My Politics" with a brief account of his Civil War service in the Confederate Cavalry and his eventual return home to New Orleans as a young "paroled prisoner [of war], without one spark of loyalty to the United States Government" (*The Negro Question* 4).

From the beginning, the manuscript record of Cable's revision of the diary allows us to follow the process of his changing "My Politics" from a more personal memoir to an essentially public document. For example, lined out and followed by an exclamatory "Bah!" (also deleted) is the second manuscript sentence, recollecting his adolescence: "My father had been dead nearly two years and my mother was a needy widow" (Diary I, 62). Cable's "Bah!" following this deleted sentence may underscore a determination from the very beginning of the revision process to rule out personal material not bearing directly on the political theme, to give the memoir as rigorously a public character as possible.

A point that Cable reiterates throughout "My Politics" is that his political writings were intended first and foremost for his fellow southerners. And, indeed, early in the process of revision from manuscript to typescript we see Cable shaping his text to ameliorate possible abrasiveness to a southern ear. Thus, recalling his adolescent attempt to memorize the Declaration of Independence, he notes in the diary draft his satisfaction that it was only the Declaration of Independence that was presented to him:

> I am glad my unsophistication was left unconfronted with the national Constitution, since it would surely, at that time, have been mistaught me. (Diary I, 63)

The passage is completely rewritten in the typescript:

> ... when I was winning my flag [the prize Cable's mother offered him for memorizing the Declaration of Independence], ... [I] had no one to tell me why there was such a sad step backward and downward between the Declaration and the Constitution. (*The Negro Question* 3)

This revision epitomizes Cable's reworking of the diary version to the public typescript version, a version that might almost be called a "position paper" crafted to reduce possible harshness to southern readers. The manuscript passage focuses unmediated negative criticism on a particular place in time. In New Orleans in 1860 the young Cable could only have been "mistaught" the Constitution. In the typed revision, Cable transmutes the passage into a sophisticated, thought-provoking observation on an intertextual relationship between the "Declaration and the Constitution." His criticism shifts from a subjective, negative judgment on an American section to an objectively verifiable statement about a relationship between two well-known public documents. Any reader can confirm the perspicacity of Cable's strictures on what he perceived as a regression from idealistic attitudes and goals from the Declaration of Independence to the Constitution. The revised version, although it shifts the level of discourse of the passage from the personal and local to the public and national, remains indirectly autobiographical in that it reveals Cable's long-standing preoccupation with legal and historical documents.

As we move through the diary manuscript of "My Politics" and compare it to the typed version that was eventually published by Arlin Turner, we continue to see Cable's attempt to ameliorate the sting of his provocative, polemical style, evidently with his Southern audience especially in mind. Thus, in the diary manuscript he recalls an adolescent self who

> . . . was for Union, slavery, and a white man's government. In other words I had not begun to think for myself. . . . (Diary I, 64)

The passage was changed in the typescript to:

> . . . I was for Union, Slavery and a White Man's Government! Secession, when it came, seemed a dreadful thing and I wondered at men and women, even if it was a necessity, rejoicing in it. I had not really begun to think for myself. (*The Negro Question* 3)

By inserting in the typed revision the sentence beginning "Secession, when it came," Cable diffused the sharp bite of the manuscript text and essentially clouded the issue that is so clear in the earlier text; that is, the statement ". . . I had not really begun to think for myself . . ." in the typescript follows directly from an expression of doubt about secession, rather than from "I was for . . . a white man's government." The issue, of course, was sensitive at the time he was writing "My Politics" because "a white man's government" was exactly what was being set up in the South in the 1880s, following the demise of Reconstruction.

Somewhat blurred in Cable's revision is a theme in which "what I was taught" is handled critically and compared to the growth of his ability to think independently. This theme emerges early in the manuscript, as in the passage quoted above in which he states that the Constitution would have been "mistaught" him in the New Orleans of his youth. Not only was this passage altered in the revision, but so was the subsequent recollection of being

> . . . taught that . . . [Jefferson Davis and the Confederate flag] stood for the right "to dissolve the political bands which connected us with another and to assume among the powers of the earth a separate and equal station, to which the laws of nature & nature's God entitled us!" (Diary I, 64)

Cable's memory here of how the Declaration of Independence was quoted to justify secession recalls his diary entry in which he stated that it was well that his "unsophistication was left unconfronted with the national Constitution . . ." (Diary I, 63). In line with this tendency to blur and diffuse some of the sharper statements about the southern milieu of his youth, the clause leading into the quotation from the Declaration of Independence is changed from the manuscript, "I was taught that . . . [Davis and the Confederate flag] stood for the right 'to dissolve . . .'" to the typescript, "They [Davis and the flag] seemed to me to stand for the right 'to dissolve . . .'" (*The Negro Question* 3). This revision, too, reminds us of Cable's notable striving to take personal responsibility for the events and course of his life. It might be noted that the education theme of "My Politics," though to some extent blurred in the process of revision, invites us to consider the memoir in the context of late nineteenth-century and early twentieth-century autobiographies, such as *The Education of Henry Adams* (1907) and Henry James's *A Small Boy and Others* (1913), which highlight and critique the education of the autobiographical narrator.

For many readers today, the most significant contextual

journal material between the first and second segments of "My Politics" in the diary is the account of Cable's first meeting with the important black historian George Washington Williams. With the exception of Philip Butcher (*George W. Cable: The Northampton Years* 96), virtually all other scholars have overlooked this meeting. Yet Cable's estimation of the importance of the contact is suggested by his comparatively lengthy, carefully turned journal entry on Williams. At the time of their meeting in January 1889, Williams was the respected author of the *History of the Negro Race in America* (1883) and *A History of the Negro Troops in the War of the Rebellion, 1861–1865* (1888). Considering how Cable's interests, professional activity, and political and social values so markedly overlapped with those of Williams, Cable's satisfaction in being able to recruit the historian into the Open Letter Club is not surprising.

> Last night I read in Worcester [Massachusetts]. G. W. Williams met me at the station and took me to his pretty rooms at "Hotel Adams" to chat 3/4 of an hour. . . . Williams is a mulatto, a christian, a man of affairs, polished, graceful, laborious, in life, author by profession, & actually making his way in white society. He is writing now the History of Reconstruction. He is a strong addition to the Open Letter Club.
>
> After the reading . . . we went to an elegant club house, Col. Williams still one of the party. . . . I am delighted with Williams, in whom I see at last a man whose *only* Africanism is his tawny skin. (Diary II, 3–4)

As with the entry on Chesnutt, the note on Williams reveals Cable, too, his habits of life and work on his travels, his preoccupations and implicit values during the very time he was in the midst of composing his political autobiography. And even more than with the Chesnutt entry, Cable's identification with Williams is striking in its transparency. To see it we need only substitute three words, "Cable" for "Williams," "southerner" for "mulatto," and "northern" for "white" to obtain in the following clause an ideal self-description by the diarist: "Williams [Cable] is a mulatto [southerner], a christian, a scholar, a man of affairs, polished, graceful, laborious, in life, author by profession, & actually making his way in white [northern] society." Cable sees in Williams the qualities he most nurtured and was most proud of in himself, including that of being a person of a cultural group perceived as marginal, southern/mulatto, who was "making his way" in mainstream, northern/white, society. The passage also epitomizes Cable's interethnic attitudes and values. He explicitly acknowledges to himself his faith in European-American cultural superiority: "I am delighted with Williams, in whom I see at last a man whose *only* Africanism is his tawny skin." At the same time, Cable could positively identify with Williams and recognize him as "a strong addition to the Open Letter Club," the distinguished group Cable established in part to work toward amelioration of American social ills, including racism. It might be noted that, considering the very positive identification Cable expressed toward Williams in this entry, at this stage, in the final year of the 1880s, Cable was almost on the verge of discarding his threadbare, nineteenth-century attitudes of European superiority.

Following the account of the meeting with Williams, Cable's record of a visit in Boston with Annie T. Fields, widow of the publisher James T. Fields, and her companion Sarah Orne Jewett, prior to a public reading at Harvard, provides the contextual journal material directly leading into the second segment of the diary manuscript of "My Politics." In this segment, which treats the period just after the Civil War, Cable describes how, through independent reading and study, he came to develop a critical attitude toward intellectual and religious justifications of slavery. His account of his emergent critique of southern religious defenses of the "right" of slaveholding indicates the future author's maturing intellectual style, especially regarding the interpretation of texts:

> Not that the letter to Philemon was all the scripture I had heard used to justify slave keeping, but that now I could have no further confidence in like arguments from other parts of scripture. They all yielded to scrutiny,

and betrayed a literalism combined, strangely enough, with a violence of inference that made them worthless. (*The Negro Question* 6)

Here Cable records an early milestone in the development of his characteristic habit of blending religious and political issues with an eye to their practical consequences for right action. The critical attitude toward willfully naive "literalism," which Cable recalls he achieved in his young manhood, foreshadows the author's later literary values. Thus, elsewhere in "My Politics," while acknowledging that his masterwork *The Grandissimes* (1880) was of course a historical novel in the most basic, literal sense, he indicates it was not to be taken too literally as simply a historical novel. It was, he makes clear, about Louisiana in the period in which it was written, the early post-Reconstruction era, as much as it was about the historical period, early nineteenth-century Louisiana, in which the plot was set. "It was impossible that a novel written by me then should escape being a study of the fierce struggle going on around me, regarded in the light of . . . past history . . ." (*The Negro Question* 14). The young man who would not be taken in by naively literal interpretation of scripture purporting to justify slavery became the author who "meant to make *The Grandissimes* as truly a political work [for its contemporary post-Reconstruction time of composition] as it has been called" (*The Negro Question* 14).

Cable's presentation of his struggle to grow beyond what he was (mis)taught in order to develop an independent stance vis-à-vis his culture reaches a climax of sorts when he shifts his focus to direct criticism toward the post-Reconstruction South of his young manhood and the relationship of that period to the earlier time of slavery. He describes how, through independent study and reflection, he came to realize that the political party he loved had been wrong about Reconstruction:

. . . the so-called Democratic party of the South was really bent upon preserving the old order—the old rule by race and class and was hopelessly at variance with the national scheme; and that . . . [the] "radical" platform [of Reconstruction]—rightly enough called radical since it

alone went to the root of the difficulty—was not for black rule and white
subjugation, but against the rule of any race over any other, simply and
arbitrarily race by race, or even class by class. (*The Negro Question* 9)

This hard-won insight is especially impressive when we consider
that it ran directly counter to the strong, conventional trends of
his culture, trends that Cable certainly recognized in himself.
With conscious, explicit knowledge of his *own* spontaneous instincts about class and race, his *own* quick willingness, as we
have seen, to stereotype the "factory-girl" and the "African," in
his political autobiography Cable shows us his painful struggle
to achieve distrust of rule of "race by race, or even class by class."

All of the material from the second segment of the diary text
of "My Politics" discussed so far was retained in the typescript
without substantial revision. Yet, in the midst of Cable's account
of how he read, studied, and worked hard to free himself of conventional views regarding slavery and Reconstruction, the autobiographer added material to his typed revision that appears to
represent an attempt to balance his critique of his society and to
show himself a true southerner, a southerner who could offer
himself as an example of one who could change and still remain
loyal. (Material upper-cased in the following quotation was added to
or significantly changed by Cable from the original manuscript text.)

Did I become a Republican? Nay, I had not yet so much as taken the
"oath of allegiance" [as an ex–Confederate soldier to the United States
government]. I could not! BEFORE I HAD QUITE DIGESTED THE
THIRTEENTH AMENDMENT, here came the Fourteenth! IF BOTH
HAD COME AT ONCE I COULD HAVE MASTERED BOTH WITH
THE ONE SAME CONTORTION OF THROAT AND STOMACH. BUT
ANDREW JOHNSON—IN MY PRESENT VIEW ONE OF THE WORST
ENEMIES THE SOUTH EVER HAD—HAD SPOILED ME, and I was
having privately a great deal of mental distress.(Diary II, 13–14; *The Negro
Question* 7)

In the section written in the second manuscript segment,
as well as elsewhere in "My Politics," Cable insists that he

never "felt the temptation to pitch my public utterances to suit the public ear" (Diary II, 16). Yet the typescript additions made to the passage quoted above, and revisions described above, suggest that if he did not "pitch" his "utterances to suit the public ear" he certainly did fine-tune them. That the "public ear" may have been more specifically a "southern ear" is suggested when we take a close look at one of the last significant revisions in the second manuscript segment. To demonstrate his arduously achieved independence of thought, Cable describes in his original handwritten text how he came to see

> . . . that the day must come when the black race must share and enjoy in common with the white the whole scale of *public* rights and advantages provided under American government. (Diary II, 17)

In the typed revision of this passage, a third "must" clause has been added to the two we see above in the manuscript:

> I saw that while private society always *must* [emphasis added] and can take care of itself and its own complete defense, the day must come when the Negro must share and enjoy in common with the white race the whole scale of *public* rights and advantages. . . . (*The Negro Question* 9)

In contrast to the original, the text pitched for "public utterance" prefaces the insight that blacks must enjoy equal rights with the proviso that "private society always must and can take care of itself and its own complete defense." The stern tone of the limiting proviso is generally foreign to the original text, although it is subtly prefigured for the typed revision of this passage by Cable's underlining of the word "public" in the original.

In the final section, Cable gives a brief account of the genesis of his various "political papers." These papers, including "Literature in the Southern States," "The Freedman's Case in

Equity," "The Silent South," "The Negro Question," and "What Shall the Negro Do?"—along with other works of fiction and nonfiction—represent the fruit of the long years of struggle he went through to establish his independence vis-à-vis his home culture. As Cable relates in contextual diary entries and in the main text of "My Politics," these papers originated in invited public oral presentations, such as commencement exercises at southern universities. The typed revision for this final part of "My Politics" follows the manuscript text rather closely, without substantial revisions. While a number of these political essays were collected in *The Silent South* ("My Politics" was originally meant to serve as the lead essay of the 1889 expanded edition), they are most readily accessible today in Arlin Turner's edition of *The Negro Question* (1958). In Turner's edition Cable's political papers are prefaced, in a way that seems fitting with Cable's original intention, by the revised version of "My Politics."

Thus, readers today may read "My Politics" alongside the essays whose immediate inception and deep sources in Cable's life the political autobiography describes. When we read "My Politics" in the context of Cable's other political essays, we might feel that these are all brave and forthright pieces. Even the revised, "public" text of "My Politics" is direct, honest, and provocative. Why should "My Politics" have been suppressed, especially the revised version, and not the other pieces, most of which were printed and even reprinted in Cable's lifetime? The directly autobiographical character of "My Politics" was evidently the reason Cable readily accepted the advice of his editors to suppress the piece. For Cable, religion, politics, fiction, and nonfiction (except for direct personal history) provided opportunities for personal expression. He may have been especially willing to forgo the publication of personal history in the late 1880s, when, as Arlin Turner has shown, Cable was suffering greatly from personal attacks by proponents of southern political orthodoxy (*George W. Cable: A Biography* 268–69). It is easy to see how "My Politics," with its focus on Cable's political development in relation to his personal history, would have provided post-Reconstruction defenders of the older southern culture plenty of ammunition to use against one they considered to be a traitor.

Yet, I think that Cable's ready agreement not to publish his political autobiography derived from a personal reticence that went deeper than political considerations. We see that reticence early on, in the diary: "I wish it were best—as I know full well it is not—that I should be known through & through by all my kind. Not even this diary can or should ever give that knowledge. There are things a man cannot tell even himself" (Diary I, 52). And we see that reticence again at the very beginning of the original manuscript of "My Politics," where Cable hand-deleted the second sentence, conveying "non-political," intimate family information, and wrote "Bah!" after it. Yet along with his clear reticence concerning personal history, Cable conveyed a counter trend, a desire for complete personal disclosure: "I wish it were best . . . that I should be known through & through." Cable even wrote in his diary a fantasy of possible future publication of the whole diary (Diary I, 52). It is my wish that this study of George Washington Cable's brave political autobiography in relation to its original diary context and manuscript revisions would meet with the author's approval, at least from that side of him that desired such disclosure.

## Notes

1.  The diary discussed in this essay is labeled "Diary George W. Cable 1888–1889 1890–1891" and is filed with the George W. Cable Collection, Manuscripts Section, Howard-Tilton Memorial Library, Tulane University. The diary is written in black ink on both front and back sides of two sets of white, blue-lined, loose leaves. Pages of the chronologically earlier of the two manuscript sets, designated section "I" for this study, measure 135 x 215 mm, are paginated 51–69, and carry dates running sporadically from "Dec. 18" [1888] (on p. 52) through "Dec. 31, 1888" (p. 68). Pages of the later manu-

script set, designated section "II" for this study, measure 108 x 178 mm, are paginated 1–82 (with some irregularities of paging), and carry dates running sporadically from "Jan. 8, 1889" (on p. 1) through "Jan. 29, '89" (p. 51). Citations to this diary specify either the first section, "I," or the second section, "II," and Cable's page number. In quotations from Cable's diary, I have used italics to represent words underlined in the original manuscript.

2. Since most readers will have easier access to the text of the typescript revision of "My Politics" published in *The Negro Question* (1958) than to the typescript itself, all of my citations to the typed revision of "My Politics" are to Turner's edition of *The Negro Question*.

## Selected Bibliography

### Manuscript Sources

Cable, George W. "Diary 1888–1889 [,] 1890–1891." Manuscript. George W. Cable Collection. Manuscripts Section, Howard-Tilton Memorial Library, Tulane University, New Orleans.

——. "My Politics." Typescript. George W. Cable Collection. Manuscripts Section, Howard-Tilton Memorial Library, Tulane University, New Orleans.

### Published Sources

Adams, Henry. *The Education of Henry Adams.* 1907. Boston: Houghton, 1918.

Augustine, Saint. *Confessions.* Trans. R.S. Pine-Coffin. Baltimore: Penguin, 1961.

Butcher, Philip. *George W. Cable: The Northampton Years.* New York: Columbia UP, 1959.

Cable, George W. *The Grandissimes.* New York: Scribner's, 1880.

——. *Madame Delphine.* New York: Scribner's, 1881.

——. *The Negro Question: A Selection of Writings on Civil Rights in the South.* Ed. Arlin Turner. 1958. New York: Norton, 1968.

——. *Old Creole Days.* New York: Scribner's, 1879.

——. *The Silent South.* 1885. Expanded ed. New York: Scribner's, 1889.

Edwards, Jonathan. *Personal Narrative.* In *Jonathan Edwards: Basic Writings,* ed. Ola Elizabeth Winslow. New York: New American Library, 1966. 81–96.

Foner, Eric. *Reconstruction: America's Unfinished Revolution, 1863–1877.* New York: Harper, 1988.

Franklin, John Hope. *George Washington Williams: A Biography.* Chicago: U of Chicago P, 1985.

James, Henry. *A Small Boy and Others.* New York: Scribner's, 1913.

Turner, Arlin. *George W. Cable: A Biography.* 1956. Baton Rouge: Louisiana State UP, 1966.

Williams, George W. *History of the Negro Race in America from 1619 to 1880.* 1883. New York: Arno, 1968.

——. *A History of the Negro Troops in the War of the Rebellion, 1861–1865.* 1888. New York: Kraus, 1969.

# At Home in the Land of Columbus: Americanization in European-American Immigrant Autobiography

*Richard Tuerk*

Attempts to formulate hard and fast rules concerning the form or content of European-American immigrant autobiographies are doomed to failure.[1] Nonetheless, it is possible to make some generalizations. First, most of these autobiographies tend to be concerned in some way with the relationship between life in the European Old World and the North American New. Often, this concern manifests itself in conflict centering on tendencies toward assimilation. The two poles of this conflict can be represented by Mary Antin on the one hand and Ludwig Lewisohn on the other. Elsewhere, I show these opposite tendencies at work in three autobiographical works, *The Promised Land* (1912) by Antin and *Up Stream* (1922) and *Mid-Channel* (1929) by Lewisohn (Tuerk, "Assimilation"). Desiring to become wholly assimilated, Antin shows herself abandoning her Old World customs and even her Old World faith to achieve her goal. And she is sure she achieves it. On the other side of the conflict, Lewisohn, finding assimilation impossible, embraces the Judaism that he had earlier abandoned in his attempts to become assimilated.

Unlike Lewisohn, most European-American immigrant autobiographers do not reject assimilation. Instead, they narrate the process by which their assimilation occurs, and they indicate how they know that that assimilation is complete. In particular, four autobiographical volumes, Jacob A. Riis's *The Making of an American* (1901), Mary Antin's *The Promised Land* (1912), M. E. Ravage's *An American in the Making* (1917), and Louis Adamic's *Laughing in the Jungle* (1932), treat the process of Americanization, although in markedly different ways.

Riis was born in Denmark, Antin in Polish Russia, Ravage in Rumania, and Adamic in Slovenia. Antin and Ravage were both Jews, Riis, Antin, and Ravage all had basically middle-class origins while Adamic was basically of peasant ancestry.

Still, as I shall show, these four authors fall into two categories according to the structure of the assimilation process in their autobiographies. Riis and Adamic, on the one hand, view their lives as a continuous progression, and their autobiographies reflect that continuity. Antin and Ravage, on the other hand, view their lives as radically discontinuous, and their autobiographies reflect that discontinuity.

In his pioneering book on American autobiography, Thomas Cooley writes: "The task of the education form, as [Henry] Adams established it for his age [in *The Education of Henry Adams* (1907;1918)], was to discover continuity among the selves one had assumed over a lifetime"; the autobiographer tried to find "Identity in a 'pluralistic' universe." For Adams and his contemporaries, "an artful life necessarily yielded evidence of linear design—like a river or a stream" (21). In another highly influential study of American autobiography, Albert E. Stone also conceives of modern autobiography as establishing an essentially consistent personality in a complex environment: "The past is re-presented by a reminiscing writer who tries to show how certain events, relationships, ideas, and institutions have become functionally and imaginatively interrelated in his or her own life" (6). Even spiritual autobiography—"characterized" by "radical splits between past and present"—tries "to express this transcendent essence of identity and the timeless dimensions of human experience" (11–15).

Thus it is surprising to discover autobiographers, writing near Adams's time, who emphasize the discontinuity of their own lives. Linear patterns that describe the usual forms of autobiography do not work exactly with this kind of narrative. To represent the pattern of such works linearly involves at least two unjoined lines. Instead of viewing continuity between Old World and New World selves, as Riis and Adamic do, many immigrant autobiographers, like Antin and Ravage, see themselves as radically discontinuous in these two different phases of their lives. In fact, some tend to see themselves as two different people with only surface similarities.

Since large portions of Riis's other writings are devoted to

Americanizing immigrant groups, one might guess that in *The Making of an American* he espouses the doctrine of total assimilation as vigorously as Antin and thus emphasizes differences between Old World and New World selves. Elsewhere, I trace Riis's shifting public attitudes toward Jews in particular, showing his change from blatant anti-Semitism early in his career to writing on behalf of Eastern European Jews when he saw how easily they became what he considered good citizens (Tuerk, "Jacob Riis and the Jews"). In "The Jews of New York" (1896), for example, he praises Jews for the thoroughness with which they become Americanized: "There is no more patriotic people than these Jews, and with reason. They have no old allegiance to forget. They saw to that over yonder," meaning in Europe (59). And in *The Battle with the Slum* (1902) he writes: "If ever there was material for citizenship, this Jew is such material. Alone of all our immigrants he comes to us without a past"; having "no country to renounce, no ties to forget," the Jew has "a passionate longing for a home to call his own, that waits only for the spark of such another love to spring into flame which nothing can quench" (192–93). These passages imply that total assimilation, total Americanization, with no allegiance to a prior land of residence, is desirable.

In his book-length study of Riis, James B. Lane insists that in Riis's "call for the Americanization of the immigrant he did not wish to blot out cultural traditions and loyalties but only to teach values and tools that would enable people to become productive citizens" (156). Although Lane's words are not true in connection with a great deal of Riis's work, as indicated above, nonetheless in his autobiography Riis repeatedly depicts himself as having become one such citizen who retains his love for his homeland. In fact, Lane asserts that "Riis's Danish background remained important to him all his life" (78), a statement true at least in the way he portrays himself in *The Making of an American*, which is surprisingly a document of the continuity of the self.

In *The Making of an American*, Riis repeatedly reaffirms his allegiance to both the United States and the land of his birth. Born in Ribe, Denmark, in 1849, he came to America in 1870. In the first chapter of his autobiography he asserts: "Alas! I am afraid that thirty years in the land of my children's birth have left me as much of a Dane as ever" and adds: "Yet, would you have it otherwise? What sort of a husband is the man going to make who begins by pitching his old mother out of the door to make room for his wife? And what sort of a wife would she be to ask or to stand it?" (7–8). He even voices regret for having left Denmark, when, recounting a trip to Europe with his family, he writes about the fields near his old home in Ribe:

> My children saw them and longed back to the hills of Long Island; and in their cold looks I felt the tugging of the chain which he must bear through life who exiled himself from the land of his birth, however near to his heart that of his choice and adoption. (399)

In fact, he shows himself remaining a patriotic Dane even when he is a patriotic American. Writing of Denmark's wars with Germany and the changing boundaries between the two countries, he says: "Gray-haired and with old-time roots in a foreign soil, I dream with them [the Danes] yet of the day that shall see it [the post that marks the frontier] pulled up and hurled over the river where my fathers beat the southern tide a thousand years" (394). He glories in his love for Denmark, seeing no discrepancy between it and his love for his adopted land: "Half heathen yet, am I? Yes, if to yearn for the soil whence you sprang is to be a heathen, heathen am I, not half, but whole, and will be all my days." However, he then declares: "He is the heathen who loves not his native land" (413), words that nicely contradict his statements concerning the Eastern European Jews' lack of allegiance to their native lands. In his last chapter he comments on a golden cross King Christian of Denmark awarded him: "I wear the cross proudly for the love I bear the flag under which I was born and the good old King who gave it to me" (426), and he recounts that he told the king that the Danes in America "were good citizens, better for not forgetting their motherland and him [the king]" (429). Thus, although demanding complete assimilation for others, in his autobiography he declares it proper that he and his fellow Danish Americans remain loyal to Denmark and her traditions.

How can one explain such a discrepancy? Perhaps he felt that the same traits that make one a good citizen of some European countries, like Denmark, also make one a good American, whereas traits brought by people like the Jews, who were deprived of citizenship in Eastern Europe, would prevent them from becoming good citizens. At any rate, in *The Making of an American* he pictures himself as acquiring in Denmark the traits that he felt made him a good American.

Riis left Denmark because his beloved Elizabeth refused his proposal. In his autobiography he never shows himself thinking of streets paved with gold or a landscape overflowing with milk and honey. Nonetheless, when recounting his first glimpse of the New World, he describes the magnificence of what he saw in terms that align him with early English explorers of North America (Marx 36–40), although he viewed a cityscape while they saw an untrammeled wilderness. Awaking to find the steamer *Iowa* anchored just off Castle Garden on Whitsuntide, 1870, he recalls seeing "a beautiful spring morning," "miles of straight streets, the green heights of Brooklyn, and the stir of ferryboats and pleasure craft on the river"—a gardenlike vision. Hopeful that "somewhere in this teeming hive" he would find "a place," he writes:

> I had a pair of strong hands, and stubbornness enough to do for two; also a strong belief that in a free country, free from the dominion of custom, of caste, as well as of men, things would somehow come right in the end, and a man get shaken into the corner where he belonged if he took a hand in the game. (35–36)

Instead of seeing America as a Promised Land in contrast to a European Egypt from which he fled, he here describes it as a place where he could start anew, with more opportunity than he had in Europe. Although he does not begin his tale in poverty in Denmark, once he arrives in America, his is in part a tale of going from rags to modest riches as a result of hard work. As such, it is an immigrant version of the *Autobiography* of Benjamin Franklin.

For Riis, American reality at first consisted of exactly what he expected: hard work coupled with frequent setbacks. He could not fulfill his dream of making a quick fortune and returning swiftly to Denmark to propose to Elizabeth again. His early life in America as he describes it involved a series of jobs both in and out of New York City. Four days after arriving, he contracted to go to the Brady's Bend Iron Works on the Allegheny River, where he worked at first as a carpenter, an occupation for which he had been trained in Denmark. Then he tried coal mining. When he returned to the surface after his first day underground, he writes, "It seemed to me that I had been dead and had come back to life. The world was never so wondrous and fair." Never again would he enter a coal mine (42–46). This is, incidentally, the only place in *The Making of an American* where Riis uses the image of rebirth. In other immigrant autobiographies, as we shall see, Americanization is often treated as a kind of rebirth. But Riis views his Americanization as a steady progress rather than the radical shift that rebirth implies.

Shortly after he arrived at Brady's Bend, Riis learned that war had broken out between France and Prussia. Immediately, he left Brady's Bend and attempted to return to Europe so that he could fight for France, which was then allied with Denmark, an episode that causes Riis to comment: "I remembered the defeat, the humiliation of the flag I loved [against Prussia in 1864],—aye! and love yet, for there is no flag like the flag of my fathers, save only that of my children and of my manhood." Moreover, he also hoped that, returning from the war a hero, he might win Elizabeth's hand (47). But unable to get passage back to Europe, he ended up without money or possessions in New York City (51). Here, he again indicates that his love for Denmark does not compromise his position as an American.

Working as a farm laborer, factory hand, and traveling sales-man, Riis finally got a job in New York as a newspaperman, the kind of position he was to fill for most of his adult life. He returned to Denmark, married Elizabeth, settled with her in New York City and then Long Island, and eventually became one of the most influential figures during the Progressive Era as a pioneering photojournalist who used his pictures to help arouse people's desire to clean up the slums. His close friend-ship with Theodore Roosevelt, for whom he wrote the official presidential campaign biography, by itself would assure him a place in the history of American reform, as would the accom-plishment he was most proud of, namely, the replacing of the Mulberry Bend area of New York City with a park.

Envisioning his entire autobiography as "the story of the making of an American" (442), he tells of a process in which his Americanization takes place through natural, gradual ac-cretion. Thus, only at the end does he tell how he found that the American "was made and finished at last." Ill at a friend's house in Elsinore, Denmark, he looks out a window at the sea with ships going by in the sunshine. "But the sunshine and the peaceful day," he writes, "bore no message to me." Then, "a ship flying at the top the flag of freedom" sailed past:

> That moment I knew. Gone were illness, discouragement, and gloom! Forgotten weakness and suffering, the cautions of doctor and nurse. I sat up in bed and shouted, laughed and cried by turns, waving my handkerchief to the flag out there. They thought I had lost my head, but I told them no, thank God! I had found it, and my heart, too, at last. I knew then that it was my flag; that my children's home was mine, indeed; that I also had become an American in truth. And thanked God, and like unto the man sick of the palsy, arose from my bed and went home, healed. (442–43)

Thus, in recreating his life, this man who spent so much time Americanizing others claims that he did not himself realize that he had become an American until he had spent about thirty years living in the New World.

In actuality, when in 1885 Riis became a citizen of the United States, he probably felt he was thoroughly Americanized. Obviously, he heightens the effect of the episode at the end of his book to justify his title and to illustrate his idea that the change from Dane to American was gradual, natural, and relatively painless. Again we see parallels between Riis's book and Franklin's *Autobiography*. According to Cooley, "Franklin's narrator begins his personal narrative by selecting events from his early history that reveal the adult in embryo" (14–15). Riis too shows in his early chapters set in Denmark that he contained the seeds of what he later became. Even his chief motivation for going to America and succeeding there—his love for Elizabeth—is present throughout his narrative.

Born in 1899, in the village of Blato in Carniola, which he calls a Slovenian duchy of Austria,[2] Louis Adamic, like Riis, recreates his life as a continuous progression in which his New World self develops from his Old World self. Elsewhere in his writings, he says that he is a total assimilationist in the long run and is sure that eventually the immigrants' descendents will become indistinguishable from other Americans; nonetheless, he advocates acculturation over the short term, strongly defending the idea that, to become good Americans, the immigrants and their children must retain and take pride in the customs and qualities of their lands of origin. In *My America* (1938), for example, he outlines a plan for increasing ethnic consciousness in immigrants and their children, calling for "a recognition of the fact that America is not purely an Anglo-Saxon country, if only by virtue of numbers," and adding: "*A new conception of America is necessary*" (emphasis Adamic's, 218). Repeatedly in *My America* he affirms his feeling that he is simultaneously a Slovenian and an American: "Clearly, I was an American from Slovenia, or a Slovenian who came to America and became an American" (137).

Strangely enough, in *Laughing in the Jungle* he is not very concerned with his ethnic identity. Tracing his life in retrospect, he indicates that the seeds for his American identity were firmly planted in the Old World, and even though he focuses on what he feels is the dissonance between American promise and American reality, he shows himself in Slovenia at the age of fifteen as already having been concerned with social problems. In fact, he left Slovenia in part because of his involvement in a secret political club "affiliated with the general revolutionary Yugoslav Nationalist Movement" (25). As a result of his political activities he was expelled from school. When his father almost enrolled him in a Jesuit school, he decided to come to America. Sailing second class on the *Niagara* with his older friend, Peter Molek, he arrived in New York on 30 December 1913. On New Year's Eve he left Ellis Island to begin his life in America.

Toward the end of *Laughing in the Jungle*, Adamic clearly indicates that the seeds of his present self were present when he was a child in Slovenia. Even his detached, ironic vision, he here implies, was present from the start. He writes that he did not come to America "to become rich," "to escape from myself or something or other; nor, like most immigrants, to slave at whatever task I could find" (325). Instead, he "had come to experience America, to explore the great jungle, to adventure in understanding—and here I was"; "the adventure," he feels, was "exciting and worth while; and there was more to come" (325–26). And then, as though to emphasize the integrity and uniformity of his self, he writes: "I was twenty-nine years old and I had been in the United States half of my life, but so far, I thought, America had scarcely touched me. I liked to think that I had not let her touch me in any vital or devastating way" (327). Thus, his adult self and child self are basically continuous as are his Old and New World self.

As a child Adamic was exposed to widely differing ideas of America. When he was eight or nine, he thought of America as "the Golden Country—a sort of Paradise—the Land of Promise in more ways than one." In the New World "one could make pots of money in a short time," he felt, "acquire immense holdings, wear a white collar, and have polish on one's boots like a *gospod*—one of the gentry—and eat white bread, soup, and meat on weekdays as well as on Sundays, even if one were but an ordinary workman to begin with" (5). His mother told him of a cousin who eventually disappeared, a man who came back with venereal disease, people who returned minus arms or legs, and a woman whose husband had been killed in a mine, but he still desired to go to the New World (8–9).

He learned more about America when he met Molek, who returned to Blato "to die" after having left for America eight years earlier (13). Although Adamic was only ten at the time, he listened carefully to Molek's tales. Having read Upton Sinclair's *The Jungle*, Molek told Adamic: "there are no jungles in the United States, so far as I know. But the whole of America is a jungle" (17). Molek's words help provide the central metaphor of Adamic's book.

About his own experiences Molek said: "America swallowed me . . . but she did not digest me" (17). To Molek the idea that America was the Promised Land was a false notion used to lure immigrants to the New World, so America could use them: "Once upon a time immigrants were called 'dung' in America; that was a good name for them," he explained to Adamic: "They were the fertilizer feeding the roots of America's present and future greatness. They are still 'dung.' The roots of America's greatness still feed on them" (20).

When he arrived in America, Adamic says that he quickly learned the truth of what Molek had told him. He realized that "In the Old Country" peasants "lived in poor but clean thatch-roofed houses, with plenty of elbow room." In America they were "compelled by their poverty to live in crowded, ill-smelling tenements. I remembered what Peter Molek had said to me: they were 'dung' in America. There was no question about this in my mind" (72).

Quickly learning English, Adamic read *The Jungle* himself when he was sixteen. He recalls that "the book made a deep impression on me. So *this* was America! For a few days I felt a sharp hatred for the whole country" (79). Still, as soon as he got a fairly good job working for a Slovenian-American newspaper, his "bitterness about America" disappeared; "The incongruities and cacophonies of American life, as I perceived them, seemed to me as sharp as ever, but I now developed a tendency to be amused by them," and he adds: "My curiosity about the country increased" (98). Thus, he explicitly assumed the ironic pose reflected in the title of his book.

The rest of *Laughing in the Jungle* is largely devoted to the development of this ironic stance. Rarely does Adamic dwell on the problems that resulted from his being an immigrant. Instead, he indicates that his problems stemmed from his poverty. In fact, he writes that at the time of the book's composition "immigration is ended and immigrants are vanishing in the melting-pot" (102), implying that he foresees rapid total assimilation for America's immigrant population.

Out of work, Adamic joined the United States Army just before World War I, serving in France after brief duty in Panama. After the war he returned to the United States and, again out of work, he became convinced "of the inevitability of superior men's frustration under democracy in America" (186). He visited Washington, D.C., where he saw the Senate in session: "After sitting in the gallery for about an hour," he writes, "the scene struck me as so funny that, for fear I would burst out laughing, I left. And looking back now, I think that it was then and there that my youthful post-war seriousness took its first good tumble" (189). Going to sea for a while, he started reading, among others, Theodore Dreiser, H. L. Mencken, and Henry Adams. Finally, he went to Los Angeles, where he lived during the rest of the period covered in *Laughing in the Jungle*. He eventually made a success for himself in and around the city, doing newspaper work, working on the docks in San Pedro, and beginning his career as a serious writer. He continued his reading, especially Mencken, after whom he consciously modeled his ironic pose and who, in 1928, accepted his "first story for the *Mercury*" (265).[3]

From the time he tells of entering the army until the end of his autobiography, Adamic rarely mentions his immigrant background. Instead, he writes as though he were a native of America, like H. L. Mencken or Sinclair Lewis, looking satirically at the land. He even admits that he rarely wrote home and then "only brief notes that I was well and content. In a letter I could not begin to tell them about America" (265).

Nonetheless, he comments on the lives of some of the immigrants he meets. He tells in particular of a friend he met shortly after he arrived in America, Steve Radin, brother of one of his classmates in Europe who was slain in a demonstration for Yugoslavian independence. Radin felt that he belonged in America "from the start," Adamic writes:

> He had been the exceptional kind of immigrant, so constructed that it was all but inevitable for him to "make good" in America. He had been adventurous, strongly egoistical, recklessly selfish, realistic and pragmatic (a "wise guy"), but at the same time capable of deluding himself and swallowing the less transparent species of hokum; a go-getter, a schemer, an opportunist, a racketeer, with a will to power and a desire for grandeur and acclaim. His values were the values of democratic America; the values of the moment. (322)

Radin became fairly wealthy before dying in a boating accident. However, even had he achieved the fame and wealth he sought, Adamic feels, Radin "would have been a frustrated man" (323). In Radin, Adamic sees a symbol of

> the whole American success idea; the idea that urged, lured, and pushed millions, native and foreign-born, to great material achievements for the sake of those achievements, while . . . as individuals and as a class, these success-bent men and women . . . were headed, sooner or later, toward some such fate, metaphorically speaking, as had finished Steve Radin—a crash in the dark. (323–24)

Although Riis repeatedly questions certain aspects of the superstructure of American society, he never shows himself questioning its substructure. He shows himself as genuinely believing that significant reform can occur through existing American institutions. Adamic, on the other hand, repeatedly shows himself questioning that substructure, including American democracy itself. The crash of 1929, he feels, has made of the United States "more of an economic, political, and social jungle than it ever was before." It has rendered

> ten million workers, including millions of my own countrymen and other immigrants . . . jobless. Their number, as I write this [in 1931], is increasing, with the end nowhere in sight. Now they are not even "dung" any longer. The jungle is too fruitful and has no further use for them. The greatest jungle in the world is inundated with "dung," and no one in the jungle knows what to do about it. (333)

Consequently, he writes: "of late I find it hard to laugh at things and conditions in the jungle." Before he "roared" himself "purple in the face," but now "the jungle . . . is too monstrous, too full of horrors and parasitism, for one to laugh in it, and at it, with amusement." People "who occasionally still laugh do not laugh naturally or pleasantly, but hysterically," and Adamic wonders whether "we are in the midst of a revolution" and whether a "tide of dissatisfaction will seize the crazy overproductive and destructive forces now loose and uncontrolled in the jungle, and try to transform the jungle into a civilization." Perhaps America is "being hooked up to history, to the epic idea that is behind Russia's experiment" in trying "to conquer chaos with planning" (334–35).[4]

Nonetheless, he concludes his book with an assertion of his own essential sameness in the midst of change:

> Meantime, personally, I still have no real complaint against America, the jungle. I have come here for excitement and adventure. I have never been hungry for more than two days since I am here. The jungle has been and is vastly interesting. Too interesting. Sometimes it is over-

whelming in its complexity and melodrama. And as I say, lately I find it difficult to laugh. But I stay and intend to remain here. (335)

Thus, he stays essentially the same detached observer he initially describes himself as having been when he first arrived in the New World. Retaining a desire for constructive change that developed in the Old World, he nonetheless views American affairs from a distance, even in the depths of the Great Depression able to laugh at what he sees, although, he admits, he now laughs less frequently.

For both Riis and Adamic, life in the New World is basically a continuation of life in the Old. Viewing their lives as a continuous progression, their autobiographies tend to mirror the usual form of the modern autobiography as they discover in themselves a continuity that links Old World and New.

Neither Mary Antin nor M. E. Ravage, however, shows such continuity. For Antin a break in continuity occurs when she enters the New World. For her, Russia, where she spent her childhood, truly "was another Egypt" (7), and America is, as the title of her book suggests, the Promised Land. In fact, she entitles the chapter in which she tells of her entrance into America "The Promised Land" (180), thus reemphasizing her central metaphor. Unlike Adamic, she does not use the term ironically.

Antin was born in 1881 in Polotzk, which by then had been part of Russia for over a century. In 1894, when she was thirteen, she went to Boston. Immediately upon telling of her arrival, she emphasizes the discontinuity between life in Old World and New:

The most ignorant immigrant, on landing, proceeds to give and receive greetings, to eat, sleep, and rise, after the manner of his own country; wherein he is corrected, admonished, and laughed at, whether by interested friends or the most indifferent strangers; and his American experience is thus begun.

Faced with a way of life radically different from anything previously experienced, the newly arrived immigrant becomes an "engaging infant," and the person established in America becomes a "nursery maid" (180). In fact, Antin writes of her own arrival in America as "my second infancy" and of "immigrant officials, school-teachers, settlement workers, and sundry other unprejudiced and critical observers" as "maiden aunts" who helped raise the newborn child (181). Even her name was changed. In Polotzk her "Hebrew name" was "Maryashe in full, Mashke for short, Russianized into Marya," and her surname was used only "on state occasions"; in America she was Mary Antin, and she "felt very important to answer to such a dignified title" (188).

Antin's use of the rebirth metaphor implies a radical discontinuity of self. It is as though, in response to what she considers two radically different environments, she sees herself as two different people. In the Old World she was irrevocably labeled "Jew" and as such severely limited in what she could do and where she could live. "Well I knew," she writes, "that Polotzk was not my country. It was *galuth*—exile." And she adds that "not a child among us was too young to feel in his own flesh the lash of the oppressor" (226). Deprived of the rights of citizenship, she found that she and her fellow Jews "had no country, . . . no flag to love" (228). Her life was more limited than the "empty and endless and dull" life of a "treadmill horse" (96). Unable to attain a secular education because of her Jewishness and unable to attain a satisfactory religious education because she was female (111), she found in America a freedom which she earlier could not have imagined.

Frequently in *The Promised Land* she emphasizes the differences between Old World limitations and New World possibilities. She even writes of "the garden of America, where opportunity waits on ambition" and where she feels that she can make her "days a triumphal march toward" any "goal" she chooses. And she feels that she has reached that goal: "The most unfriendly witness of my life will not venture to deny that I have been successful. For aside from subordinate desires for greatness or wealth or specific achievement, my chief ambition in life has been *to live*, and I have lived," something she feels that she could not do in Polotzk: "A glowing life has been mine, and the fires that blazed highest in all my days were kindled on Dover Street" in the heart of Boston's worst slums (emphasis Antin's, 355). In America, she declares, "a child of the slums owns the land and all that is good in it. All the beautiful things I saw belonged to me, if I wanted to use them; all the beautiful things I desired approached me. I did not need to seek my kingdom" (357–58). In such circumstances how could she possibly not succeed?

Antin compares herself to King David, who "was a shepherd before he became a king. I was an ignorant child in the Ghetto, but I was admitted at last to the society of the best; I was given the freedom of all America" (114). The evolution here from shepherd to king is not compared to the change from Old World to New World inhabitant. Such a comparison would imply the kind of continuity of self that Antin denies. Instead, the evolution is compared to the change from dweller in an *American* slum to member of American society. Her Old World and New World selves are discontinuous, but, considered separately, each is continuous in a way that emphasizes the discontinuity of the two. When she declares, "Outside America I should hardly be believed if I told how simply, in my experience, Dover Street merged into the Back Bay" (361–62), she again emphasizes the continuity of her American existence and the discontinuity of her Old and New World experiences.

When describing the changes in her New World self, Antin thus speaks of natural progression; when describing the changes from Old World to New World self, she speaks of rebirth. Toward the end of *The Promised Land* she recalls that Bates Hall, the reading room of the Boston Public Library, is

> where I liked to remind myself of Polotzk, the better to bring out the wonder of my life. That I who was born in the prison of the Pale should roam at will in the land of freedom was a marvel that it did me good to realize. That I who was brought up to my teens almost without a book

should be set down in the midst of all the books that ever were written was a miracle as great as any on record. That an outcast should become a privileged citizen, that a beggar should dwell in a palace—this was a romance more thrilling than poet ever sung. Surely I was rocked in an enchanted cradle. (342–43)

The implications of her language here could not be clearer: "wonder," "marvel," "miracle, "romance," "enchanted"; each of these terms emphasizes the radical discontinuity of her life. Offered new possibilities by America, she describes herself as having responded by becoming a new person. Thus, unlike Riis's and Adamic's, Antin's autobiography is a tale of two separate, distinct selves, joined merely by having the same parents and similar names.

Antin describes the rebirth in which she ceased being a creature of the Old World and became a citizen of the New as relatively quick and painless. M. E. Ravage, on the other hand, sees his rebirth as drawn out and painful. Born in Vaslui, Rumania, sometime around 1884, he came to America when he was sixteen. According to Ravage the immigrant is willing to submit to a lot—steerage, seasickness, homesickness, "even to Ellis Island inspectors." But none would consider submitting to these hardships "for a moment . . . if he suspected that he must, before he is through, become an American into the bargain. Mortal man is ready for everything except spiritual experiences." And he explains:

Vowing allegiance to the state is one thing. But renouncing your priceless inherited identity and blending your individual soul with the soul of an alien people is quite another affair. And it is this staggering experience of the spirit—this slipping of his ancient ground from under the immigrant's feet, this commingling of souls toward a new birth, that I have in mind when I speak of becoming an American. (199–200)

This process of rebirth is so painful, he explains, that those who begin to undergo it find themselves "cursing Columbus" (84).

For Ravage, Americanization was twofold. First, he became acclimated to life in the slums of New York's Lower East Side. This part of the process he found terribly painful. But just as painful was the second half of the process, when he became acclimated to life at the University of Missouri.

Like Antin, Ravage says that, before he left home, he saw America as the Promised Land and New York as "that magic city of promise" (46). In fact, he too refers to escape from bondage in Egypt, entitling the chapter in which he describes the general movement from Rumania to the United States "The Exodus" (27).

Ravage learned about America primarily from a distant relative named Couza, who, returning from New York to Vaslui, told about his own importance in the New World. Ravage was not too surprised that in America one could get rich. What amazed him was "that our humble, downtrodden people could not only vote, but be voted for and hold office in New York" (17), something impossible for Jews in Rumania. Couza spoke eloquently of the differences between life in Rumania and "the freedom and the wealth and the beauty of that City of God which was New York. There were," Couza said, "many ways of getting rich in America. . . . People got paid, it seemed, even for voting" (18). Ravage realized that, even if Couza was a "sham, America surely was no sham." Ravage was certain: "There was a country somewhere beyond the seas where a man was a man in spite of his religion and his origin" (24).

Three months after Couza left Vaslui, "America-fever had spread to the confines of the kingdom" (27). All who could left for America. Many wrote relatives in America asking for tickets for at least one family member. When answers returned that times were as hard in America as in Rumania and that the people would do well to remain in Vaslui, Ravage says that the townspeople thought the people in America "feared our competition; America was so good that they wanted her all to themselves" (32–33). The residents of Vaslui thus remained steadfast in their desire to go to America, for they knew that "Everybody who went there became a millionaire overnight, and a doctor or a teacher into the bargain. There, in America," Ravage decided, was his "future as well as" that of the rest of his family, "For it would take," he thought, "only a few weeks to make enough money to send for" them (50).

Since the older residents of Vaslui could find no way to send their children to the New World, the children "took matters into their own hands, and one fine morning Rumania awoke to hear the startling news that the Walking Movement had begun" (33). Although many of the young Rumanians who set out to walk to America never arrived there (Howe 33), Ravage and his fellow Vaslui youths who tried to go "To America on Foot" (34), as Ravage entitles his fourth chapter, did arrive, although Ravage himself traveled entirely by train and boat.

What he found matched his expectations in so few ways that he declares: "I myself was very bitterly disappointed. And, unless observation has been altogether astray with me, I think I am justified in the generalization that nearly all other new-comers are at least as disappointed as I was." He insists that the "entire Old World soul" of the immigrant "comes in conflict with America as soon as he has landed." For the American reality he finds is the Lower East Side: "It was not America in the large sense, but the East Side Ghetto that upset all my calculations, reversed all my values, and set my head swimming." Ravage was not especially impressed by his first view of New York City; it was like other large cities. And even Ellis Island was like the Hungarian border. But he writes: "I have not forgotten and I never can forget that first pungent breath of the slums which were to become my home for the next five years" (60–62). Recalling his first day in the New World, Ravage writes: "I shall never forget how depressed my heart became as I trudged through those littered streets, with the rows of pushcarts lining the sidewalks and centers of the thoroughfares, the ill-smelling merchandise, and the deafening noise" (66–67). As for so many of his fellow immigrants, his first home in "the land of

Columbus" (94) is in the midst of squalor. Still, he writes, "Somehow, even in those dark days of greenhornhood, an occasional ray would penetrate through the gloom and reveal another America than that of the slums" (87), and it is this America that he feels he eventually reached.

Like many of his fellow immigrants, Ravage worked at a succession of jobs. After a week of job hunting, he began peddling. He thought that that week "had exhausted all America's possibilities of hardship and disheartening failure. But that was because I was a greenhorn, unversed in the ways of Columbus's land." Only when he experienced one and a half months of unemployment was he "to get my American baptism—that cleansing of the spirit by suffering which every one of us immigrants must pass through to prove himself worthy of his adoption" by America: "Purification—that was what, with telling aptness, the East Side called the period of struggle, starvation, and disappointment in America, which was the lot of the green" (112).

After a while he found work as a barroom assistant and then as a sweatshop employee. His father, however, had dreamed of Ravage's becoming a doctor, and Ravage realized that to fulfill this dream he could not simply work for someone else. But he also realized that in America, unlike in Rumania, he could fulfill the dream: "The earth was young and fresh from the hand of the Maker, and as yet undivided among His children. That was another distinctive superiority of America over Rumania" (131).

So he began going to school, hoping to win a Regents' Scholarship so that he could attend college. Failing to win the scholarship, he sought a school that he could attend at his own expense. Finally, he decided to go to the University of Missouri, the first of several universities he attended on his way to becoming a political writer and biographer.

In Missouri he feels his real Americanization began. At first he was completely lost, at home neither in New York nor Missouri: "I was, indeed, a man without a country" (264). He felt that he was among "a body of people who were in nearly every way the opposite of" him (209). After a long period of alienation he made some friends, picked up what he considered some American habits, including bathing regularly and brushing his teeth, and began to feel at home. Not, however, until he went back to New York after his freshman year to earn money for the coming year did he realize how much at home he had begun to feel. Then, he decided that Missouri was in many ways better than the ghetto. He told a friend in New York that Missouri is "a bigger and a freer world than this" and that

> Those big, genuine people out in Missouri are the salt of the earth. Whatever they may think about the problem of universal brotherhood, they have solved it for their next-door neighbors. There is no need of the social revolution in Missouri; they have a generous slice of the kingdom of heaven.

While in New York that summer he wrote to his Missouri roommate "that I was aching to get back to Columbia (how apt the name was!) to take up again where I had left off the process of my transformation [into an American], and to get through with it as soon as might be" (265–66).

When he returned to Columbia that fall, he found himself no longer a stranger and outcast. People greeted him so warmly that

> It took me off my feet, this sudden geniality of my fellows toward me. I had not been aware how, throughout the previous year, the barriers between us had been gradually and steadily breaking down. It came upon me all at once. I felt my heart going out to my new friends. I had become one of them. I was not a man without a country. I was an American. (266)

Thus Ravage's book ends. For him Americanization involved a complete remaking, even of his soul. As he declares near the end of the book, "No, there was not much fun in being made

into an American. I was painfully aware of that fact myself"
(230). Describing the process, he writes:

> To be born in one world and grow to manhood there, to be thrust then
> into the midst of another with all one's racial heritage, with one's likes
> and dislikes, aspirations and prejudices, and to be abandoned to the task
> of adjusting within one's own being the clash of opposed systems of
> culture, tradition, and social convention—if that is not heroic tragedy, I
> should like to be told what is. (200)

Ravage here expresses what he feels is the discontinuity of
Old World and New World life and of those who find themselves living both of those lives. His New World self, after his
experiences in Missouri, is changed in all ways not only from
his Rumanian self but also from his New York ghetto self. His
initial "baptism" into the ways of America on the Lower East
Side proved not an end to his Americanization but merely the
beginning. And by the time he was finished, he found himself
resembling people who shortly before he had declared his ex-
act opposites. Thus, like Antin, Ravage sees his life as being
basically discontinuous, but he writes in terms of three distinct selves: a Rumanian one, a semi-Americanized New York
one, and an Americanized Missouri one.

Although the autobiographies of Jacob Riis, Louis Adamic,
Mary Antin, and M. E. Ravage are all markedly different, they
fall into two very distinct groups according to the form in
which the authors conceive of their lives. Riis and Adamic see
themselves as basically unchanged by their American experiences. Each sees his Old World self as an embryonic version
of his New World self, and each describes his progression as
an evolution proceeding along orderly lines. On the other hand,
both Antin and Ravage see almost nothing in their Old World
selves that indicates what their New World selves will be.

Why these two visions should be so different is not entirely
clear. Perhaps Antin's and Ravage's Eastern European Jewish

background has something to do with it.[5] Both Adamic and Riis had much stronger secular educations, along with greater secular possibilities, in Europe than Antin and Ravage had. Even though Adamic's people were subject to Austria, they were not entirely deprived of citizenship the way Antin and Ravage were. And Adamic did feel loyalty to a secular state, even though it was, when he lived in Europe, submerged in another state. Thus Antin and Ravage had more reason to detest Europe than did Riis and Adamic, perhaps making the idea of radical change more acceptable.

Regardless of the causes, however, these two sets of immigrant autobiographies indicate that there are at least two principal forms the immigrant experience can take in its literary retelling. That a variety of subspecies exists within these two forms is clearly suggested by the marked differences between the tales told by Riis and Adamic, on the one hand, and by Antin and Ravage on the other.

## Notes

1. For one such attempt, see Boelhower 20.
2. After World War I, Slovenia became part of Yugoslavia.
3. Adamic probably refers here to "Case History," published in Nov. 1928. He had two essays published previously in the *American Mercury*, "The Yugoslav Speech in America" (Nov. 1927) and "The Bohunks" (July 1928), but neither is really a story in the sense that "Case History" is. Incidentally, he worked the material from "Case History" into *Laughing in the Jungle*.
4. Adamic was to change his ideas about Russia markedly in the years to come when he identified himself as an anti-Communist.
5. That all Eastern European Jews who came to America did not think of their Americanization in terms of rebirth is indicated by Abraham Cahan, who in *The Education of Abraham Cahan* describes his life as basically continuous in Russia and America.

## Works Cited

Adamic, Louis. "The Bohunks." *American Mercury*, July 1928, 318–24.

———. "Case History." *American Mercury*, Nov. 1928, 287–96.

———. *Laughing in the Jungle: The Autobiography of an Immigrant in America*. New York: Harper, 1932.

———. *My America: 1928–1938*. New York: Harper, 1938.

———. "The Yugoslav Speech in America." *American Mercury*, Nov. 1927, 319–21.

Adams, Henry. *The Education of Henry Adams*. 1907. Boston: Houghton, 1918.

Antin, Mary. *The Promised Land*. Boston: Houghton, 1912.

Boelhower, William. *Immigrant Autobiography in the United States (Four Versions of the Italian American Self)*. Verona: Essedue, 1982.

Cahan, Abraham. *The Education of Abraham Cahan*. Trans. Leon Stein, Abraham P. Conan, and Lynn Davison. Introd. by Leon Stein. Philadelphia: Jewish Publication Society, 1969.

Cooley, Thomas. *Educated Lives: The Rise of Modern Autobiography in America*. Columbus: Ohio State UP, 1976.

Franklin, Benjamin. *The Autobiography of Benjamin Franklin: A Genetic Text*. Ed. J. A. Leo Lemay and P. M. Zall. Knoxville: U of Tennessee P, 1981.

Howe, Irving. *World of Our Fathers*. New York: Harcourt, 1976.

Lane, James B. *Jacob A. Riis and the American City*. Port Washington: Kennikat, 1974.

Lewisohn, Ludwig. *Mid-Channel: An American Chronicle*. New York: Harper, 1929.

———. *Up Stream: An American Chronicle*. New York: Boni, 1922.

Marx, Leo. *The Machine in the Garden: Technology and the Pastoral Ideal in America*. New York: Oxford UP, 1967.

Ravage, M. E. *An American in the Making: The Life Story of an Immigrant*. New York: Harper, 1917.

Riis, Jacob A. *The Battle with the Slum*. New York: Macmillan, 1902.

———. "The Jews of New York." *Review of Reviews*, Jan. 1896, 58–62.

———. *The Making of an American*. New York: Macmillan, 1901.

Sinclair, Upton. *The Jungle*. Ed. James R. Barrett. Urbana: U of Illinois P, 1988.

Stone, Albert E. *Autobiographical Occasions and Original Acts: Versions of American Identity from Henry Adams to Nate Shaw*. Philadelphia: U of Pennsylvania P, 1982.

Tuerk, Richard. "Assimilation in Jewish-American Autobiography: Mary Antin and Ludwig Lewisohn." *A/B: Auto/Biography Studies* 3, no. 2 (Summer 1987): 26–33.

———. "Jacob Riis and the Jews." *New-York Historical Society Quarterly* 63 (1979): 179–201.

# My House Is Not Your House: Jerre Mangione and Italian-American Autobiography

*Fred L. Gardaphe*

Contrary to the testimony of maps, there is such a place as Italian America. It is to be found in Italian houses in America. In these places, the house is, in one of several possible senses, the old country itself.

—Robert Viscusi, *"Il Caso della Casa*: Stories of Houses in Italian America"

My mother's insistence that we speak only Italian at home drew a sharp line between our existence there and our life in the world outside. We gradually acquired the notion that we were Italian at home and American (whatever that was) elsewhere. Instinctively, we all sensed the necessity of adapting ourselves to two different worlds. We began to notice that there were several marked differences between those worlds, differences that made Americans and my relatives each think of the other as foreigners.

—Jerre Mangione, *Mount Allegro*

Today Italian Americans blend easily into mainstream American life. Since leaving the immigrant ghettos of the past for new lives in the suburbs, Italian Americans no longer share identifiable geographical spaces. But for an Italian surname and a few distinctive Mediterranean physical features, it is possible to say that the Italian American has in many respects lost a publicly recognizable Italian character. If not for a renewed third-generation curiosity about the history and culture of Italian immigrants and their land of origin, sparked by the few scholars and artists of first and second generations, it would be possible to announce the total assimilation of the

Italian American. Yet there are qualities of an Italian American that persist into third and fourth generations, and this persistence can be best observed inside Italian-American houses or, as we will see, inside the writings of Italian Americans.[1] As Italian-American writers begin to build their own "houses," they come to realize an Italian-American identity that results from the interaction of two very different notions of Italian and American self in society. What is distinctive about Italian-American culture can best be perceived in these houses as they become homes.

This essay will connect the development of Italian-American autobiography to its roots in oral tradition. It will also examine representative works—particularly those of Jerre Mangione, a major figure in Italian-American letters. As we will see, Mangione's four autobiographical books provide us not only with an example of the evolution of an Italian-American identity but with a basis upon which a distinctive Italian-American tradition of autobiography is built.

It has taken three generations and over one hundred years of Italian presence in America to produce what can be called an Italian-American literature.[2] Within this literature the number of autobiographies is small in comparison to that of other major ethnic groups. The paucity of self-reflective written works can be attributed to a number of causes: the distrust of the written word (an Italian proverb warns: *Pensa molto, parla poco, e scrivi meno* [Think a lot, speak little, and write even less]), the immigrant's distrust of social and educational institutions that represent the ruling classes, and a lack of parental encouragement of children to pursue literary careers due to the need of having to earn money as soon as one is old enough to be employed.[3] In spite of the low priority given to writing by Italian Americans on the whole, a number of authors have emerged to document the Italian-American experience and create a literary tradition out of a strong oral tradition.[4] In this respect, Italian-American writers have much in common with writers who come from American-Indian and African-American traditions. The strong storytelling traditions that we find in Italian-American oral culture are filled with tales that explain the reasons for traditional rituals and provide information about how to live one's life. They also enable us to examine the evolution of the Italian American's self-concept and its progression into public discourse.

## Oral Traditions and the Self

"The conscious awareness of the singularity of each individual life is the late product of a specific civilization," writes Georges Gusdorf in his essay "Conditions and Limits of Autobiography." "Throughout most of human history, the individual does not oppose himself to all others; he does not feel himself to exist outside of others, and still less against others, but very much *with* others in an interdependent existence that asserts its rhythms in the community" (29).

The body of available literature on Italian oral traditions supports Gusdorf's observations. Telling the story of self in public was not part of any public cultural tradition that can be found south of Rome (the region from which come over 80 percent of the Italians who migrated to America). Yet, since little work has been done on oral traditions in southern Italy, we generally must look to the studies that have been done on the oral traditions of northern Italy.[5]

In *Italian Folktales in America: The Verbal Art of an Immigrant Woman*, Elizabeth Mathias and Richard Raspa present an in-depth look at what happens when a traditional tale teller, Clementina Tedesco, trained by a master storyteller from her native village of Faller in northern Italy, immigrates to America. Mathias and Raspa note that Tedesco's repertoire expanded from traditional *marchen* and legends, representing an Italian communal experience, to include personal, factual accounts of her immigration experience: "What emerged with Clementina in the new setting was a different way of communicating with others, still artistic, still startling in its power to evoke life, but no longer a part of a traditional art" (60).

In the Italian oral tradition, the self is suppressed and is not used as a source for storytelling in the communal settings of Italy, where one function of such stories was to create a temporary respite from the harsh realities of everyday peasant life. In his study of Tuscan oral traditions, Alessandro Falassi cites a proverb that reveals a second function of traditional storytelling: *La novella non è' bella se non c'è' la giuntarella* (The story isn't good if it doesn't have its moral) (37). Traditional stories served both to entertain and to inform the young, while reminding the old of traditions that have endured over the years. Personal information was expected to be kept to one's self.

Southern Italian culture is replete with aphorisms and proverbs that advise against revealing information that can be used against the self or the family: *A chi dici il tuo secreto, doni la tua libertà* (To whom you tell a secret, you give your freedom); *Di il fatto tuo, e lascia far il fatto tuo* (Tell everyone your business and the devil will do it); *Odi, vedi, e taci se vuoi viver in pace* (Listen, watch, and keep quiet if you wish to live in peace). This tendency to keep to one's self has often been misinterpreted by other American groups who see this characteristic silence or *omertà* as un-American.[6] In their study, Mathias and Raspa suggest that this behavior changes through immigration. Once the Italian storyteller is uprooted, a sense of self begins to emerge as the dominant material for storytelling. It is in this immigrant experience then that we can locate the sources of an autobiographical tradition.[7]

## From Oral to Written Traditions: Immigrants and Autobiography

The theme of flight to a better world or a promised land, found in many immigrant autobiographies and slave narratives, is one that permeates the earliest Italian-American autobiographies.[8] Arrival in America brought the immigrant to a new system of codifying cultural signifiers, a system that often conflicted with the immigrant's previous way of interpreting

life. The resulting conflicts are most obvious in the early language encounters between Italian-speaking immigrants and
English-speaking Americans.[9] This arrival also required the
immigrant to develop a new sense of self in the context of the
larger society.

The experience of leaving the old country and arriving in
the new is the primary subject of early autobiographies such
as Constantine Panunzio's *The Soul of an Immigrant* (1921),
Pascal D'Angelo's *Son of Italy* (1924), and autobiographies narrated to those who could write English such as *Rosa, the Life
of an Italian Immigrant* (1970).

Panunzio's writing contains two stories of conversions,
both of which relate to his Americanization. The first is his
conversion from Roman Catholicism to "American" religion
(Protestantism), the second to American citizenship. His use
of selections from English and American poetry to introduce
each chapter provides evidence that he has come to understand and accept "the genius of the Anglo-Saxon mind and
character of the soul of America" (vii). D'Angelo's story of his
rise from illiterate, "hunger-artist" immigrant to citizen of literary America (through his winning of a national poetry contest)
can be read as a version of the American success story modeled
after Benjamin Franklin's *Autobiography*.[10] D'Angelo's *Son of
Italy*, like many African-American slave narratives, is introduced
by an established American, who functions as both authentica-
tor and model reader. In D'Angelo's case the American is Carl
Van Doren, former editor of *The Nation*, the magazine that
awarded D'Angelo first prize in its 1922 poetry contest. Both
Panunzio's and D'Angelo's autobiographies may have been
subjected to editing; both authors refer to their inadequacy
with the English language.[11] Indeed, we can assume that each
experienced a great deal of control in preparing his work. These
writings are the earliest Italian-American autobiographies; they
also represent the insertion of Italian contents into the more
traditional American autobiographical forms of the conversion and success story.

One of the strongest Italian-American immigrant autobiographies is the story of Rosa Cavalleri, narrated to Marie Hall Ets, a social worker who met Rosa through contact at the Chicago Commons, a settlement house for poor immigrants.[12] Rosa is the illegitimate daughter of a famous Italian actress whose name Rosa refuses to reveal.[13] She was abandoned at birth by her mother and spent her early years in a Catholic orphanage before being placed into a foster home. *Rosa* documents a young girl's life in an impoverished northern Italian village and her forced immigration to America to join her husband (a marriage arranged by her stepmother, who would not allow Rosa to marry a man to whom Rosa had earlier declared her love).

It is important to keep in mind that Rosa's story comes to us through the filter of an American recorder. Although the sound and structure of Rosa's Italian-American dialect has been preserved and recorded in Rosa's consistent use of present tense, we must remember that, as an illiterate, Rosa (like many of the voices in slave narratives) had little control over what was published. Ets explains that she chose not to include the many traditional stories that Rosa had told her because they, when written down, "held little that would interest moderns." Unlike Mathias and Raspa, Ets chose to preserve only "the amazing story of her [Rosa's] life and of the fears and superstitions and beliefs of the people of her village" (7).

Rosa's story graphically depicts the poor conditions in Italy that forced hundreds of thousands of Italians to migrate. A key to understanding the effects that this migration had on the Italians can be found by examining the role that fear played in the development of Rosa's self-identity. Rosa's fear in Italy is generated by the Italian class system, which demands that the poor never look into the eyes of the rich; this fear is also present in the traditional man/woman relationship which turns females into the property of fathers, husbands, bosses, and priests. Rosa's accounts are filled with fear of men and the Italian authorities who impose their will upon hers. But there is another fear that Rosa experiences, the fear of God, and this fear is not lost in her move to America. In fact her immigrant experience

strengthens her Italian-created religious convictions. Thus for
Rosa, as for many Italian immigrants, there is the experience of
two types of fear: the fear that feeds the development of self, the
fear of God; and the fear that starves it, the fear of Man—both of
which make up her identity. Her last wish indicates the psychological transformation she experienced in the move to America:

> Only one wish more I have: I'd love to go in *Italia* again before I die.
> Now I speak English good like an American I could go anywhere—
> where millionaires go and high people. I would look the high people in
> the face and ask them what questions I'd like to know. I wouldn't be
> afraid now—not of anybody. I'd be proud I come from America and
> speak English. I would go to Bugiarno and see the people and talk to the
> bosses in the silk factory. And to Canaletto [the convent where she was
> educated]. Those sisters would not throw me out when I come from
> America! I could talk to *Superiora* now. I'd tell her, "Why you were so
> mean—you threw out that poor girl whose heart was so kind toward
> you? You think you'll go to heaven like that?" I'd scold them like that
> now. I wouldn't be afraid. They wouldn't dare hurt me now I come from
> America. Me, that's why I love America. That's what I learned in
> America: not to be afraid. (254)[14]

For Rosa, and many of the immigrants like her, leaving Italy
meant leaving a time-trapped traditional system of life that could
be escaped only by death or migration. This dynamic of Old
World sense of destiny versus New World sense of freedom from
fate, so well portrayed in Rosa's "as-told-to" autobiography, becomes a dominant theme in Italian-American autobiography.

As we will see, the American ideas of self-reliance and the
importance of developing one's self-identity outside of one's
community become staples of the Italian-American identity
as the Italian American develops a written tradition out of a
predominantly oral tradition. For in the oral tradition of Italian
Americans such as Rosa, self becomes a new and, most importantly, a safe subject for public discourse in the immigrant's new
environment. As the subject of self becomes the focus of Ital-

ian-American writing, we find that the autobiographer, now in greater control of the language of the new country, is better able to negotiate the difference between Italian and American ideas and is thus better able to forge an identity that essentially is a synthesis of the two often conflicting worldviews. The result, especially for the American-born child of Italian immigrants, is that the autobiographer, while writing the story of his or her self, also becomes a spokesperson for his or her community, developing models of self-construction that represent possible ways of moving from an Italian to an Italian-American identity. Essentially, as we will see in the evolution of the writings of Jerre Mangione, control of the American language— something immigrants of the oral tradition did not have—means greater control of the self as American. With this increased control comes the ability to create and articulate a truly Italian-American identity.

## Freedom from Destiny: The Writings of Jerre Mangione

Immigrants from southern Italy brought to America a belief in a destiny that humans were powerless to change. Such beliefs were indoctrinated by centuries of domination by outside forces. Parents could not expect that their children's lives would ever be better than their own. Proverbs such as *Fesso chi fa il figlio meglio di lui* (Only a fool makes his son better than himself) pointed to the futility of expecting progress through generations. The tension between the Sicilian's adherence to such notions of life and the American sense of freedom to become whatever one wishes can best be observed in the body of work created by Jerre Mangione.

Born in the United States in 1909, Mangione is one of the most celebrated of Italian-American writers.[15] His *Mount Allegro* has remained in print most of the years since its first appearance in 1943, a feat which has required six publishers to date and has prompted Malcolm Cowley to write in a personal letter to Mangione: "*Mount Allegro* has had more lives than any other book of our time." An American-born son of Sicilian immigrants, Mangione grew up in a multiethnic neighborhood of Rochester, New York.[16] Though originally contracted to be a memoir about life in the Rochester neighborhood, *Mount Allegro* was first published as a work of fiction over Mangione's protests.[17] Despite this initial confusion, *Mount Allegro* has survived to acquire the appropriate subtitle: *A Memoir of Italian American Life.*

*Mount Allegro* is the first of four nonfiction books by Mangione that can be read as autobiography. Each book represents a progressive stage of identity development: from Sicilian to American and eventually to Sicilian American. Our reading of the development of an Italian-American autobiographical tradition in general, and Mangione's writings in particular, can be greatly illuminated through a metaphorical paradigm that Robert Viscusi set up in his reading of Italian-American literature.

In his essay "*Il Caso della Casa*: Stories of Houses in Italian America," Viscusi employs four prototypes of Italian-American houses as metaphors for possible readings of Italian-American writings. The first prototype represents the house as shrine; the second, as villa; the third, as *palazzo*; and the fourth, as embassy. Viscusi explains that these are not stages of development so much as characteristics that can be found in the writings of Italian Americans. He tells us that ". . . any house may be all four of these at the same time, for these nouns merely name purposes, and a house, as we know, can do many things at once" (1). Viscusi's "houses" paradigm can enhance our reading of Italian-American autobiographies since many, if not all, do contain elements of all four prototypes; what varies is the degree to which each one emphasizes a specific function of a particular prototype. In short, then, early immigrant autobiographers can be seen as moving their contents into already-made houses designed by American ideas, built out of American materials, subject to American inspection/editing.

In the earlier autobiographies a large portion, if not all, of the "house" is set aside for creation of a shrine to the old country. This is followed by a period of identity crisis and a progression from inside to outside the home, represented first by villa building and then by *palazzo* building. The fourth prototype represents a politicization of the self that comes from a more confident sense of self as ambassador/participant in the larger community outside the "Little Italies" and immigrant ghettos that many first called home.[18] For Italian-American writers, autobiography becomes an essential step, perhaps even the very process by which the writer creates an American identity. In fact, for many Italian-American autobiographers, the writing of an autobiography is a major testament to their experiences of developing an American identity.

By applying Viscusi's four prototypes to our reading of Mangione's works, we can observe a developing intertextuality that takes place within the writings of one man. This evolution begins with house/autobiography as shrine and ends with house/autobiography as embassy. Although within each book there is a similar pattern of this movement, each work—interestingly enough—emphasizes one prototype over the others. Thus we can read *Mount Allegro* (1943) as shrine, *Reunion in Sicily* (1950) as villa, *A Passion for Sicilians* (1968) as palazzo, and *An Ethnic at Large* (1978) as embassy. The tension between the competing systems of Old versus New World creates the dynamic by which the development of this intertextuality occurs. The resolution of this tension culminates in Mangione's achievement of a multicultural perspective and identity.

The first prototype Viscusi identifies is the house as

Shrine. *Lares* and *penates* are what make an American house Italian American, and we have innumerable examples to choose from because anything that bears the mark of Italy can become a household god in Italian America. This extends from such obvious artifacts as the statue of Santa Rosalia or the panorama of the Golfo di Napoli to the subtle but all-enveloping atmosphere of cookery. (2)

Applying this notion to *Mount Allegro* enables us to identify specific elements of this Italian-American autobiography that work to enshrine and eventually mythicize the old country inside the Italian-American home, inside Italian-American writing. Such elements are easily distinguished in references to home decor, meals prepared, and subjects of conversation. The autobiographer, in this type of work, submerges the self in deference to a historical and at times mythical ancestral past communicated through others; Mangione becomes a memoirist who, in defining his past, dignifies his present.

As in the accounts of Rosa, fear in the old country becomes a shadow to life in the new country, despite Mangione's American birth. The source of this shadow for Mangione is the Old World notion of *destino* or destiny, a notion that was reinforced in the daily life of his Sicilian-American family, resulting from their experience of Sicily's political realities and religious practices.

Though Mangione's life and writing, in many respects, are an attempt to escape *destino*, they are nevertheless greatly affected by it. His relatives' lives are governed by traditions and myths, a way of life that Georges Gusdorf says does not foster autobiography because of a characteristic "unconsciousness of personality" that is found in even "advanced civilizations that subscribe to mythic structures . . . governed by the principle of repetition" (30). Such civilizations, Gusdorf concludes, fix their attention and energies on "that which remains, not on that which passes" (30). The Italian notion of *destino* is an example of what Gusdorf calls a theory of "eternal recurrence." Mangione writes that *destino*, a barrier that keeps his relatives from becoming Americans, contained "strong elements of fatalism" that were "ingrained in the Sicilian soul by centuries of poverty and oppression. . . . In their minds, *Destino*, the willingness to resign oneself to misfortune, was the key to survival; to refuse to believe that an almighty force predetermined the fate of all people was to court disaster" (*Ethnic* 32). Mangione can overcome this barrier only by leaving his relatives. And throughout *Mount Allegro* we get the sense that the narrator is documenting the decline of a people, the end of an era, an era that becomes history the moment the narrator separates himself from his immigrant relatives. In fact, Mangione can only write this book after he has left his home. By leaving home, then, he begins the process by which he becomes Americanized. Even the structure of Mangione's first book reveals the duality he experienced.

William Boelhower sees *Mount Allegro* composed of three movements (187). In the first movement (chapter 1), we find the narrator focusing on Gerlando (Jerre), a child protagonist questioning his identity as he begins to develop an individual personality separate from the group of grown-ups. This movement opens with his sister saying: "When I grow up I want to be an American" (1). What follows is an argument among the siblings, during which Gerlando replies: "We're Americans right now. . . . Miss Zimmerman says if you're born here you're an American." His brother argues that they are Italians; soon the argument is resolved by their father's pronouncement, "Your children will be *Americani*. But you my son are half-and-half" (1). The duality expressed at the outset of *Mount Allegro* is one that Mangione will experience throughout his life. The second movement (chapters 2 through 10) presents life in Mount Allegro through a series of anecdotes and vignettes as reported by a detached narrator who forgoes references to himself in favor of letting the relatives relate their own lives in their own words. This second movement is presented primarily through dialogue among family members as they interact and through monologues in which key personalities relate their experiences along with traditional folktales, all of which of course is filtered through the narrator who has mastered the use of English. This movement is, in essence, a synthesis of Rosa and Ets. The final movement (chapters 10 through 14) returns to what Boelhower calls a "sharp focus . . . on the now mature protagonist" (187) as he makes his way out of Mount Allegro by going off to college, then traveling to Sicily, and finally moving into the American mainstream.

First by leaving the family house in Mount Allegro and then by recreating or rebuilding it in his writing, Mangione confronts his divided self and attempts to make a whole of the two halves.[19] The residents of Mount Allegro are not part of the outside community; the interactions they have with the larger community are more often than not portrayed as confrontations which become the tales told at family gatherings. When Mangione announces his plans to leave Mount Allegro to attend college, his family expects that he will do so only to return in a position of power. The family expects him to become a doctor or a lawyer. When they realize he has the talent or temperament for neither career, a wise uncle suggests a compromise: that Gerlando (the Gerry in the book) become a pharmacist. Mangione chooses instead to become a writer; this choice signals a total break from the old world, for there is no real need in the Sicilian-American oral-based community for a writer; to become a writer was to elect becoming an outsider. As Mangione tells us in his "Comments" in *Contemporary Novelists*, the experiences that became the substance of *Mount Allegro* "accentuated for me the sharp contrast between the philosophical values of the old world and those of the new. It also succeeded in casting me in the role of outsider who, belonging to neither world, tries to create his own world by writing . . ." (571).

What accelerates the building of Mangione's American identity is a 1936 trip to Italy, recounted at the end of *Mount Allegro*. Mangione leaves America for Italy with the caution that he not travel far from American consulates, for his relatives fear that, as the son of immigrants, he might be kidnapped and forced to serve in Mussolini's army. In Sicily, Mangione is identified as the "Americano." He speaks an older dialect of Sicilian and uses words that are part of a creole invented out of necessity as Sicilians imposed their native language on the American experiences that had no Sicilian equivalent. He immediately recognizes his Sicilian relatives as versions of those back in America, physically and especially in temperament. These similarities enable him to realize that it was futile "... for anyone to believe that Sicilians could become conventional Americans in the course of a single lifetime" (265). However, he also becomes aware of a great difference between Sicilians and Sicilian Americans, especially in a time of fascism: the former still had a fear of "... speaking out of turn. It lay on their hearts and minds like a heavy poison. But Sicilians had to talk, for it was in their nature. Some talked to me because I was an American relative and would not give them away" (266). Mangione can see this fear, and he can recognize the limitations it forces the Sicilian to live with, only because he has come to understand and exercise a more "Americanized" notion of freedom and self-reliance. His experiences outside of Mount Allegro, as well as the books he had read about life in America, have enabled him to transcend the immigrant world, to free himself from *destino*.

And so, *Mount Allegro* can be read as a shrine that Mangione has built of his Sicilian-American past. The memories recorded of his many uncles and aunts, and their immigrant experiences, preserve a time that is forever gone. As a shrine, *Mount Allegro* can also be read, as Boelhower has pointed out, as a group biography. However, Mangione's work is not as revolutionary or untraditional as Boelhower and other critics would have us believe. According to Boelhower, *Mount Allegro* "... signals the very death of the genre, of the autobiographical paradigm as it is traditionally understood, for here the protagonist's time dissolves into the time of the community. Out of the ashes of the typology of the single solitary self will arise the transindividual self, the group-biography" (192). Another critic, John M. Reilly, also does not read *Mount Allegro* as an autobiography in the traditional sense. In his essay "Literary Versions of Ethnic History from Upstate New York," Reilly sees *Mount Allegro* taking on another traditional form, the memoir in which "The self serves as an armature . . . but the subject is less the unfolding of personality than it is passage through events and relationships that may be known also from other, perhaps more objective, writings" (190–91). Although both of these critics correctly point out that *Mount*

*Allegro* is not autobiography in the traditional sense, through which we observe the progression of an individual's development of self over time, a more accurate explanation of Mangione's difference can be given by noting the tradition out of which Mangione writes. Mangione's style of submerging the self, inserting the narrator as an invisible protagonist/observer, according to Ben Morreale, is a typical characteristic of control practiced by many Sicilian writers:

> Coming from an island that had been the crossroads of armies bent on world domination for centuries, having insecurities that some have translated into a psychological *paura storica*, or history of fear, the Sicilian has learned not to reveal himself. This reticence might be the core of Sicilian style in literature. ("Mangione and the Yearning for Home" 41)

Morreale's observation is crucial to reading Mangione's memoirs, his fiction, and his social histories. Morreale finds a similar style at work in the writers associated with the Sicilian school of Italian literature: Giovanni Verga, Luigi Pirandello, Giuseppe di Lampedusa, Elio Vittorini, and the contemporary Leonardo Sciascia. In all these writers the narrative self plays a subservient role to the voices of others; the self is rarely placed in a consistent dominating position over others. This narrative mask enables the true self to remain flexible and thus untraceable. It is also a politically safe position for the narrator who must negotiate his way through a repressive political system. This becomes an important stance for Mangione to take, especially when he must deal with two very different political systems: democracy in America and fascism in Italy.

The guiding principle of Mangione's style, as well as a dominant theme in his work, is that one can challenge destiny and make his or her own destiny. He writes out of a need to explain the people who have affected his notions of self; he also writes in order to bridge the gap between the Italian immigrant and the American. He knows the sophistication and the wit these illiterate immigrants are capable of communicating to each other, but not to outsiders who mistakenly equate the immigrants' struggle for self-expression in a foreign language with ignorance. That Italian immigrants had much to offer America in the process of becoming Americans led Mangione to question the viability of such ideas as the melting-pot theory:

> Was it in the chemistry of human life for my relatives to become Anglo-Saxonized—the apparent goal of the melting pot theorists? So long as they believed in freedom and democracy—and their long history showed those ideals to be as ingrained in them as their religion—was it necessary that they try to change themselves? Didn't America need their wisdom and their warmth, just as they and their children needed America's youth and vigor? (*Mount Allegro* 239).

The search for answers to these questions led Mangione on a journey into the past, first through reading, and then through travel to his ancestral homeland. The solution to the identity conflict of Sicilian versus American dramatized in *Mount Allegro* would be pursued in Mangione's second book, *Reunion in Sicily*, which through Viscusi's prototypes can be read as Mangione's villa.

Viscusi explains the house as villa prototype:

> The Villa. Aeneas, the successful immigrant, owed his prosperity to *pietas,* veneration for ancestors so profound that he left Troy actually carrying his father on his back. Here is an exorcism of guilt that really works. For the immigrant who has abandoned father and mother, there is still a symbolical path of Aeneas that lies open, and many have taken this road, choosing to build in America a home which can advertise itself, with whatever repression of absurdity, as patriarchal—*una villa padronale.* Stories of the *famiglia* which builds itself a house and so becomes a *casa* abound in Italian America. ("*Il caso*" 3)

Viscusi's second prototype invites us to consider those elements of the Italian-American autobiography that reveal idiosyncrasies pertaining to the Italian family and the American experiences that work to strengthen or weaken the traditional family structure. In the *villa* prototype we can observe the interaction of family members (within the characteristic patriarchal structure) in the writings of Italian Americans and realize the influence that the Old World patterns of interaction have on those of the New World. This prototype emerges as a result of the autobiographer leaving his childhood home, in essence reenacting the emigrant experience of his parents.

*Reunion in Sicily* documents the second of Mangione's many trips to Sicily. These trips become odysseys that reverse the typical journey paradigm found in the immigrant autobiography. With each trip, Mangione's writing creates a different house. The reunion that he experiences in Sicily goes beyond the strengthening of ties between families in two worlds; it is more a reunion of a divided self. By revealing the process of a reintegration of self, the book allows Mangione to realize that he is neither American nor Italian but a synthesis of the two which creates an Italian American.

Structured as a personal travelogue and political report, *Reunion in Sicily* (1950) opens with a confession that, in spite of receiving a Guggenheim Fellowship, Mangione is in no mood to go to Sicily. Ten years after his first visit, Mangione tells us that the goal of this project is to look at postwar life in Italy and to document the transition from dictatorship to self-government. Among the dangers he anticipates encountering is the trap of marriage. At thirty-seven years of age, Mangione is plagued by his relatives' disappointment with his bachelor state. They hope he will return from this trip to Sicily married to a good Sicilian woman. His mother tells him "Life without a wife leaves no image on the soul" (16); Mangione notes that she seems to be paraphrasing Goethe's "Italy without Sicily leaves no image on the soul." This is one of the many examples of advice his Sicilian-American relatives give to the young bachelor.

*Reunion in Sicily*, like its predecessor, includes anecdotes concerning his experiences with his Sicilian relatives. Through his discussions with them and other Sicilians he is able to document the effects that World War II had on the Italians.

Many experienced the bombing of their villages by Americans; some witnessed the brutality of Allied soldiers, brutality not normally equated with the liberation of Italy.[20]

It is a different Sicily that Mangione experiences in this trip. Political arguments may be heard in public. Fathers who believed in fascism's ability to impose order and enable progress now have sons whose hopes for a brighter future are planted in the growing communist and socialist parties that are quickly gaining strength in the more impoverished regions of southern Italy and Sicily. Rather then merely report the situation as a touring journalist, Mangione employs a more novelistic approach as he threads his narrative with dialogue, allowing Italians to speak of their experiences for themselves.

As Mangione gathers the impressions from Italians and Sicilians from all walks of life and from different classes, he begins to understand the way they view America and the stereotype of the "typical American" they have constructed based on their interactions with Americans. Though much of what he is fits their notion of the stereotypical American, there are qualities that Mangione has that do not conform to their image. By challenging their monolithic notions of what the typical American is, Mangione becomes the exception, a reminder that stereotypes are artificial constructions. Through this sometimes intense scrutiny of his parents' homeland, Mangione comes to learn about a Sicily his parents had not made him aware of. This learning results in his establishing an identity that crosses both the American and Italian cultural boundaries. Mangione can be an American in Italy and an Italian in America. In effect, his investigations into Italy enable him to deconstruct the images that both cultures have of each other:

> When you tell an Italian that many Americans own automobiles, radios, and refrigerators and that some of them have machines that clean dishes automatically, he will blink at you as though you were describing the plot of a fairy tale. "Ah," he will gasp, "the Americans must be the happiest people in the world." It would mystify him if you replied that on the whole the Italians have a better grasp of happiness. (134)

Mangione is also in the unique position of being able to view and comment on the attitudes towards Italians expressed by Americans who are present in postwar Sicily. He finds that his attitudes differ greatly from those Americans who hold ". . . a certain amount of contempt or condescension in their attitude toward the natives. The only Sicilians they seemed to like were royalists and members of the upper class. . . . The rest were generally regarded as inferiors, unworthy of their respect" (216). Observations such as these fix Mangione in the role of being a cultural mediator; he is not the typical American, nor is he the typical Italian. This middleman position, although enabling him to see events and people from a privileged insider/outsider perspective, has its disadvantages, as evidenced by his inability to continue a courtship with a beautiful Sicilian woman he had fallen in love with during his trip around Sicily. It did not take him long to realize that he was "not Sicilian enough to do justice" to the Sicilian woman.

Mangione's achievement of a true bicultural perspective, created by his newly developed ability to experience both Italy and America as both outsider and insider, comes when he realizes that he cannot possibly be a pure product of either culture. The experience of knowing his families and countries more intimately, now on both sides of the ocean, forces and enables Mangione to construct his autobiographical villa; having left in search of home (in the ancestral sense), his writing suggests that he has transcended the American as well as Italian identity as he creates a Sicilian-American identity out of the fusion of the two. This fusion can be read as the creation of his *palazzo* or house which expands to include a larger community. Viscusi explains the concept of house as

The Palazzo. To many an enlightened immigrant, then, it has seemed that it would not be enough for family to become house and for it to erect the paternal totem in the form of a rooftree. This would bear the marks of self-enclosure, even of self-damnation. House must also become community. ("*Il caso*" 5)

Using the notion of house as *palazzo* we can identify those elements of autobiography that portray the interaction of the nuclear family and its extensions within the Italian-American community. This aspect reveals the decentralization of patriarchal power that occurs as families interact with each other outside of the home. We can also examine the extent to which a geographical community mirrors the traditional family structure.

*Reunion in Sicily*, the result of Mangione's Guggenheim-sponsored trip to Italy in 1947, revealed the writer's growing interest in the human community of the world. In his proposal to the Guggenheim committee, he mentioned that what was happening in postwar (and post-Fascist) Sicily "should concern all who realize that the military liberation of a people sickened with dictatorship and war is one thing; its convalescence into a healthy, self-governing body is quite another" (3). It is Mangione's sense of the need to develop a concept of world community that motivates him to return to Sicily for a third time, close to twenty years after his second trip. This third trip is recounted in the third volume of his Sicilian-American memoirs. *A Passion for Sicilians: The World around Danilo Dolci* (1968) is undoubtedly Mangione's least autobiographical work of the four considered in this essay. In its 1972 Harper and Row paperback edition, the subtitle became the main title, more accurately identifying the focus of the writing.[21] As a social history written in the first person, this book is more an ethnography—an account of a neglected region's fight for progress against the Mafia and a stubborn, slow-moving Italian government—than a continuation of the narrative progression of Mangione's life toward an Italian-American identity. Mangione chooses to step back and record his observations of the work of Italian social activist Danilo Dolci, often called the "Ghandi of Sicily."[22] Dolci's goal was to assist Sicilians in taking control over their own lives. Having come to understand the possibilities of making one's own destiny, Mangione is able to see what needs to be done in Sicily and so can assist

Dolci with public relations materials that enable Dolci to gain public and private support for his projects.[23]

In *A Passion for Sicilians* Mangione, now considered an "unofficial" representative of America on a Fulbright Fellowship, describes the conditions of poverty that continue to plague Sicily despite the economic growth that Italy is experiencing. Because Dolci is as demanding as he is determined, Mangione often finds himself in the precarious position of having to mediate between Dolci and the Sicilians, between Dolci and the larger community of Italy, and between Dolci and the people outside of Italy. At times Mangione feels that he is being used by Dolci to strengthen Dolci's image in the world community. The events that Mangione recollects reflect the burdens placed on someone who has developed a bicultural perspective along with an ability to interact and relate well in two cultures.

Once again, Mangione depends on the people he knows best, his family, to recount the Sicilian experience. As he used their reactions to World War II for material in *Reunion in Sicily*, he turns to them for accounts of the economic situation in Sicily twenty years after the war. He also elicits their reactions to Dolci's presence in Sicily. Though his family has experienced some economic improvement, symbolized by a "luxurious bathtub and the superspeed washing machine," they have yet to make much progress, represented by the fact that "only for one hour every two days was water available" (221). When Mangione tells them that the water problem might be resolved by Dolci's work, a cousin, who was formerly a Fascist in the Mussolini era, dismisses Mangione's notions with, "Danilo Dolci, everyone knows is a Communist." Within his own family lie the various responses that Dolci's work receives in Sicily; Mangione shows us that it is impossible for his relatives to form a consensus of opinion about the man and his work. During this visit, Mangione does not spend much time with his family, much to their dismay. In effect, as in *Mount Allegro*, he must leave them in order to participate in the larger community of the outside world.

As an outsider who is writing about Dolci, Mangione is the person Dolci's detractors seek out, hoping to impress their opinions upon the eventual readers of Mangione's projected writings. By recording their opinions through the dialogue of his interaction with them, Mangione is able to present both the strengths and weaknesses of Dolci, rendering him more realistic than heroic. With a solid knowledge of Sicily's past, discovered and documented in both of his earlier books, Mangione is most concerned, as is Dolci, with Sicily's future. Mangione sees a changing Sicily this time around, a land in which Sicilians are learning to take destiny into their own hands by informing on the Mafia, protesting against government neglect, and building community centers that will train tomorrow's leaders. But the establishment of a new democracy in Italy presents many challenges to the old patriarchal structure of the family, a structure that was mirrored in the earlier Fascist regime. Mangione records the struggle in one young woman's words: "How can we ever have democracy in our society if we don't have it in the family" (260)?

In a sense, Mangione shows with this book that he has become not only a citizen of both countries but an ambassador of sorts of each country to the other. Here he presents a sense of being finally at home in both worlds. Now comfortable in this ambassadorial position, Mangione is prepared to write *An Ethnic at Large*, a book that represents Viscusi's final prototype:

> The Embassy. Nothing will serve, finally, but that the breach be healed, that the hatreds give up their furies before the gentle forces of understanding and mutual absolution, the familial communion of love. (*"Il caso"* 7)

As embassy, the Italian-American house becomes the focal point of interaction between Italian-American self and others outside the extended family of "paesani." Through this prototype the Italian-American autobiography can be read as the interaction between the Italian American and the dominant

American culture that exists outside the home. Very often this prototype emerges along with the politicization of the Italian American and the development of social confidence that comes after achieving success in the larger community. One of the chief characteristics of this prototype is the ability to transcend the anger and fear that were characteristic of the immigrant who felt isolated in the ghetto, powerless to take control of his or her American life.

Of the four works considered, Mangione's *An Ethnic at Large* (1978) contains the type of material that we most expect to find in a traditional "success story" autobiography. In it we follow the son of immigrants out of the neighborhood and into the world. Early portions of the book involve a retelling of the experiences in Mount Allegro, but now these events appear from an even greater distance both in time and space. Mangione, at age sixty-nine, reexamines his life from childhood up through age thirty-five. The result is that he now (re)presents the past in a much more Americanized context. He is much more confident in his abilities to mediate among cultures, and he reexamines his past from a unique multicultural dimension that enables him to view events from a variety of perspectives. His experiences outside Mount Allegro have politicized him without radicalizing him; he is better able to take a more central position, balancing—like a fulcrum—left and right, insider and outsider. Mangione, however, does not sit contentedly in the middle of the road. His main interest becomes examining social injustices from a nonpartisan point of view. His multicultural perspective requires that he reach beyond partisan politics for solutions to social injustices, beyond the politics of difference that divide immigrants from natives, rich from poor, black from white. And it is from this suprapolitical stance that Mangione presents not only his story but the history of the America he has experienced.

Structured chronologically, *An Ethnic at Large* charts the development of Mangione's career as a writer and civil servant and dramatizes the cross-cultural experiences he encounters in America. This book differs most noticeably from his others by eliminating the distance Mangione had earlier maintained between the overall narrative voice and the voice of the protagonist. In *An Ethnic at Large* we sense that the narrator and protagonist are one and the same; the events are recounted in more of a historical or journalistic fashion, compared to the more dramatic style of *Mount Allegro* in which the narrative voice seems at times almost omniscient, especially in the earlier family scenes. Much of *Mount Allegro* seems almost mythic, as though it could be just as alive today as it was for Mangione when he lived through it. At the opposite extreme is *An Ethnic at Large*, which is presented more as a historical document in which Mangione sets himself up as a participant in and an observer of American life. As a historical character, Mangione is entitled to recount what he has witnessed during a period of great economic and social change in America. The writing then becomes an account of the narrator's coming of age during America's roaring twenties, the Great Depression, through World War II (including visits to the White House) and the McCarthy era.

*An Ethnic at Large* begins with Mangione recounting his sense of alienation as he peers through the picket fence that separates the inner world of his Sicilian home from the outside American world. Unlike the persona of *Mount Allegro*, who viewed a self composed of two lives, Sicilian and American, the protagonist in *An Ethnic at Large* speaks of a third life, "the one I lived with myself, which gradually was to dictate the secret resolve to break away from my relatives" (13). This became a fantasy life, nurtured by daydreams and books "read clandestinely in the bathroom or under the bed" because his mother "believed that too much reading could drive a person insane" (14).

Unlike Mangione's earlier works, *An Ethnic at Large* concentrates on the development of this third life as adolescent fantasies become adult realities. Mangione's education (both in the classroom and on the streets) enables this process to occur; both types of experience figure prominently in the writer's first stage of creating an American identity. For his parents that education became a source of concern:

> The American school system, for him [Mangione's father], symbolized everything that outraged him about his adopted country. His diatribes on the subject were of such eloquence as to make us feel guilty for daring to like any of our teachers. Beneath his fury was the conviction that they were encouraging immorality, disrupting family life, and undermining his position as the head of his family. (18)

Though education created a gap between son and immigrant parents, a distance that his parents feared, Mangione would never be able to totally cut himself off from his Sicilian origins.

His early ambitions to be a writer were nurtured by his becoming the editor of his high-school paper. Mangione boldly changed the format to resemble that of *Time* magazine, a move that won the paper a silver trophy for excellence in Cornell University's annual contest for high-school papers. It also brought him recognition by Henry R. Luce, one of *Time*'s founders, who in a congratulatory letter expressed the hope of seeing Mangione in the near future. Mangione interpreted this as a job offer. Upon finding out there were no openings at the magazine for a high-school student, Mangione, encouraged by Luce, went on to major in English at Syracuse University. His work on the *Daily Orange* (the school's newspaper, for which he wrote a daily column called "Muse-ings") brought him in touch with some of the best writers of the times who passed through Syracuse. These included Edna St. Vincent Millay, Carl Sandburg, John Cowper Powys, and Thornton Wilder, among the many. Mangione soon began devoting more time to his literary pursuits than to his coursework. He resurrected *The Chap Book*, the college's literary magazine, and gained national attention when he published a Stephen Crane short story that he had discovered in the magazine files of the university library.[24] College life marks the beginning of Mangione's conscious movement away from a Sicilian identity. He even escapes an Italian fraternity in order to separate himself from those who had created "a miniature ghetto" by banding together "to fortify themselves against the fear of being surrounded by a hostile people" (36).

From college, Mangione follows a distinctly American path. His earlier encounters with mainstream American writers had strengthened his belief in the possibility of realizing his dream of becoming a writer; his bachelor's degree would enable him to realize his dream of leaving the Rochester ghetto (Mount Allegro) behind. Upon graduation he lands a job in Manhattan with *Time*; much to his dismay it is in the Business and Finance Department, in which he has scant knowledge and no interest. After he quits the job in 1931, perhaps the worst year of the Great Depression, he takes on odd clerical jobs, reviews books for *The New Republic*, works in the library of Cooper Union Institute, and eventually lands work with a New York publishing firm. All this time he is also trying to keep his literary aspirations alive.

His interest in writing and his encounters with American avant-garde artists lead him to dismiss the "art for art's sake" cult and to realize that "no writer worth his salt could turn his back on social injustice" (49). For a brief time he attends meetings of the New York John Reed Club, whose motto was "Art is a Class Weapon." Though uncomfortable with party-line politics, Mangione contributes to the cause by writing articles and reviews for such left-wing publications as *New Masses*, the *Partisan Review*, and *The Daily Worker*, most of which he published under the pen names Mario Michele and his baptismal name Gerlando. Most of his writing during the thirties, primarily book reviews, was done for *The New Republic*. His first assignment was reviewing Alberto Moravia's *The Indifferent Ones* in 1931. He continued writing for *The New Republic* and the New York *Herald Tribune* until 1937, when he left New York to work for the New Deal. In the course of this period of politicization, Mangione came to understand the terrible threat that rising European fascism presented to the world.

As he worked to understand it better, he befriended Carlo Tresca, an Italian anti-Fascist and anarchist who came to America in the early 1900s to aid the exploited Italian immigrant laborers. During this same period Mangione also read Sicilian writers, interviewed Luigi Pirandello, and convinced the publishing firm that employed him to accept the work of Italian anti-Fascist writer Ignazio Silone. Later, his left-wing publications and his friendship with Tresca proved to haunt his first trip to Italy, during which his mail was censored and his movements monitored by Fascist authorities. This first trip, recounted in both *Mount Allegro* and in *An Ethnic at Large*, both reminded him of his Sicilian influences and strengthened his fledgling identity as an American. Upon his return from Italy, Mangione (by now fiercely anti-Fascist) quit his publishing job in New York and went to Washington to join the New Deal as an "information specialist" with the U.S. Resettlement Administration, which later became the Farm Security Administration.

During this time, Mangione shared a house with two of the top executives of the Works Progress Administration's Federal Writers' Project, Henry G. Alsberg and Clair Laning. Because of his previous experience in the publishing field, Mangione was offered a job in the Federal Writers' Project as national coordinating editor.[25] A highlight that Mangione writes about during this period was receiving an invitation to Sunday supper at the White House. In 1939, the Writers' Project lost its Federal sponsorship and Mangione was among those dismissed. He took some time off to concentrate on his literary interests. In 1942 he completed *Mount Allegro*, which he began in the summer of 1939 at the Yaddo artists' retreat. By this time he had become friends with a number of American writers, including cultural critic Kenneth Burke, on whose New Jersey farm Mangione continued writing *Mount Allegro*. Encounters with writers and critics of this period served to foster Mangione's education; his frequent discussions with Burke enabled him to "gain a more intelligent perspective on the dialectics of the thirties" (*Ethnic* 270); such encounters also would strengthen Mangione's identity as an American writer who the intellectual community would judge not by his background but by his writing and his ideas.

Shortly before the United States entered World War II, Mangione was invited to join the public relations staff of the U.S. Department of Justice to help publicize the national registration of aliens of enemy nations; he was appointed special assistant to the U.S. commissioner of immigration and naturalization, in which position he became the custodian agent for a selective internment program of aliens of enemy nationality, a program sponsored by the Department of Justice, which interned ten thousand aliens, only two-hundred and fifty of whom were Italians. In that position he traveled to a number of detention centers gathering first-hand information about the conditions he observed. Mangione's sensitivity to his own ethnicity enabled him to see things from a multicultural perspective, and thus he was able to identify with the Japanese, German, and Italian Americans who were kept (some merely on grounds of suspicion) in America's versions of concentration camps.[26] Mangione refers to the experience as a reminder that "we were engaged in a war of hopelessly conflicting wills . . . that had thrust us into the shameful position of locking up people for their beliefs" (352).

In 1944, Mangione received an invitation to spend a weekend at the White House, an invitation he seriously considered refusing because of an earlier commitment to attend his parents' wedding anniversary. His parents excused his absence only after being assured that he had not been summoned to the White House for the purposes of taking on a dangerous overseas spy mission. The White House weekend episode served to mark the end of what Mangione calls his "apprenticeship as an American."

> By then I was well into the process of discovering who I was and what I was up against. I had learned how to protect myself from the bruising paradoxes of everyday American life, and how to cope with the ever-recurring sensation of being a foreigner in my own native land. That I had managed to hold my own in the American mainstream struck me as something of a miracle but one which I could in part attribute to a growing awareness of my own worth as well as to a propensity for the comic. (*Ethnic* 367)

Later, during the McCarthy era, his "foreignness," in spite
of his years of dedicated public service, would come back to
haunt him. A neighbor reported to Mangione that two government men had been questioning her and had asked if she
had seen any foreign-looking people around Mangione's apartment, to which she had replied, "Yes, his parents." During the
same period, Mangione was called to testify before an executive session of the House Un-American Activities Committee, as well as its Senate counterpart, headed by the notorious
Joseph McCarthy. Never having been a member of the Communist party, Mangione was of no further use to either committee and never heard from them again.

In the final chapter of *An Ethnic at Large*, Mangione
reveals the resolution he has come to regarding his recurring
identity crisis. Unlike those who would spend a lifetime har-
boring an anger generated by experiences of prejudice, or those
whose identities suffered conflicting self-images throughout
their entire lives, Mangione found a compromise by

> . . . becoming an ethnic at large, with one foot in my Sicilian heritage,
> the other in the American mainstream. By this cultural gymnastic
> stance, I could derive strength from my past and a feeling of hope for
> my present. Rarely did I encounter in the American world the sageness
> and love of life I found among my Sicilian relatives; but theirs was an
> old and static world which lacked the spirit of enterprise and faith in
> the future that firmly attached me to that admixture of compatriots
> known as Americans. (369–70)

With *An Ethnic at Large*, Mangione finally presents his
embassy, an embassy built by a man who can move comfortably and confidently in two worlds, whose knowledge of one
assists his movement in the other. Thus Mangione clearly establishes himself as an accomplished writer whose major works il-
luminate the Italian-American experience while providing insights into the complexities of ethnic American culture. Over
the years since the publication of *An Ethnic at Large*, Mangione
has continued to serve as an ambassador and interpreter of

Italian-American culture. He reviews books, presents talks, encourages younger writers, and continues to examine and chronicle the Italian-American experience. He is currently at work on a monumental social history of Italian Americans. *An Ethnic at Large* completed the building of his Italian-American home, or better, as Ben Morreale has observed:

> Mangione seems finally to have reached home. . . . The child in *Mount Allegro* had become an American. Yet the memory of another identity remains in those four books, like a deposit of that sea the color of wine and the pipes' lament echoing the mountains of Sicily—and the father's predictions that he would be half and half. ("Mangione and the Yearning for Home" 41)

In the same article, Morreale suggests that all of Mangione's work involves a search for this home: "In Sicilian there is no equivalent to the English word *home* with all its yearning sentiment. In American English the yearning for home looms large, as if all groups have searched for an identity once having left the home of Europe" (41). Each of Mangione's four autobiographical works essentially maps the route he has taken to reach his home. He has, in effect, found his multicultural identity through his writing. From an early shrine to villa, to *palazzo*, and finally with an embassy, Mangione has documented the evolution of not only an Italian American but of the outsider who has become insider through the American houses he has built with words.

## Conclusion

As Viscusi concluded in "*Il caso*":

> For *la casa italo-americana* must do more than offer shelf space to our old Caruso records or a place in the garden to bury the figtree in winter; it must do even more than impress our cousins; it must turn its face outward, as the embassy does, and must surely keep its inward gaze, reminding us of the astonishing doubling of our minds that makes us—American Italians, Italian Americans—what we are. (8)

A thorough history of Italian-American autobiography will require more essays and certainly deserves more book-length studies; the houses are as different as they are many. Jerre Mangione is only one of many gifted writers who came to an Italian-American identity through writing, but his works, more extensive than those of any other Italian-American writer, represent the struggles faced and the progress gained by Italians who have forged a bridge over the gap between what was Italian and what was American. Other accounts can be found in the early fiction and poetry of Italian Americans, most of which is heavily autobiographical. Pietro DiDonato's *Christ in Concrete*, Mari Tomasi's *Like Lesser Gods*, Joseph Tusiani's *Gente Mia*, Mario Puzo's *The Fortunate Pilgrim*, and Helen Barolini's *Umbertina* are a few of the many, too numerous to list here.[27] These writers, all children and grandchildren of immigrants, by writing their life stories share the process by which they have created, in James Olney's terms, their personal metaphors, their ways of seeing the world (*Metaphors* 34); they also give voice to a distinct American subculture.

## Notes

I am indebted to Jerre Mangione and A. LaVonne Brown Ruoff for their guidance in producing this article.

1.  This notion of the autobiography as house is a metaphor that appears in Robert F. Sayre's essay "Autobiography and the Making of America," in which he compares autobiography to architecture, specifically to houses:

    American autobiographers . . . are mainly different from others
    according to the ways in which America has been different. America is
    an idea. Her autobiographers are like American houses, with many
    important imitations of foreign styles—the English Puritan, the
    Palladian Historical, the Mercantile Journalistic, to suggest a few—and
    mixtures of these styles with new forms and experiences. . . . Autobi-
    ography has been a way for the builder to pass on his work and his
    lessons to later generations. . . . (155-56)

2.  Though Italians have been part of America's history since Columbus's voyage, only in retrospect can we establish a distinct

Italian-American literary tradition that begins with accounts of explorers, missionaries (Father Samuel Mazzuchelli's *Memoirs*; Sister Blandina Segale, *At the End of the Santa Fe Trail*), and statesmen.

3. In her introduction to *The Dream Book*, Helen Barolini offers an explanation of why Italian immigrants did not encourage their children to write: "When you don't read, you don't write. When your frame of reference is a deep distrust of education because it is an attribute of the very classes who have exploited you and your kind for as long as memory carries, then you do not encourage a reverence for books among your children. You teach them the practical arts not the imaginative ones" (4).

4. Barolini, in her introduction to *The Dream Book*, points out that as late as 1949, the date of the first published survey of Italian-American writers (Olga Peragallo, *Italian American Authors*), the U.S. Census counted a little over four and one-half million Italian Americans, fewer than a million of whom spoke English, a small number to expect many writers to emerge from.

5. We must keep in mind that, although the experiences of migration from Northern and Southern Italy share many similarities, they share as many differences, especially in sociopolitical development. Though the written tradition of the Italian autobiography can be traced back to Dante and continues developing through such prominent figures as Benvenuto Cellini, Giambattista Vico, Benedetto Croce, and so on, we must remember that these writers are *prominenti*, representatives of an Italian experience that differs greatly from that of the immigrant. Italian-American autobiographers, then, can be seen as creating a new tradition and are often doing something that, in the minds of most Italian immigrants, is considered "American." Giuseppe Pitre and Solomone Marino have both done important work on southern Italian folk culture that has yet to be translated into English. Their work is listed in an excellent bibliography on Italian folklore compiled by Italo Calvino in *Fiabe italiane*.

6. For example, in America *omertà* is often pointed to as an attribute of Mafia members who hold their tongues under fear of death. Unfortunately, the Mafia, as represented in American popular culture, has become the filter through which characteristics of Italian-American life have primarily been perceived.

7. For a survey of the Italian-American movement from an oral- to a literate-based culture, see Fred L. Gardaphe, "From Oral Tradition to Written Word: Toward an Ethnographic Approach to Literary Criticism."

8. William Boelhower, in *Immigrant Autobiography: (Four Versions of the Italian American Self)*, presents the most thorough analysis to date on the subject of Italian-American autobiography. Rose Basile

Green's pioneer study *The Italian-American Novel* presents some
of the earliest Italian-American writing and examines autobiographical aspects of Italian-American fiction. And in *The Ethnic I*, James
Craig Holte provides valuable information on the autobiographies
of Frank Capra, Edward Corsi, Leonard Covello, Lee Iacocca, and
Jerre Mangione.

9. For an interesting account of the Italian and English language encounter, see Robert Viscusi, "Circles of the Cyclopes: Schemes of
Recognition in Italian American Discourse."

10. For excellent discussions of the similarities between early Italian
immigrant autobiographies and the *Autobiography* of Benjamin Franklin,
see James Craig Holte, "Benjamin Franklin and Italian-American
Narratives" and his "The Representative Voice: Autobiography and
the Ethnic Experience."

11. Panunzio already had some education when he came to the United
States. D'Angelo had none; he learned English on his own while trying to survive as an unskilled laborer.

12. Cavalleri was the surname given to Rosa by Ets; Rosa's legal surname was Cassetari.

13. Rosa does not reveal the real names of those who played major roles
in her life. She fears that what she says will somehow harm those
who were still alive at the time of her telling.

14. "Bugiarno," the pseudonym given for Rosa's native village, can mean
"no lie," *bugiare* being the Italian infinitive of the verb "to lie."
"Cannaletto," or "cane bed," is the name chosen as a pseudonym
for the convent that the wild young Rosa was sent to for her education. Since Ets does not tell us whether she knew Italian, it is
anyone's guess as to whether Rosa or Ets made up these names.

15. Mangione received the 1989 Pennsylvania Governor's Award for Excellence in the Arts; among his many awards are: a Guggenheim
(1946) and a Fulbright Fellowship (1965), two National Endowment for the Arts grants (1980 and 1984), and the prestigious Italian "Empedocles" prize (1984). In 1971 Italy named Mangione
*Commendatore* and awarded him the "Star of Italian Solidarity." He
has also received two honorary degrees: Doctor of Letters from the
University of Pennsylvania, 1980; Doctor of Humane Letters from the
State University of New York at Brockport, 1986.

16. In "Finale," a new chapter to *Mount Allegro* added in 1981, Mangione
lamented the total disappearance of his old neighborhood. Today, a
historic marker, dedicated in a ceremony by the City of Rochester,
marks the site of the "Mount Allegro" area.

17. The publication of *Mount Allegro* as fiction was done against Mangione's
wishes. In response to his publisher's demands, Mangione fictionalized
his characters' names prior to publication; thus the Mangiones became

the Amorosos; Jerre becomes Gerlando (Mangione's actual given name). For a thorough account of the genre-jumping *Mount Allegro* experienced—from novel to children's literature and finally to memoir, see Boelhower's chapter on Mangione in *Immigrant Autobiography*.

18. These developmental stages of Italian-American autobiography are similar to the three stages of African-American autobiography identified by Stephen Butterfield in *Black American Autobiography*. Butterfield's stages: the slave narrative, the search for identity, and the politicized rebirth, can also be traced in Italian-American autobiography and can provide a useful framework for reading Italian-American autobiographies.

19. In "Song of the Bicentennial," poet Joseph Tusiani expresses this duality: "Two languages, two lands, perhaps two souls . . . / Am I a man or two strange halves of one" (7). For an account of how a sense of this duality can be read in ethnic American authors, see Jerre Mangione, "A Double Life: The Fate of the Urban Ethnic."

20. "A peasant woman was working in the fields and found a bomb which she thought was a dud. When she picked it up, the thing exploded and hurt her badly. An American Negro soldier . . . rushed over to help her. He was bent over her trying to stop the bleeding when a jeep full of American military policemen drove by and saw him. They must have thought the Negro was raping the woman. Anyway, they shot him dead. They never bothered to see what had happened to the woman. They tossed the Negro's body into the jeep like a sack of onions and drove away . . . " (*Reunion* 83).

21. The present edition of the book (1985) is published by Transaction Books and includes a new concluding chapter. The main title reverts to that of the first edition.

22. Danilo Dolci is a social activist born in Trieste in northern Italy. He employed nonviolent techniques in dealing with Sicilian poverty and violence in order to show how people can create their own destiny. Dolci, only partly Italian, is an accomplished poet as well as an activist.

23. Nat Scammacca is another Sicilian American who returns to Sicily. Scammacca's story, yet to be translated into English, is a moving testament to the trials and tribulations of relocating an American self in Sicilian life. His works *Due Mondi* and *Sikano l'Americano!* relate Mangione's experience in reverse. More subjective than Mangione, Scammacca bares his self and intimately presents all the effects the reverse odyssey had on his psyche.

24. "The Cry of the Huckleberry Pudding" was the story Mangione tells us first appeared in an 1892 issue of the Syracuse *University Herald*. (*Ethnic* 44n).

25. Mangione's experience in the Federal Writers' Project is documented in his *The Dream and the Deal*, a social history.

26. Mangione reports that in one Immigration and Naturalization Service camp in Missoula, Montana, there were 250 Italian civilian aliens, "residents of the United States who had been arrested because they had been pro-Fascist journalists, active members of pro-Fascist organizations, or simply because there was some reason to suspect that their loyalty to Fascist Italy might be stronger than their loyalty to the American government. Among the latter were fathers of sons fighting in the American armed forces" (*Ethnic* 343).

27. For extensive bibliographies of Italian-American literature and criticism see Rose Basile Green, *The Italian American Novel*, and Anthony Tamburri, Paul Giordano, and Fred L. Gardaphe, *From the Margin: Writings in Italian Americana*. An examination of the role autobiography plays in Italian-American fiction can be found in Samuel J. Patti, "Autobiography: The Root of the Italian-American Narrative."

## Selected Bibliography

Arrighi, Antonio A. *The Story of Antonio: The Galley Slave*. New York: Revell, 1971.

Barolini, Helen, ed. *The Dream Book: An Anthology of Writings by Italian American Women*. New York: Schocken, 1985.

———. *Umbertina*. New York: Seaview, 1979.

Boelhower, William. *Immigrant Autobiography in the United States: (Four Versions of the Italian American Self)*. Verona: Essedue, 1982.

Butterfield, Stephen. *Black Autobiography*. Amherst: U of Massachusetts P, 1974.

Calvino, Italo. *Fiabe italiane*. 2 vols. Milan: Einaudi, 1956.

Cordasco, Francesco and Salvatore LaGumina. *Italians in the United States: A Bibliography of Reports, Texts, Critical Studies and Related Materials*. New York: Oriole, 1972.

Covello, Leonard and Guido D'Agostino. *The Heart Is the Teacher*. New York: McGraw, 1958.

D'Angelo, Pascal. *Son of Italy*. New York: Macmillan, 1924.

DiDonato, Pietro. *Christ in Concrete*. 1939. New York: Bobbs, 1966.

Ets, Marie Hall. *Rosa: The Life of an Italian Immigrant*. Minneapolis: U of Minnesota P, 1970.

Falassi, Alessandro. *Folklore by the Fireside: Text and Context of the Tuscan Veglia*. Austin: U of Texas P, 1980.

Franklin, Benjamin. *Autobiography*. Ed. Max Farrand. Berkeley: U of California P, 1949.

Gambino, Richard. *Blood of My Blood: The Dilemma of the Italian Americans*. New York: Doubleday, 1974.

Gardaphe, Fred L. "From Oral Tradition to Written Word: Toward an Ethnographically Based Literary Criticism." In *From the Margin: Writings in Italian Americana*, ed. Anthony Julian Tamburri, Paul Giordano, and Fred L. Gardaphe. West Lafayette: Purdue UP, 1991.

———. "Italian American Fiction: A Third Generation Renaissance." *MELUS* 14, no.3–4 (1987): 69–85.

Green, Rose Basile. *The Italian-American Novel*. Cranbury, NJ: Associated UP, 1974.

Gusdorf, Georges. "Conditions and Limits of Autobiography." In *Auto-biography: Essays Theoretical and Critical*, ed. James Olney. Princeton: Princeton UP, 1980. 28–48.

Holte, James Craig. "Benjamin Franklin and Italian-American Narratives." *MELUS* 5, no. 4 (1978): 99–102.

———. *The Ethnic I: A Sourcebook for Ethnic American Autobiography*. New York: Greenwood, 1988.

———. "The Representative Voice: Autobiography and the Ethnic Experience." *MELUS* 9, no. 2 (1982): 25–46.

Mangione, Jerre. "Comments." In *Contemporary Novelists*, ed. D. L. Kirkpatrick. 4th ed. New York: St. Martin's, 1986. 570–72.

———. "A Double Life: The Fate of the Urban Ethnic." In *Literature and the Urban Experience*, ed. Michael C. Jaye and Ann Chalmers Watts. New Brunswick: Rutgers UP, 1981. 169–83.

———. *The Dream and the Deal: The Federal Writers' Project 1935–1943*. 1972. Philadelphia: U of Pennsylvania P, 1983.

———. *An Ethnic at Large: A Memoir of America in the Thirties and Forties*. 1978. Philadelphia: U of Pennsylvania P, 1983.

———. *Mount Allegro*. 1943. New York: Harper, 1989.

———. *Night Search*. New York: Crown, 1965.

———. *A Passion for Sicilians: The World around Danilo Dolci*. 1968. New Brunswick: Transaction, 1985.

———. *Reunion in Sicily*. 1950. New York: Columbia UP, 1984.

———. *The Ship and the Flame*. New York: A. A. Wyn, 1948.

Mathias, Elizabeth, and Richard Raspa. *Italian Folktales in America: The Verbal Art of an Immigrant Woman*. Detroit: Wayne State UP, 1985.

Mazzuchelli, Samuel. *The Memoirs of Father Samuel Mazzuchelli, O.P.* Chicago: Priory, 1967.

Morreale, Ben. "Jerre Mangione: The Sicilian Sources." *Italian Americana*. 7.1 (1981): 5–17.

———. "Mangione and the Yearning for Home." *Fra Noi*, Nov. 1986, 41.

Napoli, Joseph. *A Dying Cadence: Memories of a Sicilian Childhood*. West Bethesda, MD: Marna, 1986.

Olney, James. *Metaphors of Self: The Meaning of Autobiography.* Princeton: Princeton UP, 1972.

Panella, Vincent. *The Other Side: Growing Up Italian in America.* Garden City: Doubleday, 1979.

Panunzio, Constantine. *The Soul of an Immigrant.* New York: Macmillan, 1921.

Patti, Samuel J. "Autobiography: The Root of the Italian-American Narrative." *Annali d'Italianistica* 4 (1986): 243–48. Eng. lang. ed.

Pellegrini, Angelo. *Americans by Choice.* New York: Macmillan, 1956.

Peragallo, Olga. *Italian-American Authors and Their Contribution to American Literature.* New York: S. F. Vanni, 1949.

Puzo, Mario. *The Fortunate Pilgrim.* New York: Atheneum, 1964.

Reilly, John M. "Literary Versions of Ethnic History from Upstate New York." In *Upstate Literature: Essays in Memory of Thomas F. O'Donnell,* ed. Frank Bergmann. Syracuse: Syracuse UP, 1985. 183–200.

Sayre, Robert F. "Autobiography and the Making of America." In *Autobiography: Essays Theoretical and Critical,* ed. James Olney. Princeton: Princeton UP, 1980. 146–68.

Scammacca, Nat. *Bye Bye America: Memories of a Sicilian American.* Eng. lang. ed., Trapani, Italy: Antigruppo Siciliano & Cross-Cultural Communications, 1986.

———. *Due Mondi.* Trapani, Italy: Antigruppo Siciliano & Cross-Cultural Communications, 1979.

———. *Sikano l'Americano!* Trapani, Italy: Antigruppo Siciliano & Cross–Cultural Communications, 1989.

Segale, Sister Blandina. *At the End of the Santa Fe Trail.* 1912. Milwaukee: Bruce, 1948.

Tamburri, Anthony Julian, Paul Giordano and Fred L. Gardaphe. eds. *From the Margin: Writings in Italian Americana.* West Lafayette: Purdue UP, 1991.

Tomasi, Mari. *Like Lesser Gods.* Milwaukee: Bruce, 1949.

Tusiani, Joseph. *Gente Mia.* Stone Park, IL: Italian Cultural Center, 1978.

Vergara, Joseph. *Love and Pasta.* New York: Harper, 1968.

Viscusi, Robert. "*Il caso della casa*: Stories of Houses in Italian America." In *The Family and Community Life of Italian Americans*, ed. Richard N. Juliani. Staten Island, NY: American Italian Historical Association, 1983. 1–9.

———. "Circles of the Cyclopes: Schemes of Recognition in Italian American Discourse." In *Italian Americans: New Perspectives in Italian Immigration and Ethnicity*, ed. Lydio F. Tomasi. New York: Center for Migration Studies, 1985. 209–19.

# The Ghetto and Beyond: First-Generation American-Jewish Autobiography and Cultural History

*Steven J. Rubin*

To have a sense of history one must consider *oneself* a piece of history.

—Alfred Kazin

## I

The central problem in the study of autobiography as cultural history lies in the duality of the genre itself. Although autobiography is indeed a valid record of social history, it is also undeniably an exploration of personal identity. By its very nature, autobiography is an assertion of the power of the individual; its purpose is to express subjective awareness. At the same time it is inescapably historical, reflecting the concerns of society and culture in general. Albert Stone, for example, in *Autobiographical Occasions and Original Acts*, points out that the effort to situate one's self within a particular time and place and thereby to determine one's historical self is not only one of the essential functions of autobiography but that which distinguishes it from fiction: "The struggle to see and state one's 'circumstanced' location in time and social space, and thereby to discover one's historical self, marks the commonly accepted difference between autobiography and fiction" (6). Because autobiography re-creates a collective past, it has become a particularly useful means of understanding cultural history. Although every autobiography is unique, revealing the idiosyncrasies of individual personality, it is also general, reflecting patterns of cultural and historical development. This essential duality—existing as both subjective and objective reality—has made autobiography an especially rich mode of minority expression. For the ethnic autobiographer, self-examination and cultural analysis have always been inseparable. In the hands of an oppressed people, autobiography is often a direct response to a society that has denied them their full individual freedoms. As James Olney maintains, "autobiography renders in a peculiarly direct and faithful way the experience and the vision of a people" (13).

Like other minority writers, many Jewish authors have turned to autobiography in an effort to understand and define the ethnic experience in America as well as their own subjective identities as American Jews. For Jewish immigrant writers—like Ludwig Lewisohn (1882–1955), Anzia Yezierska (1885–1970), and Mary Antin (1881–1949)—the autobiographical form offered a means of defining an uncertain identity within a new and often alien culture. Equally important, it provided a vehicle for linking personal history with that of the group—with an entire social process. In retelling the story of their lives, they re-created the collective history of their people. "It is because I understand my history, in its larger outlines, to be typical of many," explained Mary Antin in the introduction to her autobiography, *The Promised Land* (1912), "that I consider it worth recording. . . . Although I have written a genuine personal memoir, I believe that its chief interest lies in the fact that it is illustrative of scores of unwritten lives" (xiii).

For the next generation of American-Jewish writers—the first to be born in this country—the autobiographical form has been equally important. As the process of Americanization progressed and the sons and daughters of Jewish immigrants moved as rapidly as possible to enter the mainstream of American culture, the American-Jewish experience became increasingly difficult to describe. The social, intellectual, political, and economic freedom that Jews achieved by mid-century only served to complicate the story. For writers like Alfred Kazin (*A Walker in the City*, 1951), lost for a time between the old and the new, autobiography offered a means of reclaiming the past, of telling how it was and why it was important. Similarly, Meyer Levin (*In Search*, 1950) sought in autobiography a way of defining his ambiguous relationship to two cultures, a task with which he struggled throughout his career. As the second half of the twentieth century progressed, however, American-Jewish autobiography began to reflect the more assimilated, more secure role of the American Jew generally. The brash title of Norman Podhoretz's autobiography, *Making It* (1967), for example, seemed to sum up the mood of Jewish authors in the 1960s who believed themselves comfortably secure in the wider world of American intellectual life. Yet Podhoretz's recounting of his successful journey beyond the ghetto did not imply a general turning away from the fast-disappearing traditions of the Jewish community. On the contrary, *Making It* seemed to demonstrate, perhaps for the first time, that one need not abandon one's specifically Jewish heritage in order to partake in the riches of contemporary American culture.

The most recent examples of American-Jewish autobiography are neither laments of alienation nor celebrations of success. They are expressions of cultural retrieval, of a "reconquest" of Jewishness, and of the desire to link individual identity with that of the group. The themes of return and renewed commitment, often heard in the autobiographies of Alfred Kazin and Meyer Levin, became a dominant motif in American-Jewish autobiographies of the 1970s and 1980s. Both Herbert Gold in *My Last Two Thousand Years* (1972) and Irving Howe in *A Margin of Hope* (1982), for example, delineated the forces that moved them from marginality to assimilation and then ironically back to the specifically Jewish aspects of their own, personal history.

Although very different in style and content, the autobiographies of Kazin, Levin, Gold, and Howe reveal similar efforts to articulate and to resolve the conflict between secular Americanism and Jewish consciousness. Moreover, in spite of their eclectic nature, all reflect parallel patterns of personal development as well as similar preoccupations with certain significant world events. Kazin, Levin, Gold, and Howe, for instance, were deeply affected by the traumatic events of the Holocaust, and all struggled in their autobiographies to come to some understanding—both on personal and collective terms—of the meaning of those events. The Holocaust, as Howe admitted, led to "reconsiderations" of what it meant to be a Jew, even for the most secular. The creation of the state of Israel became for each of these authors another highly meaningful world event that by necessity helped define Jewish personality. Having witnessed the death of six million fellow Jews and the subsequent establishment of a Jewish homeland, Kazin, Levin, Gold, and Howe came to understand—in spite of varied political loyalties—the significance of Israel for themselves and for the future of world Jewry.

There are other similarities as well. Each of these autobiographies reveals a corresponding mode of self-discovery, one that invariably involves a reconciliation of past and present aspects of Jewish personality, an intellectual "return" to Jewishness, and ultimately a renewed commitment to peoplehood. This "reconquest," as Howe calls it, is most clearly and specifically defined in *A Margin of Hope* (the most intellectually conceived of all the works considered in this essay), but it is also present in the autobiographies of Kazin, Levin, Gold, and—in a somewhat abbreviated form—that of Podhoretz as well. The need to articulate one's personal link to Jewish culture and history appears greater for Gold and Howe in the 1970s and 1980s than for Kazin and Levin in the 1950s; the further removed from the "source," the greater the need to reestablish one's connection. Nevertheless, this pattern of rediscovery and reaffirmation not only helps delineate personality in the autobiographies of all of the above writers but often the actual structure of their texts as well.

Although over thirty years separate the publication of these works, all share similar thematic concerns. Moreover, Kazin, Levin, Gold, and Howe (all sons of immigrants) found in autobiography the perfect vehicle for expressing those concerns.

Their autobiographies exist as records of individual lives as well as an entire social process. Each, too, reflects the changing and complex cultural history of the American Jew in the twentieth century.

## II

Born in the Brownsville section of Brooklyn in 1915, Kazin was one who "made it" in America. The son of an immigrant house painter, Kazin quickly succeeded in the wider intellectual world of Manhattan: first as a book reviewer and then as an editor of the *New Republic*; later as an author, critic, and teacher. *A Walker in the City* is the first of three autobiographical works Kazin has written to date, and the one that fully evokes his early life in Brownsville and the relationship of his past to his present self. It is also the work that most clearly defines the tension between these two aspects of personality—both through the book's theme and through its structure.

The autobiography contains two conflicting motifs, and the author establishes both of them before the narrative begins. Kazin uses as his frontispiece Alfred Stieglitz's famous photograph of crowded immigrants on board ship, "The Steerage." Yet the epigraph of *A Walker in the City* is from Whitman's poem "Crossing Brooklyn Ferry": "The glories strung like beads on my smallest sights and hearings— / on the walk in the street, and the passage over the river." Thus the reader is presented at the outset with Kazin's objective correlative for the two aspects of his personal history and the two themes he wishes to develop. On the one hand are his immigrant roots and the richness of his Jewish culture, which he presents with lyrical affection. Yet at the same time there is the pull on the young author of all that lies "beyond Brownsville," the history of America, the poetry of Whitman and Emily Dickinson, and the paintings of Thomas Eakins and Winslow Homer. *A Walker in the City* is about the immigrants in Stieglitz's photograph and about the emotional ties that bind Kazin the adult to the world of his parents and to his youth. But it is also about Kazin's own, almost compulsive need to escape his ghetto roots and his great desire to enter Whitman's America: "the great world that was anything just out of Brownsville" (172).

*A Walker in the City* is divided into four chapters, each signifying a particular landscape within Kazin's past and present Brownsville and the associations it recalls. The book's structure is not linear but emerges instead in a Proustian manner as Kazin links physical sensation with personal memory: the sights, sounds, smells, and tastes of the present transport the author back into his past.

The first chapter, "From the Subway to the Synagogue," derives its title from the direction the present narrator takes as he returns to Brownsville, exits from the subway, and strolls slowly toward his old synagogue. On the way, he pauses at each personal landmark: his former school, "I went sick with all my old fear of it"; Belmont Avenue with its open street market; Pitkin Avenue, "Brownsville's show street"; and finally the synagogue, "one of the oldest things in Brownsville and in the world." All that Kazin encounters and all that he remembers are rendered in specific, concrete terms. Again, like Proust's *Remembrance of Things Past*, sensations evoke memory, and what is remembered is recounted with great attention to detail, revealing, as Allen Guttmann notes, "an almost obsessive desire to see in the present a past that was" (90).

In the second chapter, "The Kitchen," Kazin recalls the image of his mother, the force that held the family together: "All my memories of that kitchen are dominated by the nearness of my mother sitting all day long at her sewing machine, by the clacking of the treadle against the linoleum floor. . . . The kitchen was her life. Year by year, as I began to take in her fantastic capacity for labor and her anxious zeal, I realized it was ourselves she kept stitched together" (66–67).

Kazin's evocation of past intimacy reinforces his present dislocation and allows him to relive a youth marked by familial closeness. Yet the solidarity of the immigrant family is only one aspect of the wider theme of peoplehood expressed throughout: "So it was: we had always to be together: believers and non-believers, we were a people; I was of that people. Unthinkable to go one's own way, to doubt or to escape the fact that I was a Jew. . . . The most terrible word was *aleyn*, alone" (60).

The second half of *A Walker in the City*—chapter 3, "The Block Beyond," and chapter 4, "Summer: The Way to Highland Park"—concentrates on the other side of Kazin's dichotomy, the Whitmanesque America that lies "beyond Brownsville": "*Beyond* was anything old and American—the name *Fraunces Tavern* repeated to us on a school excursion; the eighteenth-century muskets and glazed oil paintings on the wall; the very streets, the deeper you got into Brooklyn, named after generals of the Revolutionary War—Putnam, Gates, Kosciusko, DeKalb, Lafayette, Pulaski" (90).

"Beyond," too, was the world of American art and literature: the poems of Whitman and Dickinson, the paintings of Eakins, Sargent, Sloan, and Winslow Homer. But even as Kazin declares his desire to embrace "my city, my country," the book's tension reasserts itself, for in the last pages Kazin expresses once again his dominant fears of permanent alienation, of existing always on the periphery of mainstream American culture: "I felt then that I stood outside all that, that I would be alien forever, . . . I read as if books would fill my every gap, legitimize my strange quest for the American past, remedy my every flaw, let me in at last into the great world that was anything just out of Brownsville" (172).

There is a tendency to view Kazin's almost compulsive need to move "beyond" as a statement of assimilation, to see Kazin as one who willingly abandoned his past to enter, like Mary Antin, "the promised land." In fact, the circumstances of his subsequent career (successful author, critic, editor of the *New Republic*) would seem to indicate that Kazin was able to enter easily and quickly the wider world of American intellectual life. But the structure and language of *A Walker in the City*, as well as its thematic tension, indicate that this is not entirely the case. Emotionally and metaphorically, Kazin voyages backward into the past instead of forward toward an ecumenical future. *A Walker in the City*, for example, begins: "Every time I go back to Brownsville," indicating the motif of return as well as repetition. And Kazin's constant fears of somehow not being able to extend his personal boundaries beyond Brownsville are coupled with a conflicting anxiety of losing his deep emotional ties to the very culture he wishes to leave behind. Moreover, the book's language, its lyrical and at times nostalgic style, reflects the author's deep affection for the world he describes. Kazin revisits his past in order to relive it, to experience in adulthood the world he has with some ambivalence left behind.

This apparent contradiction is understandable when one reads *A Walker in the City* not as social doctrine but as self-interpretation, as a re-creation of a life, and as the equivalent of Kazin's own unresolved feelings. In a general sense, it is also a replica of the entire process of assimilation and acculturation. Accordingly, the past is seen as intellectually and materially inferior, but also as a time of familial warmth, of meaningful ceremony, and of Jewish togetherness. How to preserve the one without sacrificing the other is a question that has preoccupied American-Jewish authors for most of the twentieth century.

To fully understand the conflicting pulls of Kazin's life, one must examine his two later autobiographies, both of which help explain Kazin's link to his past, to Stieglitz's immigrants, and to "the old women in their shapeless flowered housedresses and ritual wigs" (6) that inhabited Brownsville. Both *Starting Out in the Thirties* (1965) and *New York Jew* (1978) are essentially literary and cultural memoirs, capturing the intellectual climate of the times and recalling Kazin's close associations with critics, authors, and editors. Nevertheless, the central conflict of belonging versus independence, of alienation versus assimilation, has not been resolved and is again expressed in both later works. "Lonely you were born," Kazin laments at the outset of *Starting Out in the Thirties*, "and lonely you would die—you were lonely as a Jew and lonely in a strange land" (45). And although there are few such personal confessions, as Kazin recounts his growing success and acceptance in the world "beyond," *Starting Out in the Thirties* concludes with a startling and forceful image of Jewish suffering that suddenly brings the reader full circle back to Brownsville, back to Stieglitz's photographs, back to the concept of peoplehood. As World War II came to a close, Kazin in London recalls his reaction while watching newsreels of the liberated concentration camps:

> One day in the spring of 1945, when the war against Hitler was almost won, I sat in a newsreel theater in Piccadilly looking at the first films of newly liberated Belsen. On the screen, sticks in black-and-white prison garb leaned on a wire, staring dreamily at the camera; other sticks shuffled about, or sat vaguely on the ground, next to an enormous pile of bodies, piled up like cordwood, from which protruded legs, arms, heads. A few guards were collected sullenly in a corner, and for a moment a British Army bulldozer was shown digging an enormous hole in the ground. Then the sticks would come back on the screen, hanging on the wire, looking at us.
>
> It was unbearable. People coughed in embarrassment, and in embarrassment many laughed. (166)

Kazin could not have ended his book on a more moving note, nor one that better clarifies for the reader why Kazin was moved to write a book such as *A Walker in the City* in the first place, why it was necessary for him to recapture the past of his parents' generation—and to link his own, personal history with the tragic history of his people.

*New York Jew*, Kazin's third autobiography, continues where *Starting Out in the Thirties* left off and recounts events from 1942 to 1978. Again, like *Starting Out in the Thirties*, the book is primarily a portrait of the contemporary literary and cultural scene. But as he does in his first two autobiographies, Kazin again moves back in time to explore earlier, more personal issues. Here, for instance, Kazin explains in full his choice of

Stieglitz's photograph and its deeper significance as frontispiece for *A Walker in the City*:

> I was another slave to Stieglitz's eye. I had become one from the moment I had seen his great photograph "The Steerage" and had imagined my mother as the woman who dominates the composition as she stands on the lower deck draped in an enormous towel, her back always to me. In some way Stieglitz's photographs of old New York possessed my soul, my unconscious past. His was the New York my mother and father had stumbled along as frightened young immigrants. My mother seemed to me frozen forever on that lower deck. (140)

Although *New York Jew* is mostly concerned with secular issues, the thematic tension that marked Kazin's earlier autobiographies is again evident. Written thirty-three years after the incident that dramatically concluded *Starting Out in the Thirties*, *New York Jew* once more bears witness to Kazin's deep connection to the victims of Nazi extermination. For Kazin, the Holocaust would become "the nightmare that would bring everything else into question, that will haunt me to my last breath" (39). Yet Kazin is also painfully aware of his inability to express the ineffable: "the impossibility of finding words for Jewish martyrdom." "The Jews could not state their case without seeming to overstate it," Kazin laments with frustration at the conclusion of *New York Jew*, "the world was getting tired of our complaint" (435–36).

In 1970 Kazin was moved to visit Belsen on the twenty-fifth anniversary of its liberation, and from there, on to Israel "to sweeten the pill." But even here, Kazin worries about Jewish survival: "there is no ease in Zion. There is never any safe homecoming for Jews" (424). Once again, Kazin recalls the image of Stieglitz's Jews and of their—and of his parents'—"overpowering sense of effort, of strain, of will" to survive as a people, be it in Israel or in the ghetto of Brownsville. The reader begins to understand Kazin's irrevocable bond to the fate of Jews everywhere ("We were a people; I was of that people"), as well as his emotional attachment to the Brownsville of his youth. One comprehends too the irony of the author's loving and lyrical portrayal as an adult of the place he so desperately wished to escape as a young man.

In each of Kazin's three autobiographies, the narrator presents himself as a secular being, as one who either wishes to or has succeeded in the larger world "beyond" Brownsville. But Kazin's links to his former self are undeniable, as are the implications of his past history to his present personality. And surely Kazin's choice of a title for his latest autobiography symbolically and perhaps with some degree of irony proclaims his belief in the inescapability of cultural identity.

In "The Self as History: Reflections on Autobiography," Kazin explained what he believed to be the important relationship between the personal and the historical, and the need for the autobiographer to "emphasize the self as a creature of history" (76). The autobiographic form, what Kazin called "self living history," allowed him to re-create experience that was "personal but not private." Kazin's delineation of the past, Jewish aspects of his present, American self is a significant part of his individual story and one that demonstrates his need to interpret his personal history in terms of that of the group. As we shall see, Kazin was not alone among American-Jewish autobiographers who chose to recount the events of their lives and their understanding of self in relation to a collective past and to the specifically Jewish aspects of contemporary events.

Authors have traditionally turned to autobiography for diverse reasons. In Kazin's case, there were different motivations at various points in his career. *A Walker in the City* is an attempt to reach an equilibrium between present and past selves, to understand the importance of the past through the development of the present narrator. Both *Starting Out in the Thirties* and *New York Jew* are primarily intellectual and cultural memoirs, efforts to define the author's own subjective history within the context of the world at large. Meyer Levin's *In Search* (1950) shares both of these objectives. It is an attempt to organize the chaos of contemporary history in terms of individual identity. At the same time, *In Search* is a personal inquiry; its purpose is to resolve the conflicting aspects of Levin's own personality.

The author of seventeen novels and numerous short stories, Levin sought in autobiography a means of defining his ambiguous relationship to two cultures, a task with which he struggled throughout his career. *The Old Bunch* (1937), Levin's best novel, portrayed a group of Jewish characters fighting their way out of Chicago's West Side ghetto and into the mainstream of American society. *In Search* is Levin's exploration of the duality in his own life between the secular and the Jewish aspects of self. Levin's "search" therefore was for a basis of understanding of the opposing forces within his personality and, on a larger scale, of how a Jew functions within a majority culture that is not historically his own. That which is subtly evoked or symbolically suggested in Kazin's *A Walker in the City* is here overtly stated and analyzed at every juncture. The basic dichotomy of Levin's existence and the central issue of the book is stated early: "Was I an American, or a Jew?" Levin asks; "Could one be both?" (69). *In Search* is, as Levin asserts at the outset, "a book about being a Jew." It is a long work—over five hundred pages; the tone is mostly confessional, and the mood is one of introspection. The events of the past, both political and personal, are recounted from the vantage point of the present and interpreted through Levin's acute sense of his Jewish identity. Levin was a writer who had roots in America, in Jewish traditions, and in Israel. In almost every episode he assesses each of these factors in order to develop some kind of personal equilibrium.

*In Search* is divided into three parts, each representing one aspect of the synthesis of his personality: America, Europe, and Israel. The headings also reflect Levin's physical movement, his journey from Chicago to his Old World roots in Eastern Europe, and then to Israel and an acceptance of a new, "bicultural" identity. Levin's odyssey back to what was then Poland ("the source land of European Jewry") is not unlike Kazin's return to Brownsville and similarly suggests the author's renewed connection to his ancestral roots. Levin must return to

Vilna, the place of his parents' birth, to understand his own connection with peoplehood before he can move forward to a Zionistic future in Israel.

Part 1, "America: The Self-Accused," begins with Levin's early memories of life in Chicago where social tensions between hostile minorities resulted in a premature sense of alienation: "My dominant childhood memory is of fear and shame at being a Jew" (5). Levin describes this and other vicissitudes of growing up Jewish in Chicago as well as his early years as a writer, first as a student at the University of Chicago, and then as an apprentice and a reporter for the *Chicago Daily News*. One learns of his early efforts at fiction: short stories published (with some regret) in "Jewish" journals and his first "American" novels, *Reporter* (1929) and *Frankie and Johnny* (1930). Part 1 also describes Levin's early fascination with Zionism, his first trip to Palestine, and his stay on a collective farm near Haifa—the experiences of which formed the basis of his novel *Yehuda* (1931).

In addition to the recounting of personal incidents, *In Search*, like Kazin's two later autobiographies, is a firsthand account of much of the literary and political history of three decades. Levin describes, for example, his experience as a war correspondent during the Spanish Civil War. As an ardent leftist, Levin observed with growing apprehension the threat of fascism in Europe and the events leading up to World War II. Part 1 concludes on the eve of the war and with Levin's premonition of the horror that was about to take place.

Part 2, "Europe: The Witness," is dominated by the story of the Holocaust and Levin's own discovery of the tragic fate of six million European Jews. Although the shortest of the three sections, it is in many ways the heart of the book. Levin's melancholy yet obsessive odyssey through Hitler's crematoria understandably became one of the most significant experiences of his life and helped solidify his commitment to world Jewry. As with Kazin, it is the event that places Levin's own Jewish identity into sharp perspective. Yet also like Kazin, Levin acknowledges the impossibility of expressing the horror of the Holocaust and its aftermath:

> From the beginning I realized I would never be able to write the
> story of the Jews of Europe. This tragic epic cannot be written by a
> stranger to the experience, for the survivors have an augmented view
> which we cannot attain; they lived so long so close with death that on a
> moral plane they are like people who have acquired the hearing of a
> whole range of tones outside normal human hearing. (173)

Instead Levin gives a moving account of what he discovered
as he traveled through the sites of Hitler's death camps and of
his own strained emotions as he learned of the millions dead and
the living dead who emerged. "I am sick of telling their stories,"
Levin writes of the survivors, "for there is no issue from their
dreary tales. . . . It isn't a fourth of the Bulgarian Jews and a fifth
of the Polish Jews and a third of the French who survived; they
all have death inside" (175). All this transcends memoir to become history that is at once personal and universal. Through his
attempts to interpret the world and the self within the same autobiographic structure, Levin succeeds in both personalizing history and in viewing objective events within a subjective framework. In so doing, he is able to articulate his link, not only with
the dead of Auschwitz and Dachau, but also with the whole of
the Jewish past and its future.

In Part 3, "Israel: The Released," Levin specifies the implications of his connection with Jewish history and with the
new nation of Israel. This last section recounts the filming of
*The Illegals* (1948), Levin's documentary which recorded the
clandestine flight of European Jewish survivors to Palestine,
then under British mandate. Levin's personal involvement with
the *Bricha*, as the illegal exodus was called, is told in great
detail. We learn of the difficulties and dangers that were part
of the underground movement, the multitude of heroic and
tragic episodes experienced by the voyagers, as well as the sei-
zure of the ship by the British while Levin covertly filmed the
encounter. The style is objective and reportorial; but Levin's
purpose is ultimately personal, as he describes his sense of responsibility to the European survivors and his urgent need to
be part of the future of Israel.

*In Search* concludes with Levin's philosophical reflections on the relationship between Israel and America, and with a call for mutual understanding and support between the world's two largest Jewish communities. Having his roots in both, Levin naturally wants to build a bridge between them. For his part, his "search" is concluded in Israel where his earlier doubts ("Was I an American, or a Jew") have been replaced by a renewed commitment to Judaism and a new acceptance of his "bicultural" identity. His efforts "to harmonize a multiplicity of forces" (536) have mostly succeeded. Levin remains what he always was: "a peculiar mixture of Chicago and Chassidism" (537). But now he can state without contradiction that he is both a "truth-seeking American reporter and truth-seeking son of the Torah" (537). The central dichotomy of his life—his Jewish and his American identity—is resolved through an ultimate acceptance of his "biculturalism": "I do not . . . feel that I am in an issue-less dilemma as an American and as a Jew, and that I must renounce one culture or the other. . . . [W]e know that there can be successful bicultural and multicultural personalities, and I do not see why the modern Jew shouldn't strive for such a realization, if it gives the best expression to all that is in him" (536). Furthermore, Levin concludes, Jewish civilization will continue to flourish because of a living Israel, a land which will stand as a metaphor for the survival of the Jewish people as well as for universal justice.

Although *In Search* is particular in many respects as to the specifics of Levin's experience, it is also typical of American-Jewish autobiographies in general during this period. Levin's dilemma is that of Kazin; both writers recognize the essential duality of their existence, and both strive toward a reconciliation of the opposing poles of their personalities. In the process, both Kazin and Levin rely heavily on the motif of return: Kazin to Brownsville and Levin to the birthplace of his parents in Eastern Europe. The terms and purpose of Levin's journey are clear: "I had to go there, to touch Poland before I was free. . . . Then my own journey would be rounded and complete" (369–70). The motivation for Kazin's return is less obvious but no less meaningful: it allows for a renewed connection to his past and to his former self. Like Levin, his voyage is circular and—as the opening lines indicate—repetitive; he too must somehow reconnect himself to his past for his present personality to be "rounded and complete."

Both narrators emerge, as a result of this "return," with a more unified, integrated self—one that contains elements of the present and the past. In neither case, of course, is the dichotomy completely resolved. At the conclusion of *A Walker in the City* Kazin still fears that he will remain "alien forever." Similarly, Levin's claim to have resolved the disparate aspects of his personality is somewhat mitigated by his final admission that, in spite of all his efforts to fit himself "into the world pattern," he was "still a little member of my clan, over anxious, self-centered, insecure" (171). Nevertheless, each remains at the end of his particular journey toward self-understanding mostly renewed and whole, having embraced both the uniquely Jewish and the specifically American aspects of his personality.

## III

Whereas Kazin, Levin, and other Jewish writers had earlier struggled to establish their credentials within purely "American" intellectual circles, American Jews by the mid-sixties had not only entered the mainstream of American culture but had to a large extent defined the specifics of that culture by virtue of their own contributions. Indeed, the title of Norman Podhoretz's autobiography, *Making It* (1967), accurately reflected the optimism of the decade. Like *A Walker in the City*, *Making It* describes its author's desire to escape the narrow and limited world of the Jewish ghetto. "One of the longest journeys in the world," Podhoretz claimed, "is the journey from Brooklyn to Manhattan" (3). But unlike Kazin, Podhoretz does not pause to reminisce about his past. *Making It* is not so much about the complexities of ethnic identity as it is a celebration of success in America, the proud and sometimes silly boast of a brash young man who wishes to confess the "dirty little secret" of his ambition. Podhoretz wants to share with the world his discovery that "it is better to be a success than a failure. . . . [I]t was better to be rich than to be poor. . . . [I]t was better to be recognized than to be anonymous" (xi).

Yet Podhoretz's mostly self-serving memoir is significant in that it reveals an aspect of personality previously unarticulated in American-Jewish autobiography. As Alvin Rosenfeld in his essay "Inventing the Jew: Notes on Jewish Autobiography," has correctly noted, Podhoretz was one of the first of his generation to understand that the Jewish intellectual can achieve secular success without losing his connections to the Jewish past and without agonizing over the inherent contradictions: ". . . with Podhoretz we begin to see an alternative to the Jew as *merely* secular intellectual and catch glimpses of something more, of options within the intellectual life that permit and encourage a return to Jewishness while fully maintaining a stake in the world" (147). *Making It,* however, remains predominantly superficial, an autobiography in which—as Rosenfeld states—we see only "glimpses" of more significant issues. It was left to writers such as Gold and Howe a decade or more later to explore in a serious and moving fashion themes pertaining to the development of Jewish personality in contemporary America.

By the 1970s the notion of cultural pluralism had become generally accepted by American-Jewish intellectuals. And by the 1980s few Jewish writers or critics believed there to be any contradiction between intellectual and Jew. With this new pluralism, however, came a new challenge. No longer were Jewish intellectuals preoccupied with the thought of escaping their ghetto roots. On the contrary, many now began to recognize the inevitable loss inherent in the process of acculturation. American Judaism—distinguished throughout the first half of the twentieth century by its ties to Yiddish language and culture, by segregated pockets of population, and by a distinct religious history—now seemed to be in danger of becoming lost in the vast mainstream of American culture. The Jew had, as Ludwig Lewisohn predicted in his autobiography, *Up Stream* (1922), become "another dweller on an endless Main Street" (240). What was necessary for those wishing to revive their connection with the past was a creative act of the will, an imaginative "return" to tradition. For Kazin and Levin this return, while full of ambiguity, was both physically and metaphorically within reach. Although they struggled to understand the dichotomy of their American-Jewish identities, neither had ever fully severed their ties to their Jewish pasts. Both Herbert Gold and Irving Howe, however, had early in their careers fully and successfully immersed themselves in the secular aspects of American culture. "Jewishness," Howe recalled in *A Margin of Hope*, "was not regarded as a major component of the culture I wanted to make my own" (251). Yet later in their lives, both Gold and Howe felt the need to renew their connections to Jewish history and tradition, to rediscover the Jewish forces within themselves.

Herbert Gold's *My Last Two Thousand Years* (1972), for example, is a personal account of Jewish return and renewal. Born in 1924 to immigrant parents, Gold quickly entered the mainstream of American cultural and intellectual life. But, like Levin and Kazin, Gold discovered at mid-life that he could not cut himself off from the past without sacrificing the future. *My Last Two Thousand Years* is Gold's record of that discovery, of his "retrieval" of Jewish consciousness, of his "giving birth"—as he states—"to the Jewishness within myself" (245).

Gold, the successful author of over a dozen works of fiction, begins his autobiography with a statement outlining his spiritual turning and return: "By a wide and narrow road I found my way back to an allegiance I didn't possess. Born a Jew in Lakewood, Ohio, I embraced the belief and accusation: America is enough" (7). Like Podhoretz, Gold had spent his life "making it." But unlike Podhoretz, he discovered that the rewards of success in America were not enough: "In the community of girls and the commerce of culture, I forgot I was a writer, a

Jew, a man. . . . Like the Hasidic folk singer, I was elsewhere than at home in the Diaspora" (195).

Gold begins to think through the details and circumstances of his life: graduate study, teaching positions, publication successes, travels throughout the world, two marriages, and numerous affairs. Without a sense of community or any recognizable purpose, however, Gold concludes that his life has been one of disconnection and inauthenticity: "I was joining the peculiar company of those who seize avidly upon each moment as if it and only it means life. And it meant nothing. . . . No meaning, no community" (195–96).

But Gold is eventually able to emerge Prometheus-like from the ashes of his former existence. Like Levin and Kazin, he begins to discover meaningful bonds to his past and to his people. What eventually saves Gold from total disaffection is "the reassurance of history," the knowledge that he is a Jew and as such shares a history both tragic and beautiful with others of his faith. Throughout his travels, for example, Gold encounters fellow Jews in strange places: an ancient tailor in Haiti; a Hungarian-Jewish refugee aboard a steamship to Jerusalem; old, forgotten Jews in Moscow; and young, optimistic, first-generation *Sabras* in Israel. Despite the trauma of the past and the difficulties of the present, they all seem to share the same stoic response to life and experience as that expressed to Gold by an elderly Holocaust survivor in Paris: "'I lived. I lived.' he said, still not believing it. 'I'm alive'" (108). In the lesson of Jewish survival, Gold finds hope and compassion. "I was," Gold acknowledges, "moved by my kind."

Although Gold's basic autobiographical question ("What is a Jew and why am I that thing?") is not completely answered in *My Last Two Thousand Years*, the issues of Jewish history and continuity are brought into sharp focus. By the end of the book, Gold in Jerusalem ("home at last") is uplifted by his newly discovered connection to Jewish history and to his Jewish faith, both of which link him to past generations: "I did not suddenly learn the faith of my fathers, but I learned the lesson of this faith. It wouldn't shut up my complaining, either, no more than it shut up the complaining of my fathers. But now I also had the reassurance of history which they had given me through their sons and daughters" (223).

In his two autobiographical novels, *Fathers* (1967) and *Family* (1981), Gold explores the issues of Jewish identity and history through the lives of his parents and other members of his family. In both novels, fact and fiction blend to re-create the immigrant experience in America and the relevance of that experience for Gold's understanding of his present personality. In *My Last Two Thousand Years* Gold moves further back in time, exploring the entire scope of Jewish history in order to discover his rightful place within that history. He reaches few definitive conclusions. But, like Kazin and Levin, Gold's ultimate awareness of himself as a Jew and as an American relies on an understanding of the relationship between his Jewish past and his Jewish present: "I'm not sure what my destiny as a Jew means," he concludes, "or what the destiny of the Jews means—except that it is a unique fate, a peculiar devotion to world and spirit wrapped together. And that I have at last become what I was when my Old Country father and mother in Cleveland submitted to nature and conceived me" (246).

A decade later, Irving Howe in his autobiography *A Margin of Hope* also relied heavily on the theme of spiritual return as he delineated the forces that transformed him from secular Jew to one who wished to enter the "net and memory" of Jewish experience. Howe, the quintessential "New York intellectual," had previously set down his recollection of the New York literary and political scene, first in a 1968 article for *Commentary*, "The New York Intellectuals," and then in a section of *World of Our Fathers* (1976). In *A Margin of Hope* Howe again discusses these issues as well as the central problem that preoccupied both Gold and Podhoretz: the relationship between Jewish consciousness and the life of the modern intellectual.

*A Margin of Hope* is Howe's depiction of those forces—both historical and personal—that helped form him as a writer, a socialist, and a Jew. Howe's analysis of intellectual and political currents over five decades (specifically the growth and decline of socialism and radical politics in America) occupies the major portion of the book, but his thoughts about his identity as a Jew give *A Margin of Hope* its resonance and its individuality.

Born of impoverished immigrant parents in 1920 in the Bronx, Howe acknowledges his early ties to the past and to the language of his parents:

> In the early thirties—by then I was entering my teens—the East Bronx was still a self-contained little world. . . . Yiddish was spoken everywhere. The English of the young, if unmarred by accent, had its own intonation, the stumbling melody of immigrant speech. A mile or two from my building—I did not know it then—there lived a cluster of Yiddish writers who would gather on Sundays near a big rock in Crotona Park. . . . At the corner newsstands the Yiddish daily, the *Forward*, sold about as well as the *News* and the *Mirror*. (2)

For Howe, like Kazin, the world of culture and ideas was a liberation from the ghetto, as well as "a high calling." And like Kazin, Howe believed the two worlds to be inimical. Yet also like Kazin, Howe records the past in order to relive former pleasures and rituals: "Jewishness flickered to life on Friday night, with a touch of Sabbath ceremony a few moments before dinner; it came radiantly to life during Passover, when traditional dignities shone through its ritual" (4).

But, like Podhoretz, Howe does not linger on the past. *A Margin of Hope* recounts the now familiar story of a pilgrimage from the outer reaches of New York to the inner circles of Manhattan. Howe's particular journey began at City College, "where ideology grew wild" and where he very quickly became involved with radical politics. After graduation, Howe spent several months editing *Labor Action*, a four-page weekly socialist tabloid, until he was drafted into the Army and sent to serve out his term of duty in Alaska. Upon his release,

Howe returned to New York and to writing for various leftist journals. Eventually he placed an essay in *Commentary* on Isaac Rosenfeld's *Passage from Home*, and other articles followed. By the late 1940s, Howe was writing for Dwight Macdonald's *Politics* and on occasion for *Partisan Review* until he landed a steady job as a book reviewer for *Time*. In the meantime he had begun his eclectic and very productive career as an author and critic, publishing books on such diverse topics as Sherwood Anderson and Walter Reuther and the United Auto Workers. After several years at *Time*, Howe received an academic appointment at Brandeis University and then the editorship of *Dissent*. Other professorships ensued, as did many more books.

Throughout *A Margin of Hope*, Howe talks seriously about politics, literature, the history of ideas, and—in one central chapter—the development of his Jewish consciousness. As a secular Jew, an intellectual, and a socialist, Howe early in his career gave little thought to the issues surrounding his religious affiliation: "In the years before the war people like me tended to subordinate our sense of Jewishness to cosmopolitan culture and socialist politics. We did not think well or deeply on the matter of Jewishness—you might say we avoided thinking about it. Jewishness was inherited, a given to be acknowledged. . . . But Jewishness did not form part of a conscious commitment, it was not regarded as a major component of the culture I wanted to make my own, and I felt no particular responsibility for its survival or renewal" (251).

After the war, however, the reality of the Holocaust led "to timid reconsideration of what it meant to be Jewish" ( 253). As it had for Kazin and for Levin, the horror of the Nazi concentration camps became the greatest single factor in Howe's recognition of peoplehood and his acceptance of Jewish identity. "The problems" of his own Jewishness, Howe acknowledged, "cut more deeply": "Our earlier failure to face them with sufficient candor had left us their victims, had made us 'inauthentic' Jews who gave the Jewish 'situation' neither serious thought nor unblocked emotion" (258).

Howe begins, therefore, to rediscover his relationship to his past and to his religion, a process he labels his "reconquest" of Jewishness. He is quick to point out, however, that this "reconquest" is not merely the nostalgic turning back to the roots of a middle-aged man. It is rather an existential act, "an ordeal of the will" similar to Gold's "giving birth" to his Jewishness, a process that ultimately brought Howe closer to his own, sometimes unorthodox, beliefs and to his past.

Howe's repossession of his Jewish identity manifested itself first by a commitment to the "lost cause" of Yiddish literature, which allowed him "to preserve a Jewish culture derived from the Judaic past." In the early 1950s, for example, Howe began to edit and translate Yiddish poetry and fiction with the poet Eliezer Greenberg. This led to a discovery not only of the beauty of Yiddish literature but of his own connection with Jewish history: ". . . reading more deeply in the Yiddish poets helped me to feel at ease, if not with myself, then at least with my past. It helped open memories, unclog feelings. . . . Yiddish poetry . . . helped me strike a truce with, and then extend a hand to, the world of my father" (267, 269).

Concomitant with this renewed interest in the past was Howe's increased empathy with the state of Israel, a bond that he did not feel at the time of its birth. Unlike Levin, Howe was not a committed Zionist from the first. He was not, Howe remembered, "one of those who danced in the streets when Ben Gurion made his famous pronouncement that the Jews, like other peoples, now had a state of their own" (276). But by 1967, Howe admits his pride, his "thrill of gratification" at Israel's victory.

Nevertheless, Howe's "reconquest" is both limited and, by his own admission, problematic: "How much easier my 'reconquest of Jewishness' would have been if God, with or without a clap of thunder, had appeared one day to tap me on the shoulder and declare me his own!" (277) What Howe has become, he finally concludes, is a "partial" Jew, true to himself, if to no organized group, "savoring the goodness of the thinning tradition of Yiddish" (281) and enjoying his place within the "net and memory" of Jewish history. Like Gold, Howe has come to recognize the significance of his Jewish past in terms of his present, American identity: "We were now learning to accept the ease that might come from acknowledging and even taking pleasure in ties with a past that, in any case, had become an integral part of our being" (275).

In the end Howe offers no solutions to the "problems" of Jewish personality. Nor does he put forth any program for younger Jews: "They would have to improvise and scamper about, like others before them." "My own hope," Howe concluded, "was to achieve some equilibrium with that earlier self which had started with childhood Yiddish . . . and then turned away in adolescent shame" (269). Like Gold, Howe the adult has come full circle to reclaim an important aspect of his present personality, one that includes "the world of [his] father" (269).


## IV


Not all the works examined here sustain the proper equilibrium between objective and subjective analysis. Levin's *In Search* at times lapses into needless preoccupation with self. Kazin's two later autobiographies often reflect the author's self-centered world view. Podhoretz's *Making It* remains mostly self-indulgent. But at their best, each of the works examined maintains a balance between individual awareness and historical truth, between self and the world. Levin, Kazin, Howe, and Gold have all chosen to portray the circumstances of their lives in relation to society and to their own cultural past. Although over thirty years separate their respective autobiographical works, all share similar concerns and preoccupations. Like Kazin and Levin, Gold and Howe come to understand the importance of the past and its relation to present personality. Howe's "repossession" of the Jewish aspects of self is prompted to a large degree by the historical fact of the Holocaust. It is further motivated or at least crystallized by the creation of the state of Israel. Moreover, the element of voyage, which helped solidify Kazin's and Levin's connection to their respective pasts, becomes for Howe a journey of the intellect, manifesting itself most specifically in a devotion to the dying language and literature of Yiddish. Gold embarks on a similar spiritual odyssey, although his voyage to Israel helps in a symbolic way to solidify that "return."

While the specifics of personal change are unique to each author and his particular circumstance, the theme of individual growth and development that emerges in each case is strikingly similar and one that helps distinguish first-generation American-Jewish autobiographies in general. The pattern can be summarized as follows: early estrangement from mainstream America, feelings of isolation, an identity crisis marked by the pull of dual loyalties, a journey (either physical or spiritual) of "return" to a place or culture of personal significance, a renewed connection with one's people, and finally a better understanding of self in relation to the group and its shared history. With some variation, this pattern is clearly discernable in the autobiographies of Levin, Kazin, Gold, Howe, and—to a lesser extent—Podhoretz. Moreover, it is also present in one form or another in such other American-Jewish autobiographies as Jay Neugeboren's *Parentheses: An Autobiographical Journey* (1970), Ronald Sanders's *Reflections on a Teapot: The Personal History of a Time* (1973), Paul Cowan's *An Orphan in History: Retrieving a Jewish Legacy* (1982), and Samuel Heilman's *The Gate behind the Wall: A Pilgrimage to Jerusalem* (1984).

Similarly, each of the works discussed shares the motif of journey, one that is closely linked to the theme of spiritual return. The element of voyage is a common aspect of autobiography, metaphorically suggesting the author's subjective movement toward self-discovery. There are, however, specifically Jewish aspects to each of these journeys. To begin with, each author travels back to a place of the past, indicating a connection with tradition and history that is endemic to Jews in the Diaspora. Moreover, the circular nature of their movement reflects the entire history of Jews' expulsion and return to "the promised land." This same circularity further suggests not only a personal discovery of the past but the archetypal Jewish journey of religious discovery—the annual intellectual pilgrimage of observant Jews on the eve of Yom Kippur, the Day of Atonement. Each year, through the vehicle of prayer and by means of religious repentance (or *teshuvah* in Hebrew), the Jew symbolically returns to his or her ancestral roots. (the word *teshuvah* is derived from the Hebrew verb *shub*, to return).[1]

Perhaps the most common elements repeatedly expressed in the autobiographic works of Kazin, Levin, Howe, and Gold are those associated with the two most significant occurrences in recent Jewish history: the extermination of six million European Jews and the establishment of the state of Israel. Levin's obsession with the Holocaust and his involvement with Israel are obvious. In *A Walker in the City*, Kazin mentions neither the Holocaust nor Israel. Yet one must read Kazin's three autobiographical works on a continuum rather than as separate entities. The closing references to Hitler's death camps in *Starting Out in the Thirties*, for example, leave no doubt as to the profound effect the events of the Holocaust had on the author and—in an indirect way—help to explain the purpose for Kazin's trip to Brownsville fifteen years earlier. Moreover, Kazin's journey to Israel, symbolically coming after his trip to Belsen, allowed him to share in the future of world Jewry and to reassure himself of the survival of his people. Similarly, Gold and Howe are both moved by the fate of the six million to reconsider their own sense of identity and their link to Jewish history, as well as to its future.

Interestingly, neither the Holocaust nor the creation of the state of Israel figures prominently in American-Jewish fiction.[2] The reasons for these omissions may be complex and need not be of concern for this study. The fact that autobiography more than any other form of literature reflects widely held concerns and preoccupations of American Jews, however, further illustrates the close connection between personal narration and cultural history. Autobiography, in short, is personal history that remains relevant and meaningful because it is collectively shared.

Without the demands of fiction and because of the unique nature of the genre, writers like Kazin, Levin, Gold, and Howe (as well as Podhoretz, Sanders, Neugeboren, Cowan, and others) found in autobiography the ideal form for interpreting complex ties to faith, history, and world events. For each, personal and cultural identity are inexorably intertwined. Both individually and collectively, their autobiographical works offer a valid and coherent version of the cultural and emotional development of a people. The dual nature of autobiography—its existence as both history and literature—enabled each of these authors to explore issues that were highly personal and at the same time germane to an entire generation of American Jews.

## Notes

1. The concept of *teshuvah* and its relationship to Jewish autobiography was first suggested to me by Rabbi Barry Konovitch, Sarasota, Florida. For a more detailed discussion of *teshuvah* and its significance, see *Encyclopedia Judaica* 4: 74–78.
2. Alvin Rosenfeld ("Israel and the Idea of Redemption") has observed: "By common agreement, the two most momentous events in Jewish life in the modern period are the destruction of European Jewry and the rebirth of the Jewish state. . . . One might, accordingly, expect Jewish writing over the past three or four decades to register such powerful historical eruptions in a major way. Yet that has not happened" (54). When Bernard Malamud ("An Interview") was asked to comment on the absence in American-Jewish fiction of the subject of Israel and Zionism, he responded: "Writing about Zionism wouldn't interest me. I'd rather write about Israel if I knew the country. I don't, so I leave it to the Israeli writers" (14). Saul Bellow's personal memoir, *To Jerusalem and Back* (1976), is a reasoned defense of Israel, but the subject rarely appears in his fiction. Ruth Wisse ("Reading About Jews") has commented that Bellow's memoir marks "one of the few occasions when the American Jewish writer has shared the preoccupations of ordinary Jews" (48).

## Works Cited

Antin, Mary. *The Promised Land*. New York: Houghton, 1912.

Bellow, Saul. *To Jerusalem and Back: A Personal Account*. New York: Viking, 1976.

Cowan, Paul. *An Orphan in History: Retrieving a Jewish Legacy*. Garden City: Doubleday, 1982.

Gold, Herbert. *Family: A Novel in the Form of a Memoir*. New York: Arbor, 1981.

——. *Fathers: A Novel in the Form of a Memoir*. New York: Random, 1967.

——. *My Last Two Thousand Years*. New York: Random, 1972.

Guttmann, Allen. *The Jewish Writer in America: Assimilation and the Crisis of Identity*. New York: Oxford UP, 1971.

Heilman, Samuel. *The Gate behind the Wall: A Pilgrimage to Jerusalem*. New York: Summit, 1984.

Howe, Irving. *A Margin of Hope: An Intellectual Autobiography*. New York: Harcourt, 1982.

——. *World of Our Fathers*. New York: Harcourt, 1976.

Kazin, Alfred. *New York Jew*. New York: Vintage, 1978.

——. "The Self as History: Reflections on Autobiography." In *Telling Lives*, ed. Marc Pachter. Washington, DC: New Republic, 1979. 74–89.

——. *Starting Out in the Thirties*. Boston: Little,1965.

——. *A Walker in the City*. New York: Harcourt, 1951.

Levin, Meyer. *Frankie and Johnny*. New York: John Day, 1930.

——. *In Search*. 1950. New York: Pocket Books, 1973.

——. *The Old Bunch*. New York: Simon, 1937.

——. *Reporter*. New York: John Day, 1929.

——. *Yehuda*. New York: Cape, 1931.

Lewisohn, Ludwig. *Up Stream: An American Chronicle*. New York: Boni, 1922.

Malamud, Bernard. "An Interview with Leslie and Joyce Field." In *Bernard Malamud: A Collection of Critical Essays*, ed. Leslie and Joyce Field. Englewood Cliffs: Prentice, 1975. 8–17.

Neugeboren, Jay. *Parentheses: An Autobiographical Journey.* New York: Dutton, 1970.

Olney, James. "Autobiography and the Cultural Moment: A Thematic, Historical, and Bibliographical Introduction."In *Autobiography: Essays Theoretical and Critical,* ed. James Olney. Princeton: Princeton UP, 1980. 3–27.

Podhoretz, Norman. *Making It.* New York: Random, 1967.

Proust, Marcel. *Remembrance of Things Past.* New York: Random, 1932.

Rosenfeld, Alvin. "Inventing the Jew: Notes on Jewish Autobiography." In *The American Autobiography: A Collection of Critical Essays,* ed. Albert E. Stone. Englewood Cliffs: Prentice, 1981. 133–56.

——. "Israel and the Idea of Redemption in the Fiction of Hugh Nissenson." *Midstream,* Apr. 1980, 54–56.

Sanders, Ronald. *Reflections on a Teapot: The Personal History of a Time.* New York: Harper, 1973.

Stone, Albert E. *Autobiographical Occasions and Original Acts: Versions of American Identity from Henry Adams to Nate Shaw.* Philadelphia: U of Pennsylvania P, 1982.

Wisse, Ruth R. "Reading about Jews." *Commentary,* Mar. 1980, 41–48.

Yezierska, Anzia. *Red Ribbon on a White Horse.* New York: Scribner's, 1950.

# Protest and Accommodation, Self-Satire and Self-Effacement, and Monica Sone's *Nisei Daughter*

*Stephen H. Sumida*

In the eyes of its author, *Nisei Daughter*[1] is not an example of belles lettres but a plain sort of nonfictional writing. In 1976 Monica Sone responded to an inquiry about the possibility of her taking part in the Asian-American writers' conference held that year, the American bicentennial, in her hometown, Seattle, by apologizing that she does not consider herself a "writer" but is a psychological counselor who has made a career while living in Canton, Ohio. Though she was happy to be asked to the conference, she declined that opportunity to be recognized among poets, fiction writers, and dramatists. The reprinting of her *Nisei Daughter* three years later, however, made possible its steady use and recognition (as well as criticism) beyond Sone's earlier disclaimer. A decade after the reprinting, Sone's words appeared now and again in captions and narratives for historical photo exhibits and films about Asian Americans of the state of Washington, in the observance of the state's 1989 centennial. Though displayed merely as opaque statements of fact or as illustrations of ideals and principles, Sone's words are perhaps better understood now than ever before. What her written autobiography provides, however, that the occasional use of her words as captions cannot is a sense of how her very discourse changes as her remembrance moves from early childhood in the 1920s through World War II and the Japanese-American internment.

*Nisei Daughter* runs against the grain of the assimilationist ideology that failed to dominate her, no matter that her readers today do not always note this point.[2] The incident with which the work begins introduces the theme in Sone's earliest remembered encounter with her identity as a Japanese American: "The first five years of my life I lived in amoebic bliss," she writes in the opening chapter, titled "A Shocking Fact of Life," "not knowing whether I was plant or animal, at the old Carrollton Hotel on the waterfront of Seattle. One day when I was a happy six-year-old, I made the shocking discovery that I had Japanese blood. I was a Japanese" (3). She could not in that instant consider the discovery a refutation of her being an American, and she shows no fear of her own that she is somehow not American enough. While at six she is confused by her mother's reference to race, neither she nor Mother defines "American" by race. Neither of them, that is, excludes a "Japanese," the nisei daughter, from being American. Yet her language and the incident she chooses to report directly reflect how nisei of the mainland United States came to define what it means to be a second-generation Japanese American under the traumatic pressures of an assimilationist American ideology which insists that a Japanese American reckon with race.

The incident opening the autobiography epitomizes the entire work. A recreation through Sone's adult hindsight, the beginning of *Nisei Daughter* is a carefully selected memory. It reflects some thirty years—and not merely six—of the author's experience and view of her life. The opening incident and the way it is told are thus both direct and indirect, about an actual event one Sunday at dinner in 1925 and about the entire narrative. The point of view results from Sone's act of writing as it loops back to inform its own beginning in her childhood experience.

Typically, Sone's autobiography is read as a direct, spontaneous, historical source, like a diary where entries are written on or near the days their events occur. Sone's account of her learning the "shocking fact" of her being "Japanese" is thus taken as her first of a lifetime of rebellions not only against the shocking idea itself but against the Japanese race and the culture—her parents' culture. This view is especially compelling to those readers who already believe, as the momentarily baffled six-year-old Kazuko does, that to be nisei is to have a dual identity in which a domestic American heart is ever in conflict against an alien skin. This, however, is not borne out by the remainder of the narrative. Indeed, in hindsight Sone qualifies the suggestion of an interracial, intercultural conflict between the first two generations of Japanese Americans by comically satirizing that suggestion. For the practical outcome of Mother's announcement that Kazuko (i.e., Monica Kazuko Itoi) is a "Japanese" is that she will be sent to Japanese language school after her school day at Bailey Gatzert Elementary, and so she would not be done until 5:30: "So that's what it meant to be a Japanese—to lose my afternoon play hours! I fiercely resented this sudden intrusion of my blood into my affairs" (4). Contrary to any preconceptions readers might bring to the incident that Sone rejects the culture taught at Japanese school, her protest is against something else, which her lost play hours represent in a mock-heroic, exaggerated way: "Until this shattering moment, I had thought life was sweet and reasonable. But not any more" (4). Further, this precocious coming-of-age at six (actually the burlesque of an epiphany) climaxes with Kazuko's own great fuss and protest put to action: "Why did Father and Mother make such a fuss just because we had Japanese blood? Why did we have to go to Japanese school? I refused to eat and sat sobbing, letting great big tears splash down into my bowl of rice and tea" (5). In one outcry the child denounces Japanese blood, Japanese school, and Japanese food, while the adult author smiles at the bathos of it all. Such is her present view of her first, naive response to the "shocking fact" of something she can neither choose nor change—her race.

Sone clearly uses this incident and her implicit, adult, quite humorous assessment of it to introduce her point of view and themes as well as to characterize herself. And indeed, along with the sometimes humorous tone of the narrative, there is the seriousness of Sone's themes. The truly "shocking fact of life," not that she is of "Japanese blood" but that she and her race are discriminated against because of it, is repeated many times over by the time she is thirty: in her daily life in a multiracial, multicultural city; in a comic incident when Mother is mistaken simply by race for the wife of the consul general of Japan and is treated as an aristocrat without her knowing why; in the family's visit to Grandfather Itoi and their relatives in Japan; in Monica Kazuko's search, with Mother, for a summer home, for the sake of her sister Sumiko's health, in a Seattle beachfront neighborhood where, they learn, Japanese are excluded by race; and in the internment of her, her family, and her community during World War II.

By choosing such incidents to characterize her first twenty or thirty years, Sone protests against a definition of "American" that excludes whoever is not white. Meanwhile, her definition of herself as an American is a specifically ethnic one. Besides the book's title, the very opening page of *Nisei Daughter* is an implicit testament literally to the gusto of Sone's nisei identity. She describes the meal on that Sunday afternoon in the small kitchen into which the family of six crowds. The kitchen, part of their apartment in the hotel her parents run, is "cozily comfortable," with "soy sauce splattered on the floor and elbows jabbed into the pot of rice" at the crowded table (3). The family is lined up in their usual order of seats. But there is no standing on formalities here, nothing diffident about Kazuko or alienating about being "Japanese," if being one is actually embodied in the comfort, family love, and, most explicitly, the food in this very scene. Indeed, the closest Sone comes to describing a ritual on that page is of Mother's serving the meal and Father's way of eating it: "Now we watched as Mother lifted from a kettle of boiling water a straw basket of steaming slippery noodles. She directed her information [about their having 'Japanese blood'] at Henry and me, and I felt uneasy. Father paid strict attention to his noodles, dipping them into a bowl of fragrant pork broth and then sprinkling finely chopped raw green onion over them" (3). Kazuko is at once "uneasy" about learning that she is Japanese American and yet hungry in anticipation of a hot Japanese-American meal.[3] Soon in the narrative it becomes clear that this meal itself is part of a diet that is polyethnically American, not confined to Japanese dishes. It is laden with "ham and eggs, steaks and potatoes, apple and pumpkin pies," which Father learned to cook working "in the galleys of Alaska-bound ships," and Mother's "authentic" Japanese and "superb" Chinese dishes which she, having arrived as an immigrant too young to have had much experience in cooking, learned in Seattle and not mainly in Japan. "Although we acquired tastes for different types of food," Sone notes, "we adhered mostly to a simple American menu," whatever that may mean, given the variety she relishes on these pages (13).

It does mean at least that Mother's announcement to the six-year-old and her brother Henry that they are "Japanese" must have a special meaning intimately involved with the multicultural conditions of their American lives. Kazuko's uneasiness is stirred thoroughly with her simultaneous pleasure over the unmistakably Asian meal until its end, when, eating her final course of tea poured over rice, she argues with Mother against having to attend Japanese school because it cuts off her playtime. Sone recounts how she reflected at the time: "Up to that moment, I had never thought of Father and Mother as Japanese. True, they had almond eyes and they spoke Japanese to us, but I never felt that it was strange. It was like one person's being red-haired and another black" (5).

Perhaps it is only natural that an autobiographer aiming to trace the development of her psyche and character would begin with what may be the first memorable instance casting doubt on her own identity. It is notable in Sone's case, however, that, writing in the aftermath of the war and the imprisonment of Japanese Americans, she could in her opening pages express the point from which an awareness of pluralism grew in her, contrary to widespread attempts to suppress Japanese Americanness before and in this very era. Her observation that she "had never thought of Father and Mother as Japanese" is nothing less than her first intuiting of a concept of American cultural pluralism and her first questioning of the concept of assimilation. Can't "Americans" have different colored hair, looks, and languages? Does our being "Japanese" change the meaning of "American"? Even considering what Sone, a psychologist, may understand about the development of an individual's "identity" beginning with such inchoate thoughts, it seems an especially early remembered beginning for children in general. But perhaps it indicates that the child who grows up ethnic or nonwhite in America does indeed begin early to develop an especially complex identity that seems sometimes to take rather unusually long to mature because of these factors of race and ethnicity, compared with the identities—but perhaps never realized in this regard—of those Americans who give scant thought to these aspects of themselves.[4]

However commonplace a claim it has become to some of us today—with terms and theories enabling us consciously to distinguish, say, between "pluralism" and "assimilation"— Sone's assumption that being "American" is defined by one's history, including one's ethnic history, in and of America, and is *not* limited, compromised, or lessened by one's race, ethnicity, gender, or class as elements of one's identity, is opposed by the assumptions and language of some other Japanese-American autobiographies. Roughly half of Japanese-American autobiographies run with the assimilationist American grain. Attempts at validating the self by conventional standards, they are based on assumptions about America, racial and ethnic "minorities," gender, success, and "acceptance" in line with expectations current in their time.[5] The other half, including Sone's, are subversive, however subtly and intuitively. Directly or on a revealing bias, they cut across the grain, sometimes appearing to do so either without their authors' knowing it or making special efforts to act, in their writing, as critics of society and not merely of themselves.

Embodying an initially pluralistic view of what it means to be "American," *Nisei Daughter* stands up against the examples of Daniel K. Inouye's *Journey to Washington* and Daniel Okimoto's *American in Disguise*. These two nisei autobiographies were written later than Sone's—that is, further after the war—yet in their differing ways they are demonstrations of their authors' accommodation to values and traits they assume to be essentially "American," sometimes in distinction from and even conflict against being "Japanese," in order to define themselves as Americans. When Sone's autobiography is misread as being of the same kind as these two, it would seem, for instance, that her mother was more "American" and less "Japanese" than her father, since Mother is a Christian, the daughter of a Protestant minister. In the common, assimilationist view, which Inouye and Okimoto assume, people would be measured against two assumed, fixed, and opposite standards at either end of a scale, the "American" and the "Japanese." This reductive, exclusionary, and static way of defining what it means to be "American" does not become but *is* racist in both content and structure, since the very traits by which the term *American* is thereby defined are nearly always thought to be derived from "dominant" Western European cultures even when their origins may be elsewhere.

Yet surely Inouye's is a heroic story on nearly every count: his "accommodation" to an established system is nothing less than to be elected to the U.S. Congress at the time of Hawaii's achieving statehood in 1959, subsequently becoming and remaining until today a U.S. senator. In this way his *Journey to Washington* is indeed proof that his Americanness is defined (and continues to evolve today) by the course of his history. In his autobiography he pays tribute to his parents and their origins in Japan; so Inouye, like Sone, presents his own life as part of a continuity and history ever changing and yet unbroken through several generations, including the generation of the Inouyes' infant son, whose birth inspired the senator to work on the autobiography.

But it is the language of *Journey to Washington* that expresses a view of Inouye, of Japanese Americans, and of America that is uncritically assimilationist, even while Inouye's very history and thoughts may run in other directions. The matter is somewhat complicated by Inouye's autobiography having been written with the help of a professional writer, Lawrence Elliott. So the diction of the work is not entirely Inouye's own. Inouye's two-page introduction, however, may well be as close to his solo writing as can be found in the volume, and in it he says:

> . . . [M]y life, as I see it, is not really so very different from all the millions of others that have contributed to the American melting pot. My forbears came from the Orient and it is true that their facial characteristics set them apart from Americans whose roots are in the Western world. But their problems of assimilation were exactly the same: to find work, to maintain a pride in their heritage while adapting to the culture of a strange new land, and slowly, step by painful step, to work their way up the social and economic ladder toward independence and full acceptance by their fellow-countrymen. (xix-xx)

Inouye's easy use of the terms *melting pot, assimilation,* and *acceptance* contradict what he is simultaneously trying to say about maintaining "a pride in their heritage." The "melting pot" symbolizes not the ethnic diversity many assume it means but, as Inouye himself intimates here, the sameness and uniformity that result when all the constituent elements, the different metals and minerals in the metaphor, are melted together into a single alloy, the heavily dominant or host culture, whom Inouye nonetheless democratically calls "their fellow-countrymen." The term *acceptance*, although commonly used in such a context as Inouye's statement, implies one's inferiority to the party from whom acceptance is sought. In this context, indeed, it is a term of inequality of human relationships—here, of racial inequality— despite Inouye's probable thoughts to the contrary, whereas the term *recognition*, which does not imply inequality, is what Inouye's own story of his World War II service on the U.S. Army's 442nd Regimental Combat Team implicitly demands.[6]

Okimoto's *American in Disguise* is far more overt an accommodation. It is a self-conscious, admitted apology for being Japanese American, some might say a confession, as if being born of a race and culture were a matter of making right or wrong choices. We can scarcely doubt, however, the author's sincerity in maintaining that he is telling of his racist self-hatred and in a sense perpetuating it not because he wishes to do so but because that is exactly how the America he wants to belong to defines and "conditions" him. He is only being realistic, he implies. But his tone throughout the work, rather painful to read in any case, is excruciatingly apologetic, blaming himself and his race rather than the social conditions he nonetheless knows are oppressive:

> In this white-dominated society, it was perhaps natural that white girls seemed attractive personally as well as physically. They were in a sense symbols of the social success I was conditioned to seek, all the more appealing, perhaps, because of the subtly imposed feelings of self-derogation associated with being a member of a racial minority. In the inner recess of my heart I resisted the seductive attraction of white girls because I feared I was being drawn to them for the wrong reasons. I was afraid that my tastes had been conditioned too centrally by white standards. Behind the magnetism there may have been an unhealthy ambition to prove my self-worth by competing with the best of the white bucks and winning the fair hand of some beautiful, blue-eyed blonde—crowning evidence of having made it.
>
> Such suspicions were aggravated by deep-seated resentment and fear: resentment against feeling compelled to prove myself in the white world to begin with, and fear of failing or being hurt by prejudice in the process. (200–201)

Even when Okimoto speaks for racial tolerance, his message is conflicted by his tone and diction. This expression of his dualistic habit of thought is utterly unlike Sone's sense of a whole identity, which she sustains through nearly her entire work. In his agony, Okimoto decided to marry Nancy Miller, an "Anglo-Saxon" woman from Idaho; yet even then he is driven to rationalize himself in a kind of verbalized and rarified cold sweat:

> It was probably no accident that the decision to marry, as well as the ceremony itself, took place in Japan, because it was only after I had spent several years in my ancestral homeland that I could accept myself with a dual identity. The struggle to be recognized as a "normal" American at the expense of suppressing the Japanese in me, as well as the periodic swings into rage against white Americans, ceased troubling me so much after I had accepted the fact that I am Japanese American.

In looking ahead there could very well be similar problems of identity
for my children, perhaps compounded by the actual mixing of races
(206).

Okimoto concludes his autobiography with a statement about
his children that "Physically, at least, half the disguise I have
worn will be lost" because he sees them as half-white and
himself as contributing by his choice in marriage to the breeding of the problematic race, Japanese, out of visible existence.
He concludes his statement and his book, however, with precisely the opposite conception of what the real problem is. It
is not a person's race but racism: "I hope the day will come
when they and all my country's racial minorities are no longer
made to feel any less American because of their ethnic heritage" (206), which may well be the most hopeful assertion in
the entire work.

Like Inouye's, Okimoto's autobiography is a creature of the
1960s, when assimilationist jargon, although weakening elsewhere in American society—especially with advances in civil
rights through acts of civil disobedience and protest—was given
a boost by a counter-movement, the myth of the Asian American as quiet and resourceful "model minority."[7] The "model"
in this case exemplifies how to strive for "acceptance" by
what the subject considers the "dominant" society, his or her
own being a "sub-" or "subordinate," a "minority," and, by
these very terms, an inferior culture. The model warns the
subject not to protest but to work within the established system which subjugates him or her. Following the principle of
divide and conquer, it decrees that Asian Americans are superior to minority groups who protest for social, economic, and
political justice. By the early 1970s it was infuriatingly obvious to radicalized Asian-American critics that Okimoto's pre-
sumption that his race "disguises" his being American was
outrageous. It was all the more painful because his book seemed
shockingly to mirror the thoughts of a good many Japanese
Americans about themselves.[8] The outrage, though ostensibly
aimed at Okimoto and the accommodationists he represented,

was a cry against the pervasive system of racist thought and irrationality that continually pressured him. Indeed, James A. Michener, who wrote the foreword to Okimoto's book, in his novel *Hawaii* treats ethnicity and race as disguises for an assimilationist core.[9] *American in Disguise* may indeed be seen today as evidence from the late 1960s and early 1970s that the internment, diaspora, and forced assimilation imposed upon Japanese Americans of a quarter century before was running its nasty course. As Okimoto intimates throughout his autobiography, he is a victim undergoing interrogation, and in his degree and kind of self-effacement he is unlike Inouye and Sone.

A Japanese-American autobiography published twenty years after Sone's and therefore standing upon her shoulders is Jeanne Wakatsuki Houston's *Farewell to Manzanar*.[10] Written with James Houston, this work cut through the stranglehold of self-doubting and anxiety that for thirty years had choked back the author's story about her family's and the Japanese-American people's imprisonment in concentration camps. While not the first published narrative focused on that historic experience, it was among the first in the age of television to remind the American public at large, from the narrative point of view of a former internee, of what had happened to Japanese Americans in World War II. Houston's autobiography was made into a television movie and broadcast in 1976, when, despite the mildness of its (and the published text's) treatment of racism, it was followed by a blizzard of calls, including racist ones, to television stations.[11]

Among Sone's contemporaries, authors such as Toshio Mori, Hisaye Yamamoto, and Shelley Ota wrote and published short stories and novels about Japanese Americans and their histories, including World War II and its effects on this people, while Sone worked on her autobiography. The development of a sensibility as well as certain changes in tone and language that course through *Nisei Daughter* are paralleled by the changes these three nisei fiction writers—and, later, John Okada, Kazuo Miyamoto, Yoshiko Uchida; the dramatists Wakako Yamauchi and Momoko Iko; and the poet Mitsuye Yamada—depict between pre– and post–World War II Japanese America. Here with Sone are nisei writers whose identification with Japanese America survived the internment and the racist self-doubtings it fomented. These writers either sense or face the double trauma of the nisei having to undergo, or perhaps to suspend in psychologically and spiritually dangerous ways, the ordinary crises of their coming-of-age, in their teens and twenties, while imprisoned in concentration camps.

It may be more than coincidence that most of those works of nisei autobiography and fiction which I assert run against the American grain are by women. Why this is so may have to do with ironies beyond certain rather conventional ones. It may be evidence that, during certain crises in societies dominated by men, women are freer in some senses to act. Not free in this sense, Inouye and Okimoto find problems and seek fulfillments in a "dominant," conventional view of life and of a Japanese-American "model minority" since these men themselves subscribe to that view.[12] Unlike Okimoto, who was embraced by white critics though not by Asian-American ones, the men who by choice, temperament, and character directly resisted and protested the subordination of themselves and their communities became scapegoats and pariahs until, years later in safer eras, they were seen to have been ahead of their time.[13] But, by choosing neither to fit nor directly to oppose dominant ideologies, some women and, as Ralph Ellison elucidates in the tricksterism his protagonist learns in *Invisible Man*, so-called minorities in America find ways to operate within the blind spots of hegemonic groups with interesting, sometimes deeply troublesome, and sometimes remarkably popular (though often poorly understood) results.

One such blind spot may be found in women and members of oppressed groups within America, who typically believe less than a supposed majority of men do in the complex of ideas, endemic to a male American literary canon, involving a "coming-of-age," often including disillusionment through a change from "innocence to experience" or a traumatic loss of

a seemingly boundless Edenic childhood. Not so blessed themselves, women and members of relatively powerless groups grow
up knowing that they stand in the shadows of dominant peoples
they cannot or will not aspire to be who not only recall childhood as idyllic but define the "reality" and "power" of responsible adulthood.[14]

Whereas *Huckleberry Finn* typifies, albeit in a complex and
ambiguous way, the American novel of a boy's coming-of-age
paralleled by implications for the maturing of the nation, a work
such as Maxine Hong Kingston's *The Woman Warrior* is not plot-
ted toward a climactic moment in the narrator's adolescence
when childhood and whatever it means to her is replaced by
adulthood. Instead, the narrator's childhood is characterized by a
dull oppression inflicted by continual reminders that, as a Chinese-American daughter, she is held inferior to sons. She is told
this by the aging patriarchs of Chinese America and warned of
this view by her mother. As a result, too, her own ignorance, en-
forced by her American life, also oppresses her. For instance, she
is not much concerned with considering or reporting that historically her community's patriarchs constituted what until recently was the Chinese immigrant bachelor society created by
American laws forbidding, with few exceptions, the immigration
of women from China. Whether knowing of them or not,
Kingston's narrator is oppressed not only by those laws but by
their consequences in the kind of estrangement, idealization, and
fear of women they instilled in the bachelors of Chinatown. She
is thus not prone to thinking as Huck Finn does, however naively, that one might light off to new territories to relive a care-
free youth. The antifeminism she perceives in the Chinese-
American community is like the Sitting Ghost that Brave
Orchid, the narrator's mother, vanquishes as a doctor in China
(*Woman Warrior* 65-75): antifeminism like the "ghost" suffo-
cates a person during anxiety-ridden sleep and burdens every
hour.[15] And like the white people Brave Orchid and her fellow
immigrants insult by calling them "ghosts," the pervasive reality
called antifeminism is not simplistically Chinese, in the larger,
mostly unspoken historical context of *The Woman Warrior*.

It is a fear of women that is inescapably American, embodied in all varieties of White Ghosts who teem about. It was the United States that legislated against Chinese women, indeed in a era when American women still could not vote while an enormously powerful Empress Dowager, and not a man, ruled China. In America, Kingston's narrator can look out upon no free territory of youth except in her imagination, fantasies, and stories. Only in these does she learn of female heroism and power fulfilled not so much in rebellion against an anti-feminist China as in the imagining of an idealized world where women were warriors against any injustice and one woman warrior in particular was universally known in a heroic way that no woman of the Western world was.

When we compare *The Woman Warrior* with the more usually expected dramatization of a coming-of-age, especially in what are supposed to be "memoirs," we see a critical problem. Because *The Woman Warrior* explicitly indicts the male chauvinism of Chinese America, but not the chauvinism and xenophobia of the America that created the bachelor society by excluding Chinese women, the book seems openly to reinforce anti-Chinese stereotypes while only covertly undermining the oppressed narrator's limited and ahistorical view of Chinese America. Nowhere is there a turning point where the narrator realizes and understands the conflicted, ambiguous nature of her observations and thoughts and the influence of a dominant American history and ideology upon them. Through a narrator whose naïveté and other limitations are never explicitly exposed and who appears suspiciously assimilationist, Kingston pits sexism against racism, sometimes joins various forces to combat both, and sometimes fights one at the expense of the other, in ways that have succeeded in eluding and beguiling readers since 1976. This situation results from two main problems: first, Kingston, somewhat like Sone, herself was unsettled (or undogmatic) about these issues when she wrote her first book; second, her underlying attack against American racism goes mostly undetected by those who do not even realize how little they know about American history and who therefore misinterpret Kingston's work as either conventional or revisionist "Chinese" history.

Kingston's relevance to this discussion of Sone's *Nisei Daughter* is not only in comparing their works as two different strategies for cutting across the American grain. Each in her own way performs an act of cultural criticism that slips away from conventions and standards that grip and stifle Daniel Okimoto. A historical theme, however, separates Kingston's and Sone's treatments of their respective Asian-American subjects. In her latest work, *Tripmaster Monkey: His Fake Book*, Kingston spins a joke that was sometimes told in the 1970s when Kingston and I would argue the existence and nature of pan-Asian Americanism or the interculturality within this diverse grouping itself. Kingston's Chinese-American protagonist Wittman Ah Sing turns envious of Japanese Americans because Executive Order 9066, by which President Roosevelt authorized the internment of Japanese Americans during World War II, "has given to Issei, Nisei, Sansei their American history" (*Tripmaster* 126).[16] Regretting that he lacks his own, Ah Sing wants to "plagiarize" the historically traumatic stories of his sansei friends, especially Lance Kamiyama. For Japanese-American men and women alike, particularly the issei and the nisei, the internment is indeed traumatic like no single event in Chinese-American history, and profoundly so; it marks the loss of the American possibilities that the issei, forbidden U.S. citizenship, had struggled to hand their children, possibilities the nisei in their West Coast communities had grown up assuming before the war.[17]

Here the paradigm of the loss of innocence—seen in hindsight not only as naïveté and gullibility but in symbols of wholeness—does inform Japanese-American literature, whether by women or by men. In this respect, Sone's autobiography with its Japanese American, nisei voice and sensibility differs sharply from the Chinese-American autobiography of Jade Snow Wong, *Fifth Chinese Daughter* (the title of which Sone's echoes, except that Wong refers to the order of the individual child's birth, Sone to the order of generations). Wong insists, no matter how conformist her view, that to be "American" is to be "free" and "individual," in contrast with what she thinks is her being bound by her parents' "Chinese" traditions. To Japanese Americans at the time of Wong's book, 1945, their American internment was anything but an exercise in freedom, individualism, and independence. Because the trauma of the internment is a result of it, racism is faced directly in *Nisei Daughter* in a way that does not happen in either *Fifth Chinese Daughter* or *The Woman Warrior*.[18]

In terms of understanding racism, the plot of *Nisei Daughter* as the story of a coming-of-age has as much to do with the history of the entire nisei generation as with the situation of the nisei daughter or nisei women. Yet, quite like Hisaye Yamamoto, whose short stories began to be prominently published in the postwar years when Sone completed her autobiography, Sone may have slipped by gatekeepers of convention and acceptability with the subversive, antiracist theme of her work because she as a nisei woman may have been thought safe, unthreatening, and thus acceptably readable. In Yamamoto's case, to this day readers have to be led to see certain plots and themes (for instance, sexual ones) underlying her texts, "hidden" there because common assumptions do not prepare readers to detect sex and politics within the stories of a nisei woman, even when she means these themes to be exposed. No matter the degree to which each of these authors consciously conceived and crafted her themes and styles as acts of social criticism, these elements of their work critically reveal characteristics and shortcomings of the discourse of their times. Sone wrote her autobiography in a time when terms for whatever it is that opposes accommodation were not yet devised except in ways considered most derogatory. For the Japanese-American "Resistance" or protest against the internment, notably by the "no-no boys" (whom she does not discuss directly), was smashed by the War Relocation Authority and maligned even by the internees themselves. Whether taken out of the concentration camps and imprisoned in federal penitentiaries or segregated in "hardcore" camps such as Tule Lake, the no-no boys and other resisters were stigmatized and made to this day to appear like scum.[19] Even a term I have been using, *subversive*, was yet to be coined in the literary sense current since the early 1970s, echoing the term as used in the hunt for Communists in America in the early 1950s when to be "subversive" was to be inimical to a glorified American society of consensus. Like her fellow native of Seattle and nisei author John Okada, Sone wrote when not even the term *Japanese American* itself was an established one among the people thus named today, and the terms *Japanese-American* (with the hyphen that implied a "dual identity" which Sone by her very example refutes), *American Japanese*, and *Americans of Japanese ancestry* seemed interchangeable but still problematic among a people who otherwise unambiguously called themselves *nikkei*, *issei*, *nisei*, and *sansei*, a terminology and an ordinal numbering of generations which by itself unequivocally implies a continuing history in America.[20]

It is such a sense of history that Sone establishes immediately following her recollection of her mother's telling her that they are of Japanese blood. "Father," she says, "had often told us stories about his early life": his arrival in Seattle in 1904 with the intention of earning money to study law at the University of Michigan, his labor on a railroad gang in a "virgin" land, his toil in "the potato fields of Yakima" and in the galleys of ships shuttling between Alaska and Seattle (5). Lacking the expected fortune to continue his education in law, he nonetheless bought a laundry business in what today is called the International District of Seattle and eventually became the operator of the Carrollton Hotel near the waterfront. Much later in her book Sone notes that Father held a long-term lease from the owner of the building containing the hotel (165). The state's anti-alien land laws forbade aliens ineligible for citizenship, which virtually meant only Asian immigrants, to own any real properly under the state's jurisdiction.[21] This means that Father discovered some way to buy a laundry *business* and later a hotel *business* despite his being unable to buy the real estate while still satisfying the increasingly oppres-

sive restrictions written into the land laws through the first
two decades and into the third of the century. Sone does not
explicate these points, but knowledge of the American legal
history her immigrant parents must have known all too well
is evidenced both by her passing mention of anti-Asian laws
and their practical consequences and by the consistency of her
account of her parents' settling in Seattle with this history.
Her understanding of their situations in America, for instance
with regard to the laws, contributes to the sense that, even in
racist crises, Sone does not question that before the war her
and her parents' *home*, earned by the tenacity and ingenuity
required for their settling, is first in their Carrollton Hotel,
then in a splendid house on Seattle's Beacon Hill, in the land
where they have chosen to live, America.[22] It is not some intention of theirs to leave Seattle for Tokyo for good; it is the
evacuation of Japanese Americans in 1942 that deprives them
of this home.

Mother's history complicates the family's character considerably. She did not arrive alone but with her parents the Reverend
Yohachi and Yuki Nagashima, two sisters, and two brothers.
Mother's background as the daughter of Congregationalists
from Japan conveys the peculiar impression that for her, not a
convert but born into Christianity, coming to America is an
extension of her former life in Japan.[23] Indeed, the way her father arranges her marriage to Itoi, the typical issei bachelor, is
also an extension of the duties, obligations, and travails experienced by her peers and their parents in Japan. But no tradition
simply stays the same as if caught forever in a portrait. A
change comes when Sone shifts attention from the formal
wedding photos of her parents, Mother's face "plastered white
and immobile with rice powder," to the newlywed couple's
work: "For about a year Mother helped Father haphazardly at
his dry-cleaning shop, intent on satisfying the customer's every whim. She scribbled down the strangely garbled phone
messages. More than once Mother handed Father an address
at which he was supposed to pick up clothes, and he found
himself parking his wagon in front of an empty, weed-choked

lot or cantering briskly out of the city limits as he pursued phantom house numbers" (7). It is a change from the pre-served moment, caught in the photographs of their wedding as a culmination of their youth and bachelorhood, to the ac-tive responsibility of adulthood and child rearing, a life which for the issei in Sone's account lasts up until a special event, the wedding of a nisei couple in the concentration camp called Minidoka, in Idaho, during the war.

Sone devotes the first chapter of her book to introducing her family and describing their home in the Carrollton Hotel in such a way that nothing—not the *shoyu* (soy sauce) jug in the kitchen, not the shiny piano in the living room—is for-eign to her. And why should anything or anyone in that home be foreign? It is her family, her home.[24] Whether calculated or not, the chapter makes good strategy: by treating her subject as she does, Sone illustrates the life of Japanese Americans feeling quite literally at home two decades before the war, and in doing so she gently mocks her own childish misunderstand-ing of Mother's statement that they are Japanese. "I had al-ways thought I was a Yankee," Sone jokes, "because after all I had been born on Occidental and Main Street" (18–19). The child of six begins immediately to think she has a dual iden-tity, part-Yankee, part-Japanese: "It was like being born with two heads. It sounded freakish and a lot of trouble" (19). This way of thinking is mocked by the wholeness of identity, seen in the family and their home, that Sone establishes in that very same opening chapter. This wholeness is not likely to change simply because of Mother's sending Kazuko and Henry to Japanese school. Life is already at least bicultural, and it is whole. How childish it is to think of life as culturally split asunder into a thing with "two heads" is underscored again at the end of the chapter by what is really in Kazuko's mind: "Above everything, I didn't want to go to Japanese school" (19), a protest which, it turns out, has nothing to do with race.

This is not to say, however, that Japanese school and, later, the Japan the Itois journey to visit add nothing to Sone's nisei sensibility. A recurring word in her descriptions of Japanese behavior is "restraint," as when at Japanese school, following the pupils' loud recitation of the syllabary, "Yasuda-sensei would look suspiciously at us. Our recital sounded a shade too hearty, a shade too rhythmic. It lacked something . . . possibly restraint and respect" (23–24). Here Sone's tone plays with the act of making a fine judgment of what precisely (though not very subtly) is wrong in the children's recital. And she learns indeed to judge—well enough so that we, too, may realize—that Ohashi, the principal of the school, embodies an extreme of strict decorum and is not representative of the typical issei or the typical Japanese. He is certainly not like Father (a veritable Gandhi) and Mother (appreciated by Sone throughout chapter 3 for being "An Unpredictable Japanese Lady" and who welcomes her children home in her enthusiastic English, "Well, did you guys have a good time?" which even the kids think outlandishly slangy for her [49]). Ohashi stands stiffly at attention, so fixed a picture and posture of "the best Japanese tradition" that not even visiting Japanese naval cadets and officers match him. Nearly everyone else (except Ohashi's pet student) is characterized by growing and changing, not by Ohashi's zealous ambition to remain unchanged, his "smoldering ambition to pass on this knowledge [of 'perfect samurai control'] to the tender Japanese saplings born on foreign soil" (24).[25] Sone also learns—though not in the way Ohashi might wish—how to behave in which place: "I could not use my Japanese on the people at the hotel. Bowing was practical only at Nihon Gakko [the Japanese school]. If I were to bow to the hotel patrons, they would have laughed in my face. Therefore promptly at five-thirty every day, I shed Nihon Gakko and returned with relief to an environment which was the only real one to me. Life was too urgent, too exciting, too colorful for me to be sitting quietly in the parlor and contemplating a spray of chrysanthemums in a bowl as a cousin of mine might be doing in Osaka" (28). In short, she learns that she is not "Japanese" in the rigid, static way she thought Mother meant.

The early chapters of *Nisei Daughter* thus complicate and

refine our views of the subject's Japanese-American identity. We see her as the simplistic and dualistic "two-headed" monster sprung from assimilationist assumptions and prejudices; we watch her develop a sense of irony that sustains her through tragedy, illness, and injustice, an irony implying that there is a greater understanding than the facts at hand may indicate. She learns early to recognize a tragic irony in the death of her brother Kenji of dysentery during the family's visit to Grandfather Itoi in Japan. It was Kenji, terrified of the Japanese earthquakes he had heard about from his elders, who protested early in the trip that he wanted to return home to Seattle; Kenji alone never returns. She experiences a dramatic irony, without at first knowing it, when the old Ojih-chan, grandpa, declines visiting the grandchildren in Seattle. He says it is because "when a man gets as old as I, he does not feel like moving from the place where he was born and where he had lived all his life. I long to go with you, but I'm too old now" (107). To reveal the irony, Sone here interjects that "Many years later I learned why he could not come with us. In 1924 my country had passed an Immigration Law which kept all Orientals from migrating to America since that year. Those who had come in before that time could stay, but there would be no more new ones" (107). Old age may well have had something to do with it, but it was the American law and not Japanese restraint that prevented Ojih-chan from moving to the home of the grandchildren who doted on him. Sone's mention of this law, the so-called Asian Exclusion Act of 1924, and her use of it to explain Ojih-chan's action are, like her understanding of her parents' backgrounds and the details of the leasing of the hotel, further examples of the historicity of her autobiography. This historicity helps to substantiate her pluralistic recognition of the differing historical origins of America's peoples.

In large part, too, her ironical view arises from experiences of being mistaken and misunderstood because of her race. She understands herself to be different from the stereotype of a "Japanese" others may prejudge her to be. In understanding this, she must understand others even though they do not know her. Whereas at the beginning of the work it seemed that it was Mother who (as Sone humorously suggests) cursed the child with the label of her race, when Japan invades Shanghai and Americans consequently vilify Japan, the curse of being "Japanese" comes not from within the Japanese-American individual and her family but from racists surrounding her and her race. It is deadly serious: "Gradually I learned . . . the terrible curse that went with having Japanese blood. As the nations went, so went their people. Japan and the United States were no longer seeing eye to eye, and we felt the repercussions in our daily lives" (118). She and her friends are told by the manager of a swimming club, "Sorry, we don't want any Japs around here," and all the youths can do is say, "We're not Japs. We're American citizens" before they "piled into the car and sped away trying to ignore the bruise on our pride" (119).

If Sone's first "shock" in life is being told her race at age six, and her second discovery the consequent ironical point of view of a Japanese American, her third change in the way she sees the world comes with the internment. Sone here seems to acquire a language that appears accommodationist, the language of a Pollyanna. Yet it is strikingly clear that such language arises expressly because of the straits into which the Itoi family and some 110,000 others are crammed by "reason" of their race. Having described their arrival at the Puyallup Fairgrounds, deep in mud, where animals were the previous tenants, Sone recalls how her mother spotted the first dandelions of that spring of 1942 and claimed them as hers to cultivate, "the only beautiful things around here" (174). In this moment Monica composed a poem, imitating Mother, one of whose hobbies is writing poetry:

> Oh, Dandelion, Dandelion,
> Despised and uprooted by all,
> Dance and bob your golden heads
> For you've finally found your home
> With your yellow fellows, *nali keli*, amen!

The fun of her spontaneous poem lightens the grim moment,

but it does so with an absurd laughter because the evacuation of these people from their homes is absurd. Indeed, quite in keeping with a sort of *tanka*, the conventional five-line, 31-syllable Japanese verse form Sone parodies, the poem is not escapist but is about despised and uprooted dandelions and people alike. By the belittling comparison, it is a satirical comment on the internment.[26]

The cells converted from animal pens, the mess hall, the wretched food, and, it goes without saying, the latrines—Puyallup Fairgrounds (sardonically nicknamed "Camp Harmony"), the assembly center where the issei and nisei from the vicinity of Seattle and Tacoma were held until Minidoka was ready for them in Idaho, assaulted every sense of what both generations had considered their American home. The Pollyanna in Sone indeed cheers the prospect of change when after more than three months at Puyallup the internees hear that their relocation camp is nearly ready: "We were excited at the thought of going to unknown territory, and we liked the Indian flavor of the name 'Idaho.' I remembered a series of bright, hot pictures of Idaho in the *National Geographic* magazine, the sun-baked terrain, dried-up waterholes, runty-looking sagebrush and ugly nests of rattlesnakes. I knew it wasn't going to be a comfortable experience, but it would be a change" (189). But though they begin with excitement and anticipation of adventure, Sone's words quickly sink into a parched and bristly, venomous naturalism from which she is saved by her own weak consolation that the move would at least be a change from one camp to another, indeed quite like American Indians herded into reservations. The attempted bright optimism that can be mistaken for an acquiescence to the government's will cannot be sustained. The language and tones, the veiled sarcasms of Sone's writing become self-contradicting, undercutting, and uncertain, highly unlike the confident assertions she recollects thinking or saying even when she was six.

During the internment the nisei assumed new roles and responsibilities under their most trying circumstances. To come of age is difficult enough (Sone became twenty-three in 1942 when the internment began). To be imprisoned and thus unable to enjoy or to hoist and carry the status of adulthood is worse still. To have to assume, however, a forced and unnatural responsibility because one's alien parents are suppressed and are no longer in charge is a peculiar inversion of order which Japanese Americans experienced when the bombing of Pearl Harbor made the speaking of Japanese and the leadership by the issei unwise if not dangerous to display. Much happened to the nisei at once in the internment, and much was prevented from happening. Their maturing was short-circuited and suspended. Their world in the camps was unreal, a place where, Sone laughs, they grew so accustomed to bussing their dishes and scraping their garbage into mess-hall cans that they nearly do so in a diner—and almost forget to pay for their meals—when they take an unusual leave from camp to find a wedding dress for Minnie, the brother Henry's bride-to-be (204). In the camp, Sone reflects, "we had drifted farther and farther away from the American scene. We had been set aside, and we had become adjusted to our peripheral existence" (198). This ought to have been an easily foreseeable outcome, except that officials rationalized the internment with propaganda about how it would Americanize the Japanese Americans by putting them in test tubes for democracy where they would learn a semblance of self-governance and become model citizens by some strange chemistry. Sone is not fooled by such claims. The internment literally alienates the incarcerated from "the American scene."

In *Nisei Daughter*, the highly concentrated coming-of-age of Sone and her fellow nisei occurs at the comical, nearly disastrous reception following Minnie and Henry's wedding. The reception is held in the camp's "huge recreation barracks" in order that the couple's many friends may be invited who were prevented by "rigid rules concerning town passes" from attending the wedding ceremony the previous day in the minister's apartment on the outside, at Twin Falls (210). Despite the extraordinary circumstances, Sone describes how Minnie insists on creating a picture-perfect American wedding. The reception stands outside the flow of time like the Japanese school principal Ohashi, but at a seemingly opposite extreme of cultural iconography, this side picturing an "American" ideal the camps at once dictated and denied to the internees:

> Sunday afternoon, the stage was finally set for a formal hat-and-gloves reception. The silver tea set, the coffee urn, china cups and saucers, gleaming silverware, silver trays of nuts and mints, all borrowed, were set in their proper places. Confronted with this polished glamour, the ugly bare rafters and the two by four planks crisscrossing the walls receded hastily into the background. Behind the curtain . . . [were] gallon cans of ice cream. Outdoors, the pale yellow sun was doing its best to soften the sting of the sharp March wind. It was a perfect day for a brisk walk for our guests, some of whom would be walking several miles to our end of the camp. I anticipated a delightful afternoon with people drifting in and out for the next two hours to chat with the bride and groom and the in-laws, to meet new people and to renew old acquaintances. It would be a brief return to an urban affair, a blend of laughter, the polite tinkle of silver against teacups, and soft, bouncy music. (211)

Again Sone undercuts her picture of the ideal wedding reception with the reality of their situation. The "brisk walk for our guests" may be several miles long for some: this is Sone's most sharply pointed indication of just how vast the concentration camp is. The ideal reception is an illusion, certainly in these circumstances. The thin gaiety of the nisei who host the party lasts only a bit beyond its scheduled beginning at two that afternoon. No guests arrive. The hosts wait anxiously until three, when the issei come all at once, their tardiness implying mature restraint. Then with similar restraint, discomforting to the nisei hosts, the issei politely refuse any refreshments, for these are served at a buffet, whereas the issei expect, as is their custom, to be pressed several times, individually, into accepting the tea and sweets by gently insistent hosts. The issei also expect to be entertained, something the nisei have not anticipated in their imagining an afternoon filled with the laughter and chatter of a community in reunion.

But the apparent failure of the reception is not the true point of the event in the autobiography; neither is the conventional idea that certain ceremonial events, especially weddings but also funerals, for instance, reaffirm the solidarity of the community expressly because they are reunions. What becomes evident in Sone's narration of the wedding reception is that, for these nisei, it is perhaps the first time they themselves have had to play the host—and play the host not simply to their peers but now most importantly to their elders. Placed among obviously strong moments in the autobiography—the opening incident, Monica's bout with tuberculosis, Kenji's death, the seventh of December 1941, the remembrance of a nisei killed in combat in Europe—the afternoon of the wedding reception may seem mainly humorous because of the clash of expectations of hosts and guests. But it is also a vignette of the nisei's—specifically, a nisei daughter's—growing up in the most unlikely setting of the concentration camp, and of the internment which has plucked them out of time and growth. In time the party warms up after all. The issei for a moment think that the young people are the performers of the entertainment the issei expect—rather like watching a tea ceremony—when in exasperation one nisei and then another walks to the buffet to fill individual plates to present to the guests. And at the very end, "freed of the teacups and cake plates" and released as well from their unaccustomed role as the nisei's guests (the issei, too, have been nervous as performers in the event), the issei "rushed at Minnie and the in-laws to offer their congratulations, all at once, and the babble of laughter rose to a hilarious pitch" (215).

Thus coming to terms with each other, the two generations complete their first act in new roles. The afternoon contains a moment of transmission and change: the transmission, that is, of adult social responsibility from the issei to their children. This I believe is an underlying theme in Sone's choice of that particular event. Sone's account of it stands on the idea that, as powerful as the internment was in attempting to tear apart the community, family, and Japanese-American individual, in her experience that attempt was a failure. The wedding reception demonstrates how, even within that camp, the underlying stress on both the differences and the unity between the first and second generations implies a recognition not only of the past and their shared histories but a vision of a future in lives characterized by more than the usual changes.

One of the most persistent notions about the issei is that they came to America to sojourn only long enough to make the fortune to enable them to return to Japan and live there in comfort. Ignorant of the laws forbidding issei to own real property in the western states, some young nisei and the American public at large interpreted their refraining from buying homes and land as a sign that the issei intended to remain transient.[27] Ignorant of the American naturalization laws, upheld repeatedly by the U.S. Supreme Court, forbidding the naturalization of Asians, the American public at large interpreted the issei's lack of American citizenship as their continuing loyalty by choice to Japan. Behind such discriminatory laws were both an assumption about the inability of Asians to assimilate and the intent of lawmakers to prevent Asians from settling permanently in the United States. A false impression of issei transience was both a cause for and a consequence of further series of American laws against the race. While Sone is not alone in withholding fuel for such racist legislation, ignorance of such laws is far more common than her understanding of them.

The comic incident of the wedding reception at Minidoka in a sense enacts the fulfillment, however awkward, that racist ignorance and intentions have denied the issei. Because they were denied it, the issei spent their lives in America achieving not their own but their children's U.S. citizenship. To the issei, the nisei's coming-of-age was not simply to be the attainment of adulthood; it was to be the nisei's entrance into full and mature rights, privileges, and duties of American citizenship. So, following the attack on Pearl Harbor, the thought that nisei citizenship, their birthright, had been revoked by their fellow Americans, no matter that such an act was illegal, must have brought to ruin decades of the issei's living for the sake of their children. This is part of the context Sone does not explicate but which deepens the moment nonetheless, when the nisei wait on the aging issei at the wedding reception in Camp Minidoka.

Themes such as the deep and serious intergenerational continuity underlying the tea party emerge from beneath Sone's characteristic humor and cheerfulness, her attempts to put a bright face on the thunderclouds. Curiously, when she tries to go beyond narrating such events to express her thoughts discursively, she appears not to have yet understood these very themes. This appears especially in her final chapter, "Deeper into the Land," when she returns from Wendell College in southern Indiana to Minidoka to spend Christmas with her parents. It is 1944, I assume, though Sone rarely provides dates for events in her book. Her living outside the concentration camp is precisely a meaning of the Relocation. The "Relocation" was a diaspora: once evacuated from the West Coast and interned, nisei judged qualified were sent to work or to school in scattered places around the country where, on their own and alone, they were to become as assimilated—in a sense, as invisible—as possible. Sone attempts mechanically to draw her autobiography to a rounded conclusion by alluding to its beginning when Mother says of their experience of internment that "We felt terribly bad about being your Japanese parents" (236). The nisei daughter replies; her reassurances are brittle, her language filled with clichés and jargon uncharacteristic of her until now, maybe because as the autobiography ends she is just entering that stretch of adulthood when one must realize and put into explicit words the implied themes of one's life. The explicit terms for her life as a nisei daughter, however, have not yet been created: "'No, don't say such things, Mama, please. If only you knew how much I have changed about being a Nisei. It wasn't such a tragedy. I don't resent my Japanese blood anymore. I'm proud of it, in fact, because of you and the Issei who've struggled so much for us. It's really nice to be born into two cultures, like getting a real bargain in life, two for the price of one. The hardest part, I guess, is the growing up, but after that, it can be interesting and stimulating. I used to feel like a two-headed monstrosity, but now I find that two heads are better than one'" (236).

Aside from the fact that Sone, up to this point, has never expressed any resentment of her "Japanese blood" (resentment of the intrusion of having to attend Japanese school being another matter), in the concluding chapters she struggles with having to speak as an adult with an adult, here her own mother. The concentration camp, she realizes, retarded her and her peers, kept them childlike in the contexts of the outside worlds from which they were evacuated and into which they were relocated. The internment, with its language and ideology of assimilation, shows its marks on her at the very end of her autobiography, these chapters of the first three decades of a life that has mainly run counter to that ideology. Even when they were told by officials of the Relocation that, being "Americanized," they culturally opposed their "Japanese" parents, the nisei were presumed like their parents to be alien to America and therefore were interned in order to be taught to assimilate into "American" ways.[28] This was required of them despite the tight ring of racist illogic having already assumed, in the fact of the internment, that a person of "Japanese blood," a nisei, could not be assimilated, ever, for this person would forever be at least in part a "Japanese," defined as antithetical to being "American"—"Japanese" in a way utterly unlike what Kazuko's mother meant to her six-year-old daughter. To define "American" not by birthright or naturalization but by race, to see the term *Japanese American* as indicating partly the one, partly the other culture, is to endorse the internment of Japanese Americans and pose once more a threat against the civil rights of all Americans. To define "American" not by race but by histories of diverse peoples' experiences, deeds, lineages, intellectual and cultural developments, and by their histories of integration (not assimilation) is to do as Sone explicitly does until her final chapter, which she ends with a shockingly assimilationist cliché: "The Japanese and the American parts of me were now blended into one" (238). If at the moment of her writing that sentence the evacuation and internment were to recur in actuality and not only in memory, Sone and the other nisei daughters and sons would be swept up again into prison, for now they have been made to believe and to say (if Sone is representative in her concluding thought and wording) that they think of themselves, their unified "blend," as partly and now inextricably alien to America, just as those who interned them have claimed.

I do not believe that Sone continued far beyond that postwar era and her youthful autobiography of 1953 to continue to mimic the jargon of her oppressors.[29] Yet fortunately because of the change of terms from self-satire and protest to self-effacement and accommodation, *Nisei Daughter* is valuable at the very least for being an ingenuous and retrospective record, at its conclusion a demonstration more than an interpretation, of nisei history and its basis in experience. The changes in her discourse show just how the nisei daughter and her peers bent under a very great weight. But in view of Sone's resiliency and, through most of her autobiography, her faith that we and our immigrant forebears are Americans by our histories, for the sake of my own sansei generation, our children, and the descendants of all of us Americans, I hope we learn to see Sone's parting words critically.

## Notes

1. The term *nisei* in reference to Japanese Americans means the second generation in the United States, i.e., the first generation born in this country. The term *issei* refers to the immigrant generation; the term *sansei* refers to the third generation resident in the United States, the grandchildren of the immigrants.

2. For a critical discussion of *Nisei Daughter* and especially of apparently assimilationist trends in the second half of Sone's work, see Kim (74–81). In disagreement with Kim is Fujita's extensive discussion of *Nisei Daughter*. See also S. Frank Miyamoto's introduction

to the 1979 edition of *Nisei Daughter*, which, however, is based upon assumptions (or perceptions) about "Japanese" and "Americans" which do not really fit Sone's way of defining these terms. See also Sone's own preface to the 1979 edition (xv–xvii). Yamada reviews this newer edition in *MELUS*. For another reading of *Nisei Daughter* and its contexts, see Rayson, who stresses "a split cultural identity" in the autobiographies of Japanese-American women who write about their World War II internment; she cites some recent analyses of women's autobiographies to frame her discussion.

3. The detailing of foods in Asian-American literature is commonly enough done as to be a literary device, both authenticating and authenticated by life and literature and immediately recognizable to an informed reader. Louis Chu, *Eat a Bowl of Tea*; Wing Tek Lum, "Juk"; Cathy Song, "The Youngest Daughter"; Bienvenido N. Santos, "Immigration Blues"; Frank Chin, *The Year of the Dragon*; and Jim Mitsui, "When Father Came Home for Lunch," for example, all contain passages conveying the intimacy, and not exoticism, of Asian-American food and culture.

4. The terms and concepts of "assimilation" and "pluralism" are central to such studies of American ethnicity as Boelhower's and Sollors's works. Caveats, however, are in order. Boelhower tends to see "advocates of the multi-ethnic paradigm," or proponents of pluralism, as repeating the "essentialist errors" of their opponents in defining the elements of culture in fixed and static ways (20). I would agree with him that, if his observation is true, then such a pluralism was a very naive sort to begin with; but such is no longer the case, Boelhower's own sense of cultural dynamicism and continual change being shared today by other scholars. His readings of "ethnic signs," however, are sometimes false. For instance, while his general observation (81–82) seems sound that family names imply genealogies, which imply ethnic histories that distinguish one group from another, his illustration that in Kingston's *The Woman Warrior* the Chinese immigrants are said to hide their names is not, as Boelhower thinks, because they wish to disguise their ethnicity. How can they? They are perceived as being racially Chinese, something a name change even to "Smith" cannot hide. They hide their names and true identities because they are "paper sons," illegal immigrants who assumed false names in order to qualify for entrance into America by American laws. Boelhower seems not to know this history. In Sollors, "consent" is a refinement of "assimilation," while "descent" is likewise somewhat synonymous with "pluralism." It is curious still that in his discussion of cultures of consent Sollors seems only to glance at or glimpse what Americans of "minority" groups typically have to see: that being different from oth-

ers by "descent" or race is not a matter of choice (i.e., "consent"), and yet this difference is not necessarily a bar to national harmony and unity. I note this because throughout *Beyond Ethnicity* there runs a discomfort with the concept of pluralism, and this bias is perhaps exacerbated because the opposite, "consent," sounds so affirming while "descent" is a pun on "dissent," as if it were a continual reminder of disunity.

5.  A category of Japanese-American autobiographies I do not include are by authors not so much interested in identifying themselves as Americans as in depicting themselves as Japanese in America. This is a mixed group: for instance, Yone Noguchi's *The American Diary of a Japanese Girl*, where the author presents his own observations of California through the persona of a woman visiting from Japan, and Etsu Inagaki Sugimoto's *A Daughter of the Samurai*, concerning a class and breeding not typical of the laboring immigrants but potentially insightful therefore in unusual ways. In Asian-American fiction there is the case of Onoto Watanna (Winnifred Eaton Babcock), a sister of Sui Sin Far (Edith Maude Eaton, also a fiction writer). Watanna favored setting her romantic novels (e.g., *The Wooing of Wistaria* and *A Japanese Nightingale*) in Japan and until World War II cultivated an identification with that country while her sister identified herself as Chinese American, their father being British, their mother Chinese. What these authors in these works have in common are their attempts, appealing to some degree to a popular taste for the exotic, to use Japaneseness as an opaque sign of their identity while assuming that an "American" stands in contrast, mainly because of race.

6.  Chan et al., in "Resources for Chinese and Japanese American Literary Traditions" (28–29), make this point of contrasting "recognition" and "acceptance" when discussing Kazuo Miyamoto's *Hawaii: End of the Rainbow*.

7.  Published statements and promotions of the "model minority" myth begin at least as far back as 1965, with Schmid and Nobbe, and, in 1966, Petersen, who does not ignore the World War II internment and the suffering that lies in the background of the group's "success." Such articles run unbroken to the present. For a description, survey, and critique of the myth, see Osajima.

8.  Unfavorable Asian-American criticism of Okimoto's book includes Chin et al., *Aiiieeeee! An Anthology of Asian-American Writers* (xxvii–xxviii), which also includes a similar criticism of Sone's autobiography but with the inference that her writing is shaped by the detested dual-identity concept whereas Okimoto's is more like an active perpetration of that ideology. See also Iwasaki (454) and Kim (81–84).

9. My study *And the View from the Shore: The Pastoral and the Heroic in Hawaii's Literary Traditions* (83–86) contains a discussion of Michener and the criticism I mention here.

10. For criticism of *Farewell to Manzanar*, see Kim (84–89). Kim finds in Houston a dual impulse—either to "disappear" or to "fight back"—but "the method of fighting disappearance turns out to be an attempt to assimilate, which is in effect the same as disappearing" (84).

11. Seattle bookseller David Ishii showed me a copy of the KING-TV (the NBC affiliate) call sheet following the broadcast. It contained some memorably racist responses which were repeated many times during the ensuing years of struggle over the issue of redress for the World War II internment of civilians. For a critique of the television movie, see Okamura.

12. For an interpretation of many nisei women's autobiographies as compared with men's, see Rayson, whose assumptions about a "traditional family system" (46), however, are repetitions of fixed and rigid characterizations of both "Japanese" and "American" ideals the stereotypical nature of which Sone and others subvert. This subversion is found also in the very humaneness of the visual artist Miné Okubo's remarkable *Citizen 13660*; while quite different in tone and striking appearance from *Nisei Daughter*, Okubo's book is a forerunner, in the author's prose and drawings, to the treatment of the internment in the later pages of Sone's book. Rayson discusses Okubo's autobiography and a 1972 catalog of her work, *Miné Okubo: An American Experience*, along with Sone's and Houston's autobiographies, Akemi Kikumura's oral biography, *Through Harsh Winters*, and Yoshiko Uchida's *Desert Exile*. Though Rayson states that, with one exception, nisei men have not "written autobiographically of the internment" (45), that historical event does affect Inouye and Okimoto. Moreover, a recent example of an autobiography of a nisei male with still another distinctive experience and point of view regarding the internment is Karl Yoneda's *Ganbatte*.

13. Among the male poets who wrote critically of the internment while it was occurring are Keiho Soga, Taisanboku Mori, Sojin Takei, and Muin Ozaki, in *Poets behind Barbed Wire*. Until the publication of such editions as this and, earlier, *Ayumi: A Japanese American Anthology*, ed. Janice Mirikitani, female and male issei voices of satire, protest, and outright grievance were rarely published in the United States.

14. See Rabine. I owe this reference to Bonnie Tu-Smith and her dissertation, "Alternative Visions: Perspectives on Individualism and Community in Multiethnic American Literatures, 1960s–1980s" (Washington State U, 1989).

15. Often masked in misreadings and the rapt exoticism of the narrator herself is the idea that the Sitting Ghost, or what Great Uncle, echoing the English phrase, calls "Sit Dom Kuei" (88), is no less "real" than what in Western psychology is poetically called a "homunculus" (as if a "small man" were animating a person's brain), a *cri du chat* (the "cry of the cat" of an afflicted baby), or, say, an "Oedipal complex." At one point Brave Orchid, speaking of her combat against the Sitting Ghost, enjoins her medical students, "You have to help me rid the world of this disease, as invisible and deadly as bacteria" (74). This is a reminder that bacteria and psychological complexes are no more nor less "visible" than "ghosts" and are as picturesquely and mythically named. Tricked by Kingston, Dasenbrock badly misreads "ghosts" in *The Woman Warrior* by seeing them as "spectral," superstitious auras clothing the spiritual and the corporeal (13–15) rather than as Brave Orchid's medical terminology and as the targets of blunt insults as unliteral (and unspiritual) as "You bastard!"

16. See note 1, above, for definitions of *issei*, *nisei*, and *sansei*. See also note 20, below.

17. Momoko Iko once commented to me that before World War II the nisei of the West Coast grew up actually believing that one of them could someday become president of the United States. Of course such a possibility was utterly crushed in their aspirations when they were thrown into the concentration camps.

18. See Chin, "This Is Not an Autobiography," for a condemnation of the form, and with it the content, of the Chinese-American autobiography, which he accuses of being inspired not by Chinese heroic values but by Christian confession. Of the Asian-American autobiographies I mention or discuss in this essay, the most abjectly confessional is not Chinese American but Japanese American, Okimoto's. Still, Chin's insight may well apply to every one of them at one point or another of each text.

19. Still the focus of deep conflicts among Japanese Americans today, no-no boys and other nisei draft resisters during World War II in general demanded a clarification of the status of their U.S. citizenship: if they were not American citizens (the nisei having been classified 4-C, enemy aliens), then they could not be drafted into American military service; or if they were now recognized once more as citizens of the United States and were therefore draftable, then they were wrongfully imprisoned without charges, trial, or conviction, along with every other individual locked within the concentration camps. The government, caught thus in a vise of its own making, dealt with the Resistance in several ways, including trumping up charges of draft evasion, an ignominious crime whose stain the

members of the Resistance have not yet entirely lost. See my essay, "Japanese American Moral Dilemmas in John Okada's *No-No Boy* and Milton Murayama's *All I Asking for Is My Body*."

20. *Nikkei* literally means 'Japanese American.' The terms cited here were devised by Japanese immigrants to apply directly to their lives—and implicit vision of future generations—in America. Strictly speaking, they are not "Japanese" terms but, born from an American historical experience, they are part of the American lexicon of the nikkei. The term *issei* means the 'first Japanese American generation,' not the last Japanese one. Thus Sone, the nisei daughter, is of the same nikkei culture as her issei parents, and her autobiography realizes this way of conceiving her culture and her relationship with her parents throughout most of its pages. Cultural conflicts among the issei and nisei in this sense are intracultural—dynamic instances of change and continuing development of the culture—not intercultural conflicts presumed to be between statically defined *East* and *West*.

21. The first of the anti-alien, state land laws was written into the Washington State Constitution in 1889.

22. As I write in "Japanese American Moral Dilemmas," it is a youthful and confused ignorance of the American land laws that mistakenly reinforces the protagonist's thought, in Okada's *No-No Boy*, that the issei did not buy property prior to World War II because they intended to return to Japan. Given the prevalence of such misunderstanding among urban nisei (to whom such laws seemed irrelevant until adulthood brought the responsibility of knowing better), it is rather remarkable that Sone implicitly understands the matter so consistently.

23. It is rather uncommon in Asian-American literature to see an immigrant depicted as having a consistent and yet changing or developing identity stretching from life in Asia through life in America, as can be inferred in the characterization of Sone's mother. Sone's view of her parents is reminiscent of how Bulosan, in his *America Is in the Heart*, bases his characterization of the protagonist, Carlos, on a continuous development of a moral, social, and political consciousness from childhood in the Philippines to adulthood in America. In *Upon Their Shoulders* Ota also characterizes the maturing of issei in such a way, as does Kazuo Miyamoto in *Hawaii: End of the Rainbow*.

24. In contrast, Kingston characterizes the narrator of her *Woman Warrior* as thinking her mother "Chinese" and foreign, rather than "American" and truly resident. So does Jade Snow in Wong's *Fifth Chinese Daughter*. But unlike Kingston, Wong seems to believe it—believe, that is, that "American" is defined so as to exclude her

long-resident parents and to alienate her own self both from them and from her being truly "American."

25. Late in Sone's autobiography we glimpse Ohashi relocated to Colorado following the internment (233). He becomes a bookseller. While it might momentarily seem that by being humbled he got what he deserved for his prewar stiffness, the lasting impression is sad: he has been reduced from his former stature as a larger-than-life figure, as have all the interned issei parents and elders.

26. See my comments on the issei verse form, *senryu*, in "Hawaii, the Northwest, and Asia: Localism and Local Literary Development in the Creation of an Asian Immigrants' Sensibility." Senryu is satirical verse written in the same seventeen-syllable form as haiku but with people and society rather than nature and perception as subjects. See also Honda.

27. See, in note 19 above, the fictional case of Ichiro Yamada, protagonist of Okada's *No-No Boy*. For a concise expression of the view of Asians, particularly Japanese, as reluctant sojourners to America, see Mansfield, who is sympathetic with what he calls "The great bulk of immigrants . . . from Asia [who] did not choose to leave their homes" but rather "were compelled to leave" by bad conditions of life in Asia while he somehow thinks or infers that all other "migrants"—Europeans, Latin Americans, and African Americans—came by choice, including even the slaves. Despite his expressed sympathy, the view Mansfield thus presents in 1967 thoroughly evokes an American ideology aimed since the nineteenth century to keep Asian immigrants disenfranchised and alienated, with serious consequences as well to their descendants. Chinese immigrants have been allowed naturalization beginning in World War II as a result of the two countries' alliance. South Asians and Filipinos gained their right to naturalization in 1946. But naturalization was not permitted to other Asian immigrants, the last in America to be proscribed by race, until 1952.

28. At the heart of Okada's *No-No Boy*, literally in the novel's central pages (123–26), Mr. Kanno, the magnanimous and loving father of Kenji, the veteran dying of a war wound, remembers how a young nisei sociologist scolded the issei in a concentration camp for failing to be "American" parents to their "American" nisei children. The sociologist's imputation is a base one, a bald example of "blaming the victim": he lectures that the issei are to blame for the internment of both generations because they have corrupted their children with Japaneseness. The example of the issei father, Mr. Kanno, utterly refutes this charge and illuminates how, before the war, the other issei parents, too (for instance Sone's), may have been closely bonded with their children—bonds which the internment

was meant to sever, since any nisei who believed the sociologist would hate their parents for their fate. It is absurdly ironic that, while the sociologist, an agent of the War Relocation Authority, calls the nisei "American," the nisei too are imprisoned for being "Japanese." For a recent, thorough examination of the history of the internment and relocation as a social experiment conducted by the Assistant Secretary of War John J. McCloy and his subordinates, see Drinnon.

29. Sau-ling C. Wong has observed that Sone's preface to the 1979 Edition of *Nisei Daughter* bears no overt sign that its author is aware of how conflicted are the language and assumptions or implications of the autobiography's later pages. The 1979 Preface, in contrast to the autobiography's closing pages, is in contemporary terms not of assimilation but of cultural pluralism and indeed of hegemony or political recognition and empowerment, as though the terms concluding the main work were not in conflict with such a vision.

## Works Cited

Babcock, Winnifred Eaton. [Onoto Watanna.] *A Japanese Nightingale.* New York: Harper, 1903.

————. *The Wooing of Wistaria.* New York: Harper, 1902.

Boelhower, William. *Through a Glass Darkly: Ethnic Semiosis in American Literature.* New York: Oxford UP, 1984.

Bulosan, Carlos. *America Is in the Heart.* 1946. Seattle: U of Washington P, 1973.

Chan, Jeffery Paul, et al. "Resources for Chinese and Japanese American Literary Traditions." *Amerasia Journal* 8, no. 1 (1981): 19–31.

Chin, Frank, et al., eds. *Aiiieeeee! An Anthology of Asian-American Writers.* 1974. Washington, DC: Howard UP, 1983.

————. *The Chickencoop Chinaman and* The Year of the Dragon: *Two Plays.* Seattle: U of Washington P, 1981.

————. "This Is Not an Autobiography." *Genre* 18 (Summer 1985): 109–30.

Chu, Louis. *Eat a Bowl of Tea.* 1961. New York: Lyle Stuart, 1986.

Clemens, Samuel [Mark Twain]. *Adventures of Huckleberry Finn.* New York: Charles L. Webster, 1885.

Dasenbrock, Reed Way. "Intelligibility and Meaningfulness in Multicultural Literature in English." *PMLA* 102 (1987): 10–19.

Drinnon, Richard. *Keeper of Concentration Camps: Dillon S. Myer and American Racism.* Berkeley: U of California P, 1987.

Ellison, Ralph. *Invisible Man.* New York: Random, 1952.

Fujita, Gayle Kimi. "The 'Ceremonial Self' in Japanese American Literature." Diss. Brown U, 1986.

Honda, Sachiko. "Issei Senryu." In *Frontiers of Asian American Studies: Writing, Research, and Commentary,* ed. Gail M. Nomura et al. Pullman: Washington State UP, 1989.

Houston, Jeanne Wakatsuki, and James D. Houston. *Farewell to Manzanar.* New York: Houghton, 1973.

Iko, Momoko. "The Gold Watch." [Act I.] In *Aiiieeeee! An Anthology of Asian-American Writers,* ed. Frank Chin et al. 1974. Washington, DC: Howard UP, 1983.

Inouye, Daniel K. *Journey to Washington.* Englewood Cliffs: Prentice, 1967.

Iwasaki, Bruce. "Introduction: Literature." In *Counterpoint: Perspectives on Asian America*, ed. Emma Gee. Los Angeles: Asian American Studies Center, UCLA, 1976. 452–63.

Kikumura, Akemi. *Through Harsh Winters: The Life of a Japanese Immigrant Woman*. Novato, CA: Chandler and Sharp, 1981.

Kim, Elaine H. *Asian American Literature: An Introduction to the Writings and Their Social Context*. Philadelphia: Temple UP, 1982.

Kingston, Maxine Hong. *Tripmaster Monkey: His Fake Book*. New York: Knopf, 1989.

———. *The Woman Warrior: Memoirs of a Girlhood among Ghosts*. New York: Knopf, 1976.

Lum, Wing Tek. "Juk." In *Asian-American Heritage: An Anthology of Prose and Poetry*, ed. David Hsin-Fu Wand. New York: Washington Square P, 1974. 155–56. Rpt. in *Expounding the Doubtful Points*, by Wing Tek Lum. Honolulu: Bamboo Ridge P, 1988. 91-92.

Mansfield, Mike. Foreword to *Journey to Washington*, by Daniel K. Inouye. Englewood Cliffs: Prentice, 1967.

Michener, James A. *Hawaii*. New York: Random, 1959.

*Miné Okubo: An American Experience*. Oakland Museum, 1972.

Mirikitani, Janice, ed. *Ayumi: A Japanese American Anthology*. San Francisco: Japanese American Anthology Committee, 1980.

Mitsui, Jim. "When Father Came Home for Lunch." In *Breaking Silence, an Anthology of Contemporary Asian American Poets*, ed. Joseph Bruchac. Greenfield Center, NY: Greenfield Review P, 1983. 194.

Miyamoto, Kazuo. *Hawaii: End of the Rainbow*. Rutland, VT: Tuttle, 1964.

Miyamoto, S. Frank. Introd. to *Nisei Daughter*, by Monica Sone. 1979 ed. Seattle: U of Washington P, 1979. vii–xiv.

Mori, Toshio. *Yokohama, California*. 1949. Seattle: U of Washington P, 1985.

Noguchi, Yone. *The American Diary of a Japanese Girl*. New York: Frederick A. Stokes, 1901.

Okada, John. *No-No Boy*. 1957. Seattle: U of Washington P, 1979.

Okamura, Raymond. "*Farewell to Manzanar*: A Case of Subliminal Racism." In *Counterpoint: Perspectives on Asian America*, ed. Emma Gee. Los Angeles: UCLA Asian American Studies Center, 1976. 280–83.

Okimoto, Daniel I. *American in Disguise*. Foreword by James A. Michener. New York: Walker/Weatherhill, 1971.

Okubo, Miné. *Citizen 13660*. 1946. Seattle: U of Washington P, 1983.

Osajima, Keith. "Asian American as the Model Minority: An Analysis of the Popular Press Image in the 1960s and 1980s." In *Reflections on Shattered Windows: Promises and Prospects for Asian American Studies*, ed. Gary Y. Okihiro et al. Pullman: Washington State UP, 1988. 165–74.

Ota, Shelley Ayame Nishimura. *Upon Their Shoulders*. New York: Exposition, 1951.

Petersen, William. "Success Story, Japanese American Style." *New York Times Magazine*, 9 Jan. 1966, late city ed.: 20–21, 33, 36, 38, 40–41, 43.

Rabine, Leslie W. "No Lost Paradise: Social Gender and Symbolic Gender in the Writings of Maxine Hong Kingston." *Signs* 12 (Spring 1987): 471–92.

Rayson, Ann. "Beneath the Mask: Autobiographies of Japanese-American Women." *MELUS* 14 (Spring 1987): 43–57.

Santos, Bienvenido N. *Scent of Apples*. Seattle: U of Washington P, 1981.

Schmid, Calvin F., and Charles E. Nobbe. "Socioeconomic Differentials Among Nonwhite Races." *American Sociological Review* 30 (1965): 909–22.

Soga, Keiho, Taisanboku Mori, Sojin Takei, and Muin Ozaki. *Poets Behind Barbed Wire*. Ed. Jiro Nakano and Kay Nakano. Illus. George Hoshida. Honolulu: Bamboo Ridge, 1983.

Sollors, Werner. *Beyond Ethnicity: Consent and Descent in American Culture*. New York: Oxford UP, 1986.

Sone, Monica. *Nisei Daughter*. 1953. Seattle: U of Washington P, 1979.

Song, Cathy. "The Youngest Daughter." In *Bamboo Ridge: The Hawaii Writers' Quarterly* 4 (1979): 10–11. Rpt. in *Picture Bride*, by Cathy Song. New Haven: Yale UP, 1983. 5–6.

Sugimoto, Etsu Inagaki. *A Daughter of the Samurai*. Garden City: Doubleday, 1925.

Sumida, Stephen H. *And the View from the Shore: The Pastoral and the Heroic in Hawaii's Literary Traditions*. Seattle: U of Washington P, 1991.

———. "Hawaii, the Northwest, and Asia: Localism and Local Literary Developments in the Creation of an Asian Immigrants' Sensibility." *The Seattle Review: Blue Funnel Line* 11 (1988): 9–18.

✗ ———. "Japanese American Moral Dilemmas in John Okada's *No-No Boy* and Milton Murayama's *All I Asking for Is My Body*." In *Frontiers of Asian American Studies: Writing, Research, and Commentary*, ed. Gail M. Nomura et al. Pullman: Washington State UP, 1989.

Tu-Smith, Bonnie. "Alternative Visions: Perspectives on Individualism and Community in Multiethnic American Literatures, 1960s–1980s." Diss. Washington State U, 1989.

Uchida, Yoshiko. *Desert Exile: The Uprooting of a Japanese American Family*. Seattle: U of Washington P, 1982.

———. *Picture Bride: A Novel*. New York: Simon, 1987.

Wong, Jade Snow. *Fifth Chinese Daughter*. New York: Harper, 1945.

Yamada, Mitsuye. *Camp Notes and Other Poems*. Berkeley: Shameless Hussy Press, 1976.

———. *Desert Run: Poems and Stories*. Latham, NY: Kitchen Table: Women of Color Press, 1988.

✗ ———. Review of *Nisei Daughter*. *MELUS* 7 (Fall 1980): 91–92.

Yamamoto, Hisaye. *Seventeen Syllables and Other Stories*. Latham, NY: Kitchen Table: Women of Color Press, 1988.

Yamauchi, Wakako. *And the Soul Shall Dance*. *West Coast Plays* 11–12 (1982): 117–64.

Yoneda, Karl G. *Ganbatte: Sixty-Year Struggle of a Kibei Worker*. Introd. by Yuji Ichioka. Los Angeles: UCLA Asian American Studies Center, 1983.

# Autobiography as Guided Chinatown Tour? Maxine Hong Kingston's *The Woman Warrior* and the Chinese-American Autobiographical Controversy

*Sau-ling Cynthia Wong*

Maxine Hong Kingston's autobiography, *The Woman Warrior*, may be the best-known contemporary work of Asian-American literature. Winner of the National Book Critics Circle Award for the best book of nonfiction published in 1976, *The Woman Warrior* remains healthily in print and on the reading lists of numerous college courses; excerpts from it are routinely featured in anthologies with a multicultural slant. It is safe to say that many readers who otherwise do not concern themselves with Asian-American literature have read Kingston's book.

In spite—or maybe, as we shall see, because—of its general popularity, however, *The Woman Warrior* has by no means been received with unqualified enthusiasm by Kingston's fellow Chinese Americans. A number of Chinese-American critics have repeatedly denounced *The Woman Warrior*, questioning its autobiographic status, its authenticity, its representativeness, and thereby Kingston's personal integrity. Though often couched in the emotionally charged, at times openly accusatory, language characteristic of what the Chinese call "pen wars," the critical issues raised in this debate are not merely of passing interest. Rather, they lie at the heart of any theoretical discussion of ethnic American autobiography in particular and ethnic American literature in general. It would therefore be instructive to set out the terms of the controversy and explore their theoretical ramifications, with a view to understanding the nature of Kingston's narrative enterprise in *The Woman Warrior*.

The most fundamental objection to *The Woman Warrior*

concerns its generic status: its being billed as autobiography rather than fiction, when so much of the book departs from the popular definition of autobiography as an unadorned factual account of a person's own life. Responding to a favorable review of the book by Diane Johnson in the *New York Review of Books*, Jeffery Chan notes how "a white reading public will rave over ethnic biography while ignoring a Chinese American's literary art" and attacks Knopf, "a white publishing house," for "distributing an obvious fiction for fact" (6). The thrust of Chan's message is that the autobiographical label is a marketing ploy in which the author, to her discredit, has acquiesced. Chan's stricture is echoed by Benjamin Tong, who finds *The Woman Warrior* "obviously contrived," a work of "fiction passing for autobiography" ("Critic of Admirer" 6). By way of contrast, while the unusual generic status of *The Woman Warrior* is also widely noted by non–Chinese-American critics, it is seldom cited as either a weakness or a matter of personal, as opposed to artistic, purpose.[1]

How far is Kingston personally responsible for the nonfiction label on the covers of *The Woman Warrior*? According to her, very little:

> The only correspondence I had with the publisher concerning the classification of my books was that he said that Non-fiction would be the most accurate category; Non-fiction is such a catch-all that even "poetry is considered non-fiction."

And poetry is something in whose company she would be "flattered" to see her books.[2] The entire matter might have rested here—but for some theoretical issues raised by the controversy which command an interest beyond the topical.

Although Kingston's detractors do not use the term, at the heart of the controversy is the question of fictionalization: to what extent "fictional" features are admissible in a work that purports to be an autobiography. The Chinese-American critics of *The Woman Warrior* focus their attention on the social effects of admitting fictionalization into an autobiographical work. Their concern, variously worded, is summed up most concisely, if baldly, by Katheryn Fong:

> I read your references to mythical and feudal China as fiction. . . . Your fantasy stories are embellished versions of your mother's embellished versions of stories. As fiction, these stories are creatively written with graphic imagery and emotion. The problem is that non-Chinese are reading your fiction as true accounts of Chinese and Chinese American history. (67)

Thus stated, the *Woman Warrior* "problem" is seen to rest ultimately on the readers, not the author; the basis for denouncing *The Woman Warrior* is pragmatic, response-contingent, and reader-specific. Why, then, has Kingston been implicated at all in the misreadings of her audience? It is possible to reject the very question as irrelevant, in that authors have little control over how their published works will be read. On the other hand, when critics like Chan, Tong, or Fong hold Kingston responsible for her readers' failings, they do so from a set of assumptions about ethnic literature that are grounded in a keen awareness of the sociopolitical context of minority literary creation. Such an awareness is precisely what is missing in many white reviewers' remarks on *The Woman Warrior*; moreover, the autobiographical genre, with its promise (perceived or real) of "truthfulness," by nature encourages preoccupation with a work's sociopolitical context. Thus the charge of unwarranted fictionalization must be addressed.

*The Woman Warrior* can be considered fictionalized in a number of ways. On the most obvious formal level, it violates the popular perception of autobiography as an ordered shaping of life events anchored in the so-called external world. It aims at creating what James Olney calls "a realm of order where events bear to one another a relationship of significance rather than of chronology" ("Some Versions" 247). According to an early student of the genre, autobiographies must contain, "in some measure, the germ of a description of the manners of their times" (Pascal 8–9). Although recent scholars have found the referential grounding of autobiography much more problematic and its defining essence much more elusive (e.g., Olney, "Autobiography and the Cultural Moment" 3; Bruss 2; Eakin 5), the term *autobiography* usually does evoke, at least among general readers, a chronologically sequenced account with verifiable references to places, people, and events. As one critic puts it, in more abstruse language: "Texts bound by the real insist upon an epistemological status different from works of the imagination in which the real is more nearly hypothetical" (Krupat 25). But what if the "real" that an autobiography is bound by is the "imagination" of the protagonist?[3] This is the thorny problem of generic differentiation posed by *The Woman Warrior.*

By an outwardly oriented definition of autobiography, *The Woman Warrior* is at best only nominally autobiographical: to borrow a phrase from Pascal, it is a work "so engrossed with the inner life that the outer world becomes blurred" (Pascal 9), told by a narrator who, as a child, regularly sees "free movies" on "blank walls" and "[t]alks to people that aren't real inside [her] mind" (221). The prose slips from the subjunctive to the declarative with but the slightest warning: the No Name Woman story begins with *perhaps*'s and *could have been*'s (7) but soon dispenses with these reminders of conjecture. Likewise, while the Fa Mu Lan segment in "White Tigers" is initially marked as an enumeration of the possible and desirable—"The call *would* come from a bird. . . . The bird *would* cross the sun. . . . I *would* be a little girl of seven. . . ." (24–25; my italics)—the bulk of the narration is in the simple past tense, as if recounting completed events in the actual world. Two divergent accounts are given of Brave Orchid's encounter with the Sitting Ghost (81–84, 85–86), neither of which could have been definitive since the event (or alleged event) predates the birth of the daughter/narrator. "At the Western Palace," presented as a deceptively conventional, self-contained short story, is revealed in the next chapter to be a third-hand fiction (189–90). In short, the referential grounding of *The Woman Warrior* is tenuous and presented in a potentially misleading manner. A few public places and events in the "outer" world are recognizable from what we know about author Kingston's life; all else is recollection, speculation, reflection, meditation, imagination. Verifiability is virtually out of the question in a work so self-reflexive. Presumably, then, readers who do not pay sufficient attention to the narrative intricacies of *The Woman Warrior*, especially white readers with biased expectations, will mistake fiction for fact.

The critics of *The Woman Warrior* also detect fictionalization—in the sense of "making things up"—in the way Kingston has chosen to translate certain Chinese terms. A central example is the word *ghost*, based on Cantonese *kuei* or *gwai*, a key term in the book appearing in the subtitle as well as several important episodes.[4] Kingston renders *kuei* as *ghost*. Chan and Tong ("Critic of Admirer" 6), while conceding that the character can indeed mean "ghost" (as in "spirit of the dead"), insist that it be translated as *demon* (or *devil* or *asshole*). They object to the connotations of insubstantiality or neutrality in Kingston's translation, finding it unsanctioned by community usage and lacking in the hostility toward whites indispensable to true works of Chinese-American literature.[5]

Tong further elevates the rendition of *kuei* as *ghost* into a "purposeful" act of pandering to white tastes and adds another example of "mistranslation" ("Critic of Admirer" 6): referring to "frogs" as "heavenly chickens" (77), which should have been "field chickens" in Cantonese. (*Tien*, "sky" or "heaven," and *tien*, "field" or "meadow," differ only in tone, which is phonemic in Chinese dialects.) Tong suggests that Kingston must have knowingly selected the wrong term, the one with the "familiar exotic touristy flavor" relished by "whites checking out Chinese America" ("Critic of Admirer" 6).

A more serious charge of fictionalization concerns the way Kingston handles not just single Chinese terms but Chinese folklore and legends. The story of Fa Mu Lan,[6] the woman warrior invoked as the young protagonist's patron saint, is recognizable only in bare outline to a reader conversant with traditional Chinese culture. The section on the girl's period of training in the mountains draws extensively on popular martial arts "novels" or "romances" (*wuxia xiaoshuo*) as well as from traditional fantasy lore on *shenxian* ("immortals").[7] As for the way Kingston makes use of the traditional Fa Mu Lan story, at least the version fixed in the popular "Mulan Shi" or "Ballad of Mulan,"[8] deviations from it in *The Woman Warrior* are so numerous that only a few major ones can be noted here. The tattooing of the woman warrior is based on the well-known tale of Yue Fei, whose mother carved four characters (not entire passages) onto his back, exhorting him to be loyal to his country. Also, the spirit-marriage to the waiting childhood sweetheart, a wish-fulfilling inversion of the No Name Woman's fate (7), is utterly unlikely in ancient China, considering the lowly place of women. The traditional Fa Mu Lan is never described as having been pregnant and giving birth to a child while in male disguise. The episode of the wicked baron is fabricated. The Fa Mu Lan of "Mulan Shi" is a defender of the establishment, her spirit patriarchal as well as patriotic, a far cry from a peasant rebel in the vein of the heroes of *Outlaws of the Marsh*.[9]

Because of these and other liberties Kingston has taken with her raw material, *The Woman Warrior* has been criticized by a number of Chinese Americans varying in their knowledge of traditional Chinese culture. Chinese-born scholar Joseph S. M. Lau dismisses the book as a kind of mishmash, a retelling of old tales that would not impress those having access to the originals (Lau 65–66). Writer Frank Chin, who is fifth-generation, attacks Kingston for her "distortions" of traditional Chinese culture. In a parody of *The Woman Warrior* filled with inversions and travesties, Chin creates a piece entitled "The Unmanly Warrior," about a little French girl growing up in Canton and drawing inspiration from "her imagined French ancestor Joan of Arc."

[Her] picture of Joan of Arc . . . was so inaccurate as to demonstrate that the woman has gone mad, the French people of Frenchtown on the edge

of the port city said. The French girl is writing not history, but art, the
Chinese who loved the book said, and continued: She is writing a work of
imagination authenticated by her personal experience. ("Most Popular
Book" 7)

Clearly, the personal authority of an autobiographer is not easy
to challenge. Perhaps sensing this, some of Kingston's critics concede it but blend the charge of fictionalization with that of
atypicality. Again, the projected reactions of the white audience
are kept constantly in sight. Speaking of the protagonist's account of not knowing her father's name, Chan calls this experience "unique" and expresses fears that Kingston "may mislead
naive white readers" by not giving any background on the system of naming unique to Chinese Americans. Fong complains:
"Your story is a *very personal* description of growing up in Chinese America. It is *one* story from one Chinese American woman
of one out of seven generations of Chinese Americans" (67; italics in original). Like Chan, she feels that a narrative as personal
as Kingston's must be made safe for white consumption by
means of a sobering dose of Chinese-American history; the historical information to be incorporated should emphasize the
"causes" behind the "pains, secrets, and bitterness" portrayed in
*The Woman Warrior* (67).[10] Fong lists various excerpts that she
finds especially dangerous and glosses each with a summary of
experiences considered canonical to an ideologically correct version of Chinese-American history. Without such a corrective, she
suggests, Kingston will reinforce the white readers' stereotype of
Chinese Americans as eternally unassimilable aliens, "silent,
mysterious, and devious" (67). Tong feels that Kingston's up-
bringing in the one-street Chinatown of Stockton, an agricultural
town in California's Central Valley (instead of in a bigger, geo-
graphically more distinct and presumably more "typical"
Chinatown) disqualifies her from attaining "historical and cultural insight" about Chinese America ("Chinatown Popular Culture" 233).

According to Kingston's critics, the most pernicious of the
stereotypes that might be supported by *The Woman Warrior*

is that of Chinese-American men as sexist. Some Chinese-American women readers think highly of *The Woman Warrior* because it confirms their personal experiences with sexism (e.g., Suzi Wong, Nellie Wong). Others find Kingston's account of growing up amidst shouts of "Maggot!" overstated, yet can cite little to support the charge besides *their* own personal authority.[11] Contrasting *The Woman Warrior's* commercial success with the relatively scant attention received by books like Louis Chu's *Eat a Bowl of Tea* and Laurence Yep's *Dragonwings*, both of which present less negative father images, Fong implies that Kingston's autobiography earns its reputation by "over-exaggerat[ing]" the ills of Chinese-American male chauvinism (68). She is willing to grant that a more understanding response from white readers might have given Kingston more creative license but finds the existing body of Chinese-American literature small enough to justify a more stringent demand on the Chinese-American writer, especially the woman writer.

If Chinese-American women disagree about the accuracy of Kingston's portrayal of patriarchal culture, it is hardly surprising to find male Chinese-American critics condemning it in harsh terms. Chan attributes the popularity of *The Woman Warrior* to its depiction of "female anger," which bolsters white feminists' "hallucination" of a universal female condition; and Tong calls the book a "fashionably feminist work written with white acceptance in mind" ("Critic of Admirer" 6). If Chinese-American literature is, according to the editors of *Aiiieeeee!*, distinguished by emasculation (Chin et al. xxx–xxxi), then Chinese-American writers cannot afford to wash the culture's dirty linen in public. Frank Chin declares that personal pain—merely a matter of "expression of ego" and "psychological attitudinizing"—must be subordinated to political purpose ("This Is Not an Autobiography" 112).

For Chin, the very form of autobiography is suspect because of its association with the Christian tradition of confession. Although *The Woman Warrior* does not deal with Christianity, Chin places it in a tradition of Christianized Chinese-

American autobiographies from Yung Wing's *My Life in China and America* through Pardee Lowe's *Father and Glorious Descendant* to Jade Snow Wong's *Fifth Chinese Daughter*. His rationale is that all autobiography, like religious confessions and conversion testimonials, demonstrates "admission of guilt, submission of my self for judgment," for "approval by outsiders." "[A] Chinaman can't write an autobiography without selling out." In fact, claims Chin, the autobiography is not even a native Chinese form, and Chinese-American writers have no business adopting it. Unfortunately, however, "[t]he Christian Chinese American autobiography is the only Chinese American literary tradition" ("This Is Not an Autobiography" 122–24).

Some of the generalizations made by Kingston's critics, such as the exclusively Western and Christian origin of autobiography, may be called into question by existing scholarship. According to one student of the genre, a complex autobiographical tradition does exist in Chinese literature, its origins traceable to the first century A.D., in the Han Dynasty (Larson; esp. chap. 1). Moreover, the confessional mode attributed by Chin solely to a guilt-obsessed Christianity can also be found in traditional Chinese writing (Wu). This does not invalidate Georges Gusdorf's important insight on the cultural specificity of the modern Western autobiography: the point is not to claim that the modern Western autobiography as we know it was practiced in ancient China (it was not) but merely to point out the oversimplification in many of the statements that have been made about *The Woman Warrior*. When Chin links the genre with Christian self-accusation, he overlooks the possibility that the late medieval *breakdown* of Christian dogma might have been responsible for the emergence of autobiography as an autonomous literary tradition (Gusdorf 34). Furthermore, emphasis on the confessional element represents only one school of autobiographical scholarship, the Anglo-American; there are others (Eakin 202). Even if autobiography were an entirely Western phenomenon, according to Chin's own pronouncements on the unique, nonderivative nature of Asian-

American literature (especially on its separateness from Asian literature), Chinese-American writers have a right to appropriate a genre not indigenous to the Chinese in China but indigenous to the Chinese in America. As Chin and his *Aiiieeeee!* co-editors put it in their prefatory manifesto on Chinese and Japanese-American literature, an "American-born Asian, writing from the world as Asian-American," should not be expected to "reverberate to gongs struck hundreds of years ago" (Chin et al. xxiv).

Other more or less self-contained disputes on isolated assertions by Kingston's critics could be explored. On the whole, however, one may say that the entire Chinese-American autobiographical debate touches on articles of ideology so jealously held that the existence of a variety of opinions, scholarly or otherwise, may itself be seen as a problem rather than as a possible source of solutions. Given the peremptory tone in which much of the criticism of *The Woman Warrior* has been conducted, it is important that the tacit assumptions of the critics be articulated.

The theoretical underpinnings of the hostile criticism may be summarized as a series of interlocking propositions, some concerning the nature of autobiography as a genre (regardless of the author's background), others generalizable to autobiography by all American ethnic writers, still others peculiar to Chinese-American autobiography.

First of all, autobiography is seen to be self-evidently distinguishable from fiction. If the two genres blur at all at the edges, the interaction merely takes the form of fiction providing "techniques" to render the mundane material of autobiography more attractive; the epistemological status of the narrated material is not affected. In the same way that language is considered a sort of sugarcoating on dry nuggets of fact, the autobiographer's subjectivity is seen as having little or no constitutive power; rather, it is a Newtonian body moving about in a world of discrete, verifiable—and hence incontrovertible—facts, its power being limited to the choice between faithfully recording or willfully distorting this external reality. In principle, therefore, autobiography is biography which just happens to be written by one's self. It claims no special privilege, poses no special problems.[12] Finally, the *graphe* part of *autobiography*, the act of writing, the transformation of life into text, is seen by Kingston's critics as a mechanical conveyance of facts from the autobiographer's mind to the reader's via a medium in the physical world, the process pleasant or not depending on the author's literary talents. In the case of the *Woman Warrior* debate, correspondence between word and thing is deemed so perfect that a Chinese term, *kuei*, is supposed to be translatable by only one English equivalent, with all other overtones outlawed. The arbiter here is to be the individual critic backed by the authority of "the Chinese American community" (as if Kingston herself were not a member of this community).

Recognition of a preexisting external reality, however, imposes a special obligation on the ethnic American autobiographer: to provide a positive portrayal of the ethnic community through one's self-portrayal. At the very least, the autobiographer's work should be innocent of material that might be seized upon by unsympathetic outsiders to illustrate prevalent stereotypes of the ethnic group; the author should stress the diversity of experience within the group and the uniqueness and self-definition of the individual. Ideally, an ethnic autobiography should also be a history in microcosm of the community, especially of its sufferings, struggles, and triumphs over racism. In other words, an ethnic autobiographer should be an exemplar and spokesperson whose life will inspire the writer's own people as well as enlighten the ignorant about social truths.

The collective history of the ethnic community—one does not speak of *a* history in this theoretical framework—provides the ultimate reference point for the ethnic autobiographer. Here is where the Newtonian analogy begins to break down, for the self proves, after all, to be subjective in the everyday sense of "biased" or "unreliable." Handicapped by its interiority, it cannot be the equal of other "bodies" which can be summed up as a bundle of externally ascertainable properties.

The self is epistemologically underprivileged, not privileged; to discover the validity of its private truths, it must appeal to the arbitration of the community (however defined). The history of the collectivity is ballast for the ethnic autobiographer's subjectivity; it is a yardstick against which the author can measure how representative or how idiosyncratic his or her life is, how worthy of preservation in writing. Should individual experience fail to be homologous to collective history, personal authority must yield to ideological imperatives, and the details of the narrative must be manipulated to present an improved picture. According to this logic, the ethnic woman autobiographer victimized by sexism must be ready to suppress potentially damaging (to the men, that is) material; to do less is to jeopardize the united front and prostitute one's integrity for the sake of white approval. *Bios* is of little worth unless it is "representative"—averaged out to become sociologically informative as well as edifying.

A series of mutually incompatible demands on ethnic autobiography follows from the tenets outlined above. Initially, ethnic autobiography is thought useful because its focus on the uniqueness of the individual establishes a minority's right to self-definition; a sufficient number of autobiographies will disabuse white readers of their oversimplified preconceptions. Autobiography's allegedly pure factuality is also prized for its educational value: unlike fiction, it can be counted on to "tell it like it is" and resist charges of artistic license made by doubting readers. Nonetheless, autobiography cannot, by definition, be more than *one* person's life story; thus it cannot be fully trusted. What if the single individual's life happens to confirm or even endorse white perceptions instead of challenging them? Hence the insistence that ethnic autobiography be "representative." The requirement would have been easily fulfilled if the autobiographer happened—that vexatious word again!—to have already been "representative," in the sense of conforming to a view of the group agreed upon by the members making that determination. Short of that, the "representativeness" will have to be formed out of recalcitrant material, through an editorial process true to the spirit but not necessarily the letter of the "ethnic experience."

The minute this is done, however, the attempt to make absolute the generic distinctions between autobiography and fiction ends up dissolving the boundaries altogether: autobiography loses its putative authority in fact and turns into fiction. Language loses its innocuous transmitting function and assumes the unruly power of transmutation. The individual loses his or her uniqueness and becomes a sociological category. From the effort to counter homogenization by offering depictions of diversity, a new uniformity emerges: one set of stereotypes is replaced by another. In the final analysis, the main reason the critics attack *The Woman Warrior* is not that it is insufficiently factual but that it is insufficiently fictional: that the author did not tamper more freely with her own life story. And ironically—given the critics' claimed championship of self-definition and literary autonomy—the kind of fiction they would like Kingston to have written is closely dictated by the responses of white readers.

Only when safeguards against misreadings are supplied may the autobiographical label once more be affixed with confidence, the benefits of the genre now purged of the inconvenient admixture of potential harm. The ignorance of white readers seems to be taken for granted as immutable by Kingston's critics. The possibility that the less unregenerate readers may learn to read the allusions in *The Woman Warrior*, just as generations of minority readers have learned to read the Eurocentric canon, is never once raised; nor is the possibility that a Chinese-American writer may by right expect, and by duty promote, such learning in his or her audience.

These issues naturally have their counterparts in other ethnic American literatures. The differing versions of Frederick Douglass's early life found in his autobiographies provide a classic example of how a black autobiographer might feel compelled to edit "factual" details in the interest of anticipated social effect (e.g., Gates 98–124). It is worth noting that, while critic Henry Louis Gates, Jr., justifies the "crafting or making [of a 'fictive self'] by design," citing the urgent need to establish the black man's right to speak for himself, he also finds a certain flatness of aesthetic effect when Douglass begins to substitute "one ideal essence for another." "Almost never does Douglass allow us to see him as a human individual in all of his complexity" (103, 119, 109).

Though the dilemma is shared by other ethnic American autobiographies, the conflicting claims of typicality and uniqueness take a particularly acute form in Chinese-American autobiography: at stake is not only the existence of the minority writer's voice but the possible perversion of that voice to satisfy the white reader's appetite for exoticism. Indeed, it is only within the context of the Chinese-American autobiographical tradition that both the vehemence of Kingston's critics and the novelty of the narrative undertaking in *The Woman Warrior* can be understood.

To borrow a phrase applied to early African-American writers, Chinese-American writers "entered into the house of literature through the door of autobiography" (Olney, "Autobiography and the Cultural Moment" 15). Autobiographies predominate in Chinese-American writing in English.[13] Some autobiographies are by Chinese-born writers who grew up in China (Lee, Yung, Kuo, Su-ling Wong, Wei); others are by writers born and brought up in the United States (Lowe, Jade Snow Wong, Goo, Kingston). An autobiography from the former group typically focuses on the protagonist's early experiences in China, often ending very abruptly upon his or her arrival in the United States. The author tends to believe the life depicted as representing Chinese life of a certain period or social milieu, and of interest to the Western reader chiefly for this reason rather than for its uniqueness; such a conviction may easily degenerate into the accommodating mentality of a friendly guide to an exotic culture.[14] The autobiographies in the second group, those by American-born writers, are primarily set in the United States.[15] Given the distressing tendency of white readers to confuse Chinese Americans with Chinese in China, and to attribute a kind of ahistorical, almost genetic, Chinese es-

sence to all persons of Chinese ancestry regardless of their up-
bringing, the pressure on American-born writers to likewise
"represent Chinese culture" is strong. Removed from Chinese
culture in China by their ancestors' emigration, American-
born autobiographers may still capitalize on white curiosity
by conducting the literary equivalent of a guided Chinatown
tour: by providing explanations on the manners and mores of
the Chinese-American community from the vantage point of
a "native." This stance has indeed been adopted by some, and,
in a sort of involuntary intertextuality, even those works that
do not share it will most likely be read as anthropological
guidebooks. The curse is potent enough to extend at times to
nonautobiographical literature; for a book like *The Woman
Warrior*, then, it would be all but impossible to prevent some
readers from taking the autobiographical label as a license to
overgeneralize.

A few examples will characterize the stance of the cultural
guide found among both Chinese-born and American-born autobiographers. In Lee Yan Phou's *When I Was a Boy in China*, personal narrative slows at every turn to make room for background
material; seven of the twelve chapter titles—"The House and
Household," "Chinese Cookery," "Games and Pastimes," "Schools
and School Life," "Religions," "Chinese Holidays," "Stories and
Story-Tellers"—could have come out of a general survey of
Chinese society. The individual's life serves the function of
conveying anthropological information; the freight, in fact,
frequently outweighs the vehicle. Lee directly addresses white
American readers as "you" throughout the book and consciously
assumes the persona of a tour guide: "The servants were . . . sent
out to market to buy the materials for breakfast. Let us follow
them"; "Now, let me take you into the school where I struggled
with the Chinese written language for three years" (27, 57). In
Helena Kuo's tellingly titled *I've Come a Long Way*, the tour
guide role seems to have become second nature to the author.
Like Lee, Kuo addresses her audience as "you" and constantly
takes into account their likely reactions. Her descriptions of
place are filtered through the eyes of her white readers (e.g.,

27); the similes she favors are pure *chinoiserie* (e.g., 23). In the midst of a narrative about her journalistic career, Kuo solicitously inserts a mini-disquisition on traditional Chinese painting, to ensure that her charges will not be lost in the future when she is no longer around (171).[16]

It is perhaps no accident that a good number of the autobiographies by Chinese-born writers are rather abruptly cut off soon after the author's arrival in the United States, in apparent contrast to the structure of immigrant autobiography described in William Boelhower's typology (*Immigrant Autobiography* 25-52). Unlike the European works cited by Boelhower, these do not chronicle the author's experience of encountering and coming to terms with American culture. While only further study can elucidate this observed difference, one might venture a guess on its cause: the Chinese authors may have sensed how far American interest in their life writings is based on the image of otherness, on exotic scenery and alien cultural practices. As the autobiographers become Americanized, the fascination they hold for the reader would fade; hence the sketchy coverage of their experience in the United States. [17]

Some American-born Chinese autobiographers also seem to have adopted the narrative stance of a cultural guide, though the presence of the audience is more implicit in their works than in Lee's or Kuo's. *Father and Glorious Descendant*, by Pardee Lowe (a contemporary and friend of Kuo's), abounds in descriptions of Chinatown customs and rituals, such as *tong* banquets, Chinese New Year festivities, celebration of the father's "Great Birthday," preparation of unusual (by Western standards) foods, and funeral practices. The name of the Lowes' ancestral village in China, Sahn Kay Gawk, is periodically rendered by the quaint circumlocution "The-Corner-of-the-Mountain-Where-the-Water-Falls," although that etymological information has been given on the first page of the book. Two chapters are devoted to a series of letters between Father and his cousin, written in a comically florid, heavily literal prose purporting to be a translation of classical Chinese (249–58). Lowe's handling of the English language betrays a habitual awareness of the white audience's need to be surprised and amused by the mystifying ways of the Chinese. Jade Snow Wong's autobiography, *Fifth Chinese Daughter*, shares with Lowe's an emphasis on Chinatown customs and rituals; with Lee's and Kuo's, a tendency to intersperse the narrative of her life with discursive segments of information on Chinese culture. A description of a dinner party for her American friends includes a step-by-step record of how egg foo young and tomato beef are cooked; an account of a visit to a Chinatown herbalist for her cough is interrupted by a clarification of the Chinese medical theory of humors (160–62, 224).[18]

Although there is much else in Lowe's and Wong's books besides these gestures of consideration for the sensibilities of white readers, it is undeniable that both of these authors, like their Chinese-born counterparts, are conscious of their role as cultural interpreters who can obtain a measure of recognition from whites for the insider's insight they can offer. The title of a chapter in Wong's book, "Rediscovering Chinatown," aptly epitomizes one way American-born Chinese may make peace with their cultural background in the face of intense assimilative pressures: to return to one's ethnic heritage with selective enthusiasm, reassessing once-familiar (and once-despised) sights and sounds according to their acceptability to white tastes.

As a form characterized by simultaneous subjectivity and objectivity, simultaneous expression and documentation (e.g., Stone 10–11; Sands 57), autobiography easily creates in its readers expectations of "privileged access" (Olney, "Autobiography and the Cultural Moment" 13) to the experience and vision of an entire people. From an intraethnic point of view, the writing of autobiography may be valued as a means of preserving memories of a vanishing way of life, and hence of celebrating cultural continuity and identity; in an interethnic perspective, however, the element of *display*, whether intentional or not, is unavoidable. Many "outsiders" will thus approach ethnic autobiographies with the misguided conviction that the authors necessarily speak for "their people." The practice of reading autobiography for "cultural authenticity" may be a particularly serious danger for Chinese-American autobiography, given the group's unique situation in United States society. The ancestral land of Chinese Americans, due to its long history, sophisticated civilization, and complex encounters with American imperialism in recent history, casts an inordinately strong spell on the white imagination. Moreover, Chinese Americans, who have been subjected to genocidal immigration policies,[19] are placed in the situation of permanent guests who must earn their keep by adding the spice of variety to American life—by selectively maintaining aspects of traditional Chinese culture and language fascinating to whites. In the terminology of Werner Sollors, if the essence of the American experience is the formation of a society based on "consent" rather than "descent," Chinese Americans have clearly been (and still are) excluded from participation in "consent" by the dominant group's insistence on the primacy of their "descent." The irony is that many readers from within the ethnic group itself have, like the detractors of *The Woman Warrior*, inadvertently contributed to this simplified and often condescending view by likewise positing a direct pipeline of cultural authenticity between the collectivity and the individual. The idea of overdetermination by "descent" is thus left unchallenged. Demanding "representativeness," the Chinese-American critics of Kingston differ from the white literary tourists only in the version of cultural authenticity subscribed to.

This tension between "consent" and "descent" is reminiscent of W. E. B. Du Bois's well-known concept of "double consciousness."[20] The writers are aware of themselves as "insiders" with unique experiences that cannot be fully captured by ethnic categories alone. On the other hand, they cannot but sense the "outsiders'" constant gaze upon their skin color, their physiognomy, their "difference." Their American right of "consent"—here taking the form of the freedom to create literature true to their felt lives—is perpetually called into question or qualified by reader expectations based on "descent." Some Chinese-American autobiographers have, indeed, sought distinction in their exotic "descent," allowing the dominant group's perceptions to define their identity. However, it is important to recognize that Kingston has taken an altogether different path in *The Woman Warrior*. The protagonist has eschewed the facile authority which self-appointment as guide and spokesperson could confer on her. The discursive space occupied by *The Woman Warrior* is between the two poles of the "double consciousness"; the audience the narrator addresses in the second person is composed of fellow Chinese Americans sharing the protagonist's need to establish a new Chinese-American selfhood:

> Chinese-Americans, when you try to understand what things in you are Chinese, how do you separate what is peculiar to childhood, to poverty, insanities, one family, your mother who marked your growing with stories, from what is Chinese? What is Chinese tradition and what is the movies? (6)

Boelhower writes:

> In the mixed genre of autobiography, . . . the question of identity involves matching the narrator's own self-perception with the self that is recognized by others, so as to establish a continuity between the two (self and world), to give a design of self-in-the-world. ("Brave New World" 12)

If the "others" are the potential "misreaders" among her white audience, Kingston is in truth far less obsessed than her critics with "the self that is recognized by others." There are, of course, other "others" in the protagonist's lonely struggle: her Chinese family, relatives, fellow "villagers," whose perceptions of her do not match her self-perceptions either. "Descent" notwithstanding, connection to them has to be forged, which can take place only after an initial recognition of dif-

ference. Neither American nor Chinese culture, as given, offers a resting place; the protagonist of *The Woman Warrior* has
to discover that there is "[n]o higher listener. No higher listener but myself" (237). Her project is to reach "an avowal of
values and a recognition of the self by the self—a choice carried out at the level of essential being—not a revelation of a
reality given in advance but a corollary of an active intelligence" (Gusdorf 44). This project is so bold, so unfamiliar, that
even her fellow Chinese Americans sometimes mistake it for
the accommodationism of earlier autobiographers. For resemblances can indeed be found between *The Woman Warrior* and
its predecessors—like Lee, Kingston retells Chinese tales
heard in childhood; like Kuo, she makes general remarks on
Chinese culture; like Lowe, she speaks of unusual Chinese
foods; like Wong, she recounts experiences of sexist oppression. The crucial question is whether these resemblances are
merely superficial or whether they bespeak a basic common-
ality in autobiographical stance. Only a careless reader, I submit, would be able to conclude that Kingston's stance in *The
Woman Warrior* is that of the trustworthy cultural guide.

For the "native" in this case, having been born and raised
in "ghost country" without benefit of explicit parental instruc-
tion in cultural practices, is barely more enlightened than an
"outsider" would be: "From the configuration of food my
mother set out, we kids had to infer the holidays" (215). Quite
unlike the generalizations about Chinese culture in *I've Come
a Long Way* or *Father and Glorious Descendant*, which are
meant to be encapsulations of superior knowledge, those in
*The Woman Warrior* bespeak a tentative groping toward understanding. From fragmentary and haphazard evidence, the
protagonist has to piece together a coherent picture of the culture she is enjoined to preserve against American influence.
The effort is so frustrating that she exclaims in exasperation:
"I don't see how they kept up a continuous culture for five
thousand years. Maybe they didn't; maybe everyone makes it
up as they go along" (216). But the point, of course, is that the
Chinese who remain in Chinese-dominant communities would

have no trouble at all transmitting culture through osmosis. It is the protagonist's American-born generation who must "make it up as they go along." The emigrant parents' expectation of a "continuous culture" is, if entirely human, ahistorical and therefore doomed. (So, one might add, is the critics' similar demand for cultural authenticity. Purity is best preserved by death; history adulterates.)

Given *The Warrior Woman*'s situation in the broader cultural timescape of Chinese America, then, the so-called distortions of traditional Chinese culture found in the text are simply indications of how far removed from it the protagonist has become. As Deborah Woo rightly observes, "where culture is problematic as a source of identity, cultural ignorance itself is part of what is authentic about the experience" (186). Thus the substitution of "heavenly chicken" for "field chicken" is not exoticization but an example of how a young Chinese child in an English-dominant society may misunderstand a tonal language. The protagonist's cosmological speculations on the omnipresent number six (91), involving a misinterpretation of *dai luk* (which in Cantonese pronunciation can be "the big six," a nonexistent collocation, or "the big continent/the mainland"), betray her "craving for coherence" in the face of a bewildering mass of unexplained cultural data (Hsu 434). It is not an actual Chinese fortune-teller who confuses the homophones, which might have justified the charge of willful distortion on Kingston's part; the phrase "the Big Six" is framed by the young girl's meditation on her mother's life, the fortune-teller a fictive one whom she imagines her mother consulting.

It is, in fact, essential to recognize that the entire *Woman Warrior* is a sort of meditation on what it means to be Chinese American. To this end, the protagonist appropriates whatever is at hand, testing one generalization after another until a satisfactory degree of applicability to her own life is found. As she says of the differing versions of the No Name Woman's story: "Unless I see her life branching into mine, she gives me no ancestral help" (10). The aphoristic statements about Chinese ways interspersed in the narrative—"Women in the old China did not choose" (7); "Chinese communication was loud, public" (13); "Among the very poor and the wealthy, brothers married their adopted sisters, like doves" (14)—are not offered for the benefit of readers hungry for tidbits of anthropological information. Rather, they are threads in a larger tapestry of inferences, some sturdy, some thin, which the protagonist weaves for her own use. Rejecting the theory that the aunt is a "wild woman" (9) or a passive rape victim, the narrator decides on a version relevant to her life in an immigrant family: a story of assertion of "private life" (14) against the harsh demands of group survival.

Even with material that tempts with its air of certainty, the protagonist finds it necessary to tailor-make meanings from altered details. Thus she spurns the simplistic lesson of the traditional Fa Mu Lan tale, creating instead a potentially subversive woman warrior to whom even traditions yield. While the heroine of "Mulan Shi" sees herself merely as a second-best substitute for an aged father (there being no elder son to take his place), the little girl in "White Tigers" is a *chosen* one, destined to be called away by "immortals." Martial artists typically pass on their skills to sons or male disciples; the old couple in the mountains, in contrast, devote years exclusively to her training. For the traditional Mulan, the campaigns are but a detour; at the end of the poem, the erstwhile general puts on makeup, ready to resume her interrupted feminine life. Kingston's Fa Mu Lan chooses wifehood and motherhood in the midst of battle. Her fellow villagers know of her identity before her triumphant return from battle (43); their relinquishment of their precious sons to her army is thus an affirmation of faith in her female power. Of course, the very necessity of male disguise means that the narrator's fantasized challenge to patriarchy can never be complete; in the last analysis, she would like to be remembered for "perfect filiality" (54). Yet even Fa Mu Lan's return to her parents' house has an element of active choice. All in all, working within the constraints of internalized values, the protagonist has done her best to make of unpromising material an inspiring, if not entirely radical, tale.

The treatment of the T'sai Yen story (241–43) follows much the same pattern of sifting out details to arrive at a relevant meaning. Kingston's retelling omits a crucial scene in the original "Eighteen Stanzas for a Barbarian Reed Pipe":[21] T'sai Yen's painful leave-taking from her half-barbarian sons. Though by now attached to her captor and heartsick at the prospect of never seeing her children again, T'sai Yen nevertheless chooses Han lands as her real home, negating the twelve years spent in the steppes as a mere unfortunate interlude. Herself a half-barbarian to her China-obsessed parents ("Whenever my parents said 'home,' they suspended America" [116]), the narrator might have found such a detail too close for comfort, and too contrary in spirit to her own undertaking of forming a Chinese-American self. Thus we find a shift of emphasis: the last pages of *The Woman Warrior* celebrate not return from the remote peripheries to a waiting home but the creation of a new center through art. Singing a song that transcends cultural boundaries, T'sai Yen can now leave "her tent to sit by the winter campfires, ringed by barbarians" (243).

As with the "Eighteen Stanzas," the moral that the protagonist draws from the assorted Chinese ghost stories diverges from the one intended by the source. No automatic authority on Chinese culture simply by virtue of "descent," the protagonist must resort to public, written texts in her quest for meanings not forthcoming in her mother's private oral tradition. (Contrary to one critic's judgment that the Mandarin transliteration of some names in *The Woman Warrior* betrays how Kingston passes library research for her Cantonese mother's bedtime stories,[22] Kingston does not attempt to cover her trails, as any self-respecting cultural guide would. She provides dates with the Mandarin names and identifies the source, "the research against ghost fear published by the Chinese Academy of Science" (Zhongguo Kexueyuan Wenxueyanjiusuo 104). The lesson she constructs to make sense of her experiences in a frugal immigrant family—"Big eaters win" (105)—bears little relation to the political allegory of the Communist-compiled anthology. But what matters is not the fit (for which Procrustean beds are notorious). The most useful lesson the protagonist can learn from her research is that a passive staking of her life on some preestablished reality, like looking up *Ho Chi Kuei* (237–38) in a dictionary filled with decontextualized definitions, will always prove fruitless.

The narrator's methodology of self-redemption is thus remarkably consistent. Over and over, we find her forgoing the security of ready-made cultural meanings, opting instead to painstakingly mold a new set suited to her condition as a Chinese-American woman. The many questions about "facts" plaguing the narrator—Were there an Oldest Daughter and Oldest Son who died in China (120)? Did Brave Orchid cut her frenum (190)? Did the hulk exist or was he made up (239)?— function much like a series of Zen *koan*, frustrating because impossible to answer by appeal to an external authority (mother, in this case). In the end, realization of their very impossibility frees her to explore the fecund uncertainties of her Chinese-American existence.

The readers who fault *The Woman Warrior* for not being more responsible toward "facts" would do well to meditate on their own *koan*. To read departures from traditional material found in *The Woman Warrior* as Kingston's cynical manipulations of naïve white readers, as her critics have done, is not only to fly in the face of textual evidence but to belittle the difficulty and urgency of the imaginative enterprise so necessary to the American-born generation: to make sense of Chinese and American culture from its own viewpoint (however hybrid and laughable to "outsiders"), to articulate its own reality, and to strengthen its precarious purchase on the task of self-fashioning. The Fa Mu Lan story itself, which many of Kingston's critics take to be a fixed and sacred given, actually exists in a multitude of Chinese texts differing from each other in purpose as well as detail.[23]

Kingston's critics have been measuring *The Woman Warrior* "against some extra-textual order of fact," not realizing that this order is "based in its turn on other texts (dignified as documents)" (Eakin 23): an ideologically uplifting version of Chinese-American history revising earlier racist texts, a version of the Fa Mu Lan legend sufficiently hoary to be considered "historical." The critics' concern is understandable in view of widespread ignorance about the sociopolitical context of Chinese-American literary creation, the inherent duality of the autobiographical genre (which encourages reading for "cultural authenticity"), the existence of autobiographies by both Chinese- and American-born writers promising privileged glimpses into the group's secret life and the apparent similarities between them and Kingston's work. These issues are, indeed, vital ones generalizable to other ethnic American autobiographies, even to all ethnic American literatures. Nevertheless, intent on liberating Chinese-American writers from one set of constraints, Kingston's detractors have imposed another, in the meantime failing to take note of the most fundamental freedom of all that *The Woman Warrior* has wrested from a priori generic categories and cultural prescriptions: the freedom to create in literature a sui generis Chinese-American reality.

I am grateful to King-Kok Cheung, Samuel Cheung, Maxine Hong Kingston, Kathy Lo, Stephen Sumida, Shelley Wong, Deborah Woo, and Yiheng Zhao for their assistance in the writing of this essay, and to James Payne for his many valuable suggestions on revision. I am solely responsible for its content.

## Notes

1. For example, both Juhasz and Rabine relate the unconventional narrative structure of *The Woman Warrior* to the feminist act of creating identity, although their interpretations differ.

2. Personal communication to the author from Kingston, 21 May 1988; quoted with her permission.

3. On the "real" and the "imaginary," Kingston writes: "My idea [in *The Woman Warrior* and *China Men*] was to invent a new form for telling my stories and thoughts. I needed a form in which I could have real, true human beings who have very imaginative minds tell their lives and dreams. My real characters have artful minds, the minds of fiction writers and storytellers." Personal communication to the author, 21 May 1988; quoted with Kingston's permission.

4. For example, Brave Orchid's encounter with the "Sitting Ghost"; the Chinese stories of big eaters who devour ghosts and other monsters (104–6); the protagonist's girlhood interactions with many types of "ghosts" (113–16); and Moon Orchid's reunion with her husband, both now having entered the "land of ghosts" (178).

5. For a reading of the multilayered significance of the term *ghost*, see Sato, who demonstrates how Kingston's rendering of *kuei* focuses many aspects of Chinese-American life and is hardly a "whitewashed" usage.

6. This version of the name appears to be a composite of Cantonese and Mandarin transliterations, *Fa Muk Lan* and *Hua Mu Lan*—another "impurity"?

7. The prolonged training in still "stances" and feats of balance (like sleeping on a rope), the copying of animal movements, and the gaining of control over normally involuntary bodily functions are standard fare in *wuxia xiaoshuo*. The "calling" of a chosen one for spiritual discipline, the hermit's retreat on misty mountains, the magic water gourd, and the cultivation of immortality are images from *shenxian* stories, which have passed fully into the Chinese popular mind. These and other features from folk traditions found in *The Woman Warrior* would be familiar to children growing up in a Chinese community.

8. A translation of "The Ballad of Mulan" may be found in Liu and Lo 77–80 (cited in Chua).

9. *Outlaws of the Marsh*, a classic in Chinese literature, is based on oral tales depicting peasant heroes who form "righteous armies" to defy the corrupt imperial government. The earliest extant written version dates from the sixteenth century. The English title of Shapiro's recent translation, rather than the older *Water Margin*, is used here.

10. Note that in her next book, *China Men*, Kingston has included a list of discriminatory legislation against Chinese Americans. "The reviews of my first book made it clear that people didn't know the history—or that they thought I didn't. While I was writing about

*China Men,* I just couldn't take that tension any more" (Pfaff 26; cited in Kim xvii).

11. Fong cites her relationship with a "warm, generous and loving father" (68–69) to support her complaint against *The Woman Warrior.*

12. The critics of *The Woman Warrior* supply almost a textbook example of the assumptions about autobiography, common prior to the recent shifting of critical focus from *bios* to *autos,* described by Olney, "Autobiography and the Cultural Moment" 20.

13. Chinese-American literature has a large Chinese-language component, the exclusive domain of immigrant writers, which is only beginning to be studied and translated. This component falls outside the scope of this essay, but one should note that it contains very few autobiographies.

    A partial list (in chronological order) of works explicitly presented as autobiography, of varying literary interest and popularity, include Lee Yan Phou's *When I Was a Boy in China* (1887), Yung Wing's *My Life in China and America* (1909), Helena Kuo's *I've Come a Long Way* (1942), Pardee Lowe's *Father and Glorious Descendant* (1943), Jade Snow Wong's *Fifth Chinese Daughter* (1945), Su-ling Wong (pseud.) and Earl Herbert Cressy's *Daughter of Confucius: A Personal History* (1952), Jade Snow Wong's *No Chinese Stranger* (1975, Thomas York-Tong Goo's *Before the Gods* (1976), Maxine Hong Kingston's *The Woman Warrior* (1976), and Katherine Wei and Terry Quinn's *Second Daughter: Growing Up in China, 1930-1949* (1984).

14. See Kim's discussion of "ambassadors of goodwill" in her chapter on early Asian immigrant writers (24–29).

15. Goo, who undergoes assimilation into Chinese culture in China, is an exception to this pattern.

16. A passage in Korean American Younghill Kang's fictionalized autobiography, *East Goes West* (1937), provides an interesting gloss on the practice of "cultural guiding," which is apparently generalizable from Chinese to other Asian-American autobiographies. Kim, an older Korean exile, advises the protagonist Chungpa Han to retain his classical Oriental learning: "You have to eat. And to eat, you must enter into the economic life of Americans. . . . In making a living, Oriental scholarship may help you more than your American education. . . . [I]n such a field, you would have the advantage. There would be less competition. . . . *You must be now like a Western man approaching Asia.* . . . As a transplanted scholar, this is the only road I could point to, for your happy surviving" (277–78; my italics). Despite his rhetoric of cultural catholicity, what Kim is suggesting is really a kind of self-Orientalization.

17. This possibility is further explored in my "Immigrant Autobiography: Some Questions of Definition and Approach."

18. Recipes are again included in the sequel to *Fifth Chinese Daughter,*

*No Chinese Stranger* (e.g., 187–88). In the latter, Wong and her husband lead tours to the Far East, thus making cultural interpretation their trade.

19. The Chinese Exclusion Act, passed in 1882 to keep out Chinese laborers, as well as subsequent anti-Chinese measures (including antimiscegenation laws and laws prohibiting laborers' wives from entering), created a "bachelor society" unable to reproduce itself. The situation did not begin to change until the Exclusion Act was repealed in 1943.

20. This concept has been related by more than one scholar (e.g., Rubin 75; Rampersad 13) to the duality of autobiography.

21. Rorex and Fong provide a complete translation of the poem as well as color illustrations from a traditional scroll. Kingston's use of the T'sai Yen material is discussed in greater detail in my forthcoming "Kingston's Handling of Traditional Chinese Sources."

22. Statement delivered by Marlon Hom at the roundtable discussion, "Asian American Literature: State of the Art and Criticism," Fifth National Conference of the Association for Asian American Studies, 26 Mar. 1988, Washington State University, Pullman.

23. According to Zhao 77–79, since the Tang dynasty (618–907) there have been many versions of the Fa Mu Lan story, some poetic, others operatic or novelistic. One Qing dynasty (1644–1911) version features a sister; another adds a cowardly cousin. During the Anti-Japanese War (1937–45), the Fa Mu Lan story was frequently staged as plays, with the moral modified to emphasize nationalism (even though the "original" heroine was not Han but a member of a northern tribe.) I have seen a film version from the 1960s sung in *huangmeidiao*, a variety of popular Chinese opera, available in videotape rental outlets serving Chinese-American communities. This version includes statements on the equality of the sexes reflecting modern, Westernized ideas.

## Works Cited

Boelhower, William. "The Brave New World of Immigrant Autobiography." *MELUS* 9, no. 2 (1982): 5–23.

———. *Immigrant Autobiography in the United States.* Verona: Essedue, 1982.

Bruss, Elizabeth. *Autobiographical Acts: The Changing Situation of a Literary Genre.* Baltimore: Johns Hopkins UP, 1976.

Chan, Jeffery Paul. "Jeff Chan, Chairman of SF State Asian American Studies, Attacks Review." *San Francisco Journal,* 4 May 1977, 6.

Chang, Diana. *Frontiers of Love.* New York: Random, 1956.

Chin, Frank. "The Most Popular Book in China." *Quilt* 4 (1984): 6–12.

———. "This Is Not an Autobiography." *Genre* 18, no. 2 (1985): 109–30.

Chin, Frank, Jeffery Paul Chan, Lawson Fusao Inada, and Shawn Wong, eds. *Aiiieeeee! An Anthology of Asian-American Writers.* 1974. Rpt. Washington, DC: Howard UP, 1983.

Chu, Louis. *Eat a Bowl of Tea.* Seattle: U of Washington P, 1961.

Chua, Cheng Lok. "Golden Mountain: Chinese Versions of the American Dream in Lin Yutang, Louis Chu, and Maxine Hong Kingston." *Ethnic Groups* 4 (1982): 57.

Chuang Hua (pseud.). *Crossings.* New York: Dial, 1968.

Eakin, John Paul. *Fictions in Autobiography: Studies in the Art of Self-Invention.* Princeton: Princeton UP, 1985.

Fong, Katheryn M. "To Maxine Hong Kingston: A Letter." *Bulletin for Concerned Asian Scholars* 9, no. 4 (1977): 67–69.

Gates, Henry Louis, Jr. *Figures in Black: Words, Signs, and the "Racial" Self.* New York: Oxford UP, 1987.

Goo, Thomas York-Tong. *Before the Gods.* New York: Helios, 1976.

Gusdorf, Georges. "Conditions and Limits of Autobiography." Trans. James Olney. In Olney, *Autobiography* 28–48.

Hsu, Vivian. "Maxine Hong Kingston as Psycho-Autobiographer and Ethnographer." *International Journal of Women's Studies* 6, no. 5 (1983): 429–42.

Johnson, Diane. "Ghosts." Rev. of *The Woman Warrior,* by Maxine Hong Kingston. *New York Review of Books,* 3 Feb. 1977, 19+.

Juhasz, Suzanne. "Maxine Hong Kingston: Narrative Technique and Female Identity." In Rainwater and Scheik 173–89.

Kang, Younghill. *East Goes West: The Making of an Oriental Yankee.* Chicago: Follett, 1937.

Kim, Elaine H. *Asian American Literature: An Introduction to the Writings and Their Social Context.* Philadelphia: Temple UP, 1982.

Kingston, Maxine Hong. *China Men.* New York: Knopf, 1980.

———. *The Woman Warrior: Memoirs of a Girlhood among Ghosts.* 1976. New York: Random, 1977.

Krupat, Arnold. "The Indian Autobiography: Origins, Type, and Function." *American Literature* 53, no. 1 (1981): 22–42.

Kuo, Helena. *I've Come a Long Way.* New York: Appleton, 1942.

Larson, Wendy Ann. "Autobiographies of Chinese Writers in the Early Twentieth Century." Diss. U of California, Berkeley. 1984.

Lau, Joseph S.M. [Liu Shaoming]. "Tangrenjie de xiaoshuo shijie" ["The Fictional World of Chinatown"]. *Ming Pao Monthly* 173 (1980): 65–66.

Lee, Yan Phou.*When I Was a Boy in China.* Boston: Lothrop, 1887.

Lim, Genny, ed. *The Chinese American Experience: Papers from the Second National Conference on Chinese American Studies (1980).* San Francisco: Chinese Historical Society of America and Chinese Culture Foundation, 1980.

Liu, Wu-Chi, and Irving Yucheng Lo, trans. *Sunflower Splendor: Three Thousand Years of Chinese Poetry.* Bloomington: Indiana UP, 1975.

Lowe, Pardee. *Father and Glorious Descendant.* Boston: Little,1943.

Olney, James. "Autobiography and the Cultural Moment: A Thematic, Historical, and Bibliographical Introduction." In Olney, *Autobiography* 3–27.

———, ed. *Autobiography: Essays Theoretical and Critical.* Princeton: Princeton UP, 1980.

———. "Some Versions of Memory/Some Versions of Bios: The Ontology of Autobiography." In Olney, *Autobiography* 236–67.

Pascal, Roy. *Design and Truth in Autobiography.* Cambridge: Harvard UP, 1960.

Pfaff, Timothy. "Talk with Mrs. Kingston." *New York Times Book Review*, 18 June 1980.

Rabine, Leslie W. "No Lost Paradise: Social Gender and Symbolic Gender in the Writings of Maxine Hong Kingston." *Signs: Journal of Women in Culture and Society* 12, no. 3 (1987): 471–92.

Rainwater, Catherine, and William J. Scheik, eds. *Contemporary American Women Writers: Narrative Strategies.* Lexington: UP of Kentucky, 1985.

Rampersad, Arnold. "Biography, Autobiography, and Afro-American Culture." *Yale Review* 73, no. 1 (1983): 1–16.

Rorex, Robert A., and Wen Fong. *Eighteen Songs of a Nomad Flute: The Story of Lady Wen-Chi.* New York: Metropolitan Museum of Art, 1974.

Rubin, Steven J. "Ethnic Autobiography: A Comparative Approach." *Journal of Ethnic Studies* 9, no. 1 (1981): 75–79.

Sands, Kathleen Mullen. "American Indian Autobiography." In *Studies in American Indian Literature: Essays and Course Designs,* ed. Paula Gunn Allen. New York: MLA, 1983. 55–65.

Sato, Gayle K. Fujita. "Ghosts as Chinese-American Constructs in Maxine Hong Kingston's *The Woman Warrior.*" In *Haunting the House of Fiction: Feminist Perspectives on Ghost Stories by American Women,* ed. Lynette Carpenter and Wendy K. Kolmar. Knoxville: U of Tennessee P, 1991. 193–214

Shapiro, Sidney, trans. *Outlaws of the Marsh.* Beijing: Foreign Language Press, 1980.

Sollors, Werner. *Beyond Ethnicity: Consent and Descent in American Culture.* New York: Oxford UP, 1986.

Stone, Albert. "Autobiography in American Culture: Looking Back at the Seventies." *American Studies International* 19, no. 3–4 (1981): 3–14.

Tong, Benjamin R. "Chinatown Popular Culture: Notes toward a Critical Psychological Anthropology." In Lim 233–41.

———. "Critic of Admirer Sees Dumb Racist." *San Francisco Journal,* 11 May 1977, 6.

Wei, Katherine, and Terry Quinn. *Second Daughter: Growing Up in China, 1930–1949.* New York: Holt, 1984.

Wong, Jade Snow. *Fifth Chinese Daughter.* 1945. Rev. ed. New York: Harper, 1950.

———. *No Chinese Stranger.* New York: Harper, 1975.

Wong, Nellie. Review of *The Woman Warrior*. *Bridge* 6, no. 4 (1978–79): 46–48.

Wong, Sau-ling C. "Immigrant Autobiography: Some Questions of Definition and Approach." In *American Autobiography: Retrospect and Prospect*, ed. Paul John Eakin. Madison: U of Wisconsin P, 1991. 142–70.

———. "Kingston's Handling of Traditional Chinese Sources." *Approaches to Teaching Kingston's The Woman Warrior*, ed. Shirley Geok-lin Lim. New York: MLA, 1991.

Wong, Shawn. *Homebase*. New York: I. Reed, 1979.

Wong, Su-ling (pseud.), and Earl Herbert Cressy. *Daughter of Confucius: A Personal History*. New York: Farrar, 1952.

Wong, Suzi. Review of *The Woman Warrior*. *Amerasia Journal* 4, no. 1 (1977): 165–67.

Woo, Deborah. "Maxine Hong Kingston: The Ethnic Writer and the Burden of Dual Authenticity." *Amerasia Journal* 16, no. 1 (1990): 173–200.

Wu, Pei-Yi. "Self-Examination and Confession of Sins in Traditional China." *Harvard Journal of Asiatic Studies* 39, no. 1 (1979): 5–38.

Yep, Laurence. *Dragonwings*. New York: Harper, 1975.

Yung, Wing. *My Life in China and America*. New York: Holt, 1909.

Zhao, Jingshen. *Minzu wenxue xiaoshi* [*A Brief History of National Literature*]. N.p.: Shijie Shuju, 1940.

Zhongguo Kexueyuan Wenxueyanjiusuo [Chinese Academy of Science, Institute of Literary Studies]. *Bupagui de gushi* [*Stories of Those Who Are Not Afraid of Ghosts*]. Hong Kong: San Lian, 1961.

# Autobiography and Ethnic Politics: Richard Rodriguez's *Hunger of Memory*

*Raymund A. Paredes*

Probably no work by a Mexican-American writer has attracted so much national interest as Richard Rodriguez's intellectual autobiography, *Hunger of Memory* (1982). The *New York Times* and the *Los Angeles Times* gave the volume front-page attention in their Sunday book reviews while *Time*, *Newsweek*, and other leading magazines also featured it prominently. Rodriguez appeared on various television talk shows and, perhaps most tellingly, sat for a lavish *People* magazine interview, complete with photographs of the author jogging in the shadow of the Golden Gate Bridge and celebrating his literary success in a chic San Francisco restaurant. While the works of most gifted Mexican-American writers go largely unnoticed by the national—and especially eastern—media, *Hunger of Memory* created something of a sensation. Ten years later, the book is still in print, frequently cited and anthologized, and Rodriguez leads a highly visible career as an essayist and journalist on Mexican-American subjects.

The extraordinary media attention brought to bear on *Hunger of Memory* is attributable primarily to Rodriguez's denunciation of ethnic activism and his corresponding endorsement of conservative cultural and political positions at a time when Reaganism was sweeping liberal and further-left values aside. In his attacks on affirmative action and bilingual programs and his support of traditional American education, institutionalized religion, and ethnic assimilation, Rodriguez quickly emerged as the designated "Hispanic" intellectual of the 1980s. In a national climate turning chilly towards minorities, Rodriguez eloquently justified, from the dominant political point of view at least, a retreat from a national agenda to address minority concerns.

Not surprisingly, the largely political response to *Hunger of Memory* stands at odds with Rodriguez's own characterization of his work. He concedes that it is "necessarily political" (7), but, attentive to the dictates of modern American academic criticism—and *Hunger of Memory* is very much an academic's book—Rodriguez prefers to emphasize the literary, esthetic qualities of his autobiography. Put another way, he wishes to regard it essentially as a carefully circumscribed account of his personal and educational experiences. Having been trained conservatively in English literature, Rodriguez seeks to establish himself as a literary artist rather than a polemicist, but there is a scent of disingenuousness about him as he attempts to justify his political views. Which brings us to the question of how Rodriguez marshalls autobiographical form, and attendant literary and rhetorical devices, to validate his political and cultural choices and to vindicate a particular ideology.

As autobiography, *Hunger of Memory* follows a literary form immediately recognizable to any experienced reader of American literature: the conversion narrative.[1] This literary form, of course, appears in virtually all literary traditions, but it has especially thrived in a country that prides itself on opportunity, mobility, and individualism; the conversion narrative lends itself particularly well to the depiction of these phenomena. In the American colonial period, conversion narratives commonly manifested a religious emphasis, with the authors chronicling their rise from depravity to a state of grace. The conversion narrative proved flexible as well as enduring and was eventually taken up with great success by a number of immigrant autobiographers toward the end of the nineteenth century. In these works, the nature of the conversion experience often ran from benighted, impoverished foreigner to sophisticated, proudly—even defiantly—bourgeois American. Perhaps the classic example of the type is Mary Antin's best-selling *The Promised Land* (1912), whose opening lines read: "I was born, I have lived, and I have been made over. . . . I am absolutely other than the person whose story I have to tell" (xi).

Antin recounts a childhood of anti-Semitism in Polotzk,

Russia, and an adolescence of measureless opportunity in Boston. Antin sheds her "impossible Hebrew name, Maryashe," soon after entering an American school and then proceeds to jettison her Jewish identity altogether. A lover of language and poetry, Antin delights in her growing mastery of English. In a familiar pattern of heedless assimilation, Antin never connects her readiness to cast off her ethnic heritage to her childhood experiences of bigotry and barely questions the socializing aspects of her American education; she merely celebrates its accessibility.

Antin recalls an incident with a "great, hulky colored boy" that exemplifies her romanticized, uncritical depiction of American life. The young man had treated Antin roughly, and her father had set the police on him. After a night in jail, the teenager emerges with a fresh "respect for the rights and persons of his neighbors." For Antin, the episode is wonderfully instructive, demonstrating that all are "free, and all treated equally, just as it said in the Constitution. . . . Three cheers for the Red, White and Blue!" (260). Experiences such as these so exhilarate Antin that she is only too willing to abolish, to escape from—at least so much as she is able—her personal and cultural history. "I want to forget—sometimes I long to forget," Antin writes. "I want now to be of to-day. It is painful to be consciously of two worlds" (xiv).

I mention Antin because her autobiography, in form, substance, and its naive rendering of social conditions and relations, so closely anticipates *Hunger of Memory*. Like *The Promised Land*, Rodriguez's work traces its author's passage from modest origins to a comfortable position among the intellectually and socially prominent. For both, education is the means of conversion.

I do not wish to suggest that Rodriguez duplicates the pattern of Antin's autobiography; after all, some seventy turbulent years had passed between the publication of the two books to modify further the formula of the conversion narrative. It is a commonplace of contemporary criticism to locate in the literary products of advanced capitalism qualities of intense alienation from the circumstances of one's life, often accompanied by a romantic recollection of one's past; certainly *Hunger of Memory* exhibits these features to distinguish it from Antin's autobiography. Another powerful modifying influence in Rodriguez's work has been the rise of ethnic consciousness. Over the past generation, ethnic accounts have supplanted immigrant writing as the most prevalent treatments of "otherness" in American autobiographical expression. And, as Werner Sollors has demonstrated, these works have generally adopted a conversion pattern that moves from "shallow assimilationist to reborn ethnic" (31–32). The striking example is *The Autobiography of Malcolm X* (1965), in which the author describes his younger self "in [his] zoot and conk" trying very hard to suppress his blackness. After a familiar process of education, in this case largely self-administered, Malcolm X recognizes that his blackness is inassimilable and so begins the tortuous journey towards ethnic pride. The conventional immigrant pattern of assimilation is thus reversed, and Malcolm X is transformed into a vehement black nationalist. A similar pattern of development may be found in numerous other black and ethnic autobiographies. Among Mexican-American works, Oscar Zeta Acosta's two volumes, *The Autobiography of a Brown Buffalo* (1972) and *The Revolt of the Cockroach People* (1973), most compellingly depict the experience of ethnic rebirth.

In *Hunger of Memory*, Rodriguez reverts to an older formula of conversion. He rejects ethnic consciousness as an effective antidote for social injustice in American life, but he cannot ignore it; it has been, after all, one of the most powerful social and cultural forces in the United States since the 1960s. Apart from his preference for the traditional Latin liturgy of the Catholic church, nothing reveals Rodriguez's rigid conventionalism more clearly than his adherence to the doctrine of assimilation. In a key passage from *Hunger of Memory*, he recalls the occasion when several nuns from his elementary school visit his parents to suggest that they speak English at home in order to facilitate their son's comprehension of it. Coming from representatives of the church, the suggestion carries great force, and so the parents acquiesce. The shift in language undermines family intimacy, a loss justified by Richard's dramatic academic progress in the first grade. Soon Ricardo becomes "Rich-heard," and his last name is Americanized as "Road-ree-guess." The experience of conversion injures, but it is an injury inflicted and sanctioned by his beloved church and, in any event, Rodriguez points out, childhood involves "inevitable pain." Rodriguez embraces his assimilated self vehemently. When, as an adult, he observes ethnic nationalists promoting their political and educational agenda, he excoriates them as middle-class malcontents "filled with decadent self-pity, obsessed by the burden of public life" (27). And he dismisses minority university students eager to exhibit their continuing allegiance to their ethnic communities as engaging in "clownish display."

Rodriguez insists that ethnicity is a private, individual matter which is degraded by public, collective exhibitions. As he attacks ethnic activism, he assures his readers that he desires not to abolish ethnicity but only to locate it properly in American culture. His perception of its proper place, however, has the effect of isolating and containing ethnic consciousness, of depleting its capacity for restructuring American life. In treating his own experience of Mexican-American culture, he relegates it to a distant, unthreatening childhood that he may recollect at his leisure and reconstruct as he pleases.

We can see at this point that *Hunger of Memory* represents still another variety of conversion narrative and, in comparison with *The Promised Land*, a different sort of rhetorical strategy for the validation of assimilation. Whereas Mary Antin discards a cultural experience of bigotry and oppression, Rodriguez forsakes one of love and stability. Antin's autobiography is a record of flight and realization, Rodriguez's one of relinquishment and realization. In emphasizing how much he has given up, Rodriguez hopes to make the achievement of "public identity" (he prefers to avoid the provocative political connotation of the term "assimilation") all the more precious. "I remember what was so grievously lost," he writes, "to define what was necessarily gained" (6).

But what exactly was so "grievously lost"? The reader cannot know because Rodriguez's evocation of his ethnic childhood is extremely superficial. He reveals little about those informal individual and group experiences that convey a sense of culture. Beyond some nicely rendered observations of his family's religious practices and displays of mutual affection, Rodriguez tells us hardly anything about living inside ethnic culture: nothing about children's games or rhymes, nothing of a grandparent's cure for *empacho*. He recalls no legends, no *corridos*, no stories of the Mexican Revolution; he repeats hardly any Spanish words or phrases although he tells us that Spanish had been his first language. Rodriguez presents a childhood bereft of culture, a quality especially curious in a work so forthcoming about the author's personal life. It may be that Rodriguez's claim to a rich Mexican-American past, beyond its usefulness as a political device and a rhetorical gesture, is a fabrication, a "nameless Eden where he never was." Or it may be that, in his eagerness to adopt a successful public identity, Rodriguez has relieved his memory of most of what he has left behind, a possibility that contradicts the implication of his book's title.

In characterizing *Hunger of Memory* as a conversion narrative, I have sought to place the work in an extensive tradition of American autobiographical expression. Rodriguez himself prefers to describe his book as a "middle-class pastoral," a hybrid designation conveying Rodriguez's bourgeois American consciousness and his affinity for "classic"—particularly English—literature. In its nostalgic presentation of childhood, its admiration for simple human values, and its studied courtliness of language and manner, *Hunger of Memory* resembles the conventional pastoral. But for Rodriguez the conventional pastoral, with its lofty, aristocratic point of view, is inherently condescending toward precisely the modest folk and experiences it purports to celebrate. Of humble origin himself, Rodriguez finds this quality offensive: hence the "middle-class" pastoral.

However, Rodriguez's preferred angle of perception is not without its own dangers. He argues that the middle class "is tempted by the pastoral impulse to deny its difference from the lower class" and claims that this temptation must be resisted "because in trying to imitate the lower class, the middle class blurs the distinction so crucial to social reform" (6). Rodriguez never explains precisely how the "pastoral impulse" tempts the middle class; nor does he define the nature of the "distinction" necessary to social reform. The reader must surmise that he believes social reform is possible only when the relative benefits and deprivations of the two classes are clearly recognized. The goal of Rodriguez's middle-class pastoral would thus seem to be the depiction of the poor compassionately but authentically and without underestimating their isolation. Such a literary undertaking would be laudable particularly if it induced political action on behalf of the poor, but Rodriguez's work has the opposite effect. His assertions of sympathy for the poor are undermined by his own eager abandonment of his ethnic traditions and his failure to present any details of lower-class culture that the reader may admire. Moreover, Rodriguez delineates class differences so rigidly that lower and middle classes seem hopelessly alienated, utterly unable to communicate across class lines. Rodriguez vivifies this problem with examples from his own experience. He recalls returning home from college to encounter a "bewildering silence" between himself and his parents. He remembers a summer job among numerous Mexican laborers to whom he could find nothing to say. As for social reform, which Rodriguez claims to support, *Hunger of Memory* offers few likely prospects. He proposes little in the way of an agenda and, in any event, shows no inclination toward participation, no desire even to help correct the flaws he correctly identifies in existing social programs. As he recounts his life, Rodriguez quickly assumes the role of that quintessentially modern literary figure: the solitary observer, immune to involvement in anything he surveys. This is distressing enough in itself without having to recall Rodriguez's habit of belittling ethnic social activists.

As Rodriguez practices the form, the effect—as opposed to the intention—of the middle-class pastoral is to discourage activism on behalf of the working classes and to reaffirm middle-class privilege. Rodriguez's contention that the middle-class pastoral is "a more difficult hymn" than the conventional aristocratic version because of the former's tendency to exaggerate its kinship with the poor is without substance. *Hunger of Memory* never demonstrates any such inclination, nor does it manifest any tension between the forces of assimilation and the allegiances of ethnicity and class. *Hunger of Memory*, like traditional autobiographical narratives of conversion, accepts the process of transformation without hesitation. Ultimately, Rodriguez's claim for his middle-class pastoral is best understood as an attempt to magnify his literary accomplishment and to obscure the regressiveness of his political and cultural views behind a pretense of formal innovation.

As I indicated at the beginning of this essay, *Hunger of Memory* is a self-consciously academic work, replete with sophisticated literary and cultural references and eager to establish its intellectual respectability. Rodriguez's scholarly training is particularly evident in the way he characterizes various public impressions of himself and his work and, more important, in the way he develops his autobiographical persona. For example, he reveals that "among certain leaders of the Ethnic Left," he is considered a "brown Uncle Tom, interpreting the writing on the wall to a bunch of cigar-smoking pharaohs" (4). After he declines to teach a course in minority literature at Berkeley, "Hispanic" students come to regard him as "some comic Queequeg, holding close to [his] breast a reliquary containing the white powder of a dead European civilization" (162). Rodriguez's self-portrait varies considerably from these scornful characterizations, but it is similarly constructed out of his academic store of literary figures and cultural types.

Predictably, Rodriguez's conception of his autobiographical self derives primarily from English sources, one of which he came across while reading randomly in the British Museum, "too distracted" to finish his dissertation. The source is Richard Hoggart's *The Uses of Literacy* (1957), a wide-ranging examination of traditional working-class culture and its transformation by popular literature and other forms of mass media. For Rodriguez, Hoggart's finest achievement is his delineation of the "scholarship boy," a young man who lifts himself—or, perhaps more precisely, who is lifted—out of working-class culture through the experience of education. Some scholarship boys become relatively "declassed" and make themselves quite at home in the circle of intellectuals and scholars; some others are able to function comfortably among the intellectually elite while maintaining easy and respectful relationships with their working-class relatives. A third group, with which Hoggart is especially concerned, is beset with doubt and anxiety, feeling uprooted and ill at ease in any social environment. This last type of scholarship boy is "enormously obedient to the dictates of the world of school" (241). His bookishness is often considered effeminate by other members of the working class, and he is likely to be closer to his mother than to his father. This scholarship boy rarely laughs and dislikes his physical appearance. As he progresses in his education, he becomes uncomfortable in his parents' house; he comes to despise the popular magazines and novels lying about the living room. In time, he pulls himself away psychologically from his mother and father; his teachers become his true parents. He cannot return home.

Rodriguez properly recognizes himself in this last variety of scholarship boy. He frequently questions his intellectual gifts and readily admits his natural submissiveness to authority, particularly his teachers. He confesses his feelings of sexual inferiority and estrangement from his father. He tells of his teenage anxieties regarding his weight and lack of athletic skills. He remembers his embarrassment over his parents' poor English and lack of learning. And very early in *Hunger of Memory*, Rodriguez announces that his mother and father are no longer his parents in a cultural sense.

Although Rodriguez follows Hoggart closely in his self-portrayal as a scholarship boy, he largely ignores Hoggart's suggestion that the scholarship boy is both a victim and a tool of the educational system. Hoggart quotes Herbert Spencer's comment that "established systems of education . . . are fundamentally vicious" in that they "encourage *submissive receptivity* instead of *independent activity*" (243). A moment later, Hoggart cites Hazlitt's view that men "do not become what by nature they are meant to be, but what society makes them. The generous feelings, and high propensities of the soul are, as it were, shrunk up, seared, violently wrenched, and amputated, to fit us for our intercourse with the world . . . "(244). Ever the perfectly docile scholarship boy, Rodriguez refuses to question the political and social motives of the educational system that shapes him. Nor does he make the obvious connection between Hoggart's apprehension over the increasing rate of homogenization in modern, urban, technologically advanced society and his own advocacy of language and cultural assimilation. In adopting Hoggart's figure for his purposes, Rodriguez disregards any qualities that might undermine his political positions. Throughout *Hunger of Memory*, Rodriguez insists that no one can live dual roles—public and private identities, participation in both working and middle classes—comfortably. Consequently, he mentions nothing about Hoggart's second variety of scholarship boy who manages, like many consciously ethnic Americans, to function successfully in several communities simultaneously.

While the third scholarship boy doubtless represents Rodriguez's closest literary approximation of his authentic self, he does not by any means constitute Rodriguez's most provocative, ideologically interesting conception of his autobiographical persona. Rodriguez begins *Hunger of Memory* with these lines: "I have taken Caliban's advice. I have stolen their books. I will have some run of this isle." The Caliban in question, of course, is the elusive aborigine—presumably modeled after certain types of American natives much discussed in contemporaneous European travel literature—of Shakespeare's late play, *The Tempest*. Over the years, Caliban has aroused tremendous critical scrutiny of a political nature, to the point where he has become a sort of ideological litmus test for critics. The traditional view regards him "as natural man, a primitive whose name seems to echo the 'cannibals' of Montaigne's famous essay" (Frye, introd. to *The Tempest* 16). In fact, Caliban is not a cannibal at all although doubts about the extent of his humanity are raised by his desire to murder his master Prospero and to "rape" Prospero's daughter, Miranda. Traditional critics have also emphasized the descriptions of Caliban as subhuman, offered by various characters: "mooncalf," "puppy-headed monster," and "thing of darkness" to name only three. All in all, Caliban's subjugation is, once again in the traditional view, understandable if not pardonable: his violent passions must be held in check. Not until the end of *The Tempest*, when he acknowledges Prospero's superiority and announces that he will "be wise hereafter, / And seek for grace," does Caliban seem truly human and capable of redemption.

In an instructive example of how cultural and social circumstances shape critical perspective, another group of critics, many like Frantz Fanon and Roberto Fernández Retamar from countries with long histories of colonization, have regarded Caliban quite differently. For these writers, the longstanding debate over Caliban's humanity skirts the more critical issues of his enslavement and the theft of his land by European colonizers. Caliban's life symbolizes the history of the oppressed peoples everywhere, but not in wholly negative terms. He is, to be sure, a slave but not always a compliant one. When he first appears in *The Tempest*, he balks at Prospero's order to fetch wood. Caliban never "yields a kind answer" to his master and, having been forced to learn Prospero's language, uses it to curse him. As he plots to murder Prospero, he encourages his co-conspirator Stephano to first seize and burn the master's books "for without them / He's but a sot" (III, ii). Caliban intuits that knowledge is power and that Prospero has used his learning treacherously. Revisionist critics have argued that Caliban's wish to murder Prospero is justifiable as an act of resistance and that his intention to "rape" Miranda is the oppressors' inflammatory interpretation of an aborigine's sexual interest in one of their own. Furthermore, for all his hideousness and insolence, Caliban is indispensable. "We cannot miss him," admits Prospero. He "does make our fire . . . and serves in offices / That profit us" (I, ii). The key to truly understanding Caliban is to discard the biased, conventionally European view of *The Tempest* and to consider him from the perspective of the colonized. Seen from this angle, Caliban ceases to be a deformed and dim-witted culprit and emerges instead as the "unconquerable master" of his island.[2]

In the opening sentence of *Hunger of Memory*, Rodriguez seems to be aligning himself with the revisionist interpreters of Caliban. His claim that he has "stolen their books" suggests a spirit of defiance while his remark that he "will have some run of this isle" suggests a refusal to surrender his autonomy. But Rodriguez soon reveals himself to be neither a revisionist critic nor a defiant Caliban. In a quite conventional manner, Rodriguez is drawn to Caliban largely for the latter's utility as a symbol of ethnic exoticism and sheer physical ugliness. In emphasizing his swarthy and severe "Mayan" features, Rodriguez establishes that he too, like Caliban, is a "thing of darkness." Skin color is an issue of great concern to Rodriguez, so much so that he devotes an entire chapter to it. In "Complexion," Rodriguez traces his anxiety about his brown skin to the prejudices of family members who associated swarthiness with ugliness and poverty. Inevitably, Rodriguez internalizes this attitude and comes to despise his appearance. As a highly self-conscious adolescent, he never dates and seldom participates in typical high-school activities. His self-hatred reaches such proportions that he tries to scrape off his brown skin with his father's straight razor. The young Rodriguez regards himself with the same loathing that Prospero and Miranda manifest towards Caliban. With only a trace of irony, Rodriguez presents his physical self as a "monster."

In the last several pages of "Complexion," however, Rodriguez charts his movement towards a sense of self-esteem. He relates this process to the development of an appropriate public identity and the realization that his relatives were quite wrong: there is no necessary connection between dark skin and either ugliness or poverty. As a working-class child, Rodriguez had endured helplessly such epithets as "greaser" and "dirty Mexican." But as he assumes bourgeois values and manners, as he evolves into an educated, sophisticated, and stylish adult, he encounters distinctly different responses to his appearance. At a Bel Air cocktail party, a stranger admires his exotic Indian features and encourages Rodriguez to consider a career in high-fashion modeling. In New York, a bellboy notes his brown skin and asks if he had been vacationing in the Caribbean. In Rodriguez's rendering of a contemporary, bourgeois Caliban, exoticism becomes a saleable commodity and swarthiness a mark of leisure. Ultimately in *Hunger of Memory*, Rodriguez's Caliban undergoes a process not merely of conversion and transformation but of transfiguration. Rodriguez has taken Shakespeare's deformed savage and rid him of his insolence, his misguided hostility to civilization, his capacity for physical violence. Rodriguez's Caliban metamorphoses into a proper scholarship boy, eager to learn from his master and to become such a man as Prospero himself might countenance.

Clearly, then, the opening sentences of *Hunger of Memory* are misleading. Rodriguez's Caliban steals no book but rather timidly absorbs those texts that are given him. He will have "some run of the isle" because he has been culturally and socially assimilated and poses no threat to Prospero's descendants. Rodriguez's highly conditioned imagination can barely accommodate the possibility of an aggressive, liberated Caliban and, once having entertained the possibility of such a figure, can certainly not sustain his development. At the most fundamental level, Rodriguez, unlike the Caliban of the revisionists, does not recognize, however crudely, that education, books, and language can be used as tools of domination. In the end, Rodriguez's autobiographical persona resembles perfectly the self-loathing colonized figure described in many recent Third World cultural studies.

In characterizing *Hunger of Memory*, Rodriguez explains that it is not only an account of his education and personal experience but a book about language. In the most literal sense,

*Hunger of Memory* is about Rodriguez's sometimes agonizing movement from Spanish to English and the benefits of American culture he enjoyed as a consequence. But *Hunger of Memory* is also a book that intends to demonstrate Rodriguez's literary mastery of English as conclusive proof, as if further proof were needed, of his assimilation. "What I needed to learn in school," writes Rodriguez, "was that I had the right—and the obligation—to speak the public language of *los gringos*" (19). His commitment to English is so strong that he opposes bilingual programs on the grounds that they postpone "learning the language of public society" (19).

Because Rodriguez considers his autobiography an act of literature rather than straightforward personal history, he aims to create a style worthy of literary art. *Hunger of Memory* contains some fine writing and powerful imagery, as when he describes his appearance: "My face is mournfully long, in the classic Indian manner; my profile suggests one of those beak-nosed Mayan sculptures—the eaglelike face upturned, open-mouthed, against the deserted primitive sky" (115). The language of *Hunger of Memory* is sometimes insidious—Rodriguez, for example, invariably refers to bilingual programs as "schemes"—but its more conspicuous quality is a carefully crafted elegance intended to underscore Rodriguez's connection to the tradition of classic English literature. The movement of *Hunger of Memory* is deliberate; Rodriguez aptly describes his book as "six chapters of sad, fuguelike repetition" (7). Here is a passage in which he describes the inevitable decline of family intimacy:

> Intimacy is not trapped within words. It passes through words. It passes. The truth is that intimates leave the room. Doors close. Faces move away from the window. Time passes. Voices recede into the dark. Death finally quiets the voice. And there is no way to deny it. No way to stand in the crowd, uttering one's family language (39).

These few sentences exemplify not only Rodriguez's style but the use of style in the service of rhetoric. The slow pace of

*Hunger of Memory*—achieved by such devices as repetition; short, abrupt sentences; and sentence fragments—gives the work a thoughtful, even painful, quality as if Rodriguez had weighed carefully his political, social, and cultural choices and then paid the price of his decisions. But, in fact, as in the passage above, the appeal to the reader is sentimental rather than rational. The deliberateness of *Hunger of Memory* creates a rhetorical condition of understatement and reassurance. The passage above is both charming and, in its particular way, poignant; it quietly and seemingly innocuously conveys Rodriguez's contention that the intimacies of families and ethnic communities are delicate and short-lived while the pressures of the crowd, which is to say, the dominant class, are irresistible. Once again, relentlessly, Rodriguez makes his point that there is no attractive, realistic alternative to assimilation.

In *Black Skin, White Masks*, Frantz Fanon delineates how, in conditions of colonialism, the colonized young people are taught to reject the culture of their families, to regard their colonizers as their ancestors, and to prefer life among the colonizers. In his essays on culture, Antonio Gramsci writes about the importance of the "radical intellectual" who, in taking on the cause of the oppressed, must constantly fight against his own academic training. These are familiar writers and ideas, but they seem not to have touched Rodriguez. He announces, in the manner of Caliban appropriating Prospero's books, that Montaigne, Shakespeare, and Lawrence are his now, but what of Fanon and Gramsci, of Fernández Retamar and José Martí? Writers, of course, reveal their ideology as much by what they do not say and acknowledge as by what they do. Rodriguez, both as writer and as autobiographical persona, is willfully disconnected from an entire tradition of thought that treats the impact of historical, social, and cultural circumstances on individual identity. The problem is not so much that Rodriguez fails to embrace this body of work but that he seems indifferent to its existence. Consequently, he overestimates the autonomy of his consciousness and tends to interpret social and cultural phenomena as functions of his own experience.

*Hunger of Memory* is not a work of proselytization; it exists to confirm traditional American notions about ethnic loyalty, and in so doing, to validate and strengthen Rodriguez's public identity. And because of its animating political purposes, Rodriguez has constructed a remarkably uncritical autobiographical persona, one who never challenges the justice of a national culture that demands, as he sees it, the relinquishment of his ethnic past. Rodriguez never wonders where his relatives acquired their distaste for dark complexions (a legacy of Spanish colonialism, perhaps?) or why, among the nations of the world, the United States so systematically discourages the practice of languages other than English. Precisely because Rodriguez refuses to engage critically the surrounding culture, *Hunger of Memory* is full of contradictions and garbled polemics. Even as Rodriguez celebrates the achievement of a public identity, the enduring impression of him is at his family's Christmas dinner, perhaps its last, standing forlornly, an irrevocable silence yawning between him and his Mexican father.

## Notes

1. My discussion of the conversion narrative is indebted to Werner Sollors, *Beyond Ethnicity*.
2. See Fernández Retamar, "Caliban."

## Works Cited

Acosta, Oscar Zeta. *The Autobiography of a Brown Buffalo.* San Francisco: Straight Arrow Books, 1972.

———. *The Revolt of the Cockroach People.* San Francisco: Straight Arrow Books, 1973.

Antin, Mary. *The Promised Land.* Boston: Houghton, 1912.

Fanon, Frantz. *Black Skin, White Masks.* Trans. Charles Lam Markmann. New York: Grove, 1967.

Fernández Retamar, Roberto. "Caliban: Notes toward a Discussion of Culture in Our America." Trans. Lynn Garafola, David Arthur McMurray, and Robert Márquez. *Massachusetts Review* 15, no. 1–2 (1974): 7–72.

Frye, Northrop. Introduction. *The Tempest.* By William Shakespeare. Baltimore: Penguin, 1959.

Hoggart, Richard. *The Uses of Literacy.* 1957. New York: Oxford UP, 1970.

Malcolm X. *The Autobiography of Malcolm X.* With the assistance of Alex Haley. New York: Grove, 1965.

Rodriguez, Richard. *Hunger of Memory: The Education of Richard Rodriguez.* Boston: Godine, 1982.

Sollors, Werner. *Beyond Ethnicity: Consent and Descent in American Culture.* New York: Oxford UP, 1986.

# The School of Caliban:
# Pan-American Autobiography

*José David Saldívar*

A new turbulence is at work everywhere, and Caliban is wide awake.
—George Lamming

Caliban can still participate in a world of marvels. . . .
—Aimé Césaire

. . . I lack language.
The language to clarify
My resistance to the literate.
—Cherríe Moraga

Caliban is in control, metamorphosing a linguistics of mastery with masterful sound.
—Houston Baker, Jr.

The title of this essay, "The School of Caliban," carries several related senses which are essential to my comparative cultural analysis of some Latin American, Afro-Caribbean, African-American, and Chicano/a writers. I use the phrase to suggest a group of writers, scholars, and professors of literature who are engaged under a common political influence, a group whose different (imagined) national communities and symbologies are linked by their derivation from a common and explosive reading of Shakespeare's play *The Tempest*. At the same time, I use the phrase emblematically not just for the group's shared subaltern subject positions but for the "schooling" that their enrollment in such an institution provides. This essay's task in part is to answer the broad question: do the Americas have a common autobiographical discourse? I will trace the cultural reworkings of *The Tempest* by three prominent Caribbean writers: George Lamming, from Barbados; Aimé Césaire, from Martinique; and Roberto Fernández Retamar, from Cuba. Then I will try to establish the literal and figurative centrality of Caliban to a line of Chicano/a and African-American writers not usually seen as instances of Calibanic inheritance: Ernesto Galarza, Richard Rodriguez, Cherríe Moraga, and Houston Baker, Jr.

To be sure, George Lamming, from Barbados, is one of the first great investigators of Caliban's deformation of mastery in the New World. His chief subject in his autobiographical text, *The Pleasures of Exile* (1960), is a "descriptive reflection" on the predicament of a group of writers from the English-speaking Caribbean who arrived in Great Britain as part of what he calls a "larger migrating labor force" (6). The text, moreover, focuses "on the colonial character of their relation to the metropole" (6).

Along with Roberto Fernández Retamar, Lamming is the supreme commentator, the author from Our America, who pulls Old World colonialist and New World colonized writing into a coherent and continuous line; this is the role he has played in Fernández Retamar's larger constructions of the literatures of the Americas.[1] Lamming delivers an exciting postcolonial autobiography by exploring his and a group of Caribbean writers' experiences in Britain within the frame of reference of *The Tempest*. It is the frame, Lamming stresses, "within which the meaning of our total experience, at the time, could be located" (6). Lamming's revisionist tactic in *The Pleasures of Exile* is to rewrite Shakespeare's *The Tempest* from the colonialist subject's standpoint. As Rob Nixon suggests, Lamming and other Caribbean and African writers "on the one hand . . . hailed Caliban and identified themselves with him; on the other, they were intolerant of received colonial definitions of Shakespeare's value" (561). Lamming recalls how his teachers in Barbados "followed the curriculum as it was. He did what he had to do: Jane Austen, some Shakespeare, Wells's *Kipps*, and so on. What happened was that they were teaching exactly whatever the Cambridge Syndicate demanded. That was the point of it. These things were directly connected. Papers were set in Cambridge and our papers were sent back there to be corrected. We had to wait three to four months. Nobody knew what was happening till they were returned" (Lamming qtd. in Munro and Sanders 6).

Lamming not only describes his own childhood cultural dependency; in the process he challenges directly the colonialist readings of *The Tempest*. In his searing chapters "A Monster, A Child, A Slave" and "Caliban Orders History," for example, he suggests that European and British hegemony provides Shakespeare's dominant discursive contexts. For Lamming, Shakespeare's *The Tempest* is simply "an expression of the perfect colonial concern" (96). At the same time, the play is also about Caliban's enslavement as the means of supplying food and labor on which Prospero and his daughter, Miranda, are completely dependent. As Lamming says, "It is in his relationship to Caliban, as a physical fact of life that we are allowed to guess some of Prospero's needs. He needs his slave. Moreover, he must be cautious in his dealings with him, for Caliban contains the seed of revolt" (98).

What is especially significant in this reading is that *The Tempest* describes the colonialist hegemony in the New World through Prospero's native violence, for Prospero is always trying to achieve his colonialist legitimacy through what Lamming calls "sadism": "After the slaves were encamped in Haiti torture became a common method of persuading them to work. In some cases they were roasted, others were buried alive up to their neck, their heads smeared with sugar that the flies might devour them; they were . . . made to eat their excrement, drink their urine, lick the saliva of other slaves" (98). Likewise, in Shakespeare's play, Lamming asserts, "There is a similar sadism in Prospero whenever he is moved to threaten Caliban for his rebellion" (99). To support his political reading of *The Tempest*, Lamming cites the following:

Prospero: For this, be sure, tonight thou shalt have cramps
Side stitches that shall pen thy breath up; urchins
Shall, for that vast of night that they may work,
All exercise on thee; thou shalt be pinch'd.
As thick as honeycomb, each pinch more stinging
Than bees that made them. (I, ii, 325–30)

Prospero's sadism, Lamming contends, has been signally ignored by European and North American Shakespeare critics, who have tended to listen exclusively to Prospero's voice. After all, Prospero speaks their language of empire. In other words, Shakespeare's *The Tempest* has been interpreted through critical practices that are complicitous, whether consciously or not, with a Eurocentric colonialist ideology.

But what changed this colonialist interpretation of *The Tempest*? According to Lamming, two historical events destroyed Prospero's domination in the New World: "a profound revolutionary change initiated by Toussaint L'Overture in the Haitian war of independence" (6) and Fidel Castro's overturning of Prospero in Cuba in 1959. As Lamming states, "The Caribbean remained for Europe and the United States, an imperial frontier until, like a bolt from the blue, Fidel Castro and the Cuban revolution reordered our history, and called attention to the obvious and difficult fact that people lived there. The Cuban revolution was a Caribbean response to that imperial menace which Prospero conceived as the civilizing mission" (6–7).

For Lamming, Prospero's defeat by Caliban in the Caribbean can no longer be glossed over. Unlike the colonialist Prospero who "forgot that foul conspiracy / Of the beast Caliban and his confederates / Against my life" (IV, i, 139–41), the postcolonial Prospero can no longer contain Caliban's revolt and can no longer complete, in a smoothed-over narrative, the colonialist project. Prospero's version of history, after the Cuban Revolution, can thus no longer remain authoritative: "The dialogue which Caliban now offers Prospero is an important occasion; for it is based upon and derives from a very great drama. I would describe that drama as the release of two-thirds of the world's population from the long and painful purgatory of un-awareness. . . . The world from [which] our reciprocal ways of seeing have sprung was once Propsero's world. It is no longer his. Moreover, it will never be again. It is ours, the legacy of many centuries, demanding of us a new kind of effort, a new kind of sight for viewing the possible horizons of our own century" (203). The establisher of the coherence and continuity of Caliban in the New World, Lamming functioned, too, as the agent who gave Caribbean and United States minority discourses a new, bold protagonist.

Since 1939, Aimé Césaire, with his famous anti-colonialist poem "Notebook of a Return to the Native Land," a poem about his native Martinique, about colonial oppression, and about African sources, has communicated to his readers the urgent need for decolonization and used his negritude aesthetics to counter Prospero's ideology of racial superiority. Throughout his career (he has held the elected posts of mayor of Fort-de-France and deputy to the French National Assembly), Césaire has oscillated between the political periphery and center, dialoging between Martinique and France.

Aesthetically, he has also been central in producing an alternative art aimed back at France and the metropole. Together with his collaborator, Michel Leiris, Césaire has opened a debate with the First World that has continued during the subsequent decades. In 1969, he focused the debate by freely rewriting *The Tempest* with a play of his own entitled *A Tempest*. As with his earlier poetry and essays, he remains concerned with these questions: How has European knowledge about the world been shaped by a totalitarian will to power? And how have Western writers been enmeshed in colonial situations?

Like Lamming, Césaire makes Caliban the protagonist in *The Tempest*, what one could call a noninstrumental protagonist. As Césaire tells us, "I was trying to de-mythify [Shakespeare's] tale. To me Prospero is the complete totalitarian. I am always surprised when others consider him the wise man who 'forgives'. . . . Prospero is the man of cold reason, the man of methodical conquest—in other words, a portrait of the enlightened European."

Not surprisingly, Césaire's protagonist "is the man who still is close to his beginnings, whose link with the natural world has not yet been broken. Caliban can still participate in a world of marvels, whereas his master can merely 'create' them through his acquired knowledge. At the same time, Caliban is also a rebel—the positive hero, in a Hegelian sense" (Césaire qtd. in Belhassen 176).

Like Shakespeare's *The Tempest*, Césaire's *A Tempest* has a shipwreck, an irritable father, and a character who manipulates the plot. The old conventions are here, but mainly Césaire "writes back" at an imperial discourse from the subject(ed) position of a Caribbean Caliban whose actuality has been distorted and denied:

> Prospero, you're a great magician:
> you're an old hand at deception.
> And you lied to me so much,
> about the world, about yourself,
> that you ended up by imposing on me
> an image of myself:
> underdeveloped, in your words, incompetent,
> that's how you made me see myself!
> And I loathe that image . . . and it's false!
>
> . . . .
>
> And I know that one day my bare fist, just
> that, will be enough to crush your world. The
> old world is falling apart! (Césaire 71)

Beyond his general stance as an oppositional voice, Césaire's Caliban makes use of other contemporary Pan-American subaltern approaches. Most significant is Caliban's refusal to see himself within the European "signifying system." At the beginning of Césaire's play, for instance, Caliban challenges Prospero directly:

> Call me X. That would be best. Like a man
> without a name. Or, to be more precise, a
> man whose name has been stolen. You talk about history . . . well,

that's history, and everyone knows it! Every time you
call me it reminds me of a basic fact, that fact that you've
stolen everything from me, even my identity.
Uhuru! (Césaire 18)

Throughout *A Tempest*, Caliban offers his defiant counterdiscourse
to Prospero: Caliban reminds him again and again not only of his
Afro-Caribbean roots ("Call me X") but of how he showed Prospero
all the marvelous qualities of the isle.

In Césaire's play, it is also remarkable how Caliban contests
its true beginnings. We are made aware that Caliban has his
own story and that it does not begin where Prospero begins. A
theatrical space of resistance is therefore opened behind
Prospero's narrative, a gap that allows us to see that Prospero's
narrative (or Shakespeare's narrative) is not simply history,
not simply the way things were, but a particular version. In
his own space, Césaire's Caliban, or rather, "X," is allowed to
tell his story. Prospero and Caliban are seen not only as ar-
chetypes of the colonizer and colonized, as the cultural mate-
rialists stress in their allegorical rewritings of *The Tempest*,
but Prospero, in Caliban's response, is also represented by
Césaire as a colonial historian, and such a convincing and
subtle historian that other histories have to fight their way
into his official document.[2]

In brief, *A Tempest* is a Caribbean landscape in which ideological and cultural transformations occur. Césaire's play makes
demands. As with his poetry, his play makes readers search for
dictionaries in several languages, for encyclopedias, atlases, and
African sources. To complicate matters, Césaire even counters
Prospero's white magic and the tradition it reflects. Against the
Western cultural complex of Neoplatonism, hermeticism, and
occult philosophy, he offers the reader Afro-Caribbean *lo real
maravilloso*: he counters Prospero's magic with "Eshu," an African god. In the end, he forces his audience to construct readings
that are familiar both to new historicists and to cultural materi-
alists but that must be shaped from a comparative global cultural situation. Césaire's world, like Lamming's and, as we will
see, Fernández Retamar's, is Caribbean—hybrid and heteroglot.

Fernández Retamar also institutionalized a powerful reading of Shakespeare's *The Tempest*—in his autobiographical
pamphlet "Caliban"—but he went farther than Lamming and
Césaire by giving the reader a cultural critique of typically colonial Latin-American writers such as Jorge Luis Borges, Carlos
Fuentes, and Emir Rodríguez Monegal.[3] His adamantly anti-
colonialist form of Pan-American studies puts forward a radical
oppositional criticism of alterity which merits our close scrutiny,
for "Caliban" may be read as a long meditation on the problem
of critical cosmopolitanism itself as well as in the mapping
out of the paradoxes of the dialectics of otherness.

First and foremost, Fernández Retamar is a loyal, though critical, disciple of the Hegelian Fanon of *Black Skins/White Masks*
(1952). To say this, however, does not mean that his interpretive
essays tend only toward a dialectical and psycho-analytical reading of colonialism and the racial problematic. His theories tend
to agree with Fanon's deconstruction of the neutrality of language, for in his own hybrid manifesto-autobiography, "Caliban,"
he offers us an astute and painful elaboration of what it means to
speak the language of the dominant class: "Right now as we are
discussing [a recent polemic regarding Cuba]," he tells us, "as I
am discussing with those colonizers, how else can I do it except
in one of their languages, which is now also *our* language, and
with so many of their conceptual tools" (11). Within this
Fanonian reading of language and domination, Fernández
Retamar shows us in a starkly confessional and public discourse
how the master (Prospero) imposes his language, his system of
thought and values, and even his conceptual models on the indigenous inhabitants of the Americas (Caliban). The slave thus
becomes trapped within these systems of thought and behavior.

What, then, is significant about Fernández Retamar's allegorical text? "Caliban," in its most general intention, popularized and completed a total shift in perspective about the
Americas that Lamming and Césaire had begun—in opposition to ruling culture or hegemony in the New World—for no
longer are we to see history from the viewpoint of that familiar protagonist, Prospero, but rather we are to rethink our
American culture and identity from the perspective of the Other,

a protagonist excluded, ruled, exploited, Caliban. As inhabitants of the same geopolitical space as Caliban, we are to resist what Stephen Greenblatt has described as Prospero's refashioning of our inner lives, and thus fight against Prospero's "disciplinary techniques" of mind control, coercion, and anxiety.[4]

"Caliban" is also about the role of Pan-American writers and intellectuals in a postcolonial world—how intellectuals and writers in their work in and on culture choose either to involve or not to involve themselves in the political work of social change and criticism. Said differently, intellectuals (Ariels), according to Fernández Retamar, can side either with Prospero and help to fortify ruling culture and hegemony, or they can side with Shakespeare's "mis-shapen knave," Caliban, "our Symbol" and help to resist, limit, and alter domination in the Americas. To extend this line of thought, I will devote the remainder of this essay to analyzing four contemporary Chicano/a and African-American hybrid autobiographical works by Richard Rodriguez, Ernesto Galarza, Cherríe Moraga, and Houston Baker, Jr., within Fernández Retamar's Calibanic frame of reference.

While much has been written about Rodriguez's autobiography, *Hunger of Memory* (1982), little has been written about Galarza's *Barrio Boy* (1971), Moraga's *Loving in the War Years* (1983), or Baker's *Modernism and the Harlem Renaissance* (1987), and what has been written about these works often lacks a Calibanic viewpoint. Written against the background of contemporary American history and the global movement of change, the experimental narratives of these four writers reflect the impact of events in Our America. Their context is ethnocentric, homophobic, and racist America: concrete and intolerably continuing. My view is that their narratives are written, considered, and experienced by Caliban (Shakespeare's anagram for cannibal) who desires either to participate in the historical process of hegemony or to participate in resistance to domination.

Within this Calibanic context, for whom do Rodriguez, Galarza, Moraga, and Baker write? In what circumstances? These are the questions whose answers can provide us with the ingredients for making a politics of interpretation. But if we do not want to ask and answer the questions in simply an abstract way, we must show why these questions are relevant to the present, for as this essay has mapped out, writing, criticism, and autobiographical discourse are not merely related to but are integral parts of the currents and practices of our postcolonial world.

I will first analyze Richard Rodriguez's controversial autobiography, *Hunger of Memory*, not because I particularly agree with him or his work but because the hegemonic literary public in the United States has by now legitimized him and his work.[5] In the words of Ramón Saldívar, "Rodriguez has become in the span of a few years' time the voice of 'Hispanic America' as his many short articles on a variety of topics and in various publications, such as a recent one in the *Wall Street Journal* on language policy indicate" ("Ideologies of the Self" 26).

*Hunger of Memory* is his first attempt at full-scale autobiography. His prologue, aptly called "Middle-Class Pastoral," answers eloquently the question "who writes?": "[A] dark-skinned . . . comic victim of two cultures . . . a middle-class man" (3). His chapter about sexual and ethnic passing, "Mr. Secrets," answers the question "for whom is the writing done?": "I write today," he tells us, "for a reader who exists in my mind only phantasmagorically. Someone with a face erased; someone of no particular race or sex or age or weather. A gray presence. Unknown, unfamiliar. All that I know about him is that his society, like mine, is often public, 'un gringo'" (182). Yet, paradoxically, he pretends to join Caliban's school of cultural resistance, which Lamming, Césaire, and Fernández Retamar have described: "I have taken Caliban's advice. I have stolen their books. I will have some run of this isle. . . . (In Beverly Hills will this monster make a man?)" (3). Can our misshapen, suburban knave pass himself off so easily as an intellectual-writer who leans toward Caliban and against Prospero?

Instead of writing his autobiography in a straight narrative line, Rodriguez focuses on specific subjects. He presents chapters on the Borgesian public and private self, on Catholicism, the scholarship boy, Mexican braceros, eroticism, jogging, on the small world of academia in the San Francisco Bay Area, and on Sunday brunches. This structure of cohesive, autonomous essays allows him to meditate on the brutal process of his own "normalization," summarized in the subtitle, *The Education of Richard Rodriguez*.[6] Far from celebrating his Americanization, however, Rodriguez's autobiography is a highly marketable lyric of rhetorical angst. The main subject of his narrative is his estrangement from his working-class parents because of his education at Stanford University, Columbia University, and the University of California, Berkeley, and his subsequent rise in ruling culture: "What preoccupies me is immediate," he writes, "the separation I endure with my parents in loss. This is what matters to me: the story of the scholarship boy who returns home one summer from college to discover bewildering silence, facing his parents. This is my story. An American story" (5). Nevertheless, he never makes clear in his confession why his gain—becoming a public citizen— should be his parents' loss of a son. His father, for instance, asks perhaps the most important question in the book: "I don't know why you feel this way. We have never had any of the chances before" (172). Rodriguez's ahistorical autobiography, one may conclude, sins against his father's historical insight.

What is even more unsettling in *Hunger of Memory* is the author's claim that education necessarily causes alienation, but his thesis is false: education does not have to cut us off from our world, community, and family. Rather, education can provide us with critical understanding. As postcolonial intellectuals—as Ariels—who have a choice to make between Prospero and hegemony on the one hand, and Caliban and resistance on the other, we must involve ourselves in the political work of social change. As Frank Lentricchia has said in *Criticism and Social Change*, "We might do it very well because we have the technical knowledge of the insider. We have at our disposal an intimate understanding of the expressive mechanisms of culture" (Lentricchia 7).

In short, I am not convinced by what Rodriguez calls his "act of contrition" (153). Although he continually tells us that he suffers from a sense of the subaltern's lack of advantage, from the evidence of his chapters it is clear that he suffers more from a profound sense of snobbery and bad taste. As he tells us freely in his own pen, "I am filled with the gaudy delight, the monstrous grace of the nouveau riche" (137). Seen in this light, Richard Rodriguez is not a Calibanic protagonist in Lamming's, Césaire's, and Fernández Retamar's sense; rather, he has become, in Renato Rosaldo's words, "an icon of collaboration with the English-only movement and the conservative right wing" (28).

Furthermore, Rodriguez's autobiography is not depicted in the "biographical time" that chronicles its subject in what Mikhail Bakhtin has called "the flow of history" (116) but, as Ramón Saldívar suggests, it is structured "on the archetypal pattern of redemption, albeit in Rodriguez's case a secular redemption" ("Ideologies of the Self" 28). In other words, Rodriguez narrates— as in Christian hagiography—only the extraordinary moments of his Chicano life. He eschews the whole of human life. What he in fact dramatizes for us are two images of the self: that of the sinner before rebirth and that of the saint after crisis and rebirth, joined by a period of purification through redemption. It is therefore not surprising to the reader that we last see Richard Rodriguez leaving the last supper with his family at Christmas—ready to redeem our Chicano sins of barbarism and ready to be reborn as the hero of the conservative English-Speaking Union and its ilk. Rodriguez's *Hunger of Memory* in my view is significant not for its poetic representation of the adventures of "language acquisition," as Paul Zweig emphasized (*New York Times Book Review* 1), but for its thematization of the *muy mal educado*—the case history of ruling cultural normalization in the United States.

Against this background of the alienated Ariel intellectual-writer who sides with the disciplinary techniques of Prospero, we may better understand Galarza's *Barrio Boy*, Moraga's *Loving in the War Years*, and Baker's *Modernism and the Harlem Renaissance* as signs of independence from their enslavers. Of all the recent experimental autobiographical narratives written by Chicanos and African Americans, these three make the most valid and serious reversal of trends and influences: in the past from the phallocentric metropole to the barrio, now from the politicized and feminist barrio to the homophobic metropole. In these three works, Caliban, the negative of the master-slave relationship, assumes powerful consciousness. Caliban curses the oppressor, be it Díaz's Mexico or Teddy Roosevelt's America in Galarza's case, the bourgeois categories of family and lover for Moraga, or the monumentalists for Baker.

Of all the interesting Chicano activist-historians (with the possible exception of Américo Paredes), Galarza had the surest literary gift and the most committed intellectual ambition. So it is natural to think of him as a great historian—and not merely because we recognize him as an artist. As Alfred Kazin said in his book about classical American writers, *An American Procession*, "A great historian is not the most *immediately* influential writer of history, not the most painstaking specialist in history, but the writer who, within the discipline of scholarship, has more than any other created our image of History. The great historian, the great dramatists and analysts of history, are closest to what history means to us. Since History, as an intellectual order in the mind, is the creation of historical *writers*, it follows that it is such writers who have made history" (emphasis Kazin's; 280–81). This is precisely what Galarza accomplishes in *Barrio Boy*; he creates our activist image of Chicano history.

*Barrio Boy* is so accomplished, subtle, and persuasive in its own historical way that it may take under its wing Galarza's more famous social science books.[7] It has gathered his life; his emergent oppositional values of resistance and struggle; his contempt for ruling-class authority; his courageous family; and his fellow campesino travelers, north from Mexico, into a single document of the great transformation of Mexican life after the Mexican Revolution, offering the key to the transformation of Mexicanos into Chicanos. His account of his "double acculturation," it can be argued, has already become the great allegory of history of his epoch.

"History," said Fredric Jameson, "is what hurts, it is what refuses desire and sets inexorable limits to individuals as well as to collective praxis" (102). Galarza, throughout his remarkable life, believed that. As he said in one of his many letters to his sister, Nora Lawson:

> As far back as I can remember, people have come to me for help. Most of what I have learned has been in one way or another related to personal and collective problems that these people posed. . . . I don't know how many opportunities I have had to make money, as for instance the job of assistant manager for Standard Oil in Venezuela when I was barely out of college. Each time such a chance has come my way, my problem was whether I should take it so that I might be able to do something for those I loved—sending you to college, for instance. But I have always resolved the conflict against the advantages to my family, and always because I could not see myself cutting myself off from the other world that really bore me—my mother's world and that of her people. (Galarza qtd. in Muñoz 2)

*Barrio Boy* succeeds precisely as a work of Calibanic history because Galarza can present the actors of history who taught him how to serve his people. His book, nominally intended as oral "thumbnail sketches" for his wife, Mae, and his daughters, Karla and Eli Lu, is a committed scholar's inside story of an emergent group, a leading demographic group in California, and a new type of cultural citizen. Once you become aware of the autobiography as a performed dialogue spoken to the masses of young men and women who, like Galarza, had been uprooted by the Mexican Revolution to travel north from Mexico, you find nothing strange in thinking of Galarza as the master of his literary trade and willing agent and maker of our History. How crafty he is in the driving spirit of struggle against ruling-class authority in both Mexico and the United States. In the full freedom of the cultural conversation, he plays his life as a young child over and over, and rehearses facts. Broadly speaking, he seeks to create a travel narrative, to prove a case against the "psychologists, psychiatrists, social anthropologists and other manner of 'shrinks' [who] have spread the rumor that these Mexican immigrants and their off-spring have lost [their] self-image" (1). Everything in the life of young Ernesto—his countries, Mexico and the United States; his ancestors; his generation; and his particular subject: an individual's participation in one of the grandest migrations of modern times—finally arranges itself as a wonderful travel narrative to produce a particular effect. Chicanos have never lost their sense of self; they have always been the agents who built the greatness of America through their labor and struggle.

Galarza's purpose was always to write Calibanic history. In *Barrio Boy*, he cleverly turned himself into a character, not the mature scholar-activist, Dr. Ernesto Galarza, but "little Ernie," who "was never told, and . . . never [was] asked, about getting into the *lucha*" of history (229). He became, however, inextricably and willingly involved, first as a witness to history, then as a chronicler of history through memory. So *Barrio Boy* draws always on history in order to portray young Ernesto as a type of new global citizen. He is by turns an example of the human species in the revolutionary Americas, the barrio boy who did odd jobs (as a drug store clerk, a messenger, field and cannery worker, and court interpreter) in the homemade ghettos of the United States; the translator of North American ruling culture to his proletarian Mexican family, the sensitive, Gramscian "organic intellectual" fighting for farm workers' rights in the labor camps of California.[8] As he says at the end of *Barrio Boy*, "When troubles made it necessary for the *barrio* people to deal with the American uptown, the *Autoridades*, I went with them to the police court, the industrial accident office, the county hospital, the draft board, the county clerk . . ." (256).

*Barrio Boy* is also the story of young Ernesto's working-class acculturations in Mexico and in Sacramento, California. Born in a small village "in the wild, majestic mountains of the Sierra de Nayarit" (3) in 1905, he records his life story in its geopolitical context. Caught up in the unsettling events of the Mexican Revolution (1910–17), he, his mother, Doña Henriqueta, and his uncles, Gustavo and José, migrate slowly, in stages, from one workplace to another, from Jalco to Tepic to Mazatlán, to Nogales, finally settling in the barrios of Sacramento. What we read in the five parts of the autobiography are in fact the stages of a travel narrative—on the road forming the organizing centers for the development of his private and political self.

The earliest episodes of *Barrio Boy* are set about 1905 in Jalco, and the latest episode is centered on the author's first summer as a migrant labor organizer in rural California, daydreaming of the high school he will attend in the fall. The episodes I enjoy the most, however, are those high adventures on the road (chapters 3 and 4) that Galarza vividly records for us. In these middle chapters, young Ernesto encounters people of all social classes, religions, ages, and nationalities at the height of the Mexican Revolution. This is important for us, because as Ramón Saldívar suggests, as the Mexican Revolution shattered the rigid boundaries of prerevolutionary society, Ernesto was able to experience at first hand the breakdown of social distance between the individual and the collective ("Ideologies of the Self" 30). His acculturation was shaped in the midst of these revolutionary experiences. His book, it can be argued, renders these complex intersections of the self in both a private and a public revolutionary world.

Throughout his early acculturation in Mexico, aided by the *dichos*, *corridos*, proverbs, legends, and folklore of his mother and her mountain people, Galarza's sense of self is strong, resilient, and historical. Like his uncle José, he is never silenced by society or made into a passive victim. Rather, like Uncle José, he is self-assured and always vocal. He speaks the "vernacular rhythms" of Caliban. As Galarza says of José, "He imitated pig grunts, Relámpago's [the community's mule] braying, Coronel [his *gallo*] sounding his morning call. . . . Out of the double row of small sequence holes of his harmonica, José sucked and huffed the repertoire of *corridos* and lullabies and marches he carried in his head" (47). Thus *Barrio Boy* is a celebration of orality, strength, and struggle—what his mother, Doña Henriqueta, called *hacerle la lucha* (literally translated, "to do struggle"), for "every morning," she taught him, "was a new round in the match between us and the city" (134).

In broad terms, *Barrio Boy* is about the author's education in resistance to entrenched authority in both Mexico and the United States. Even language itself, Ernesto philosophizes, clues us in to the intense battle between those who had authority and power and those who had none: "I came to *feel* certain words rather than to know them. They were words which came from the lips of jalcotecanos with accents of suspicion, of fear, and of hatred. Those words were *los rurales*, the *jefe político*, the *señor gobernador, las autoridades, el gobierno*. When a stranger rode into Jalco, people stopped talking. Every detail about him and his horse was observed for a clue as to whether he was one of the *autoridades*" (59). In the early sections, then, we catch glimpses of an emergent political consciousness, an ideology of resistance to power in all its manifestations. Later on, he continues to question power by following the example of his uncle José's resistance to religious authority: José "composed comical versions of *Dominus vobiscum* and other bits of the ritual. The priest heard about this and expelled him because his translations were disrespectful. One of them was to the effect that if you were an awful sinner, just invite the priest to dinner" (50). As this passage illustrates, Galarza's autobiography is narrated in what Hayden White has defined for historiography as the mode of irony. It is sophisticated, self-conscious, subversive, and skeptical (37–38).

Once on the road, having been uprooted by the Mexican Revolution, young Ernesto's acculturation begins to shift from a rural Mexican education to an urban, United States education. From the enclosure of the dark musty rooms of their first residence in the lower part of Sacramento, a "prison even more confining than the alley [off of which they lived] in Tucson" (133), the Galarza family slowly begin to explore their brave new world in the barrios of California's capital. As Galarza tells us about his wanderings with his mother:

> It was a block in one direction to the lumber yard and the grocery store; half a block in the other to the saloon and the Japanese motion picture theater. In between were the tent and awning shop, a Chinese restaurant, a secondhand store, several houses like our own. We noted by the numbers on the posts at the corners that we lived between 4th and 5th

streets on L. Once we could fix a course from these signs up and down and across town we explored further. On Sixth near K there was the Lyric Theater with a sign we easily translated into Lirico. . . . Navigating by these key points and following the rows of towering elms along L Street, one by one we found the post office on 7th and K; the cathedral, four blocks farther east; and the state capitol with its golden dome. (197)

As the passage points out, the process of acculturation in the barrio is at first a conscious act of translation. Later, the acculturation becomes an unconscious imaging and projecting of the "real" that serves as the compass of their new identities as Mexicans in the United States. In this manner, "with remarkable fairness and never-ending wonder we kept adding to our list of pleasant and repulsive in the ways of the Americans. It was my second acculturation" (205). Again, as in Mexico, Ernesto deciphers who has power and is, at once, skeptical about the class differences between the *ricos* and the *pobres*:

These were the boundaries of the lower part of town, for that was what everyone called the section of the city between Fifth Street and the river and from the railway yards to the Y-street levee. Nobody ever mentioned an upper part of town; at least, no one could see the difference because the whole city was built on level land. We were not lower topographically, but in other ways that distinguished between Them, the uppers, and Us, the lowers. (198)

Galarza, to be sure, never quit fighting this invidious difference between the "uppers" and the "lowers."

I always experience a social pleasure in reading *Barrio Boy*, the social pleasure of reading a work of everyday life made up literally from historical facts—that is, the world of oral and print record. It is the social pleasure of seeing behind the actors and agents. In young Galarza's case it is both the struggle of Mexican campesinos during the Mexican Revolution, and the struggle of emergent Americans in the barrios of California. In Galarza's words, the cultural conversation is always cast in terms of social struggle, for "We still called it [in the American barrios] *hacerle la lucha*, the daily match with job-givers, lay-offs, the rent, groceries, and the seasons. I was never told, and I never asked, about getting into the *lucha*" (229). Ernesto Galarza never deviated from engaging in this American struggle, and for that we can place him squarely in the school of Caliban.

Two more examples of Caliban's deformation of mastery and resistance to domination are Cherríe Moraga's autobiography *Loving in the War Years* and Houston Baker, Jr.'s literary study *Modernism and the Harlem Renaissance*. As Moraga makes patently clear in her title, her points of reference are not language and discursive signs but battle and the ideological "war of positions."[9] Her monument of the self in the process of becoming has the form of dispatches from the front lines rather than that of language because she wants to deal with gender, empowerment, sensuous culture and the libidinal economy, not relations of meaning. Neither Rodriguez's dichotomy between the public and private self nor Galarza's semiotics of resistance can totally account for the intrinsic intelligibility of conflicts that Moraga's autobiography records.

Explicitly, Moraga's hybrid text employs a higher degree of critical observation than either Rodriguez's or Galarza's. In fact, one may read Moraga's narrative, *Loving in the War Years*, as the first sustained instance of radical Chicana feminist theory. Such critical reflection in her book encompasses not only literature but sociology, politics, and the philosophy of desire. She subverts traditional narrative order and coherence by writing in her introductory section, "Amar en los años de guerra," that "The selections are not arranged chronologically in terms of when each piece was written [1976–83]. Rather I have tried to create a kind of emotional/political chronology" (i). Traditional historical time and space is here immediately displaced by a bristling "emotional/political" chronotope where the personal is always political.

In a courageous, frank, and sometimes brutal narrative, Moraga describes growing up in southern California, and in so doing gives us what it means to be a Chicana lesbian in the 1970s and 1980s. In celebrating her sexual difference as a source of her creative energy, she traces its beginnings back to her mother, Elvira. Because she views her Anglo-American father, Joseph Lawrence, as "bland," passionless, and passive, without a real sense of history, she naturally chooses her mother's working-class culture. In many ways, *Loving in the War Years* is a socially symbolic critique of the law of the father. "I'd stare across the top of my glass of milk and the small yellow kitchen table," Moraga recalls, "and as far back as I could imagine into that wide rolling forehead, I saw nothing stirring. For the life of me, there wasn't a damn thing happening in that head of his" (8).

Moraga's autobiography is an experimental narrative about her personal and political reconciliation with her grandmother and mother—her recognition that these women gave her a power of voice. *Loving in the War Years* thus may also be read as another powerful meditation on the Ariel-Caliban relationship in the Americas, for Moraga demands that, for the native intellectual to reject the influences of Prospero, she must first make a claim toward Caliban's mother (Sycorax). The "breakdown" (124) and breakthrough in Moraga's text is that she uses this voice to expose the unrelenting homophobia in the Chicano and Anglo communities which she belongs to. She elaborates, moreover, how that homophobia is related to the struggle of all women of color.

Using a remarkable rhetoric of conversion, Moraga establishes in *Loving in the War Years* a distinction between a naive self before becoming "a woman identified subject," and one who has been awakened to the evils of racism and heterosexism.[10] As she tells us early on, "When I finally lifted the lid to my lesbianism, a profound connection with my mother reawakened in me. It wasn't until I acknowledged and confronted my own lesbianism in the flesh, that my heartfelt identification with and empathy for my mother's oppression—due to being poor, uneducated, and Chicana—was realized" (52).

What is particularly moving and powerful in Moraga's autobiography is her notion that liberation comes only after realizing that class struggle and sexual struggle cannot be separated from racial struggle. Throughout *Loving in the War Years*, she takes great pains to show us how her sexual practice is a "poverty." In addition, the hope and praxis that she writes about is continually promoted in her book by a political notion of desire. As she tells us, "my lesbianism first brought me into writing. My first poems were love poems. That's the source— *el amor, el deseo*—that brought me into politics" (iv). Desire, as such, gives her access to a revolutionary energy capable of negating the one-dimensional society of Prospero which has successfully domesticated its opposition. On another level, Moraga refuses to become part of the heterosexual world, which she sees as a mask for the origins of capitalism. For Moraga, heterosexuality is nothing but the assignment of economic roles: there are producer subjects and agents of exchange (males) on the one hand, productive earth and commodities on the other (females). In *Loving in the War Years*, Moraga confronts this identification of women as commodities by refusing to enter into it and by making conscious the consequences of that refusal: "Lesbianism as a sexual act can never be construed as reproductive sex. It is not work. It is purely about pleasure and intimacy. How this refutes, spits in the face of, the notion of sex as rape, sex as duty! In stepping outside the confines of the institution of heterosexuality, I was indeed choosing sex freely" (125). Clearly, Moraga negates the feminine body as the site of productivity (sexual, economic, and cultural). Her lesbianism, as such, constitutes a resistance to the use value placed upon the feminine body as a site of reproductive work.

Finally, it is her notion of desire that has crucial consequences for us. If the primary function of memory is to serve the "pleasure principle," as Herbert Marcuse asserted in *Eros and Civilization*, then "memory of gratification is at the origin of all thinking, and the impulse to recapture past gratification is the hidden driving power behind the process of thought" (Marcuse 29). History, from this point of view, is that which refuses desire. This historical lesson is the critical reflection of Caliban, herself, that Moraga dramatizes for us in *Loving in the War Years*, for, like Caliban, Moraga "lack[s] language.

/ The language to clarify/ My resistance to the literate. / Words are a war to me" (63). In short, the paradigm for this linguistic reality that Moraga writes about is *The Tempest*: survival, for Moraga, demands that Chicanas resist the master's language, for after all, Prospero's conquest in the Americas is fundamentally a male conquest, written from the male's perspective. *Loving in the War Years* may in the end thus serve as a corrective to Lamming's, Césaire's, and Fernández Retamar's masculinist rewritings of *The Tempest*, for she forces us to return to the question of Ariel's choice between Caliban and Prospero. Before Ariel can choose Caliban, "our symbol," Moraga suggests, she must share in Caliban's "identification with" Sycorax.

No study of the school of Caliban in the Americas would be complete without a brief discussion of Houston Baker, Jr.'s contributions to cultural studies and to the study of African-American cultural forms. In his ground-breaking *Blues, Ideology and Afro-American Literature: A Vernacular Theory* (1984), Baker offered a theoretical framework for African-American literature. Baker here used the "blues" as a vernacular paradigm of American culture. He related the themes and attitudes found in the blues directly to American social and literary history as well as to African-American expressive culture.

But it is in Baker's hybrid autobiographical study, *Modernism and the Harlem Renaissance* (1987), where he explicitly joins Lamming, Césaire, and Fernández Retamar in rewriting Shakespeare's *The Tempest*. As in his earlier study of African-American "vernacular tropes," he focuses on the development of an African-American "sound" or "voice." Indeed, he proposes a unique African-American brand of modernism against which the Harlem Renaissance can be measured as a resounding success. He perceives the Harlem Renaissance as a crucial moment in a movement, predating the 1920s, when African Americans embraced the task of self-determination and in so doing gave forth a distinctive form of expression bound up in two strategies: "mastery of form," which camouflages the political task at hand, and "deformation of mastery," through which an artist defies the norm. In rich detail, Baker traces these strategies to Booker T. Washington's *Up from Slavery*, with its formal mastery of the minstrel mask, and to W. E. B. Du Bois's *Souls of Black Folk*, with its evocation and celebration of African heritage and folk traditions. Baker concludes his extended essay, a mixture of analysis and personal testimony, by arguing that Alain Locke's *The New Negro* was the first "national book" wherein African-American formal mastery of voice and deformation of mastery coalesce.

But how are these African-American narratives related to Shakespeare's *The Tempest*? And why is Baker's study an example of Calibanic resistance? In Baker's view, *The Tempest* is especially significant for vernacular "racial" writing because it contains "the venerable trope of Prospero and Caliban—figures portrayed in terms of self-and-other, the West and the Rest of us, the rationalist and the debunker, the colonizer and the indigenous people." Further, *The Tempest*, for Baker, is simply about "Language, writing, ideology, race and a host of other Western signs . . ." ("Caliban's Triple Play" 389).

Given his previous work on the blues as a vernacular trope in African-American literature, it is not surprising that Caliban turns out to be the first "vernacular" voice represented in Western culture. In his short, whirling chapter on *The Tempest*, Baker contends that as readers we need to respond to the "sound" Caliban offers us, a consideration of what the full politics of deformation and mastery surrounding him amount to.

Baker's rewriting of *The Tempest* is unabashedly political and undeniably persuasive in its presentation of Caliban as "an instructor in a first voice," resonant with "'a thousand twangling instruments' *in* nature." Like a maroon in Jamaica, or Nat Turner in the American South, Caliban, Baker asserts, performs a powerful "drama of deformation" in *The Tempest*. Against the scene of Prospero's "intruding tongue," Caliban talks back through a unique vernacular rhythm. Hence, according to Baker, "[w]hat batters our ears—if Caliban is newly interpreted—is the three-personed god of 'natural' meanings, morphophonemics, and, most importantly, metamorphoses"

(*Modernism and the Harlem Renaissance* 56), what Baker has
called Caliban's "triple play." Thus Caliban is a precursor for
the "Rest of us" because he "transforms an obscene situation,
a tripled metastatus into a signal self/cultural expression" (55-
56). In short, Caliban's triple play is a form of what Baker calls
"supraliteracy," that is to say, "a maroon or guerrilla action
carried out within linguistic territories of the erstwhile masters, bringing forth *sounds* that have been taken for hooting,
but which are, in reality, racial poetry" ("Caliban's Triple
Play" 394).

Baker's vernacular reading of *The Tempest* and of the Harlem
Renaissance has to be seen as part of a larger project which Baker
has been instrumental in creating: the "writing/righting" of American literature and history, in the broad sense. Such a process
involves a "talking back" to the masters not in the hermeneutics
of the overseers (deconstruction, the New Rhetoric of the ratio-
nalists) but in Caliban's debunking vernacular rhythms.

Hence the importance of a hybrid narrative like Houston
Baker's. What we read in *Modernism and the Harlem Renaissance* is a critique of ahistorical, needlessly abstract, formal-
istic theory in the United States. Its style and method—the
interplay of scholarly text, personal testimony, and family
photographs; the mixture of genres, methods, and styles—cap-
ture the complex reality of African-American experience. Quite
consciously, he concludes by designing an alternative mode
of expression to the one usually encountered in the works of
literary criticism or social science. It is a personal rendering
of the African-American experience brought together by what
he calls the "[s]toried sounds that have come through my lineage" (*Modernism and the Harlem Renaissance* 101). It is
only through a recognition of the "storied sounds" told to the
author by his father, Houston A. Baker, Sr.; his grandparents,
Elizabeth and John Smith; his wife, Charlotte Pierce Baker;
and her parents that we can approach the "complex field of
sounding strategies in Afro-America that are part of a family"
(104–5).

The Calibanic self that Baker's text describes does not exist in empty space but in an organic human collective, in what he calls the family. For this reason, the Calibanic self that he lays bare is not alienated from itself like Rodriguez's self. It is in his own folk. "To be exterior meant to be for others, for the collective, for one's own people," says Bakhtin in reference to a certain kind of canonical autobiography (135). To be for the collective meant also to be for the Calibanic self, we might add, from Galarza's, Moraga's, and Baker's perspective.

## Notes

I am grateful to the Faculty Senate of the University of California, Santa Cruz, for a Faculty Research Grant and to Houston Baker, Jr., and Cherríe Moraga for their support of this essay and their example of committed scholarship.

1.  See Roberto Fernández Retamar's "Caliban: Notes toward a Discussion of Culture in Our America."
2.  For two recent cultural materialist readings of *The Tempest*, see Francis Barker and Peter Hulme's "Nymphs and Reapers Heavily Vanish" in *Alternative Shakespeare*, ed. John Drakakis, and Terrence Hawkes's *That Shakespearean Rag: Essays on a Critical Process*.
3.  For a more complete reading of Fernández Retamar's project, see my "The Dialectics of Our America" in *Do the Americas Have a Common Literature?* ed. Gustavo Pérez Firmat.
4.  See Stephen Greenblatt's *Shakespearean Negotiations: The Circulation of Social Energy in Renaissance England*.
5.  It seems self-evident that American readers are more likely to be familiar with those Ariel writers-intellectuals who lean toward Prospero's aesthetics than with those who practice Caliban's deformation of mastery. Rodriguez in particular has become a favorite with American professors of composition and rhetoric. Selections from *Hunger of Memory* are now anthologized in virtually all new first-year college "readers" in the country.
6.  The term "normalization" is Michel Foucault's. In *Discipline and Punish: The Birth of the Prison*, Foucault writes, "In a sense, the power of normalization imposes homogeneity; but it individualizes by making it possible to measure gaps, etc." (184).

7. See Ernesto Galarza's *Merchants of Labor, Spiders in the House and Workers in the Fields,* and *Farm Workers and Agribusiness in California, 1947–1960.* These are penetrating critiques of the bracero program.

8. In his *Prison Notebooks,* Antonio Gramsci divides intellectuals into "organic intellectuals," which any new progressive class needs to organize a new social order, and "traditional intellectuals," who have a tradition going back to an earlier historical period.

9. For an excellent discussion of Cherríe Moraga's *Loving in the War Years* as a "war of positions," see Ramón Saldívar's *Chicano Narrative: The Dialectics of Difference.*

10. According to Werner Sollors, ethnic autobiographies in the United States usually adopt a conversion pattern that moves from "shallow assimilationist to reborn ethnic." See Sollors's *Beyond Ethnicity: Consent and Descent in American Culture.*

# Works Cited

Baker, Houston, Jr. *Blues, Ideology and Afro-American Literature: A Vernacular Theory.* Chicago: U of Chicago P, 1984.

———. "Caliban's Triple Play." In *"Race," Writing and Difference,* ed. Henry Louis Gates. Chicago: U of Chicago P, 1986. 381–95.

———. *Modernism and the Harlem Renaissance.* Chicago: U of Chicago P, 1987.

Bakhtin, Mikhail M. *The Dialogic Imagination: Four Essays.* Trans. Caryl Emerson. Ed. Michael Holquist. Austin: U of Texas P, 1981.

Barker, Francis, and Peter Hulme. "Nymphs and Reapers Heavily Vanish." In *Alternative Shakespeare,* ed. John Drakakis. London: Methuen, 1985. 191–205.

Belhassen, S. "Aimé Césaire's *A Tempest.*" In *Radical Perspectives in the Arts,* ed. Lee Baxandall. Harmondsworth, England: Penguin, 1972.

Césaire, Aimé. *Aimé Césaire: The Collected Poetry.* Trans. Clayton Eschleman and Annette Smith. Berkeley: U of California P, 1983.

———. *A Tempest.* Trans. Richard Miller. New York: UBU, 1986.

Du Bois, W. E. B. *The Souls of Black Folk: Essays and Sketches.* 1903. Greenwich, CT: Fawcett, 1961.

Fanon, Frantz. *Black Skin, White Masks.* Trans. Charles Markmann. New York: Grove, 1967.

Fernández Retamar, Roberto. "Caliban: Notes toward a Discussion of Culture in Our America." Trans. Lynn Garafola, David Arthur McMurray, and Robert Márquez. *Massachusetts Review* 15, no. 1–2 (1974). 7–72.

Foucault, Michel. *Discipline and Punish: The Birth of the Prison.* Trans. Alan Sheridan. New York: Vintage, 1979.

Galarza, Ernesto. *Barrio Boy: The Story of a Boy's Acculturation.* 1971. Notre Dame: Notre Dame UP, 1977.

———. *Farm Workers and Agribusiness in California, 1947–1960.* Notre Dame: Notre Dame UP, 1977.

———. *Merchants of Labor.* 1964. Santa Barbara, CA: McNally & Lofton, 1978.

———. *Spiders in the House and Workers in the Fields.* Notre Dame: Notre Dame UP, 1970.

Gramsci, Antonio. *Selections from the Prison Notebooks of Antonio Gramsci.* Trans. Quintin Hoare and Geoffrey Smith. New York: International, 1971.

Greenblatt, Stephen. *Shakespearean Negotiations: The Circulation of Social Energy in Renaissance England.* Berkeley: U of California P, 1988.

Hawkes, Terrence. *That Shakespearean Rag: Essays in a Critical Process.* London: Methuen, 1986.

Jameson, Fredric. *The Political Unconscious: Narrative as a Socially Symbolic Act.* Ithaca: Cornell UP, 1981.

Kazin, Alfred. *An American Procession.* New York: Knopf, 1984.

Lamming, George. *The Pleasures of Exile.* London: Allison & Busby, 1960.

Lentricchia, Frank. *Criticism and Social Change.* Chicago: U of Chicago P, 1983.

Locke, Alain, ed. *The New Negro.* 1925. Preface by Robert Hayden. New York: Atheneum, 1968.

Marcuse, Herbert. *Eros and Civilization: A Philosophical Inquiry Into Freud.* New York: Random, 1955.

———. *Reason and Revolution: Hegel and the Rise of Social Theory.* Boston: Beacon, 1960.

Moraga, Cherríe. *Loving in the War Years: Lo que nunca pasó por sus labios.* Boston: South End P, 1983.

Muñoz, Carlos. "Galarza: Scholar on the Ramparts." Lecture. Stanford, CA: Stanford Center for Chicano Research, 1987.

Munro, Ian, and Reinhard Sanders. *Kas-Kas: Interviews with Three Caribbean Writers in Texas: George Lamming, C. L. R. James, Wilson Harris.* Austin: African and Afro-American Research Institute, U of Texas, 1972.

Nixon, Rob. "Caribbean and African Appropriations of *The Tempest.*" *Critical Inquiry* 13 (1987): 557–78.

Rodriguez, Richard. *Hunger of Memory: The Education of Richard Rodriguez.* Rev. ed. New York: Bantam, 1983.

Rosaldo, Renato. "Others of Inventions: Ethnicity and Its Discontents." *Village Voice Literary Supplement* 82 (Feb. 1990): 27–29.

Saldívar, José David. "The Dialectics of Our America." In *Do the Americas Have a Common Literature?* ed. Gustavo Pérez Firmat. Durham: Duke UP, 1990. 62–84.

————. "The Limits of Cultural Studies." *American Literary History* 2, no. 2 (Summer 1990): 251–66.

Saldívar, Ramón. *Chicano Narrative: The Dialectics of Difference.* Madison: U of Wisconsin P, 1990.

————. "Ideologies of the Self: Chicano Autobiography." *Diacritics* 15, no. 3 (Fall 1985): 25–34.

Shakespeare, William. *The Tempest.* Ed. Northrop Frye. New York: Penguin, 1987.

Sollors, Werner. *Beyond Ethnicity: Consent and Descent in American Culture.* New York: Oxford UP, 1986.

Washington, Booker T. *Up from Slavery.* New York: Doubleday, 1901.

White, Hayden. *Metahistory: The Historical Imagination in Nineteenth-Century Europe.* Baltimore: Johns Hopkins UP, 1973.

Zweig, Paul. "The Child of Two Cultures." *New York Times Book Review,* 5 Apr. 1982, 1.

# Contributors

Keith E. Byerman, professor of English at Indiana State University, is an associate editor of *Black American Literature Forum*. His *Fingering the Jagged Grain: Tradition and Form in Recent Black Fiction* was published by the University of Georgia Press in 1986. Professor Byerman is currently at work on a book on W. E. B. Du Bois.

Frances Smith Foster, professor of American literature at the University of California, San Diego, is author of *Witnessing Slavery: The Development of the Ante-Bellum Slave Narrative* (Greenwood, 1979) and *A Brighter Coming Day: A Frances Ellen Watkins Harper Reader* (Feminist Press, 1990).

Fred L. Gardaphe, professor of English at Columbia College in Chicago, is contributing editor (with Anthony J. Tamburri and Paul Giordano) of *From the Margin: Writings in Italian Americana*, Purdue University Press, 1991. He is founder (with Tamburri and Giordano) and review editor of the journal *VIA, Voices in Italian Americana*. His articles on Italian-American literature have appeared in *MELUS, Misure critiche*, and other journals.

Raymund A. Paredes, professor of English and associate vice-chancellor for academic development at the University of California, Los Angeles, has published many articles on Chicano literature and is editor of *Aztlan: A Journal of Chicano Studies*. Professor Paredes is coeditor of the *Heath Anthology of American Literature* (1990). He is currently finishing a book on Chicano literature for Arundel Press.

James Robert Payne, associate professor of English at New Mexico State University, has served as Senior Fulbright Lecturer in American Literature at Wroclaw University in

Poland. A past chair of MELUS: The Society for the Study
of the Multi-Ethnic Literature of the United States, Professor Payne was guest editor of the special multicultural
American autobiography issue of *A/B: Auto/Biography
Studies* (Summer 1987) and has served as a member of the
editorial committee of that journal. His *Joseph Seamon
Cotter, Jr.: Complete Poems* was published by the University of Georgia Press in 1990.

Steven J. Rubin is a professor of English at the University of
South Florida. He has taught English and foreign languages
at the University of Michigan; the Institute for American
Universities, Aix-en-Provence, France; the Florida State
University Florence Study Center; and, as part of the
Fulbright program, the University of Paris. He has published a book on Meyer Levin; numerous articles on such
authors as I. B. Singer, Mary Antin, Phillip Roth, Bernard
Malamud, Richard Wright, Ralph Ellison, and Camara
Laye; and several translations of French West African
poetry. He is the editor of *Writing Our Lives: Autobiographies of American Jews, 1890–1990* (The Jewish Publication Society, 1991).

A. LaVonne Brown Ruoff, professor of English at the Univer-
sity of Illinois at Chicago, is the author of *American
Indian Literatures* (MLA, 1990) and *Literatures of the
American Indian* (Chelsea House, 1990). She has edited
*Redefining American Literary History* (MLA, 1990) with
Jerry W. Ward, Jr., and *The Moccasin Maker* (1913; Univer-
sity of Arizona Press, 1987) by E. Pauline Johnson (Mohawk).
Professor Ruoff is the general editor of the American Indian
Lives Series, University of Nebraska Press, and has directed
three NEH Summer Seminars for College Teachers on
American Indian Literatures (1979, 1983, 1989). In 1986 the
Society for the Study of the Multi-Ethnic Literature of the
United States gave her its annual award for outstanding
contributions to the field.

José David Saldívar, associate professor of American litera-
ture at the University of California, Santa Cruz, has pub-
lished essays on Gabriel García Márquez (*Latin American
Literary Review*), on Tomás Rivera (*Crítica*), on Alberto
Ríos (*Denver Quarterly*), and on Chicano poetic theory
(*Confluencia*). He is editor of *The Rolando Hinojosa
Reader: Essays Historical and Critical* (Arte Público Press,
1985), and *Criticism in the Borderlands: Studies in Chicano
Literature, Culture, and Ideology*, coedited with Héctor
Calderón (Duke University Press, 1991). He is the author
of *The Dialectics of Our America: Geneology, Cultural
Critique, and Literary History* (Duke University Press,
1991).

Stephen H. Sumida, associate professor of English language
and literature and faculty associate of the Program in
American Culture, University of Michigan, Ann Arbor,
has published *Asian American Literature of Hawaii: An
Annotated Bibliography* (with Arnold T. Hiura, 1979) and
*And the View from the Shore: Literary Traditions of
Hawai'i* (University of Washington Press, 1991) and has
coedited anthologies, articles, and reviews in professional
journals for Asian-American studies and American literature. Professor Sumida has worked extensively in coordinating Asian Pacific–American literary and interdiscipli-
nary conferences, and he has served in MELUS, on the
Modern Language Association's Committee for the Literatures and Languages of America, on the international and
the minority scholars' committees of the American Studies Association, and on the executive council of the Association for Asian American Studies.

Richard Tuerk, professor of literature and languages at East
Texas State University, has published a book on Henry David
Thoreau and articles on Emerson, Thoreau, Melville,
Hawthorne, Mark Twain, Sadakichi Hartmannn, Saul
Bellow, Elias Tobenkin, Jacob A. Riis, Michael Gold, and

Mary Antin. He has also published a survey of Jewish-American literature as part of the collection *Ethnic Perspectives in American Literature,* edited by Robert J. Di Pietro and Edward Ifkovic (MLA, 1983). Professor Tuerk is past treasurer and chair of MELUS.

Sau-ling Cynthia Wong is associate professor in the Asian American Studies Program, Department of Ethnic Studies, University of California, Berkeley. A native of Hong Kong, she received her Ph.D. in English and American literature from Stanford University and has published on Asian-American literature and Chinese immigrant literature. She is completing a book-length thematic study of Asian-American literature entitled *From Necessity to Extravagance: Contexts and Intertexts in Asian American Literature.*

# Index